FUNDAMENTALS OF

ENGLISH GRAMMAR

Third Edition

WORKBOOK

W9-AJO-385

Longman

longman.com

Betty Schrampfer Azar
with Stacy Hagen

**Fundamentals of English Grammar, Third Edition
Workbook**

Copyright © 2003, 1992, 1985 by Betty Schrampfer Azar
All rights reserved.

No part of this publication may be reproduced,
stored in a retrieval system, or transmitted
in any form or by any means, electronic, mechanical,
photocopying, recording, or otherwise,
without the prior permission of the publisher.

Azar Associates
Shelley Hartle, Editor
Susan Van Etten, Manager

Pearson Education, 10 Bank Street, White Plains, NY 10606

Vice president of instructional design: Allen Ascher
Editorial manager: Pam Fishman
Project manager: Margo Grant
Development editor: Janet Johnston
Vice president, director of design and production: Rhea Banker
Director of electronic production: Aliza Greenblatt
Executive managing editor: Linda Moser
Production manager: Ray Keating
Production editor: Robert Ruvo
Director of manufacturing: Patrice Fraccio
Senior manufacturing buyer: Edie Pullman
Cover design: Monika Popowitz
Illustrations: Don Martinetti
Text composition: Carlisle Communications, Ltd.
Text font: 10.5/12 Plantin

ISBN: 0-13-013633-6

Printed in the United States of America
9 10 11–CRK–10 09 08

Contents

PRACTICES

Chapter 4 THE PRESENT PERFECT AND THE PAST PERFECT

Chapter 5 ASKING QUESTIONS

PRACTICES

Chapter 6   NOUNS AND PRONOUNS

Chapter 7   MODAL AUXILIARIES

PRACTICES

Chapter 8   CONNECTING IDEAS

PRACTICES

Chapter 11   COUNT/NONCOUNT NOUNS AND ARTICLES

PRACTICES

Chapter 12   ADJECTIVE CLAUSES

Chapter 13   GERUNDS AND INFINITIVES

PRACTICES

Chapter 14 NOUN CLAUSES

PRACTICES

Appendix 1 PHRASAL VERBS

Appendix 2 PREPOSITION COMBINATIONS

PRACTICES

CHAPTER 1
Present Time

◇ **PRACTICE 1. Interview questions and answers.**
   Directions: Complete the sentences with appropriate words.

SPEAKER A: Hi. My name ___is___ Kunio.

SPEAKER B: Hi. My ___name is___ Maria. I _____ glad to meet you.

KUNIO: I _____ glad to _____ you, too. Where _____?

MARIA: I _____ from Mexico. Where _____?

KUNIO: I _____ Japan.

MARIA: Where _____ living now?

KUNIO: On Fifth Avenue in an apartment. And you?

MARIA: I _____ living in a dorm.

KUNIO: What _____ you studying?

MARIA: Business. After I study English, I'm going to attend the School of Business Administration. How _____ you? What _____ your major?

KUNIO: Engineering.

MARIA: What _____ you like to do in your free time?

KUNIO: I read a lot. How _____ you?

MARIA: I like to get on the Internet.

KUNIO: Really? What _____ you do when you're online?

MARIA: I visit many different Web sites. It _____ a good way to practice my English.

KUNIO: That's interesting. I _____ to get on the Internet, too.

MARIA: I have to _____ your full name on the board when I introduce you to the class. How _____ spell your name?

KUNIO: My first name _____ Kunio. K-U-N-I-O. My family name _____ Akiwa.

MARIA: Kunio Akiwa. _____ that right?

KUNIO: Yes, it _____. And what _____ your name again?

MARIA: My first name _____ Maria. M-A-R-I-A. My last name _____ Lopez.

KUNIO: Thanks. It's been nice talking to you.

MARIA: I enjoyed it, too.

◇ PRACTICE 2. Present verbs. (Charts 1-1 and 1-2)

Directions: Use the given verb to complete each sentence that follows. Use the simple present or the present progressive.

1. *sit*   I _____am sitting_____ at my desk right now.

2. *read*   I _____ the second sentence in this exercise.

3. *look*   I _____ at sentence 3 now.

4. *write* Now I _____ the right completion for this sentence.

5. *do*   I _____ a grammar exercise.

6. *sit*   I usually _____sit_____ at my desk when I do my homework. And

           right now I _____am sitting_____ at my desk to do this exercise.

7. *read*   I often _____ the newspaper, but right now I

           _____ a sentence in my grammar workbook.

8. *look*   I _____ at the newspaper every day. But right now I

           _____ at my grammar workbook.

9. *write* When I do exercises in this workbook, I _____ the answers in

           my book and then I check them in the *Answer Key.*★ Right now I _____

           an answer in the book.

10. *do*   I _____ grammar exercises every day. Right now I

           _____ Practice 2 in this workbook.

◇ PRACTICE 3. Forms of the simple present. (Charts 1-1 and 1-2)

Directions: Review the basic forms of the simple present tense by completing the sentences with the correct form of the verb *speak*.

PART I: STATEMENT FORMS

1. I *(speak)* _____speak_____ English.

2. They *(speak)* _____ English.

3. He *(speak)* _____ English.

4. You *(speak)* _____ English.

5. She *(speak)* _____ English.

PART II: NEGATIVE FORMS

6. I *(speak, not)* _____do not (don't) speak_____ your language.

7. They *(speak, not)* _____ English.

8. She *(speak, not)* _____ English.

9. You *(speak, not)* _____ English.

10. He *(speak, not)* _____ English.

★The *Answer Key* to these practices is in the back of this book.

11. *(you, speak)* ___Do you speak___ English?

12. *(they, speak)* _____ English?

13. *(he, speak)* _____ English?

14. *(we, speak)* _____ English?

15. *(she, speak)* _____ English?

◇ PRACTICE 4. Forms of the present progressive. (Charts 1-1 and 1-2)
Directions: Review the basic forms of the present progressive by completing the sentences with the correct form of the verb *speak*.

PART I: STATEMENT FORMS

1. I *(speak)* ___am speaking___ English right now.

2. They *(speak)* _____ English right now.

3. She *(speak)* _____ English right now.

4. You *(speak)* _____ English right now.

5. He *(speak)* _____ English right now.

PART II: NEGATIVE FORMS

6. I *(speak, not)* ___am not speaking___ English right now.

7. They *(speak, not)* _____ English right now.

8. She *(speak, not)* _____ English right now.

9. You *(speak, not)* _____ English right now.

10. He *(speak, not)* _____ English right now.

PART III: QUESTION FORMS

11. *(you, speak)* ___Are you speaking___ English right now?

12. *(he, speak)* _____ English right now?

13. *(they, speak)* _____ English right now?

14. *(we, speak)* _____ English right now?

15. *(she, speak)* _____ English right now?

◇ PRACTICE 5. Present verbs: questions. (Charts 1-1 and 1-2)
Directions: Complete the questions with *Does he* or *Is he*.

1. ___Is he___ a student?

2. ___Does he___ have class now?

3. _____ know his teachers?

4. _____ in the classroom?

5. _____ like school?

6. _____ a hard worker?

7. _____ tired?

8. _____ study every day?

9. _____ need help with his homework?

10. _____ studying right now?

◇ PRACTICE 6. Present verbs: questions. (Charts 1-1 and 1-2)
Directions: Complete the questions with ***Does she*** or ***Is she***.

1. ____*Is she*____ at work?

2. ____*Does she*____ work five days a week?

3. _____ working right now?

4. _____ sitting at her desk?

5. _____ come to the office every day?

6. _____ like her job?

7. _____ on the phone?

8. _____ in a meeting?

9. _____ work overtime often?

10. _____ working overtime now?

◇ PRACTICE 7. Simple present. (Charts 1-1 and 1-2)
Directions: Complete the sentences with ***do, does,*** or ***Ø.****

1. Jack ____*does*____ not work at his father's store.

2. ____*Do*____ you have a job?

3. Kate ____*Ø*____ works at a restaurant.

4. _____ she work the day shift or night shift?

5. Denise and Scott _____ own a small company that does home repairs.

6. They _____ have different job skills.

7. They _____ not do the same work.

8. Denise _____ enjoys painting, and Scott _____ prefers woodworking.

9. Scott _____ not like painting very much.

10. They _____ get along well with each other.

11. _____ they plan to work together for a long time? Yes. They're married.

_____

*Ø = "nothing."

◇ **PRACTICE 8. Simple present and present progressive. (Charts 1-1 and 1-2)**
   Directions: Complete the sentences with **does**, **do**, **am**, **is**, **are**, or **Ø**.

   A: What _____is_____ that? What _____ you looking at?
                  1   2

   B: It _____ a very rare and valuable book.
             3

   A: _____ it yours?
            4

   B: No. It _____ not belong to me. It _____ belongs to my cousin.
                  5   6

   He _____ collects old books.
            7

   A: That _____ an interesting hobby. _____ you a collector, too?
                 8   9

   _____ you collect old books?
          10

   B: I _____ have the interest but not the money. Rare old books _____
            11   12

   expensive to collect. I _____ becoming interested in stamps, though. Stamps
                                   13

   _____ not as expensive as rare books. I _____ want to collect stamps from
          14   15

   the 1800s.

   A: I _____ thinking about collecting stamps, too. _____ you want to get
            16   17

   together sometime and talk about it?

   B: Yes. Let's do that.

◇ **PRACTICE 9. Simple present. (Charts 1-1 and 1-2)**
   Directions: Complete the sentences with **does**, **do**, **is**, **are**, or **Ø**.

   1. A turtle _____Ø_____ lays eggs.

   2. _____Do_____ snakes lay eggs?

   3. _____ an alligator lay eggs?

   4. _____ an alligator a reptile?

   5. _____ turtles and snakes reptiles?

   6. Turtles, snakes, and alligators _____

      all reptiles.

   7. Almost all reptiles _____ lay eggs.

   8. Reptiles _____ cold-blooded.

   9. They _____ prefer warm climates.

   10. Their body temperature _____ the same as the temperature of their surroundings.

   11. _____ reptiles like to lie in the sun? Yes, they do.

◇ **PRACTICE 10. Simple present and present progressive. (Charts 1-1 and 1-2)**
Directions: Complete the sentences with *does, do, is, are,* or *Ø.*

1. A mosquito _____is_____ flying around Sam's head.

2. Mosquitoes _____ pests.

3. They _____ bother people and animals.

4. _____ a male mosquito bite?

5. No, male mosquitoes _____ not bite.

6. Only female mosquitoes _____ bite animals and people.

7. A female mosquito _____ lays 1000 to 3000 eggs each year.

8. How long _____ mosquitoes live?

9. A female mosquito _____ lives for 30 days.

10. A male mosquito _____ not live as long as a female.

11. How long _____ a male mosquito live?

12. It _____ dies after 10 or 20 days.

13. Beverly _____ wearing mosquito repellent.

14. The mosquito repellent _____ smells bad, but it _____ works.

15. The mosquito repellent _____ effective.

16. Mosquitoes _____ stay away from people who _____ wearing mosquito repellent.

17. _____ you ever wear mosquito repellent?

18. _____ mosquito repellent work?

Directions: Add the word in *italics* to the sentences. Put the word in its usual midsentence position. Write Ø if no word is needed in a blank.

1. *usually*   Ann ____**usually**____ stays ____**Ø**____ at night.

2. *usually*   Ann ____**Ø**____ is ____**usually**____ at home at night.

3. *always*   Bob ____✓____ stays _____ home in the evening.

4. *always*   He _____ is ____✓____ at his desk in the evening.

5. *usually*   He ____✓____ doesn't _____ go out in the evenings.

6. *always*   But he _____ doesn't ____✓____ study every evening.

7. *sometimes*   He ____✓____ watches _____ a little TV.

8. *never*   He ____✓____ stays _____ up past midnight.

9. *never*   He _____ is ____✓____ up past midnight.

10. *usually*   Does _____ Ann ____✓____ study _____ at night?

11. *always*   Does _____ Bob ____✓____ study _____ at night?

12. *always*   Is _____ Bob ____✓____ at home at night?

◇ PRACTICE 12. Frequency adverbs. (Chart 1-3)

Directions: Add the given words to the sentence. Put the adverbs in their usual midsentence position. Change the verb from negative to affirmative (i.e. statement form) as necessary.

1. *Sentence:* **Jane doesn't come to class on time.**

   a. *usually*   Jane ____**usually doesn't come**____ to class on time.

   b. *ever*   Jane ____**doesn't ever come**____ to class on time.

   c. *seldom*   Jane ____**seldom comes**____ to class on time.

   d. *sometimes*   Jane ____sometimes comes____ to class on time.

   e. *always*   Jane ____always comes____ to class on time.

   f. *occasionally*   Jane ____occassionaly comes____ to class on time.

   g. *never*   Jane ____never comes____ to class on time.

   h. *hardly ever*   Jane ____hardly ever comes____ to class on time.

2. *Sentence:* **Jane isn't on time for class.**

   a. *usually*   Jane ____usually isn't____ on time for class.

   b. *rarely*   Jane ____is rarely____ on time for class.

   c. *always*   Jane ____isn't always____ on time for class.

   d. *frequently*   Jane ____frequen isn't____ on time for class.

   e. *never*   Jane ____is never____ on time for class.

   f. *ever*   Jane ____isn't ever____ on time for class.

   g. *seldom*   Jane ____is seldom____ on time for class.

◇ **PRACTICE 13. Frequency adverbs. (Chart 1-3)**

Directions: Use the given information to complete the sentences. Use a frequency adverb for each sentence.

Kim's Day	S	M	T	W	Th	F	S
1. wake up late	X	X	X	X	X	X	X
2. skip breakfast		X	X		X		
3. visit friends	X	X		X		X	X
4. be on time for class		X	X	X	X		
5. surf the Internet				X			
6. talk on the phone	X	X	X	X		X	X
7. do homework			X			X	
8. be in bed early							

1. Kim _____ *always wakes* _____ up late.

2. She _____ breakfast.

3. She _____ friends.

4. She _____ on time for class.

5. She _____ the Internet.

6. She _____ on the phone.

7. She _____ homework.

8. She _____ in bed early.

◇ **PRACTICE 14. Frequency adverbs. (Chart 1-3)**

Directions: Complete each sentence with an appropriate frequency adverb from the list.

always	*often* OR *usually*	*sometimes*
never	*seldom* OR *rarely*	

1. I watch TV in the evening five or six times a week.

→ I ___ *often* OR *usually* ___ watch TV in the evening.

2. I let my roommate borrow my car only one time last year.

→ I ___ *seldom* OR *rarely* ___ let my roommate borrow my car.

3. Maria eats cereal for breakfast seven days a week.

→ Maria ___ *always* ___ eats cereal for breakfast.

4. Four out of five visitors to the museum stay for three hours or longer.

→ Museum visitors _____ stay for at least three hours.

5. We occasionally have quizzes in Dr. Rice's history class.

→ Dr. Rice _____ gives quizzes in her history class.

6. If the teacher is on time, the class begins at 8:00 A.M. Once in a while, the teacher is a few minutes late.

→ The class _____ begins at 8:00 A.M.

7. The train from Chicago has been late ninety percent of the time.

→ The train from Chicago is _____ on time.

8. In the desert, it rains only two or three days between May and September every year.

→ It _____ rains in the desert in the summer.

9. James asks me to go to the sailboat races every year, but I don't accept his invitation because I think sailboat racing is boring.

→ I _____ go to sailboat races with James.

10. Every time I go to a movie, I buy popcorn.

→ I _____ buy popcorn when I go to a movie.

11. Andy and Jake work in the same office and are friends. They go to lunch together four or five times a week.

→ Andy and Jake _____ go out to lunch with each other.

12. Most of the time Andy and Jake don't discuss business when they go to lunch with each other.

→ They _____ discuss business during lunch.

◇ PRACTICE 15. Frequency adverbs. (Chart 1-3)

Directions: Complete each sentence with an appropriate frequency adverb from the list and the simple present of the given verbs.

always	*often* OR *usually*	*sometimes*
never	*seldom* OR *rarely*	

1. Every time Pat rents a video, she chooses a comedy.

→ Pat *(choose)* _____**always chooses**_____ a comedy to rent.

2. I almost always watch soccer matches on TV. I go to a soccer match only once a year.

→ I *(go)* _____ to a soccer match.

3. I take the bus to work once a week or once every two weeks.

→ I usually carpool to work, but I *(ride)* _____ the bus.

4. The doctor told Mari to exercise four times a week, but she works long hours and exercises only a couple of times a month.

→ Mari (*exercise*) _____ .

5. My roommate eats only vegetarian food, and I like beef and chicken. We always cook separate meals.

→ I (*eat*) _____ my roommate's meals.

6. The little boy in the street is begging for food. He comes from a poor family and never gets enough to eat.

→ The little boy (*be*) _____ hungry.

7. On most Sundays, my family gets together for a big dinner.

→ My family (*get*) _____ together for a big dinner on Sundays.

8. Usually Jane can get right to work on her computer when she turns it on, but every once in a while she gets an error message.

→ Jane (*get*) _____ an error message when she turns on her computer.

9. Peter tries to finish his homework before he goes to bed, but he usually falls asleep.

→ Peter (*finish*) _____ his homework before he falls asleep and decides to go to bed.

10. My friends like to play video games, but I don't join them because the games are too violent.

→ I (*play*) _____ video games with my friends.

11. Jenny's job starts at 8:00. Most days of the week, Jenny arrives around 7:30.

→ Jenny (*arrive*) _____ at work early.

12. I like to relax every night by taking a long, hot bath.

→ I (*take*) _____ a long, hot bath in the evening.

◇ PRACTICE 16. Simple present: final -S/-ES. (Charts 1-4 and 1-5)
Directions: Write **-s/-es** in the blanks where necessary. If the verb does not need **-s/-es**, use Ø. Change **-y** to **-i** if necessary.

1. Alan like _s___ to play soccer.

2. My son watch _es___ too much TV.

3. Rita do _es___ n't like __Ø___ coffee.

4. Monkeys climb __Ø___ trees.

5. Do _____ you like _____ to climb trees?

6. Do _____ Paul like _____ to cook?

7. Paula like _____ to dance.

8. Mike wash _____ his own clothes.

9. Yuki go _____ to school at seven.

10. Tina get _____ her work done on time.

11. Tina and Pat get _____ their work done.

12. Do _____ Bill get _____ his work done?

13. Eric do _____ n't get it done on time.

14. Ahmed carry _____ a briefcase to work.

15. Janet play _____ tennis every day.

16. A turtle is another animal that live _____ near water.

17. Bees make _____ honey.

18. A bee visit _____ many flowers in one day.

19 A frog catch _____ flies with its tongue.

20. Frogs are small green animals that live _____ near water.

◇ **PRACTICE 17. Simple present: final -S/-ES. (Charts 1-4 and 1-5)**

Directions: Read the paragraph. Then complete the paragraph about Sam's day using *he* in place of *I*. You will need to change the verbs.

SAM'S DAY:

    I leave my apartment at 8:00 every morning. I walk to the bus stop and catch the 8:10 bus. It takes me downtown. Then I transfer to another bus, and it takes me to my part-time job. I arrive at work at 8:50. I stay until 1:00, and then I leave for school. I attend classes until 5:00. I usually study in the library and try to finish my homework. Then I go home around 8:00. I have a long day.

Sam _____ **leaves** _____ his apartment at 8:00. _____ **He walks** _____ to the bus stop and

_____ the 8:10 bus. It takes him downtown. Then _____ to

another bus, and it takes him to his part-time job. _____ at work at

8:50. _____ until 1:00, and then _____ for school.

_____ classes until 5:00. _____ usually _____ in the

library and _____ to finish his homework. Then _____ home around

8:00. _____ a long day.

◇ **PRACTICE 18. Pronunciation: final -S/-ES. (Charts 1-5 and 6-1*)**
Directions: Put the verbs under the correct endings for pronunciation.

✓cooks	stays	hates	misses
✓promises	seems	travels	draws
invites	watches	picks	introduces

/s/	/z/	/əz/
cooks		promises

_____

*See Chart 6-1, p. 157, in the Student Book for information about the pronunciation and spelling of final -*s*/-*es*.

◇ **PRACTICE 19. Pronunciation: final -S/-ES. (Charts 1-5 and 6-1)**
Directions: Provide the pronunciation for the verb ending: /s/, /z/, or /əz/.

1. he need/ **z** /
2. she take/ **s** /
3. the bus pass/   /
4. John love/   /
5. Pam listen/   /

6. she add/   /
7. he dress/   /
8. it fit/   /
9. the teacher enjoy/   /
10. the baby kiss/   /

11. she realize/   /
12. her dad spend/   /
13. she think/   /
14. he wonder/   /
15. my manager suggest/   /

◇ **PRACTICE 20. Spelling: final -S/-ING. (Charts 1-4, 1-5, and 2-5)**
Directions: Fill in the blanks with the simple present and present progressive forms of the verbs.

1. buy   __buys__   __is buying__
2. come   __comes__   __is coming__
3. open   _____   _____
4. begin   _____   _____
5. stop   _____   _____
6. die   _____   _____
7. rain   _____   _____
8. dream   _____   _____
9. eat   _____   _____

10. enjoy   _____   _____
11. write   _____   _____
12. try   _____   _____
13. stay   _____   _____
14. hope   _____   _____
15. study   _____   _____
16. lie   _____   _____
17. fly   _____   _____
18. sit   _____   _____

◇ **PRACTICE 21. Non-action verbs. (Chart 1-5)**
Directions: Choose the correct sentence.

1. (a.) We want to have an answer.
   b. We are wanting to have an answer.

2. a. The students think their grammar class is challenging.
   b. The students are thinking their grammar class is challenging.

3. a. Look! An eagle is flying overhead.
   b. Look! An eagle flies overhead.

4. a. The eagle is over there! Are you seeing it?
   b. The eagle is over there! Do you see it?

5. a. Now I believe my English is better.
   b. Now I am believing my English is better.

6. a. I'm doing this exercise now.
   b. I do this exercise now.

7. a. My parents are owning two cars at this time.
   b. My parents own two cars at this time.

8. a. This is fun. I am having a good time.
   b. This is fun. I have a good time.

9. a. We are having a new computer now.
   b. We have a new computer now.

10. a. I'm not knowing the answer to your question right now, but I'll find out.
    b. I don't know the answer to your question right now, but I'll find out.

11. a. My family is preferring chicken to red meat.
    b. My family prefers chicken to red meat.

12. a. I need to borrow some money.
    b. I am needing to borrow some money.

◇ **PRACTICE 22. Simple present and present progressive.** (Charts 1-1 → 1-6)
Directions: Complete the sentences with the simple present or present progressive form of the verbs in the list. Each verb is used only once.

belong	need	see	✓take
bite	play	shine	understand
drive	prefer	sing	watch
look	rain	✓snow	write

1. Look outside! It _____is snowing_____ . Everything is beautiful and all white.

2. My father _____takes_____ the 8:15 train into the city every weekday morning.

3. On Tuesdays and Thursdays, I walk to work for the exercise. Every Monday, Wednesday, and
   Friday, I _____ my car to work.

4. A: Charlie, can't you hear the telephone? Answer it!
   B: You get it! I _____ my favorite TV show. I don't want to miss
      anything.

5. A: What kind of tea do you like?
   B: Well, I'm drinking black tea, but I _____ green tea.

6. I'm gaining weight around my waist. These pants are too tight. I _____ a
   larger pair of pants.

7. A: Dinner's ready. Please call the children.
   B: Where are they?
   A: They _____ a game outside in the street.

8. It's night. There's no moon. Emily is outside. She _____ at the sky. She
   _____ more stars than she can count.

9. Michael has a good voice. Sometimes he _____ with a musical group in
   town. It's a good way to earn a little extra money.

10. A: Ouch!

   B: What's the matter?

   A: Every time I eat too fast, I _____ my tongue.

11. Nadia always _____ in her diary before bed.

12. Thank you for your help in algebra. Now I _____ that lesson.

13. This magazine is not mine. It _____ to Colette.

14. I can see a rainbow because the sun _____ and it _____

   _____ at the same time.

◇ **PRACTICE 23. Simple present and present progressive. (Charts 1-1 → 1-6)**
   Directions: Complete the sentences with the simple present or present progressive form of the verb.

   Rosa is sitting on the train right now. She *(take/not/usually)* <u>usually doesn't take</u>
   ₁

   the train, but today her son *(need)* _____ her car. She *(enjoy)*
   ₂

   _____ the ride today. There *(be)* _____ so many people
   ₃   ₄

   to watch. Some people *(eat)* _____ breakfast. Others *(drink)*
   ₅

   _____ coffee and *(read)* _____ the newspaper. One
   ₆   ₇

   woman *(work)* _____ on her laptop computer. Another *(hug)*
   ₈

   _____ her baby. Two teenagers *(play)* _____ computer
   ₉   ₁₀

   games. One of them *(wave)* _____ his hand in excitement. A clown *(walk)*
   ₁₁

   _____ up and down the aisles and *(entertain)* _____ the
   ₁₂   ₁₃

   children. Rosa *(smile)* _____ . The train ride *(take, usually)*
   ₁₄

   _____ her longer than driving, but it *(be)* _____ a more
   ₁₅   ₁₆

   enjoyable way for her to travel.

◇ **PRACTICE 24. Error analysis. (Charts 1-1 → 1-6)**
   Directions: Correct the sentences.

1. My friend ~~don't~~ *doesn't* speak English well.

2. I am not believing you.

3. My sister's dog no bark.

4. Our teacher is always starting class on time.

5. Look! The cat gets up on the counter.

6. Is Marie has enough money?

7. We are not liking this rainy weather.

8. Mrs. Gray is worry about her daughter.

9. My brother no has enough free time.

10. Is Jim drive to school every day?

11. He always hurrys in the morning. He no wanting to be late.

12. Anna have usually dinner at eight.

◇ **PRACTICE 25. Present verbs: questions and short answers. (Chart 1-7)**
   Directions: Complete the questions with *do, does, am, is,* or *are.* Then complete both the affirmative and negative short answers.

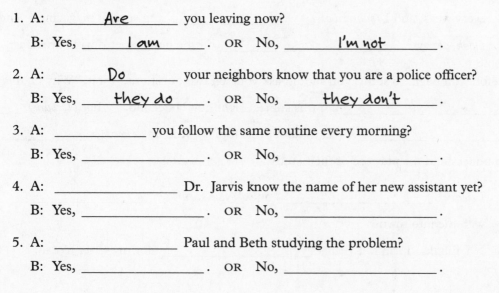

1. A: _____ Are _____ you leaving now?
   B: Yes, _____ I am _____ . OR No, _____ I'm not _____ .

2. A: _____ Do _____ your neighbors know that you are a police officer?
   B: Yes, ____ they do ____ . OR No, ____ they don't ____ .

3. A: _____ you follow the same routine every morning?
   B: Yes, _____ . OR No, _____ .

4. A: _____ Dr. Jarvis know the name of her new assistant yet?
   B: Yes, _____ . OR No, _____ .

5. A: _____ Paul and Beth studying the problem?
   B: Yes, _____ . OR No, _____ .

6. A: _____ they understand the problem?

   B: Yes, _____ . OR No, _____ .

7. A: _____ Mike reading the paper and watching television at the same time?

   B: Yes, _____ . OR No, _____ .

8. A: _____ you listening to me?

   B: Yes, _____ . OR No, _____ .

9. A: _____ that building safe?

   B: Yes, _____ . OR No, _____ .

10. A: _____ you and your co-workers get together outside of work?

    B: Yes, _____ . OR No, _____ .

◇ **PRACTICE 26. Review: present verbs. (Charts 1-1 → 1-7)**

   Directions: Use either the simple present or the present progressive of the verbs in parentheses to complete the sentences.

1. A: Hi! What *(you, do)* ___are you doing___ ?

   B: I *(watch)* _____ an exercise video. I *(want)* _____

   to lose a little weight before my vacation.

   A: I really *(enjoy)* _____ exercising. I *(go)* _____ to

   an aerobics class three times a week. It *(be)* _____ really fun. I also

   (run) _____ every morning before school.

   B: Stop! You *(make)* _____ me feel bad!

2. A: I like to read. How about you? *(you, read)* _____ a lot?

   B: Yes, I _____ . I *(read)* _____ at least one novel

   every week, and I *(subscribe)* _____ to several magazines. And I

   (look, always) _____ at the newspaper during breakfast.

3. Before you begin to study, you should ask yourself two questions. First, "Why *(I, study)*

   _____ this subject right now?" Second, "What *(I, want)* _____

   _____ to learn about this topic?" Students *(need)* _____

   to understand the purpose of their study.

4. A: I *(leave)* _____ now. *(you, want)* _____ to go

   with me into town?

   B: No, thanks. I can't. I *(wait)* _____ for my sister to call.

5. A: Shhh.

   B: Why? *(the baby, sleep)* _____ ?

   A: Uh-huh. She *(take)* _____ her afternoon nap.

   B: Okay, I'll talk softly. I *(want, not)* _____ to wake her up.

6. Ann is a painter. She *(go)* _____ to the opening of every new art show

   in the city. She *(like)* _____ to see the latest work of other artists. Right

   now she *(prepare)* _____ for a show of her new paintings next

   month.

7. It *(be)* _____ a cool autumn day today. The wind *(blow)* _____ ,

   _____ and the leaves *(fall)* _____ to the ground.

8. My roommate *(eat)* _____ breakfast at exactly seven o'clock every

   morning. I usually *(eat, not)* _____ breakfast at all. What time

   (you, eat) _____ in the morning?

9. A: *(you, shop)* _____ at this store every week?

   B: No, I _____ . I *(shop, usually)* _____ at the

      store near my apartment.

   A: Why *(you, shop)* _____ here now?

   B: I *(try)* _____ to find something special for my father's birthday

      dinner.

10. In cold climates, many trees *(lose)* _____ their leaves in winter. They *(rest)*

    _____ for several months. Then they *(grow)* _____

    new leaves and flowers in the spring. Some trees *(keep)* _____ their leaves

    during the winter and *(stay)* _____ green all year long. In some regions of

    the earth, trees *(grow, not)* _____ at all. For example, some desert areas

    (have, not) _____ any trees. The largest area of the world without trees

    (be) _____ Antarctica. No trees *(grow)* _____ in

    Antarctica.

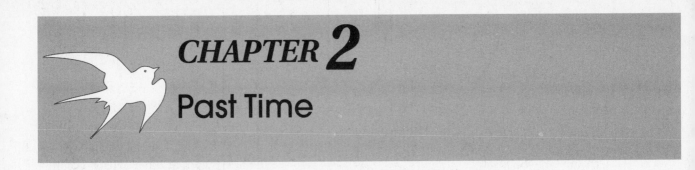

CHAPTER 2
Past Time

◇ PRACTICE 1. Simple past. (Charts 2-1 → 2-7)

Directions: Change the sentences to past time. Use simple past verbs and **yesterday** or **last**.

PRESENT	PAST
every day	*yesterday*
every morning	*yesterday morning*
every afternoon	*yesterday afternoon*
every night	*last night*
every week	*last week*
every Monday, Tuesday, etc.	*last Monday, Tuesday, etc.*
every month	*last month*
every year	*last year*

1. I **walk** to my office **every morning**.

   → I _____walked_____ to my office _____yesterday_____ **morning**.

2. I **talk** to my parents on the phone **every week**.

   → I _____talked_____ to my parents on the phone _____last_____ **week**.

3. The post office **opens** at eight o'clock **every morning**.

   → The post office _____ at eight o'clock _____
   morning.

4. Mrs. Hall **goes** to the fruit market **every Monday**.

   → Mrs. Hall _____ to the fresh fruit market _____ **Monday**.

5. The company managers **meet** at nine o'clock **every Friday morning**.

   → The executives _____ at nine o'clock _____
   Friday morning.

6. I **make** my own lunch and **take** it to work with me **every morning**.

   → _____ **morning**, I _____ my own lunch and
   _____ it to work with me.

7. Mr. Clark **pays** his rent on time **every month**.

→ Mr. Clark _____ his rent on time _____ **month**.

8. The baby **falls** asleep at three o'clock **every afternoon**.

→ _____ **afternoon**, the baby _____ asleep at three o'clock.

9. The last bus to downtown **leaves** at ten o'clock **every night**.

→ The last bus to downtown _____ at ten o'clock _____ **night**.

◇ PRACTICE 2. Simple past: regular and irregular verbs. (Charts 2-2 and 2-7)
Directions: Write the simple past form of the given verbs.

1. start	started	16. bring	
2. go	went	17. break	
3. see		18. eat	
4. stand		19. watch	
5. arrive		20. build	
6. win		21. take	
7. have		22. pay	
8. make		23. leave	
9. finish		24. wear	
10. feel		25. open	
11. fall		26. decide	
12. hear		27. plan	
13. sing		28. write	
14. explore		29. teach	
15. ask		30. hold	

◇ PRACTICE 3. Simple past forms. (Charts 2-1 → 2-3)
Directions: Use the given words to create questions and answers.

1. *you/answer*

A: The teacher asked a question. ___Did you answer___ it?

B: Yes, ___I did___. ___I answered___ it. OR

No, ___I didn't___. ___I didn't answer___ it.

2. *he/see*

    A: Tom went to the celebration. _____ the fireworks?

    B: Yes, _____ . _____ the fireworks. OR

       No, _____ . _____ the fireworks.

3. *they/watch*

    A: The game was on TV. _____ it?

    B: Yes, _____ . _____ the game. OR

       No, _____ . _____ the game.

4. *you/understand*

    A: You went to a lecture. _____ it?

    B: Yes, _____ . _____ the lecture. OR

       No, _____ . _____ the lecture.

5. *you/be*

    A: _____ at home last night?

    B: Yes, _____ . _____ at home last night. OR

       No, _____ . _____ at home last night.

◇ PRACTICE 4. Present and past negatives. (Chapter 1 and Charts 2-1 → 2-3)

Directions: The sentences in quotation marks contain incorrect information. Complete the unfinished sentences by using correct information: first in a negative sentence, then in an affirmative sentence.

1. "You flew to school yesterday."

    No, I ___ *didn't fly* ___ to school yesterday. I ___ *walked/took the bus* ___ .

2. "Lemons are sweet."

    No, lemons _____ sweet. They _____ .

3. "Astronauts walked on Mars in 1969."

    No, astronauts _____ on Mars in 1969. They _____

    in 1969.

4. "You were a baby in the year 2000."

    No, I _____ in 2000. I _____ years old in 2000.

5. "Buddha came from China."

    No, Buddha _____ from China. Buddha _____

    from Nepal.

6. "Coffee comes from cocoa beans."

No, coffee _____ from cocoa beans. It _____ .

7. "You slept outdoors last night."

No, I _____ outdoors last night. I _____ .

8. "Ice is hot."

No, ice _____ hot. It _____ .

9. "Dinosaurs disappeared a hundred years ago."

No, dinosaurs _____ a hundred years ago.

They _____ ago.

◇ **PRACTICE 5. Simple past: questions. (Charts 2-2 and 2-3)**
   Directions: Write past tense questions using the italicized words and ***did, was,*** or ***were.***

1. *he/study*   ___Did he study___ yesterday?

2. *he/sick*   ___Was he sick___ yesterday?

3. *she/sad*   _____ yesterday?

4. *they/eat*   _____ yesterday?

5. *they/hungry*   _____ yesterday?

6. *you/go*   _____ yesterday?

7. *she/understand* _____ yesterday?

8. *he/forget*   _____ yesterday?

◇ **PRACTICE 6. Simple past: questions. (Charts 2-2 and 2-3)**
   Directions: You took your driver's test yesterday. A friend is asking you questions about it. Fill in the blanks with ***did, was,*** or ***were.***

1. ___Did___ you pass your driver's test yesterday?

2. _____ you nervous?

3. _____ your hands shake?

4. _____ you practice a lot for it?

5. _____ the license examiner friendly?

6. _____ you make any silly mistakes?

7. _____ the car easy to drive?

8. _____ you go on an easy route?

◇ PRACTICE 7. Simple past: regular and irregular verbs. (Charts 2-2 and 2-7)

Directions: Complete the sentences by using the simple past of the verbs below. Use each verb only once.

call	hold	sell	swim
fight	jump	✓shake	teach
freeze	ride	stay	think

1. Paul _____shook_____ the soft drink so hard that it sprayed all over his clothes.

2. Carol didn't want to go on vacation with us, so she _____ home alone all week.

3. Since I hurt my knee, I can't go jogging. Yesterday, I _____ in the pool for an hour instead.

4. I was terrified just standing over the pool on the high diving board. Finally, I took a deep breath, held my nose, and _____ into the water.

5. The climber, who was fearful of falling, _____ the rope tightly in both hands.

6. Johnny pushed Alan down on the floor, and the two boys _____ for a few minutes. Neither boy was hurt.

7. Before Louise started her own company, she _____ chemistry at the university.

8. It was extremely cold last night, and the water we put out for the cat _____ solid.

9. Before I made my decision, I _____ about it for a long, long time.

10. Carlos _____ your house three times to ask you to go to the movie with us, but there was no answer, so we went without you.

11. My car wouldn't start this morning, so I _____ my bicycle to work.

12. I needed money to pay my tuition at the university, so I _____ my motorcycle to my cousin.

◇ PRACTICE 8. Regular verbs: pronunciation of -ED endings. (Chart 2-4)

Directions: Practice pronouncing final **-ed** by saying the words in the list aloud.

1. stopped = stop/t/
2. robbed = rob/d/
3. wanted = want/əd/
4. talked = talk/t/
5. lived = live/d/
6. needed = need/əd/
7. passed = pass/t/*
8. pushed = push/t/
9. watched = watch/t/
10. thanked = thank/t/

11. finished = finish/t/
12. seem = seem/d/
13. killed = kill/d/
14. turned = turn/d/
15. played = play/d/
16. continued = continue/d/
17. repeated = repeat/əd/
18. waited = wait/əd/
19. added = add/əd/
20. decide = decide/əd/

◇ PRACTICE 9. Regular verbs: pronunciation of -ED endings. (Chart 2-4)

Directions: Write the correct pronunciation. Then practice pronouncing final **-ed** by saying the words in the list aloud.

1. talked = talk/ t /
2. lived = live/ d /
3. waited = wait/ əd /
4. played = play/   /
5. added = add/   /
6. needed = need/   /
7. killed = kill/   /
8. finished = finish/   /
9. seemed = seem/   /
10. repeated = repeat/   /

11. continued = continue/   /
12. watched = watch/   /
13. passed = pass/   /
14. decide = decide/   /
15. stopped = stop/   /
16. turned = turn/   /
17. thanked = thank/   /
18. wanted = want/   /
19. robbed = rob/   /
20. pushed = push/   /

◇ PRACTICE 10. Spelling and pronunciation of -ED endings. (Charts 2-4 and 2-5)

Directions: Add **-ed** to each verb. When necessary, add or change letters to correct the spelling. Then circle the correct pronunciation of **-ed** for the given verb.

1. walk _ed_ (/t/) /d/ /əd/
2. pat _ted_ /t/ /d/ (/əd/)
3. worr~~y~~ _ied_ /t/ (/d/) /əd/
4. stay _____ /t/ /d/ /əd/
5. visit _____ /t/ /d/ /əd/
6. die _____ /t/ /d/ /əd/
7. trade _____ /t/ /d/ /əd/
8. plan _____ /t/ /d/ /əd/

9. open _____ /t/ /d/ /əd/
10. hurry _____ /t/ /d/ /əd/
11. rent _____ /t/ /d/ /əd/
12. try _____ /t/ /d/ /əd/
13. enjoy _____ /t/ /d/ /əd/
14. stop _____ /t/ /d/ /əd/
15. need _____ /t/ /d/ /əd/

---

*The words "passed" and "past" have the same pronunciation.

◇ PRACTICE 11. Regular verbs: pronunciation of -ED endings. (Chart 2-4)
Directions: Practice pronouncing final -ed by reading the sentences aloud.

1. I **watched** TV. Jean **listened** to the radio. Nick **waited** for the mail.
   watch/t/   listen/d/   wait/əd/

2. I **tasted** the soup. It **seemed** too salty.
   taste/əd/   seem/d/

3. James **planned** for his future. He **saved** money and **started** his own business.
   plan/d/   save/d/   start/əd/

4. I **asked** a question. Joe **answered** it. Then he **repeated** the answer for Ted.
   ask/t/   answer/d/   repeat/əd/

5. I **stared** at the sculpture for a long time. Finally, I **touched** it.
   stare/d/   touch/t/

6. Mary **prepared** a long report for her boss. She **completed** it late last night.
   prepare/d/   complete/əd/

7. After Dick **parked** the car, I **jumped** out and **opened** the door for my mother.
   park/t/   jump/t/   open/d/

8. After I **finished** reading Rod's poem, I **called** him and we **talked** for an hour.
   finish/t/   call/d/   talk/t/

9. Earlier today, I **cleaned** my apartment.
   clean/d/

10. I **washed** the windows, **waxed** the wood floor, and **vacuumed** the carpet.
    wash/t/   wax/t/   vacuum/d/

11. I **crossed** my fingers and **hoped** for good news.
    cross/t/   hope/t/

◇ PRACTICE 12. Spelling of -ING and -ED forms. (Chart 2-5)
Directions: Complete the chart. Refer to Chart 2-5 if necessary.

END OF VERB	DOUBLE THE CONSONANT?	SIMPLE FORM	-ING	-ED
-e	NO	*excite*	*exciting*	*excited*
Two Consonants		*exist*		
Two Vowels + One Consonant		*shout*		
One Vowel + One Consonant		ONE-SYLLABLE VERBS *pat*		
		TWO-SYLLABLE VERBS (STRESS ON **FIRST** SYLLABLE) *visit*		
		TWO-SYLLABLE VERBS (STRESS ON **SECOND** SYLLABLE) *admit*		
-y		*pray* *pry*		
-ie		*tie*		

◇ **PRACTICE 13. Spelling of -ING. (Chart 2-5)**
    Directions: Add **-ing** to the verbs and write them in the correct columns.

1. hit	4. take	7. learn	10. smile	13. begin
2. come	5. hop	8. listen	11. stay	14. win
3. cut	6. hope	9. rain	12. study	15. write

Double the consonant. (stop → stopping)	Drop the -e. (live → living)	Just add -ing. (visit → visiting)
hitting		

◇ **PRACTICE 14. Spelling of -ING and -ED. (Chart 2-5)**
    Directions: Spell the **-ing** and **-ed** forms of the verbs. (The simple past/past participle of irregular verbs is given in parentheses.)

		-ING	-ED
1.	ride	riding	(ridden)
2.	start	starting	started
3.	come		(came)
4.	happen		
5.	try		
6.	buy		(bought)
7.	hope		
8.	keep		(kept)
9.	tip		
10.	fail		
11.	fill		
12.	feel		(felt)
13.	dine		
14.	mean		(meant)
15.	win		(won)
16.	learn		
17.	listen		
18.	begin		(began)

◇ **PRACTICE 15. Spelling of -ING. (Chart 2-5)**

Directions: Write one "t" or two "t"s in the blanks to spell the **-ing** verb form correctly. Then write the simple form of the verb in each sentence.

SIMPLE FORM

1. I'm wai t___ ing for a phone call.
1. ___wait___

2. I'm pe tt___ ing my dog.
2. ___pet___

3. I'm bi ____ ing my nails because I'm nervous.
3. _____

4. I'm si ____ ing in a comfortable chair.
4. _____

5. I'm wri ____ ing in my book.
5. _____

6. I'm figh ____ the urge to have some ice cream.
6. _____

7. I'm wai ____ ing to see if I'm really hungry.
7. _____

8. I'm ge ____ ing up from my chair now.
8. _____

9. I'm star ____ ing to walk to the refrigerator.
9. _____

10. I'm permi ____ ing myself to have some ice cream.
10. _____

11. I'm lif ____ ing the spoon to my mouth.
11. _____

12. I'm ea ____ ing the ice cream now.
12. _____

13. I'm tas ____ ing it. It tastes good.
13. _____

14. I'm also cu ____ ing a piece of cake.
14. _____

15. I'm mee ____ ing my sister at the airport tomorrow.
15. _____

16. She's visi ____ ing me for a few days. I'll save some cake and ice cream for her.
16. _____

◇ PRACTICE 16. Spelling of irregular verbs. (Chart 2-7)

   Directions: The given verbs are in the present tense. Write the past tense of these verbs.

PART I.

buy   b <u>o</u> u g <u>h</u> t

bring   br __ __ __ __ t

teach   t __ __ __ t

catch   c __ __ __ __ t

fight   f __ __ __ t

think   th __ __ __ __ t

find   f __ __ __ d

PART II.

swim   sw __ __

drink   dr __ __ __

sing   s __ __ __

ring   r __ __ __

PART III.

blow   bl __ __

draw   dr __ __

fly   fl __ __

grow   gr __ __

know   kn __ __

throw   thr __ __

PART IV.

break   br __ __ __

write   wr __ __ __

freeze   fr __ __ __

ride   r __ __ __

sell   s __ __ __

steal   st __ __ __

PART V.

hit   h __ __

hurt   h __ __ __

read   r __ __ __

shut   sh __ __

cost   c __ __ __

put   p __ __

quit   q __ __ __

PART VI.

pay   p __ __ d★

say   s __ __ d★

★ The pronunciations of *paid* and *said* are different.
    Paid rhymes with *made*.
    Said rhymes with *red*.

◇ **PRACTICE 17. Irregular verbs. (Chart 2-7)**

Directions: Complete the sentences with the simple past of the given irregular verbs. There may be more than one possible completion.

begin	*drive*	*hurt*	*ring*	*think*
build	*eat*	*keep*	*rise*	*write*
come	*fall*	*lead*	*shut*	
do	*freeze*	*pay*	*steal*	
drink	*have*	*run*	*take*	

1. Sue _____drank/had_____ a cup of coffee before class this morning.

2. We _____ a delicious dinner at a Mexican restaurant last night.

3. When it _____ to rain yesterday afternoon, I _____ all of the windows in the apartment.

4. The phone _____ eight times before anybody answered it.

5. My brother and his wife _____ to our apartment for dinner last night.

6. The architectural firm that I work for designed that building. My brother's construction company _____ it. They took two years to complete it.

7. When Alan slipped on the icy sidewalk yesterday, he _____ down and _____ his back. His back is very painful today.

8. Alice called the police yesterday because someone _____ her bicycle while she was in the library studying. She's very angry.

9. There was a cool breeze last night. I opened the window, but Colette got cold and _____ it.

10. Ted _____ his car across Canada last summer.

11. Rita _____ faster than anyone else in the footrace.

12. None of the other runners was ever in front of Rita during the race. She _____ all of the other runners in the race from start to finish.

13. Greg is very cheap. I was surprised when he _____ for my dinner.

14. It was really cold yesterday. The temperature was three below zero.* I nearly _____ to death when I walked home!

_____

*Note: -3°F (Fahrenheit) equals -20°C (Centigrade or Celsius).

15. Jason _____ an excellent job in gluing the broken vase together.

16. The sun _____ at 6:21 this morning.

17. I _____ about going to Florida for my vacation, but I finally decided to go to Puerto Rico.

18. My friend _____ a note and passed it to me in class.

19. My mother _____ all the letters I wrote to her while I was in England. She didn't throw any away.

20. An earthquake destroyed the old bridge, so the town _____ a new one across the river.

◇ PRACTICE 18. Irregular verbs. (Chart 2-7)
Directions: Complete the sentences with the simple past of any of the given irregular verbs. There may be more than one possible completion.

break	draw	give	quit	steal
buy	fall	grow	read	teach
choose	feel	hear	shake	
cut	find	lose	sleep	
dig	forget	meet	speak	

1. A: Why isn't Bill here for the meeting? He's supposed to give the weekly report.
   B: I ____ spoke ____ to him on the phone last night, and he said he'd be here.

2. After I gave a large bone to each of my three dogs, they went to separate corners of the backyard and _____ holes to bury their bones.

3. After looking at all the chairs, I finally _____ the red one. It was a difficult decision.

4. The players are depressed because they _____ the game last weekend. Next time they'll play better.

5. A: How can you take a three-month vacation? What about your job?
   B: I won't be going back to that job ever again. I _____ yesterday.

6. Laurie has circles under her eyes because she _____ only two hours last night. She was studying for her final exams.

7. Matt lost his watch. He looked everywhere for it. Finally, he _____ it in his pants that were in the washing machine. He had washed his watch, but it was still ticking.

8. Joy was barefoot. She stepped on a piece of broken glass and _____ her foot.

9. Danny and I are old friends. We _____ each other in 1985.

10. My father _____ me how to make furniture.

11. The student with the highest grade point average _____ a speech at the graduation ceremony. She _____ about her hopes for the future of the world.

12. I didn't have a garden, so I _____ tomatoes in a pot on the balcony outside my apartment.

13. Paul was in a hurry to get to class this morning. He _____ to comb his hair.

14. Last week I _____ an interesting book about the volcanoes in Iceland.

15. When Erica and I were introduced to each other, we _____ hands.

16. Mike is in jail because he _____ a car.

17. When I heard about Sue's problem, I _____ sorry for her.

18. The students all _____ pictures of their teacher, but few of the drawings looked like her. She tried not to laugh at the pictures.

19. A few minutes ago, I _____ on the radio about a bad plane accident.

20. Joe had an accident. He _____ off the roof and _____ his leg.

◇ PRACTICE 19. Review: past questions and negatives. (Charts 2-1 → 2-3)
Directions: Rewrite the subjects and verbs that appear in boldface to create questions and negative statements. Omit the rest of each sentence.

	QUESTION	NEGATIVE
1. **I rode** a bus.	Did I ride	I didn't ride
2. **She sat** down.		
3. **We were** on time.		
4. **They tried** hard.		

5. **He was** late. _____ _____

6. **They cut** some paper. _____ _____

7. **She threw** a ball. _____ _____

8. **We did** our work. _____ _____

◇ PRACTICE 20. Simple present and past: questions. (Chapter 1, Charts 2-1 → 2-5, and preview of Chapter 5)

Directions: Create questions using the SIMPLE PAST or the SIMPLE PRESENT.

SITUATION: Your cousin, Susan, has a new friend. She was with her new friend last night. You have several questions.

1. *what/do last night?* A: ___What did you do last night?___
   B: I went to a concert with my new friend.

2. *what/your friend's name?* A: ___What is your friend's name?___
   B: Robert.

3. *he/nice?* A: _____
   B: Yes, he's very nice.

4. *how/your evening?* A: _____
   B: Fine.

5. *where/you/go?* A: _____
   B: To a concert.

6. *you/enjoy it?* A: _____
   B: Very much.

7. *the music/loud?* A: _____
   B: Yes, very loud! I loved it.

8. *what time/you/get home?* A: _____
   B: Around midnight.

9. *what/you/wear?* A: _____
   B: Nothing special. Just some jeans and a sweater.

10. *what/he/be like?* A: _____
    (his personality) B: He's funny and friendly. He's really nice.

11. *what/he/look like?* A: _____
    B: He has dark hair and is medium height.

12. *you/want to go out with* A: _____
    him again? B: Yes. I like him a lot.

◇ PRACTICE 21. Review: simple present, present progressive, and simple past forms. (Chapter 1 and Charts 2-1 → 2-7)

Directions: Complete the chart with the correct forms of the verbs.

EVERY DAY	NOW	YESTERDAY
1. He **is** here every day.	He ____is____ here now.	He ____was____ here yesterday.
2. I __think__ about you every day.	**I'm thinking** about you now.	I ____thought____ about you yesterday.
3. We **play** tennis every day.	We _____ tennis now.	We _____ tennis yesterday.
4. I _____ juice every day.	I _____ juice now.	I **drank** juice yesterday.
5. He _____ every day.	He **is teaching** now.	He _____ yesterday.
6. She _____ every day.	She _____ now.	She **swam** yesterday.
7. You **sleep** late every day.	You _____ now.	You _____ late yesterday.
8. He _____ every day.	He **is reading** now.	He _____ yesterday.
9. They _____ hard every day.	They _____ hard now.	They **tried** hard yesterday.
10. We **eat** dinner every day.	We _____ dinner now.	We _____ dinner yesterday.

◇ PRACTICE 22. Simple present and simple past. (Chapter 1 and Charts 2-1 → 2-7)

Directions: Use the simple present or the simple past form of the verb in parentheses as appropriate. Complete the short answers to the questions.

1. A: *(you, hear)* ____Did you hear____ the thunder last night?

   B: No, I ____didn't____ . I *(hear, not)* ____didn't hear____ anything all night. I *(be)* ____was____ asleep.

2. A: Listen! *(you, hear)* ____Do you hear____ a siren in the distance?

   B: No, I ____don't____ . I *(hear, not)* ____don't hear____ anything at all.

3. A: That's a nice bookshelf. *(you, build)* _____ it?

   B: No, I _____ . My uncle *(build)* _____ it for me.

4. A: I have a question. *(a fish, be)* _____ slippery to hold?

   B: Yes, _____ . It can slip right out of your hand.

   A: How about frogs? *(they, be)* _____ slippery?

   B: Yes, _____ .

   A: What about snakes?

   B: I *(know, not)* _____ . I've never touched a snake.

5. A: I *(want)* _____ to go to the mall later this afternoon and look for a new

   bathing suit. *(you, want)* _____ to go with me?

   B: I can't. I *(have)* _____ an appointment with my English teacher. Besides,

   I *(buy)* _____ a new bathing suit last year. I *(need, not)* _____

   _____ a new one this year.

6. I always *(offer)* _____ to help my older neighbor carry her groceries into her

   house every time I see her return from the store. She *(be)* _____ always very

   grateful. Yesterday, she *(offer)* _____ to pay me for helping her, but of

   course I *(accept, not)* _____ the offer.

7. Last Monday night, I *(take)* _____ my sister and her husband to my favorite

   restaurant for dinner and *(find)* _____ the doors locked. I *(know, not)*

   _____ it then, but the restaurant *(be, not)* _____ open on

   Mondays. We *(want, not)* _____ to eat anywhere else, so we *(go)*

   _____ back to my house. I *(make)* _____ a salad and *(heat)*

   _____ some soup. Everyone *(seem)* _____ satisfied even

   though I *(be, not)* _____ a wonderful cook.

8. My daughter is twenty-one years old. She *(like)* _____ to travel. My wife and

   I *(worry)* _____ about her a little when she *(be)* _____ away from

   home, but we also *(trust)* _____ her judgment.

   Last year, after she *(graduate)* _____ from college, she *(go)*

   _____ to Europe with two of her friends. They *(travel, not)* _____

   _____ by train or by car. Instead, they *(rent)* _____

   motor scooters and *(ride)* _____ slowly through each country they visited.

   While she *(be)* _____ away, my wife and I *(worry)* _____

   about her safety. We *(be)* _____ very happy when we *(see)* _____ her

   smiling face at the airport and *(know)* _____ that she was finally safe at home.

◇ PRACTICE 23. Past progressive. (Charts 2-8 and 2-9)

Directions: Complete the sentences by using the past progressive of the given verbs. Use each verb only once.

✓hide look read sing sit talk watch

1. Jack's wife arranged a surprise birthday party for him. When Jack arrived home, several people ____were hiding____ behind the couch or behind doors. All of the lights were out, and when Jack turned them on, everyone shouted "Surprise!"

2. The birds began to sing when the sun rose at 6:30. Dan woke up at 6:45. When Dan woke up, the birds _____ .

3. I _____ a video last night when my best friend called.

4. While we _____ on the phone, the power went out.

5. The bus driver looked at all the passengers on her bus and noticed how quiet they were. Some people _____ newspapers or books. Most of the people _____ quietly in their seats and _____ out the windows of the bus.

◇ PRACTICE 24. Past progressive. (Charts 2-8 and 2-9)

Directions: Complete the sentences. Use the simple past for one clause and the past progressive for the other.

ACTIVITY IN PROGRESS	NADIA	GEORGE	BILL
play soccer	break her glasses	score a goal	hurt his foot
hike	find some money	see a bear	pick up a snake
dance	trip and fall	meet his future wife	get dizzy

1. While Nadia ____was playing____ soccer, she ____broke____ her glasses.

2. George ____scored____ a goal while he ____was playing____ soccer.

3. Bill _____ his foot while he _____ soccer.

4. While Nadia _____ , she _____ some money.

5. George _____ a bear while he _____ .

6. Bill _____ a snake while he _____ .

7. Nadia _____ and _____ while she _____ .

8. While George _____ , he _____ his future wife.

9. While Bill _____ , he _____ dizzy.

◇ PRACTICE 25. Past progressive vs. simple past. (Charts 2-8 and 2-9)

Directions: Complete the sentences with the verbs in parentheses. Use the simple past or the past progressive.

1. It *(begin)* _____began_____ to rain while Amanda and I *(walk)*

   _____were walking_____ to school this morning.

2. While I *(wash)* _____ dishes last night, I *(drop)*

   _____ a plate and *(break)* _____ it.

3. I *(see)* _____ Ted at the student cafeteria at lunchtime yesterday. He *(eat)*

   _____ a sandwich and *(talk)* _____ with some

   friends. I *(join)* _____ them.

4. While I *(walk)* _____ under an apple tree a few days ago, an apple

   (fall) _____ and *(hit)* _____ me on the head.

5. Robert didn't answer the phone when Sara called. He *(sing)* _____

   his favorite song in the shower and *(hear, not)* _____ the phone ring.

6. A: I saw a whale!

   B: Really? Great! When?

   A: This morning. I *(walk)* _____ on the beach when I *(hear)*

   _____ a sudden "whoosh!" It *(be)* _____ the spout of

   a huge gray whale.

7. A: There was a power outage in our part of town last night. *(your lights, go out)* _____

   _____ too?

   B: Yes, they did. It *(be)* _____ terrible! I *(take)* _____ a

   shower when the lights went out. My wife *(find)* _____ a flashlight and

   rescued me from the bathroom. We couldn't cook dinner, so we *(eat)* _____

   sandwiches instead. I *(try)*

   _____ to read some

   reports by candlelight, but I couldn't

   see well enough, so I *(go)*

   _____ to bed

   and *(sleep)* _____ .

   How about you?

8. Yesterday Tom and Janice *(go)* _____ to the zoo, where they *(see)*

_____ many kinds of animals and *(have)* _____ a few

adventures. While they *(walk)* _____ by an elephant, it *(begin)*

_____ to squirt water at them, so they run behind a rock and *(dry)*

_____ themselves. Later, while they *(pass)* _____

the giraffe area, one of the tall, purple-tongued animals *(lower)* _____ its

head toward Tom and *(start)* _____ to nibble on his green hat. Janice

said, "Shoo!"* At that point, the giraffe *(stretch)* _____ its head toward

Janice and *(try)* _____ to eat her ice cream cone. Janice *(let, not)*

_____ the giraffe have the ice cream because she *(stand)*

_____ right in front of a sign that said, "DO NOT FEED THE

ANIMALS." She *(point)* _____ at the sign and *(say)* _____

to the giraffe, "Can't you read?"

◇ PRACTICE 26. Past time using time clauses. (Chart 2-10)
Directions: Combine the two sentences in any order, using the time expression in parentheses.
<u>Underline</u> the time clause.

1. I gave Alan his allowance. He finished his chores. *(after)*
   → *I gave Alan his allowance <u>after he finished his chores.</u>* OR
   → *<u>After Alan finished his chores,</u> I gave him his allowance.*

2. The doorbell rang. I was climbing the stairs. *(while)*

3. The firefighters checked the ashes one last time. They went home. *(before)*

4. The Novaks stopped by our table at the restaurant. They showed us their new baby. *(when)*

5. We started to dance. The music began. *(as soon as)*

6. We stayed in our seats. The game ended. *(until)*

7. My father was listening to a baseball game on the radio. He was watching a basketball game

   on television. *(while)*

---

*"Shoo! Shoo!" means "Go away! Leave!" When the woman *shooed* the giraffe, that means she said "Shoo! Shoo!" and made
the giraffe leave.

◇ PRACTICE 27. Past verbs. (Charts 2-1 → 2-10)
Directions: Complete the sentences with the correct form of the verbs in parentheses.

Last Friday was a holiday. It *(be)* _____ Independence Day, so I didn't
                                              1

have to go to classes. I *(sleep)* _____ a little later than usual. Around ten, my
                                            2

friend Larry *(come)* _____ over to my apartment. We *(pack)* _____
                              3   4

a picnic basket and then *(take)* _____ the bus to Forest Park. We *(spend)*
                                          5

_____ most of the day there.
          6

When we *(get)* _____ to the park, we *(find)* _____ an empty
                          7   8

picnic table near a pond. There were some ducks on the pond, so we *(feed)* _____
                                                                                          9

them. We *(throw)* _____ small pieces of bread on the water, and the ducks
                            10

(swim) _____ over to get them. One duck was very clever. It *(catch)*
                  11

_____ the bread in midair before it *(hit)* _____ the water.
          12   13

Another duck was a thief. It *(steal)* _____ bread from the beaks of other ducks.
                                                14

While we *(feed)* _____ the ducks, Larry and I *(meet)* _____
                          15   16

a man who usually *(come)* _____ to the park every day to feed the ducks. We
                                    17

(sit) _____ on a park bench and *(speak)* _____ to him for fifteen
              18   19

or twenty minutes.

After we *(eat)* _____ our lunch, I
20

(take) _____ a short nap under a tree.
21

While I *(sleep)* _____ , a
22

mosquito *(bite)* _____ my arm. When I
23

(wake) _____ up, my arm itched, so I
24

scratched it. Suddenly I *(hear)* _____ a
25

noise in the tree above me. I *(look)* _____
26

up and *(see)* _____ an orange and gray
27

bird. After a few moments, it *(fly)* _____
28

away.

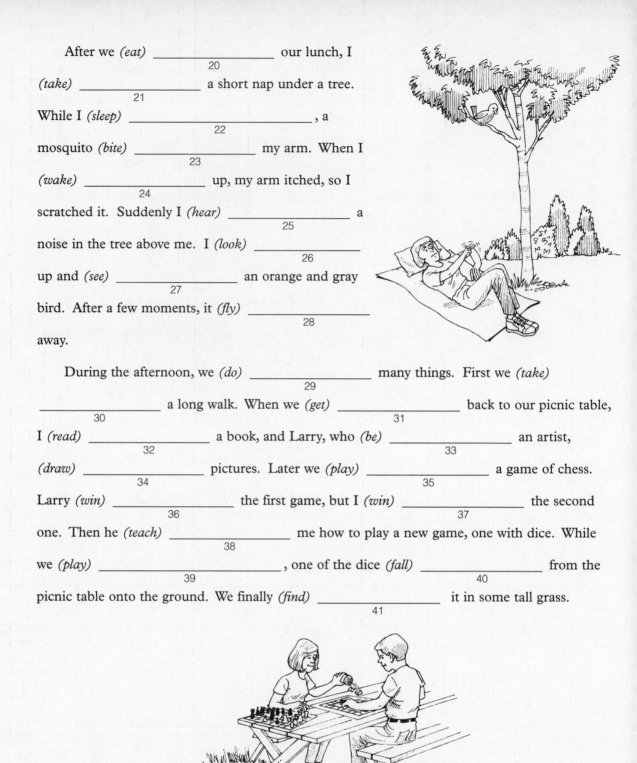

During the afternoon, we *(do)* _____ many things. First we *(take)*
29

_____ a long walk. When we *(get)* _____ back to our picnic table,
30   31

I *(read)* _____ a book, and Larry, who *(be)* _____ an artist,
32   33

(draw) _____ pictures. Later we *(play)* _____ a game of chess.
34   35

Larry *(win)* _____ the first game, but I *(win)* _____ the second
36   37

one. Then he *(teach)* _____ me how to play a new game, one with dice. While
38

we *(play)* _____ , one of the dice *(fall)* _____ from the
39   40

picnic table onto the ground. We finally *(find)* _____ it in some tall grass.
41

In the evening, we *(join)* _____ a huge crowd to watch the fireworks display.
42

The fireworks *(be)* _____ beautiful. Some of the explosions *(be)* _____
43   44

very loud, however. They *(hurt)* _____ my ears. When the display *(be)*
                                        45
_____ over, we *(leave)* _____ . All in all, it *(be)* _____
        46   47   48
a very enjoyable day.

◇ **PRACTICE 28. Past habit with USED TO. (Chart 2-11)**
    Directions: Using the given information, complete the sentences. Use **used to**.

1. When James was young, he hated school. Now he likes school.

    → James ____*used to hate school*____ .

2. Ann was a secretary for many years, but now she owns her own business.

    → Ann _____ , but now she owns her own business.

3. Rebecca had a pet rat when she was ten. The rat died, and she hasn't had another rat as a pet
    since that time.

    → Rebecca _____ as a pet.

4. Before Adam got married, he went bowling five times a week.

    → Adam _____ five times a week.

5. When we raised our own chickens, we had fresh eggs every morning.

    → We _____ every morning when we raised
    our own chickens.

6. When Ben was a child, he often crawled under his bed and put his hands over his ears when
    he heard thunder.

    → Ben _____ and
    _____ when he heard thunder.

7. When I lived in my home town, I went to the beach every weekend. Now I don't go to the beach every weekend.

    → I _____ to the beach every weekend, but now I don't.

8. Adam has a new job. He has to wear a suit every day. When he was a student, he always wore jeans.

    → Adam _____ a suit every day, but now he does.

9. Sara has two cats that she enjoys as pets. In the past, she hated cats. These are her first pets.

    → Sara _____ cats. She _____

    pets, but today she enjoys her two cats.

10. Now you have a job every summer. Have you always worked during summers?

    → What _____ in summer?

◇ PRACTICE 29. Error analysis. (Chapter 2)
   Directions: Correct the errors.

                 didn't stay
1. They ~~don't stayed~~ at the park very long last Saturday.

2. They are walked to school yesterday.

3. I was understand all the teacher's questions yesterday.

4. We didn't knew what to do when the fire alarm ringed yesterday.

5. I was really enjoyed the baseball game last week.

6. Mr. Rice didn't died in the accident.

7. I use to live with my parents. but now I have my own apartment.

8. My friends were went on vacation together last month.

9. I didn't afraid of anything when I am a child.

10. The teacher was changed his mind yesterday.

11. Sally love Jim, but he didn't loved her.

12. Carmen no used to eat fish, but now she does.

◇ **PRACTICE 30. Past verbs. (Chapter 2)**

Directions: Complete the sentences with the simple past or the past progressive of the verbs in parentheses.

Late yesterday afternoon while I *(prepare)* ___**was preparing**___ dinner, the doorbell
                                            1

(ring) _____ . I *(put)* _____ everything down and *(rush)*
             2   3

_____ to answer it. I *(open)* _____ the door and *(find)*
        4   5

_____ a delivery man standing in my doorway. He *(hold)*
        6

_____ an express mail package and *(need)* _____ me to sign
            7   8

for it. While I *(deal)* _____ with the delivery man, the phone *(ring)*
                               9

_____ . I *(excuse)* _____ myself and *(reach)* _____
        10   11   12

for the phone. While I *(try)* _____ to talk on the phone and sign for the
                                    13

package at the same time, my young son *(run)* _____ up to me to tell me about
                                                          14

the cat. The cat *(try)* _____ to catch a big fish in my husband's prized
                                15

aquarium. The fish *(swim)* _____ frantically to avoid the cat's paw.
                                    16

I *(say)* _____ an abrupt goodbye to the telemarketer on the phone and
                    17

(hang) _____ up. I *(thank)* _____ the delivery man and *(shut)*
                   18   19

_____ the door. I *(yell)* _____ at the cat and *(shoo)*
       20   21

_____ her away from the fish. Then I *(sit)* _____ down in an easy
       22   23

chair and *(stay)* _____ there until I *(begin)* _____ to feel calm
                        24   25

again. But as soon as I *(feel)* _____ like everything was under control, the
                                         26

doorbell *(ring)* _____ again. Then the phone *(ring)* _____ . Then
                       27   28

my son said, "Mom! Mom! The dog is in the refrigerator!" I couldn't move. "What's next?" I

said aloud to no one in particular.

CHAPTER 3
Future Time

◇ PRACTICE 1. Present, past, and future. (Chapters 1, 2, and 3)
    Directions: Complete the sentences with the given verbs. Use the simple present, the simple past, and ***be going to/will***.

1. *arrive*   a. Joe   *arrives*   on time **every day**.

               b. Joe   *arrived*   on time **yesterday**.

               c. Joe   *is going to arrive*   on time **tomorrow**.   OR

                   Joe   *will arrive*   on time **tomorrow**.

2. *eat*   a. Ann _____ breakfast **every day**.

            b. Ann _____ breakfast **yesterday**.

            c. Ann _____ breakfast **tomorrow**.   OR

                Ann _____ breakfast **tomorrow**.

3. *arrive, not*   a. Mike _____ on time **every day**.

                     b. Mike _____ on time **yesterday**.

                     c. Mike   *isn't going to arrive*   on time **tomorrow**.   OR

                      Mike _____ on time **tomorrow**.

4. *eat?*   a. _____ you _____ breakfast **every day**?

            b. _____ you _____ breakfast **yesterday**?

            c. _____ you _____ breakfast **tomorrow**? OR

              _____ you _____ breakfast **tomorrow**?

5. *eat, not*   a. I _____ breakfast **every day**.

              b. I _____ breakfast **yesterday**.

              c. I _____ breakfast **tomorrow**.   OR

               I _____ breakfast **tomorrow**

◇ PRACTICE 2. WILL and BE GOING TO. (Charts 3-1 → 3-3)
Directions: Complete the chart with the correct forms of the verbs.

be going to		will	
I ___am going to___ leave.		I ___will___ leave.	
You _____ leave.		You _____ leave.	
Mr. Rose _____ leave.		He _____ leave.	
We _____ leave.		We _____ leave.	
Our parents _____ leave.		They _____ leave.	
The boys (not) _____ leave.		They (not) _____ leave.	
Ann (not) _____ leave.		She (not) _____ leave.	
I (not) _____ leave.		I (not) _____ leave.	

◇ PRACTICE 3. BE GOING TO. (Chart 3-2)
Directions: Complete the sentences by using a pronoun + a form of *be going to*.

1. I ate lunch with Alan today, and ___I'm going to eat___ lunch with him tomorrow too.

2. Jason wasn't in class today, and ___he isn't going to be___ in class tomorrow either.

3. The students took a quiz yesterday, and _____ another quiz today.

4. Margaret walked to school this morning, and _____ to school tomorrow morning too.

5. It isn't raining today, and according to the weather report, _____ tomorrow either.

6. We're in class today, and _____ in class tomorrow too.

7. You didn't hitchhike to school today, and _____ to school tomorrow either.

8. I didn't get married last year, and _____ married this year either.

9. Peter didn't wear a clean shirt today, and _____ a clean one tomorrow either.

◇ PRACTICE 4. WILL. (Chart 3-3)
Directions: Read the paragraph. Change all the verbs with *be going to* to *will*.

        will
The Smiths ~~are going to~~ celebrate their 50th wedding anniversary on December 1 of this

year. Their children are planning a party for them at a local hotel. Their family and friends are

going to join them for the celebration.

Mr. and Mrs. Smith have three children and five grandchildren. The Smiths know that two of their children are going to be at the party, but the third child, their youngest daughter, is far away in Africa, where she is doing medical research. They believe she is not going to come home for the party.

The Smiths don't know it, but their youngest daughter is going to be at the party. She is planning to surprise them. It is going to be a wonderful surprise for them! They are going to be very happy to see her. The whole family is going to enjoy being together for this special occasion.

◇ PRACTICE 5. Questions with WILL and BE GOING TO. (Charts 3-1 → 3-3)
Directions: Use the given information to complete the questions. Write the question forms for both *will* and *be going to*.

1. Nick is thinking about *starting* an Internet company. His friends are wondering:

   <u>Will Nick start</u> _____ an Internet company?

   <u>Is Nick going to start</u> _____ an Internet company?

2. The teacher, Mr. Jones, is thinking about *giving* a test. His students are wondering:

   _____ a test?

   _____ a test?

3. Jacob is thinking about *quitting* his job. His co-workers are wondering:

   _____ his job?

   _____ his job?

4. Mr. and Mrs. Kono are thinking about *adopting* a child. Their friends are wondering:

   _____ a child?

   _____ a child?

5. The Johnsons are thinking about *moving*. Their friends are wondering:

   _____ ?

   _____ ?

6. Dr. Johnson is thinking about *retiring*. Her patients are wondering:

   _____ ?

   _____ ?

◇ **PRACTICE 6. WILL. (Chart 3-3)**
   Directions: Complete the dialogues. Use ***will***.

1. A: *(you, help)* _____Will you help_____ me tomorrow?
   B: Yes, _____I will*_____ .   OR   No, _____I won't_____ .

2. A: *(Paul, lend)* _____ us some money?
   B: Yes, _____ .   OR   No, _____ .

3. A: *(Jane, graduate)* _____ this spring?
   B: Yes, _____ .   OR   No, _____ .

4. A: *(her parents, be)* _____ at the ceremony?
   B: Yes, _____ .   OR   No, _____ .

5. A: *(I, benefit)* _____ from this business deal?
   B: Yes, _____ .   OR   No, _____ .

◇ **PRACTICE 7. WILL PROBABLY. (Chart 3-4)**
   Directions: Complete the sentences with ***will*** or ***won't***. Also use ***probably***.

1. The clouds are leaving, and the sun is coming out. It _____probably won't_____
   rain anymore.

2. The weather is cold today. There's no reason to expect the weather to change. It
   _____will probably_____ be cold tomorrow too.

3. Sam, Sharon, and Carl worked hard on this project. They _____
   turn in the best work. The other students didn't work as hard.

4. Ronald is having a very difficult time in advanced algebra. He didn't understand anything
   that happened in class today, and he _____ understand
   tomorrow's class either.

5. Jan skipped lunch today. She _____ eat as soon as she gets
   home.

6. I don't like parties. Mike really wants me to come to his birthday party, but I _____
   _____ go. I'd rather stay home.

_____

*Pronouns are NOT contracted with helping verbs in short answers.
   CORRECT: *Yes, I will.*   INCORRECT: *Yes, I'll.*

7. Conditions in the factory have been very bad for a long time. All of the people who work on the assembly line are angry. They _____ vote to go out on strike.

8. We are using up the earth's resources at a rapid rate. We _____ continue to do so* for years to come.

◇ PRACTICE 8. WILL PROBABLY. (Chart 3-4)
Directions: Complete the sentences.

PART I. Use a pronoun + *will/won't*. Use *probably*.
1. I went to the library last night, and ____I'll probably go____ there tonight too.

2. Ann didn't come to class today, and ____she probably won't come____ tomorrow either.

3. Greg went to bed early last night, and _____ to bed early tonight too.

4. Jack didn't hand his homework in today, and _____ it in tomorrow either.

5. The students had a quiz today, and _____ one tomorrow too.

PART II. Use a pronoun + *be going to/not be going to*. Use *probably*.
6. I watched TV last night, and ____I'm probably going to watch____ TV tonight too.

7. I wasn't at home last night, and _____ at home tonight either.

8. It's hot today, and _____ hot tomorrow too.

9. My friends didn't come over last night, and _____ over tonight either.

10. Alice didn't ride her bike to school today, and _____ it to school tomorrow either.

◇ PRACTICE 9. Sureness about the future. (Chart 3-4)
Directions: Decide if the speaker is 100%, 90%, or 50% sure.

1. ___90%___ You'll probably hear from our office tomorrow.

2. _____ Gino may not finish his assignment on time.

3. _____ My roommate will transfer to another university next year.

Do so means "do that thing I just talked about." In this sentence, do so = use up the earth's resources at a rapid rate.

4. _____ My roommate is probably going to change her major.

5. _____ Julia may join a health club next month.

6. _____ I will probably join a health club too.

7. _____ Karen and Lee are not going to continue dating each other.

8. _____ Maybe they will remain friends.

◇ PRACTICE 10. Sureness about the future. (Chart 3-4)

Directions: Answer each question by using the word in parentheses. Pay special attention to word order.

1. A: Are Joel and Rita going to have a simple wedding? *(probably)*

   B: Yes. Joel and Rita _____*are probably going to have*_____ a simple wedding.

2. A: Are they going to invite a lot of people? *(probably not)*

   B: No. They _____

   a lot of people.

3. A: Will they get married in Rita's garden? Or will they get married at a place of worship?

   (may, maybe)

   B: They're not sure. They _____ in Rita's garden.

   _____ they _____ at a place of worship.

4. A: Is Rita going to rent her wedding dress? *(may)*

   B: She's trying to save money, so she's thinking about it. She _____ her

   wedding dress.

5. A: Will she decide that she wants a wedding dress of her very own? *(probably)*

   B: She _____ that she wants a wedding dress of her very own.

6. A: Will Joel feel very relaxed on his wedding day? Will he be nervous? *(may not, may)*

   B: Joel _____ very relaxed on his wedding day. He _____

   _____ a little nervous.

7. A: Are they going to go on a honeymoon? *(will)*

   B: Yes. They _____ on a honeymoon immediately after the

   wedding, but they haven't told anyone where they are going to go.

8. A: Will they go far away for their honeymoon? *(probably not)*

   B: They _____ far. They have only a few days before

   they need to be back at work.

◇ PRACTICE 11. WILL. (Chart 3-5)

Directions: Complete the dialogues with *will* and a verb from the list. Use each verb only once.

✓ answer	hold	move	take
get	leave	read	turn off

1. At the office: A: The phone's ringing.

                  B: I <u>'ll answer it</u> .

2. At home: A: The baby won't stop crying.

                  B: I _____ her.

3. At the doctor's   A: I feel hot.

    office: B: I _____ your temperature.

4. At work: A: These boxes are in the way.

                  B: I _____ them.

5. At home: A: The oven's still on.

                  B: I _____ it _____ .

6. At a restaurant: A: You paid the bill. I _____ the tip.

                  B: Thanks!

7. At home: A: The mail's here.

                  B: I _____ it.

8. At a fast-food   A: I don't have my glasses. I can't read the menu board.

    restaurant: B: I _____ it to you.

◇ PRACTICE 12. BE GOING TO vs. WILL. (Chart 3-5)

Directions: Complete the sentences with either *be going to* or *will.**

1. (Speaker B is planning to listen to the news at six.)

A: Why did you turn on the radio?

B: I <u>'m going to</u> listen to the news at six.

2. (Speaker B didn't have a plan to show the other person how to solve the math problem, but she is happy to do it.)

A: I can't figure out this math problem. Do you know how to do it?

B: Yes. Give me your pencil. I <u>'ll</u> show you how to solve it.

_____

*Usually *be going to* and *will* are interchangeable: you can use either one of them with little difference in meaning. Sometimes, however, they are NOT interchangeable. In this exercise, only one of them is correct, not both. See Chart 3-5, p. 63, in the *FEG 3e* student book.

3. *(Speaker B has made a plan. He is planning to lie down because he doesn't feel well.)*

   A: What's the matter?

   B: I don't feel well. I _____ lie down for a little while. If anyone calls,
   tell them I'll call back later.

   A: Okay. I hope you feel better.

4. *(Speaker B did not plan to take the other person home. He volunteers to do so only after the other
   person talks about missing his bus.)*

   A: Oh no! I wasn't watching the time. I missed my bus.

   B: That's okay. I _____ give you a ride home.

   A: Hey, thanks!

5. *(Speaker B already has a plan.)*

   A: Why did you borrow money from the bank?

   B: I _____ buy a new pickup.* I've already picked it out.

6. *(Speaker B does not have a plan.)*

   A: Mom, can I have a candy bar?

   B: No, but I _____ buy an apple for you. How does that sound?

   A: Okay, I guess.

7. *(Speaker B has already made her plans about what to wear. Then Speaker B volunteers to help.)*

   A: I can't figure out what to wear to the dance tonight. It's informal, isn't it?

   B: Yes. I _____ wear a pair of nice jeans.

   A: Maybe I should wear my jeans, too. But I think they're dirty.

   B: I _____ wash them for you. I'm planning to do a load of laundry in
   a few minutes.

   A: Gee, thanks. That'll help me out a lot.

◇ PRACTICE 13. BE GOING TO vs. WILL. (Chart 3-5)
   Directions: Complete the sentences with either *be going to* or *will*.

   1. A: Can I borrow this book?

      B: Sure. But I need it back soon.

      A: I __'ll_____ return it to you tomorrow. Okay?

   2. A: I __'m going to_____ wear a dark suit to the wedding reception. How about you?

      B: I'm not sure.

   3. A: What are you doing with that picture?

      B: It doesn't look good in this room. I _____ hang it in our bedroom.

   ──────────
   *A *pickup* is a small truck.

4. A: Can you meet me for dinner after work?

   B: I'd like to, but I can't. I _____ work late tonight.

5. A: It's grandfather's eighty-fifth birthday next Sunday. What _____

   you _____ give him for his birthday?

   B: I _____ give him a walking stick that I made myself.

6. A: Gee, I'd really like an ice cream cone, but I didn't bring any money with me.

   B: That's okay. I _____ buy one for you.

   A: Thanks!

7. A: Why are you looking for a screwdriver?

   B: One of the kitchen chairs has a loose screw. I _____

   _____ fix it.

SCREW

8. A: The computer printer isn't working again! What am I going to do?

   B: Calm down. Give Tom a call. He _____

   fix it for you. He just fixed my printer.

SCREWDRIVER

9. A: Why is Nadia going to leave work early today?

   B: She _____ pick up her husband at the airport.

10. A: Achoo! Your cat is making me sneeze.

    B: I _____ put her outside.

    A: Thanks.

11. A: Do you have any plans for Saturday?

    B: I _____ help some friends move to their new home.

12. A: Your pants have ink on them.

    B: They do? I don't have another pair.

    A: Don't worry. I have some spot remover. I _____ get it for you.

◇ **PRACTICE 14. Past and future time clauses. (Charts 2-10 and 3-6)**
   Directions: <u>Underline</u> the time clauses.

   1. <u>After I did my homework last night</u>, I went to bed.

   2. I'm going to go to bed <u>after I do my homework tonight</u>.

   3. Before Bob left for work this morning, he locked the door.

   4. Before Bob leaves for work this morning, he's going to lock the door.

   5. I'll call you after I get home this evening.

   6. I called my friend after I got home last night.

   7. Class will begin as soon as the teacher arrives.

   8. As soon as the teacher arrived, class began.

   9. When the rain stops, we'll go for a walk.

   10. We went for a walk when the rain stopped.

◇ **PRACTICE 15. Future time clauses. (Chart 3-6)**
   Directions: Combine the ideas of the two given sentences into one sentence by using a time clause. Use the word in parentheses to introduce the time clause.

   1. *First:*   I'm going to finish my homework.
      Then: I'm going to go to bed.
      (after)   _____After I finish_____ my homework, _____I'm going to go_____ to bed.

   2. *First:*   I'll finish my homework.
      Then: I'm going to go to bed.
      (until)   _____I'm not going to go_____ to bed _____until I finish_____ my homework.

   3. *First:*   Ann will finish her homework.
      Then: She will watch TV tonight.*
      (before)   _____ TV tonight, _____ her
      homework.

   4. *First:*   Jim will get home tonight.
      Then: He's going to read the newspaper.
      (after)   _____ the newspaper _____
      home tonight.

   5. *First:*   I'll call John tomorrow.
      Then: I'll ask him to my party.
      (when)   _____ John tomorrow, _____ him
      to my party.

   _____
   *A noun usually comes before a pronoun:
      *After **Ann** eats dinner, **she** is going to study.*
      Ann *is going to study after* **she** *eats dinner.*

6. *First:* Mrs. Fox will stay in her office tonight.
   Then: She will finish her report.

   (until) _____ in her office tonight _____

   _____ her report.

7. *First:* I will get home tonight.
   Then: I'm going to take a hot bath.

   (as soon as) _____ home tonight, _____

   a hot bath.

8. *First:* I'm going to be in Bangkok.
   Then: I'm going to go to a Thai-style boxing match.

   (while) _____ in Bangkok, _____ to a

   Thai-style boxing match.

◇ **PRACTICE 16. IF-clauses. (Chart 3-6)**

Directions: Using the given ideas, complete each sentence by using an *if*-clause. Use a comma if necessary.*

1. Maybe it will rain tomorrow.

   _____*If it rains tomorrow,*_____ I'm going to go to a movie.

2. Maybe it will be hot tomorrow.

   _____ I'm going to go swimming.

3. Maybe Adam will have enough time.

   Adam will finish his essay tonight _____ .

4. Maybe I won't get a check tomorrow.

   _____ I'll e-mail my parents.

5. Perhaps the weather will be nice tomorrow.

   We're going to go on a hike _____ .

6. Maybe Gina won't study for her test.

   _____ she'll get a bad grade.

7. Maybe I will have enough money.

   I'm going to go to Hawaii for my vacation _____ .

8. Maybe I won't study tonight.

   _____ I probably won't pass the chemistry exam.

_____

*Notice the punctuation in the example. A comma is used when the *if*-clause comes before the main clause. No comma is used when the *if*-clause follows the main clause.

◇ **PRACTICE 17. Time clauses and IF-clauses. (Chart 3-6)**

Directions: Combine the ideas in the two sentences into one sentence by using the word in *italics* to make an adverb clause. Omit the words in parentheses from your new sentence. <u>Underline</u> the adverb clause.

1. *when*   a. I'll see you Sunday afternoon.
             b. I'll give you my answer (then).*

       → When I see you Sunday afternoon, I'll give you my answer. OR
         I'll give you my answer <u>when I see you Sunday afternoon</u>.

2. *before*   a. I'm going to clean up my apartment (first).
             b. My friends are going to come over (later).

3. *when*   a. The storm will be over (in an hour or two).
             b. I'm going to do some errands (then).

4. *if*   a. (Maybe) you won't learn how to use a computer.
             b. (As a result), you will have trouble finding a job.

5. *as soon as* a. Joe will meet us at the coffee shop.
             b. He'll finish his report (soon).

6. *after*   a. Sue will wash and dry the dishes.
             b. (Then) she will put them away.

7. *if*   a. They may not leave at seven.
             b. (As a result), they won't get to the theater on time.

◇ **PRACTICE 18. Review: past and future. (Chapters 2 and 3)**

Directions: Read Part I. Use the information in Part I to complete Part II with appropriate verb tenses. Use ***will*** (not ***be going to***) for future time in Part II. Use the simple present for present time.

PART I.

(1) Yesterday morning was an ordinary morning. I got up at 6:30. I washed my face and brushed my teeth. Then I put on my jeans and a sweater. I went to the kitchen and started the electric coffee maker.

---

*When you combine the sentences, omit the word in parentheses.

(2) Then I walked down my driveway to get the morning newspaper. While I was walking to get the paper, I saw a deer. It was eating the flowers in my garden. After I watched the deer for a little while, I made some noise to make the deer run away before it destroyed my flowers.

(3) As soon as I got back to the kitchen, I poured myself a cup of coffee and opened the morning paper. While I was reading the paper, my teenage daughter came downstairs. We talked about her plans for the day. I helped her with her breakfast and made a lunch for her to take to school. After we said goodbye, I ate some fruit and cereal and finished reading the paper.

(4) Then I went to my office. My office is in my home. My office has a desk, a computer, a radio, a fax, a copy machine, and a lot of bookshelves. I worked all morning. While I was working, the phone rang many times. I talked to many people. At 11:30, I went to the kitchen and made a sandwich for lunch. As I said, it was an ordinary morning.

PART II.

(1) Tomorrow morning ___will be___ an ordinary morning. I ___'ll get___ up at 6:30. I ___'ll wash___ my face and ___brush___ my teeth. Then I _____ probably _____ on my jeans and a sweater. I _____ to the kitchen and _____ the electric coffee maker.

(2) Then I _____ down my driveway to get the morning newspaper. If I _____ a deer in my garden, I _____ it for a while and then _____ some noise to chase it away before it _____ my flowers.

(3) As soon as I _____ back to the kitchen, I _____ myself a cup of coffee and _____ the morning paper. While I'm reading the paper, my teenage daughter _____ downstairs. We _____ about her plans for the day. I _____ her with her breakfast and _____ a lunch for her to take to school. After we _____ goodbye, I _____ some fruit and cereal and _____ reading the paper.

(4) Then I _____ to my office. My office _____ in my home. My office _____ a desk, a computer, a radio, a fax, a copy machine, and a lot of bookshelves. I _____ all morning. While I'm working, the phone _____ _____ many times. I _____ to many people. At 11:30, I _____ to the kitchen and _____ a sandwich for lunch. As I said, it _____ an ordinary morning.

◇ PRACTICE 19. Using BE GOING TO and the present progressive to express future time.
(Chart 3-7)

Directions: Rewrite the sentences by using *be going to* and the present progressive.

1. I'm planning to stay home tonight.

_____I'm going to stay_____ home tonight.

_____I'm staying_____ home tonight.

2. They're planning to travel across the country by train this summer.

_____ across the country by train this summer.

_____ across the country by train this summer.

3. We're planning to get married in June.

_____ married in June.

_____ married in June.

4. He's planning to start graduate school next year.

_____ graduate school next year.

_____ graduate school next year.

5. She's planning to go to New Zealand next month.

_____ to New Zealand next month.

_____ to New Zealand next month.

6. My neighbors are planning to build their dream home this spring.

_____ their dream home this spring.

_____ their dream home this spring.

◇ PRACTICE 20. Using the present progressive to express future time. (Chart 3-7)

Directions: Complete the sentences with the present progressive. Use each verb in the list only once. Notice the future time expressions in *italics*.

arrive	come	meet	see	take
attend	get	plan	speak	✓ travel
call	leave	prepare	study	

1. Kathy _____is traveling_____ to Caracas *next month* to attend a conference.

2. A: Your apartment is so neat! Are you expecting guests?

B: Yes. My parents _____ *tomorrow* for a two-day visit.

3. A: Do you have any plans for lunch today?

   B: I _____ Shannon at the Shamrock Cafe *in an hour.* Want to join us?

4. A: I _____ a bicycle for my son for his birthday *next month.* Do you

      know anything about bikes for kids?

   B: Sure. What do you want to know?

5. Amanda likes to take her two children with her on trips whenever she can, but she

   _____ not _____ them with her to El Paso, Texas, *next week.* It's

   strictly a business trip.

6. A: What are your plans for the rest of the year?

   B: I _____ French in Grenoble, France, *this coming summer.* Then I'll be

      back here in school in the fall.

7. A: Why are you packing your suitcase?

   B: I _____ for Los Angeles *in a couple of hours.*

8. My regular dentist, Dr. Jordan, _____ a conference in Las Vegas *next*

   week, so I _____ her partner, Dr. Peterson, when I go in for my

   appointment *next Friday.*

9. A: Do we have a test in English class tomorrow?

   B: No. Don't you remember? We're going to have a guest lecturer.

   A: Really? Who? Are you sure we don't have a test?

   B: A professor from the Department of Environmental Sciences _____

      to our class tomorrow morning.

   A: Great! That sounds interesting. And it's a lot better than having a test.

10. A: My sister and her husband _____ over to my house for dinner

      tomorrow night. It's my sister's birthday, so I _____ a special

      birthday dinner for her. I _____ her favorite food: roast beef and

      mashed potatoes.

    B: That's nice. She'll like that.

11. A: I'm going to call the doctor. You have a fever, chills, and a stomach ache.

    B: No, don't call a doctor. I'll be okay.

    A: I'm worried. I _____ the doctor! And that's it!

◇ **PRACTICE 21. Using the simple present to express future time. (Chart 3-8)**
Directions: Use any of the verbs in the list to complete the sentences. Use the simple present to express future time.

arrive	*depart*	*get in*	*open*
begin	*end*	*land*	*start*
close	*finish*	*leave*	

1. A: What time _____does_____ class _____begin/start_____ tomorrow morning?

   B: It _____begins/starts_____ at eight o'clock sharp.

2. A: The coffee shop _____ at seven o'clock tomorrow morning. I'll meet you there at 7:15.

   B: Okay. I'll be there.

3. A: What time are you going to go to the airport tonight?

   B: Tom's plane _____ around 7:15, but I think I'll go a little early in case it gets in ahead of schedule.

4. A: What's the hurry?

   B: I've got to take a shower, change clothes, and get to the theater fast. The play _____ in forty-five minutes, and I don't want to miss the beginning.

5. A: What time _____ the dry cleaning shop _____ this evening? If I don't get there in time, I'll have nothing to wear to the banquet tonight.

   B: It _____ at 6:00. I can pick up your dry cleaning for you.

   A: Hey, thanks! That'll really help!

6. A: What time should we go to the theater tomorrow night?

   B: The doors _____ at 6:00 P.M., but we don't need to be there that early. The show _____ at 8:00. If we _____ at the theater by 7:15, we'll be there in plenty of time. The show _____ around 10:30, so we can be back home by a little after 11:00.

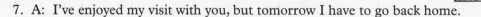

7. A: I've enjoyed my visit with you, but tomorrow I have to go back home.

   A: What time _____ your flight _____ tomorrow?

   B: It _____ at 12:34 P.M. I want to be at the airport an hour early, so we should leave here around 10:30, if that's okay with you.

   A: Sure. What time _____ your flight _____ in Mexico City?

   B: It's about a three-hour flight. I'll get in around 4:30 Mexico City time.

◇ **PRACTICE 22. Using BE ABOUT TO. (Chart 3-9)**
Directions: Write sentences using **be about to**. Use each verb in the list only once.

break	leave	✓rain	ring	write

1. A: What does it usually mean if the sky is cloudy and dark?

   B: It usually means that it _____is about to rain_____ .

2. A: What does it probably mean if Jack is standing by the front door with his car keys in his hand?

   B: It means that he _____ the house.

3. A: What does it mean if the teacher picks up a piece of chalk?

   B: It probably means that she _____ on the board.

4. A: You're in the kitchen. The oven timer has only a few seconds left. What does that mean?

   B: The timer _____ .

5. A: The heavy snow is making the tree branches hang down. One is almost touching the ground. What's going to happen?

   B: The branch _____ probably

   _____ .

◇ **PRACTICE 23. Parallel verbs. (Chart 3-10)**
Directions: Complete the sentences with the verbs in parentheses.

1. My classmates are going to meet at Danny's and *(study)* _____study_____ together tonight.

2. Tomorrow the sun will rise at 6:34 and *(set)* _____ at 8:59.

3. Last night, I was listening to music and *(do)* _____ my homework when Kim stopped by.

4. Next weekend, Nick is going to meet his friends downtown and *(go)* _____ to a soccer game.

5. My pen slipped out of my hand and *(fall)* _____ to the floor.

6. Alex is at his computer. He *(write)* _____ e-mails and *(wait)* _____ for responses.

7. Every morning without exception, Mrs. Carter *(take)* _____ her dog for a walk and *(buy)* _____ a newspaper at Charlie's newsstand.

8. Before I *(go)* _____ to your boss and *(tell)* _____ her about your mistake, I want to give you an opportunity to explain it to her yourself.

9. Next month, I *(take)* _____ my vacation and *(forget)* _____ about everything that is connected to my job.

10. Kathy thinks I was the cause of her problems, but I wasn't. Someday she *(discover)* _____ the truth and *(apologize)* _____ to me.

◇ PRACTICE 24. Error analysis. (Chapter 3)
Directions: Correct the errors.

1. My friends will ~~to~~ join us after work.

2. Maybe the rain stops soon.

3. On Friday, our school close early so teachers can go to a workshop.

4. My husband and I will intend to be at your graduation.

5. Our company is going to sells computer equipment to schools.

6. Give grandpa a hug. He's about to leaving.

7. Mr. Scott is going to retire and moving to a warmer climate.

8. If your soccer team will win the championship tomorrow, we'll have a big celebration for you.

9. I maybe won't be able to meet you for coffee.

10. I bought this cloth because I will make some curtains for my bedroom.

11. I moving to London when I will finish my education here.

12. Are you going go to the meeting?

13. I opened the door and walk to the front of the room.

14. When will you be going to move into your new apartment?

◇ **PRACTICE 25. Verb tense review. (Chapters 1 → 3)**

Directions: Complete the sentences by using a form of the words in parentheses.

1. It's getting late, but before I *(go)* _____go_____ to bed, I *(finish)* _____

_____ my homework and *(write)* _____ a couple of e-mails.

2. While I *(make)* _____ dinner last night, some grease *(spill)*

_____ out of the frying pan and *(catch)* _____ on

fire. When the smoke detector on the ceiling *(start)* _____ to buzz, my

roommate *(run)* _____ into the kitchen to find out what was wrong. He

(think) _____ that the house was on fire!

3. Mark is obsessed with video games. He *(play)* _____ video games morning,

noon, and night. Sometimes he *(cut)* _____ class to play them. Right now he

(do, not) _____ very well in

school. If he *(study, not)* _____

_____ harder and *(go)*

_____ to class every day, he *(flunk)*

_____ out of school.

4. Sometimes my daughter, Susie, has temper

tantrums. She *(cry)* _____ and

(stomp) _____ her feet when she

(get) _____ angry. Yesterday when

she *(get)* _____ angry, she *(pick)* _____ up a toy car and

(throw) _____ it at her little brother. Luckily, the car *(hit, not)* _____

_____ him. Susie *(feel)* _____ very bad. She *(apologize)*

_____ to her brother and *(kiss)* _____ him.

5. It's October now. The weather *(begin)* _____ to get colder. It *(begin)*

_____ to get cold every October. I *(like, not)* _____

winter, but I *(think)* _____ autumn is beautiful. In a couple of weeks, my

friend and I *(take)* _____ a weekend trip to the country if the

weather *(be)* _____ nice. We *(drive)* _____ through the

river valley and *(enjoy)* _____ the colors of fall.

6. Jane *(meet)* _____ me at the airport when my plane *(arrive)* _____ tomorrow.

7. If I *(see)* _____ Mike tomorrow, I *(tell)* _____ him about the party.

8. I go to New York often. When I *(be)* _____ in New York, I usually *(see)* _____ a Broadway play.

9. When I *(be)* _____ in New York next week, I *(stay)* _____ at the Park Plaza Hotel.

10. Cindy and I *(go)* _____ to the beach tomorrow if the weather *(be)* _____ warm and sunny.

11. Jack *(watch)* _____ a football game on TV right now. As soon as the game *(be)* _____ over, he *(mow)* _____ the grass in the back yard.

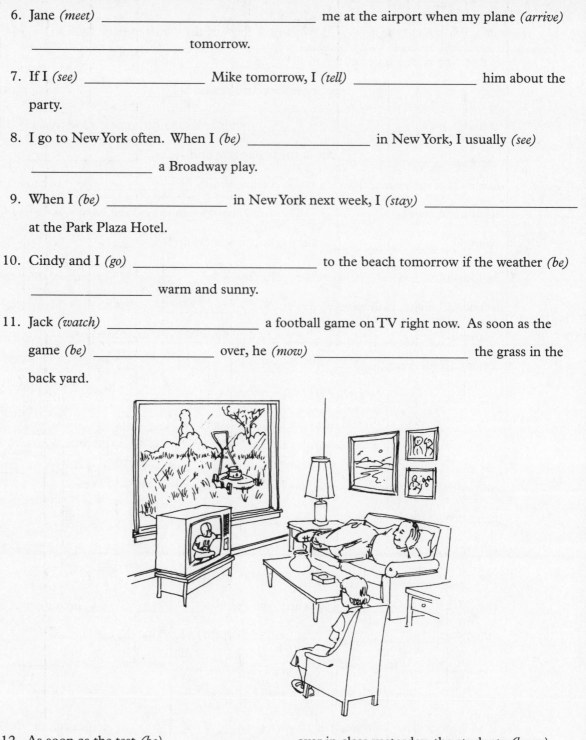

12. As soon as the test *(be)* _____ over in class yesterday, the students *(leave)* _____ the room.

13. As soon as I *(get)* _____ home every day, my children always *(run)* _____ to the door to meet me.

14. A: I'll lend you my bike if I *(need, not)* _____ it tomorrow.
    B: Thanks.

15. A: Everyone in the office *(plan)* _____ to come to the annual company

    picnic tomorrow. *(you, come)* _____?

    B: Of course!

16. A: How *(you, get, usually)* _____ to work?

    B: I *(take)* _____ the commuter train every morning.

17. This morning, Bob *(comb)* _____ his hair when the comb *(break)*

    _____ . So he *(finish)* _____ combing his hair with his

    fingers and *(rush)* _____ out the door to class.

18. I'm exhausted! When I *(get)* _____ home tonight, I *(read)* _____

    _____ the paper and *(watch)* _____ the news. I *(do, not)*

    _____ any work around the house.

19. Yesterday I *(see)* _____ the man who stole the radio from my car last Friday. I

    (run) _____ after him, *(catch)* _____ him, and *(knock)*

    _____ him down. A passerby *(go)* _____ to call the police. I

    (sit) _____ on the man while I *(wait)* _____ for them to come.

    After they *(get)* _____ there and *(understand)* _____ the

    situation, they *(put)* _____ handcuffs on him and *(take)* _____

    him to jail.

20. A: My cousin *(have)* _____ a new cat. She now *(have)* _____

    four cats.

    B: Why *(she, have)* _____ so many?

    A: To catch the mice in her house.

    B: *(you, have)* _____ any cats?

    A: No, and I *(get, not)* _____ any. I *(have, not)* _____

    _____ mice in my house.

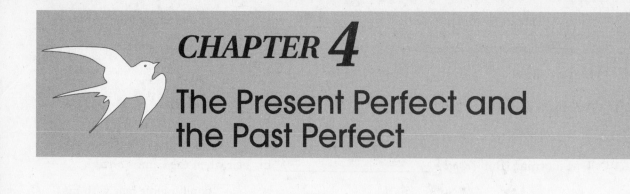

CHAPTER 4

The Present Perfect and the Past Perfect

◇ **PRACTICE 1. Forms of the present perfect.** (Charts 4-1 → 4-3)

Directions: Complete the dialogues with the given verbs and any words in parentheses. Use the present perfect.

1. *eat*   A: *(you, ever)* ___Have you ever eaten___ pepperoni pizza?

          B: Yes, I ___have___. I ___have eaten___ pepperoni pizza many times. OR

          No, I ___haven't___. I *(never)* ___have never eaten___ pepperoni pizza.

2. *talk*   A: *(you, ever)* _____ to a famous person?

          B: Yes, I _____. I _____ to a lot of famous people. OR

          No, I _____. I *(never)* _____ to a famous person.

3. *rent*   A: *(Erica, ever)* _____ a car?

          B: Yes, she _____. She _____ a car many times. OR

          No, she _____. She *(never)* _____ a car.

4. *see*   A: *(you, ever)* _____ a shooting star?

          B: Yes, I _____. I _____ a lot of shooting stars. OR

          No, I _____. I *(never)* _____ a shooting star.

5. *catch*   A: *(Joe, ever)* _____ a big fish?

          B: Yes, he _____. He _____ lots of big fish. OR

          No, he _____. He *(never)* _____ a big fish.

6. *have*   A: *(you, ever)* _____ a bad sunburn?

        B: Yes, I _____ . I _____ a bad sunburn several times. OR

          No, I _____ . I *(never)* _____ a bad

          sunburn.

◇ **PRACTICE 2. The present perfect. (Charts 4-1 → 4-3)**
    Directions: Complete the sentences with the present perfect of the verbs in parentheses.

1. A cell phone is so convenient. I *(want)* _____**have wanted**_____ one since they were
   available for sale.

2. I quit eating meat when I was in college. I *(be)* _____ a strict
   vegetarian for several years and feel very healthy.

3. We got a dog because we live in an isolated area. She *(be)* _____ a
   wonderful watchdog for us.

4. We *(fly)* _____ that airline many times because the service is excellent.

5. Our neighbors *(pick up, not)* _____ their mail yet. They may
   not be back from their trip.

6. Vivian *(change)* _____ her hair color so many times that no one can
   remember her natural color.

7. Our teacher *(correct, already)* _____ our tests, but she
   (return, not) _____ them yet.

8. A: Jose left two messages on my answering machine. I wonder what he wants.

    B: Maybe he just wants to talk. He said he *(talk, not)* _____
   to you in a long time.

9. My parents *(need)* _____ a new car for several months. They *(look)*
   _____ in lots of car showrooms, but they can't agree on what kind of car
   to buy.

10. A: *(you, have)* _____ your flu shot this year? I got mine last week.

    B: No, but I will. I *(get)* _____ one every year for the past three years.
   My doctor says it's a good idea after the age of 50.

◇ PRACTICE 3. Review: irregular verbs. (Charts 2-6, 2-7, and 4-1)
Directions: Write each verb in the correct group.

✓ring	put	quit	have	shut	teach
✓hurt	drink	stick	swim	sink	pay
✓win	stand	upset	find	let	bring
feed	keep	meet	sing	catch	set
weep	sit	cut	buy	fight	think

GROUP I. Simple form, simple past, and past participle are the same.

Example: cost → cost → cost

hurt	hurt	hurt

GROUP II. The vowel changes: i → a → u.

Example: begin → began → begun

ring	rang	rung

GROUP III. Simple past and past participle are the same.

Example: find → found → found

win	won	won

◇ **PRACTICE 4. The present perfect. (Charts 4-1 → 4-3)**
Directions: Complete the sentences with the present perfect of the verbs in the list and any words in parentheses. Use each verb only once.

eat	look	save	✓use
give	play	sleep	wear
improve	rise	speak	win

1. People _____**have used**_____ leather to make shoes for hundreds of years.

2. The night is over. It's daytime now. The sun _____.

3. I *(never)* _____ golf, but I'd like to. It looks like fun.

4. Our team is great. They _____ all of their games so far this year. They haven't lost a single game.

5. Amy must be mad at me. She *(not)* _____ one word to me all evening. I wonder what I did to make her angry.

6. The cat must be sick. He *(not)* _____ any food for two days. We'd better call the vet.

7. Our teacher _____ us a lot of tests and quizzes since the beginning of the term.

8. We put a little money in our savings account every month. We want to buy a car, but we *(not)* _____ enough money yet. We'll have enough in a few more months.

9. *(you, ever)* _____ outdoors for an entire night? I mean without a tent, with nothing between you and the stars?

10. My aunt puts on a wig whenever she goes out, but I *(never)* _____ a wig in my whole life.

11. Paul's health _____ a lot since he started eating the right kinds of food, exercising regularly, and handling the stress in his life. He's never felt better.

12. I can't find my keys. I _____ everywhere—in all my pockets, in my briefcase, in my desk. They're gone.

◇ **PRACTICE 5. The present perfect vs. the simple past.   (Charts 4-3 and 4-4)**
   Directions: Write **F** if the activity or situation is finished and **C** if it continues to the present.

   1. __C__ My grandfather *has worked* since he was in high school.

   2. __F__ My grandmother *worked* for 20 years.

   3. __F__ I *finished* my work two hours ago.

   4. __F__ I *have already finished* my work, so I'm leaving the office.

   5. _____ My father *has been* sick since yesterday.

   6. _____ Jane *was* sick last Monday.

   7. _____ Tom *has already left.* He's not here.

   8. _____ Tom *left* five minutes ago.

   9. _____ I *have known* Max Shell since we were children.

   10. _____ The baby *has had* a fever since midnight. I think I'll call the doctor.

   11. _____ The baby *had* a fever all night, but he's better now.

   12. _____ I *have had* the flu several times in my lifetime.

   13. _____ I *had* the flu last year.

   14. _____ Sue *has had* the flu since last Friday.

◇ **PRACTICE 6. Review: irregular verbs.   (Charts 2-6, 2-7, and 4-1)**
   Directions: Complete the sentences with the simple past and the present perfect of the given verbs.

   1. *begin*   I ____began____ a new diet and exercise program last week. I
                   ____have begun____ lots of new diet and exercise programs in my lifetime.

   2. *bend*   I _____ down to pick up my young son from his crib this morning. I
                   _____ down to pick him up many times since he was born.

   3. *broadcast* The radio _____ news about a terrible earthquake in Iran
                   last week. The radio _____ news about Iran every day
                   since the earthquake occurred there.

   4. *catch*   I _____ a cold last week. I _____ a lot
                   of colds in my lifetime.

   5. *come*   A tourist _____ into Mr. Nasser's jewelry store after lunch. A lot of
                   tourists _____ into his store since he opened it last year.

   6. *cut*   I _____ some flowers from my garden yesterday. I
                   _____ lots of flowers from my garden so far this summer.

   7. *dig*   The workers _____ a hole to fix the leak in the water pipe. They
                   _____ many holes to fix water leaks since the earthquake.

8. *draw*　　　The artist _____ a picture of a sunset yesterday. She

　　　　　　　_____ many pictures of sunsets in her lifetime.

9. *feed*　　　I _____ birds at the park yesterday. I _____ birds

　　　　　　　at the park every day since I lost my job.

10. *fight*　　　We _____ a war last year. We _____ several

　　　　　　　wars since we became an independent country.

11. *forget*　　　I _____ to turn off the stove after dinner. I _____

　　　　　　　_____ to turn off the stove a lot of times in my lifetime.

12. *hide*　　　The children _____ in the basement yesterday. They _____

　　　　　　　_____ in the basement often since they discovered a secret place there.

13. *hit*　　　The baseball player _____ the ball out of the stadium yesterday. He

　　　　　　　_____ a lot of home runs since he joined our team.

14. *hold*　　　My husband _____ the door open for me when he entered the

　　　　　　　restaurant. He _____ a door open for me many times since

　　　　　　　we met each other.

15. *keep*　　　During the discussion yesterday, I _____ my opinion to myself. I

　　　　　　　_____ my opinions to myself a lot of times in my lifetime.

16. *lead*　　　Mary _____ the group discussion at the conference. She

　　　　　　　_____ group discussions many times since she started going to

　　　　　　　conferences.

17. *lose*　　　Eddie _____ money at the racetrack yesterday. He _____

　　　　　　　_____ money at the racetrack lots of times in his lifetime.

18. *meet*   I _____ two new people in my class yesterday. I _____

a lot of new people since I started going to school here.

19. *ride*   I _____ the bus to work yesterday. I _____

the bus to work many times since I got a job downtown.

20. *ring*   The doorbell _____ a few minutes ago. The doorbell _____

_____ three times so far today.

21. *see*   I _____ a good movie yesterday. I _____ a lot of

good movies in my lifetime.

22. *steal*   The fox _____ a chicken from the farmer's yard. The fox _____

_____ three chickens so far this month.

23. *stick*   I _____ a stamp on the corner of the envelope. I _____

_____ lots of stamps on envelopes in my lifetime.

24. *sweep*   I _____ the floor of my apartment yesterday. I _____

the floor of my apartment lots of times since I moved in.

25. *take*   I _____ a test yesterday. I _____ lots of tests in

my life as a student.

26. *upset*   The Smith children _____ Mr. Jordan when they broke his window.

Because they are careless and noisy, they _____ Mr. Jordan

many times since they moved in next door.

27. *withdraw*   I _____ some money from my bank account yesterday. I

_____ more than three hundred dollars from my

bank account so far this month.

28. *write*   I _____ a letter to a friend last night. I _____

lots of letters to my friends in my lifetime.

◇ **PRACTICE 7. The present perfect vs. the simple past. (Chart 4-4)**
Directions: Fill in the blanks with the present perfect or simple past form of the verb.

1. I *(go)* _____went_____ to Toronto last year for business. I *(go)* _____have gone_____

there several times since then.

2. I *(live)* _____ in British Columbia from 1998 to 2000.

3. My friend, Joe, *(live)* _____ in Vancouver since 2000.

4. Before Joe *(move)* _____ to Vancouver, he *(work)* _____ on cruise ships as a cook.

5. My college roommate came from Ghana. We *(room)* _____ together for three years, and then she *(return)* _____ home.

6. My grandfather *(be)* _____ a great golfer for most of his life, but he *(die)* _____ last year.

7. My father *(play)* _____ competitive golf for most of his life and really enjoys it.

8. Since my husband began working the night shift, he *(sleep, not)* _____ very well.

9. When I lived in Alaska, the long daylight hours *(make)* _____ it difficult for me to sleep.

10. Since I was a child, I *(enjoy)* _____ collecting rocks from the beach.

11. When I was a child, my friends *(collect)* _____ rocks with me.

◇ **PRACTICE 8. Review: irregular verbs. (Charts 2-6, 2-7, and 4-1)**
   Directions: This is a review of irregular verbs. Complete the sentences with the simple past or the present perfect of the given verbs and any words in parentheses.

1. *go*   a. I _____ **have gone** _____ to every play at the local theater so far this year.

   b. My whole family _____ **went** _____ to the play last weekend.

2. *give*   a. Jane _____ **gave** _____ me a ride home from work today.

   b. *(she, ever)* _____ **Has she ever given** _____ you a ride home since she started working in your department?

3. *fall*   a. I _____ down many times in my lifetime, but never hard enough to really hurt myself or break a bone.

   b. Mike _____ down many times during football practice yesterday.

4. *break* a. *(you, ever)* _____ a bone in your body?

   b. I _____ my leg when I was ten years old. I jumped off the roof of my house.

5. *shake* a. In my entire lifetime, I *(never)* _____ hands with a famous movie star.

   b. In 2000, I _____ hands with a famous soccer player.

6. *hear* a. I _____ you practicing your trumpet late last night.

b. In fact, I _____ you practicing every night for two weeks.

7. *fly* a. Mike is a commercial airline pilot. Yesterday he _____ from Tokyo to Los Angeles.

b. Mike _____ to many places in the world since he became a pilot.

8. *wear* a. Carol really likes her new leather jacket. She _____ it every day since she bought it.

b. She _____ her new leather jacket to the opera last night.

9. *build* a. *(you, ever)* _____ a piece of furniture?

b. My daughter _____ a table in her woodworking class at the high school last year.

10. *teach* a. Ms. Kent _____ math at the local high school since 1995.

b. She _____ in Hungary last year on an exchange program.

11. *find* a. In your lifetime, *(you, ever)* _____ something really valuable?

b. My sister _____ a very expensive diamond ring in the park last year.

12. *drive* a. After I took Danny to school, I _____ straight to work.

b. I'm an experienced driver, but I *(never)* _____ a bus or a big truck.

13. *sing*   a. I _____ a duet with my mother at the art benefit last night.

               b. We _____ together ever since I was a small child.

14. *run*   a. I (*never*) _____ in a marathon race, and I don't intend to.

               b. I'm out of breath because I _____ all the way over here.

15. *tell*   a. Last night, my brother _____ me a secret.

               b. He _____ me lots of secrets in his lifetime.

16. *stand*   a. When I visited the United Nations last summer, I _____ in the main gallery and felt a great sense of history.

               b. Many great world leaders _____ there over the years.

17. *spend*   a. I _____ all of my money at the mall yesterday.

               b. I don't have my rent money this month. I (*already*) _____ _____ it on other things.

18. *make*   a. I consider myself fortunate because I _____ many good friends in my lifetime.

               b. I _____ a terrible mistake last night. I forgot that my friend had invited me to his apartment for dinner.

19. *rise*   a. The price of flour _____ a lot since February.

               b. When his name was announced, Jack _____ from his seat and walked to the podium to receive his award.

20. *feel*   a. I _____ terrible yesterday, so I stayed in bed.

               b. I _____ terrible for a week now. I'd better see a doctor.

◇ PRACTICE 9. SINCE vs. FOR. (Chart 4-5)
Directions: Complete the sentences with *since* or *for*.

1. David has worked for the power company ____*since*____ 1999.

2. His brother has worked for the power company ____*for*____ five years.

3. I have known Peter Gow _____ September.

4. I've known his sister _____ three months.

5. Jonas has walked with a limp _____ many years.

6. He's had a bad leg _____ he was in the war.

7. Rachel hasn't been in class _____ last Tuesday.

8. She hasn't been in class _____ three days.

9. My vision has improved _____ I got new reading glasses.

10. I've had a toothache _____ yesterday morning.

11. I've had this toothache _____ thirty-six hours.

12. I've had a cold _____ almost a week.

13. Jane hasn't worked _____ last summer when the factory closed down.

14. I attended Jefferson Elementary School _____ six years.

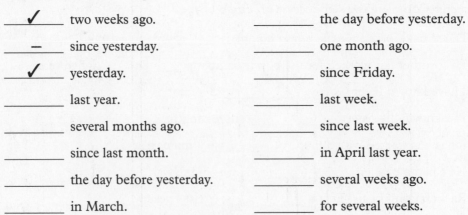

◇ **PRACTICE 10. Present perfect with SINCE and FOR. (Chart 4-5)**
Directions: Rewrite the sentences using *since* or *for*.

1. I was in this class a month ago, and I am in this class now.
   → *I have been in this class for a month.*

2. I knew my teacher in September, and I know her now.

3. Sam wanted a dog two years ago, and he wants one now.

4. Sara needed a new car last year, and she still needs one.

5. Our professor was sick a week ago, and she is still sick.

6. They live in Canada. They moved there in December.

7. I know Mrs. Brown. I met her in 1999.

8. Tom works at a fast-food restaurant. He got the job three weeks ago.

◇ **PRACTICE 11. Present perfect and simple past with time words. (Charts 4-1 → 4-5)**
Directions: Check all the phrases that correctly complete the sentences. Mark those that don't with a dash. The first item has been started for you.

1. The Petersons took a trip

____✓____ two weeks ago.

____—____ since yesterday.

____✓____ yesterday.

_____ last year.

_____ several months ago.

_____ since last month.

_____ the day before yesterday.

_____ in March.

2. The Petersons have been out of town

_____ the day before yesterday.

_____ one month ago.

_____ since Friday.

_____ last week.

_____ since last week.

_____ in April last year.

_____ several weeks ago.

_____ for several weeks.

◇ PRACTICE 12. SINCE-clauses. (Chart 4-5)

Directions: Complete the sentences with the words in parentheses. Use the present perfect or the simple past.

1. Carol and I are old friends. I *(know)* __have known__ her since I *(be)* __was__ a freshman in high school.

2. Maria *(have)* _____ a lot of problems since she *(come)* _____ to this country.

3. I *(experience, not)* _____ any problems since I *(come)* _____ here.

4. Since the semester *(begin)* _____ , our teacher *(give)* _____ four tests.

5. Mike *(be)* _____ in school since he *(be)* _____ six years old.

6. My mother *(be, not)* _____ in school since she *(graduate)* _____ from college in 1978.

7. Since I *(start)* _____ doing this exercise, I *(complete)* _____ six sentences.

8. Since soccer season *(begin)* _____ , our son *(have, not)* _____ _____ much free time.

9. Our long-distance phone calls *(become)* _____ less expensive since we *(change)* _____ to a different telephone company.

10. Our phone bill *(rise)* _____ since we *(buy)* _____ a cell phone.

◇ PRACTICE 13. The present perfect progressive. (Charts 4-6 and 4-7)

Directions: Use the given information to complete the dialogues. Use the present perfect progressive.

1. Eric is studying. He started to **study** at seven o'clock. It is now nine o'clock.
   A: How long __has Eric been studying__ ?
   B: He __'s been studying__ for __two hours__ .

2. Kathy is working at the computer. She began to **work** at the computer at two o'clock. It is now three o'clock.
   A: How long __has Kathy been working at the computer__ ?
   B: She __'s been working__ since __two o'clock__ .

3. It began to **rain** two days ago. It is still raining.

A: How long _____?

B: It _____ for _____.

4. Liz is reading. She began to **read** at ten o'clock. It is now ten-thirty.

A: How long _____?

B: She _____ for _____.

5. Boris began to **study** English in 2001. He is still studying English.

A: How long _____?

B: He _____ since _____.

6. Three months ago, Nicole started to **work** at the Silk Road Clothing Store.

A: How long _____?

B: She _____ for _____.

7. Ms. Rice started to **teach** at this school in September 2001.

A: How long _____?

B: She _____ since _____.

8. Mr. Fisher **drives** a Chevy. He bought it twelve years ago.

A: How long _____?

B: He _____ for _____.

9. Mrs. Taylor is **waiting** to see her doctor. She arrived at the waiting room at two o'clock. It is now three-thirty.

A: How long _____?

B: She _____ for _____.

10. Ted and Erica started to **play** tennis at two o'clock. It's now four-thirty.

A: How long _____?

B: They _____ since _____.

◇ PRACTICE 14. The present perfect progressive. (Charts 4-6 and 4-7)
Directions: Choose the correct verb form.

1. Where have you been? I _____ for you for over an hour!
   A. am waiting   (B.) have been waiting

2. I'm exhausted! I _____ for the last eight hours without a break.
   A. am working   B. have been working

3. Shhh! Susan _____ . Let's not make any noise. We don't want to wake her up.
   A. is sleeping   B. has been sleeping

4. Annie, go upstairs and wake your brother up. He _____ for over ten hours. He has chores to do.
   A. is sleeping   B. has been sleeping

5. Erin has never gone camping. She _____ in a tent.
   A. has never slept   B. has never been sleeping

6. This is a great shirt! I _____ it at least a dozen times, and it still looks like new.
   A. have washed   B. have been washing

7. Aren't you about finished with the dishes? You _____ dishes for thirty minutes or more. How long can it take to wash dishes?
   A. have washed   B. have been washing

8. We _____ to the Steak House restaurant many times. The food is excellent.
   A. have gone   B. have been going

◇ PRACTICE 15. ALREADY, STILL, YET, ANYMORE. (Chart 4-8)
   Directions: Choose the correct completion.

1. I haven't finished my homework yet. I'm _____ working on it.
   A. already   (B.) still   C. yet   D. anymore

2. *Top Rock Videos* used to be my favorite TV show, but I have stopped watching it. I don't watch it _____ .
   A. already   B. still   C. yet   D. anymore

3. I don't have to take any more math classes. I've _____ taken all the required courses.
   A. already   B. still   C. yet   D. anymore

4. I used to nearly choke in an airplane because of all the smoke in the cabin. But smoking is now forbidden by law on all domestic flights. You can't smoke in an airplane _____ .
   A. already   B. still   C. yet   D. anymore

5. I'm not quite ready to leave. I haven't finished packing my suitcase _____ .
   A. already   B. still   C. yet   D. anymore

6. "Don't you have a class at two?"
   "Yeah, why?"
   "Look at your watch."
   "Oh my gosh, it's _____ past two! Bye!"
   A. already   B. still   C. yet   D. anymore

7. Don't sit there! I painted that chair yesterday, and the paint isn't completely dry _____ .
   A. already   B. still   C. yet   D. anymore

8. 1448 South 45th Street is Joe's old address. He doesn't live there _____ .
   A. already   B. still   C. yet   D. anymore

9. Mr. Wood is eighty-eight years old, but he _____ goes into his office every day.
   A. already   B. still   C. yet   D. anymore

10. "Are you going to drive to Woodville with us for the street festival Saturday?"
"I don't know. I might. I haven't made up my mind _____."
A. already   B. still   C. yet   D. anymore

◇ **PRACTICE 16. ALREADY, STILL, YET, ANYMORE. (Chart 4-8)**
Directions: Complete the sentences with **already**, **yet**, **still**, or **anymore**.

1. A: Has Dennis graduated _____ yet _____?

   B: No. He's still in school.

2. A: I'm hungry. How about you? Did you eat _____?

   B: No. Did you?

   A: Nope. Let's go eat lunch.

3. A: Do you _____ live on Fifth Street?

   B: Not anymore. I moved.

4. A: Has Karen found a new apartment _____?

   B: Not that I know of. She's still living on Elm Street.

5. A: Do you _____ love me?

   B: Of course I do! I love you very much.

6. A: Is the baby _____ sleeping?

   B: Yes. Shhh. We don't want to wake him up.

7. A: Is the baby asleep _____?

   B: I think so. I don't hear anything from the nursery. I put him down for his nap fifteen
   minutes ago, so I'm pretty sure he's asleep by now.

8. It started raining an hour ago. We can't go for a walk because it's _____
   raining. I hope it stops soon.

9. Look! The rain has stopped. It isn't raining _____. Let's go for a walk.

10. I didn't understand this chapter in my biology book when I read it yesterday. Since then, I've
    read it three more times, but I _____ don't understand it.

11. A: Is Anne home _____?

    B: No, she isn't. I'm getting worried. She was supposed to be home at eight. It's almost
    nine, and she _____ isn't here.

    A: Don't worry. She'll probably be here any minute.

12. A: I'm going to have another sandwich.

   B: What? You just ate three sandwiches!

   A: I know, but I'm not full _____ . I'm _____ hungry.

13. A: Would you like to see today's newspaper?

   B: Thanks, but I've _____ read it.

14. A: Did you try to call Peter again?

   B: Yes, but the line was _____ busy. I'll try again in a few minutes.

15. A: How does Dick like his job at the cafe?

   B: He doesn't work there _____ . He found a new job.

16. A: Is your younger sister a college student?

   B: No. She's _____ in high school.

17. A: When are you going to make Tommy's birthday cake?

   B: I've _____ made it.

18. A: How did you do on your calculus exam?

   B: I haven't taken it _____ . The exam is tomorrow. I'm _____

   studying for it.

◇ **PRACTICE 17. Verb tense review. (Chapters 1 → 4)**
   Directions: Read the conversation between Ann and Ben. Complete the sentences with the words in parentheses.

   BEN: I *(need)* _____ need _____ to find a job. Where *(be)* _____ a good place for a
                    1   2

   student to work?

   ANN: *(you, work, ever)* _____ at a restaurant?
                                              3

   BEN: Yes. I *(work)* _____
                              4

   at several restaurants. I *(have)*

   _____ a job as a
          5

   dishwasher last fall.

ANN: Where?

BEN: At The Bistro, a little cafe on First Street.

ANN: How long *(you, work)* _____ there?
                                    6

BEN: For two months.

ANN: I *(work)* _____ in a lot of restaurants, but I *(have, never)*
                      7

_____ a dishwashing job. How *(you, like)*
              8

_____ your job as a dishwasher?
              9

BEN: I *(like, not)* _____ it very much. It *(be)* _____ hard
                                    10   11

work for low pay.

ANN: Where *(you, work)* _____ at present?
                                          12

BEN: I *(have, not)* _____ a job right now. I *(have, not)*
                            13

_____ a job since I *(quit)* _____ the dishwashing one.
              14   15

ANN: *(you, look)* _____ for a part-time or a full-time job?
                                16

BEN: A part-time job, maybe twenty hours a week.

ANN: I *(go)* _____ to Al's Place tomorrow to see about a job. The restaurant
                      17

(look) _____ for help. Why don't you come along with me?
                18

BEN: Thanks. I think I *(do)* _____ that. I *(look, never)*
                                    19

_____ for a job at Al's Place before. Maybe the pay *(be)*
              20

_____ better than at The Bistro.
        21

ANN: I *(know, not)* _____ . We *(find)* _____ out when
                                22   23

we *(go)* _____ there tomorrow.
                  24

◇ **PRACTICE 18. The present perfect vs. the past perfect. (Chart 4-9)**
Directions: Complete the sentences with the word in parentheses. Use the present perfect or the past perfect.

1. I am not hungry. I *(eat, already)* _____ have already eaten _____ .

2. I was not hungry. I *(eat, already)* _____ had already eaten _____ .

3. It's ten o'clock. I *(finish, already)* _____ my

homework, so I'm going to go to bed.

4. Last night I went to bed at ten o'clock. I *(finish, already)* _____
   my homework.

5. By the time* I went to bed last night, I *(finish, already)* _____
   my homework.

6. Sam's parties usually start late, so I was surprised that his party *(start, already)* _____
   _____ by the time I got there.

7. Look at all the people who are here! The party *(start, already)* _____
   _____ .

8. Carol missed her plane yesterday because of a traffic jam on her way to the airport. By the
   time she got to the airport, her plane *(leave, already)* _____ .

◇ **PRACTICE 19. The past progressive vs. the past perfect. (Chart 4-9)**
   Directions: Complete the sentences with the words in parentheses. Use the past progressive or the
   past perfect.

1. When I left for school this morning, it *(rain)* _____ **was raining** _____ , so I used my
   umbrella.

2. By the time class was over this morning, the rain *(stop)* _____ **had stopped** _____ , so I
   didn't need my umbrella anymore.

3. Last night I started to study at 7:30. Dick came at 7:35. I *(study)* _____
   when Dick came.

4. Last night I started to study at 7:30. I finished studying at 9:00. Dan came at 9:30. By the
   time Dan came, I *(finish)* _____ my homework.

5. When I walked into the kitchen after dinner last night, my wife *(wash)* _____
   the dishes, so I picked up a dish towel to help her.

6. By the time I walked into the kitchen after dinner tonight, my husband *(wash, already)*
   _____ the dishes and *(put)* _____ them
   away.

_____
by the time = before.

◇ PRACTICE 20. The past perfect. (Chart 4-9)

Directions: Read the passage and <u>underline</u> the past perfect verbs and their modifying adverbs **always** and **never**. Then complete the sentences that follow the passage. Use the past perfect in your completions.

(1) Alan Green got married for the first time at age 49. His new life is very different because he has had to change many old habits. For example, before his marriage, he <u>had always watched</u> TV during dinner, but his wife likes to talk at dinnertime, so now the TV is off.

(2) Until his marriage, Alan had always read the front page of the newspaper first, but his wife likes to read the front page first, too, so now Alan reads the sports page first.

(3) Until he got married, he had never let anyone else choose the radio station in the car. He had always listened to exactly what he wanted to listen to. But his wife likes to choose what's on the radio when she's in the car with him.

(4) When he was a bachelor, Alan had always left his dirty socks on the floor. Now he picks them up and puts them in the laundry basket.

(5) Before he was married, he'd never put the cap back on the toothpaste. He left it off. His wife prefers to have the cap back on. She also squeezes from the bottom of the tube, and Alan doesn't. Alan can't remember to put the cap back on, so now they have separate toothpaste tubes.

(6) Alan had never shared the TV remote control with anyone before he got married. He still likes to have control of the TV remote, but he doesn't say anything when his wife uses it.

Complete these sentences.

1. Until Alan got married, he ___*had always watched*___ TV during dinner.

2. Before his marriage, he _____ the front page of the newspaper first.

3. Prior to getting married, he _____ other people choose the station on his car radio.

4. Until he began married life, he _____ his dirty socks on the floor.

5. Before getting married, he _____ the toothpaste cap back on.

6. Until he had a wife who also liked to use the TV remote control, he _____ _____ the remote with anyone.

Directions: Complete the sentences with the words in parentheses.

1. A: *(you, enjoy)* ___Did you enjoy___ the concert last night?

   B: Very much. I *(go, not)* ___hadn't gone___ to a concert in a long time.

2. A: *(you, see)* _____ John yesterday?

   B: Yes, I did. It *(be)* _____ good to see him again. I *(see, not)*

   _____ him in a long time.

3. A: Hi, Jim! It's good to see you again. I *(see, not)* _____ you in weeks.

   B: Hi, Sue! It *(be)* _____ good to see you again, too. I *(see, not)*

   _____ you since the end of last semester. How's everything going?

4. A: *(you, get)* _____ to class on time yesterday morning?

   B: No. By the time I *(get)* _____ there, it *(begin, already)* _____

   _____ .

5. A: I called Ana, but I couldn't talk to her.

   B: Why not?

   A: She *(go, already)* _____ to bed, and her sister didn't

   want to wake her up for a phone call.

6. A: You're a wonderful artist. I love your watercolor paintings of the river valley.

   B: Thank you. I *(paint)* _____ the same valley many times because

   it has such interesting light at different times of the day.

7. A: I had a scare yesterday. I *(watch)* _____ the news when a

   tornado warning flashed on the screen.

   B: What *(you, do)* _____ ?

   A: I *(run)* _____ to the basement of the house.

8. A: *(you, go)* _____ out to eat last night?

   B: No. By the time I *(get)* _____ home, my husband *(make, already)*

   _____ dinner for us.

   A: How *(be)* _____ it?

   B: Terrific! We *(have)* _____ chicken, rice, and a salad. While we *(eat)*

   _____ , George Drake *(stop)* _____ by to visit us,

   so we *(invite)* _____ him to join us for dinner.

◇ PRACTICE 22. Error analysis. (Chapters 1 → 4)

Directions: Correct the errors.

                                been

1. Where have you been? I've ∧ waiting for you for an hour.

2. Anna have been a soccer fan since a long time.

3. Since I have been a child, I liked to solve puzzles.

4. Have you ever want to travel around the world?

5. The family is at the hospital since they hear about the accident.

6. My sister is only 30 years old, but her hair has began to turn gray.

7. Jake has been working as a volunteer at the children's hospital several times.

8. Steve has worn his black suit only once since he has bought it.

9. My cousin is studying for medical school exams since last month.

10. The students are hearing rumors about their teacher's engagement for a week.

11. I don't know the results of my medical tests already. I'll find out soon.

12. Jean has been try to get online to go Internet shopping for an hour.

13. By the time Michelle unlocked the door and got into her apartment, the phone already

stopped ringing.

CHAPTER 5
Asking Questions

◇ **PRACTICE 1. Preview: asking questions. (Charts 5-1 → 5-13)**

Directions: Pretend that you are interviewing Anna, a member of your class. Write your name on the first line, and then complete the dialogue with appropriate questions.

1. ME: Hi. My name is _____ . Our teacher has asked me to interview you so that I can practice asking questions. Could I ask you a few questions about yourself?

    ANNA: Sure.

2. ME: Well, first of all, ____*what is your name*_____ ?

    ANNA: Anna.

3. ME: _____ ?

    ANNA: Yes, that's my first name.

4. ME: _____ ?

    ANNA: Polanski.

5. ME: _____ ?

    ANNA: P-O-L-A-N-S-K-I.

    ME: Let me make sure I have that right. Your first name is Anna, A-N-N-A. And your last name is Polanski, P-O-L-A-N-S-K-I. Right?

    ANNA: That's right.

6. ME: _____ ?

    ANNA: Poland.

7. ME: _____ ?

    ANNA: Warsaw. My hometown is Warsaw.

8. ME: _____ ?

    ANNA: Two weeks ago. I came to this country two weeks ago.

9. ME: _____ ?

    ANNA: To study. I came here because I wanted to study at this school.

10. ME: _____ ?

    ANNA: Biochemistry.

11. ME: _____?
    ANNA: I'm going to stay here for four years, or until I graduate.

12. ME: _____?
    ANNA: I'm living at my aunt and uncle's house.

13. ME: _____?
    ANNA: No, it isn't far from school.

14. ME: _____?
    ANNA: I'd say about ten blocks.

15. ME: _____?
    ANNA: Sometimes I take the bus, but usually I walk.

16. ME: You're lucky. I live far away from the school, so it takes me a long time to get here every day. But that's my only big complaint about living here. Otherwise, I like going to this school a lot. _____?
    ANNA: Very much.
    ME: Well, thanks for the interview. I think I have enough information for the assignment. Nice to meet you.
    ANNA: Nice to meet you, too.

◇ **PRACTICE 2. Yes/no questions. (Chart 5-1)***

Directions: Write the correct question form. Use the information in B's response to create each question.

		helping verb	subject	main verb	rest of sentence
1. SIMPLE PRESENT	A:	Do	you	like	coffee?
	B: Yes, I like coffee.				

		helping verb	subject	main verb	rest of sentence
2. SIMPLE PRESENT	A:				
	B: Yes, Tom likes coffee.				

		helping verb	subject	main verb	rest of sentence
3. PRESENT PROGRESSIVE	A:				
	B: Yes, Ann is watching TV.				

		helping verb	subject	main verb	rest of sentence
4. PRESENT PROGRESSIVE	A:				
	B: Yes, I'm having lunch with Rob.				

---

*Question forms of tenses and modals can be found in the following charts in the *FEG 3e* student book:
   Simple present and present progressive: Chart 1-2, p. 4
   Simple past: Chart 2-2, p. 26
   Past progressive: Chart 2-9, p. 39
   Simple future: Charts 3-2, p. 56, and 3-3, p. 59
   Modal *can:* Chart 7-2, p. 191

		helping verb	subject	main verb	rest of sentence
5.	SIMPLE PAST	A: _____	_____	_____	_____
		B: Yes, Sara walked to school.			

		helping verb	subject	main verb	rest of sentence
6.	PAST PROGRESSIVE	A: _____	_____	_____	_____
		B: Yes, Ann was taking a nap.			

		helping verb	subject	main verb	rest of sentence
7.	SIMPLE FUTURE	A: _____	_____	_____	_____
		B: Yes, Ted will come to the meeting.			

		helping verb	subject	main verb	rest of sentence
8.	MODAL: *CAN*	A: _____	_____	_____	_____
		B: Yes, Rita can ride a bicycle.			

		form of *be*	subject	rest of sentence
9.	MAIN VERB: *BE* SIMPLE PRESENT	A: _____	_____	_____
		B: Yes, Ann is a good artist.		

		form of *be*	subject	rest of sentence
10.	MAIN VERB: *BE* SIMPLE PAST	A: _____	_____	_____
		B: Yes, I was at the wedding.		

◇ PRACTICE 3. Yes/no questions and short answers. (Charts 5-1 and 5-2)

Directions: Complete Speaker A's questions with **do**, **does**, **is**, or **are**. Complete Speaker B's short answers.

1. A: I need a flashlight. _____Do_____ you have one?

   B: No, _____I don't_____ .

2. A: _____ Africa the largest continent?

   B: No, _____ . Asia is.

3. A: _____ ants eat other insects?

   B: Yes, _____ .

4. A: _____ you going to be in class tomorrow?

   B: Yes, _____ .

5. A: _____ all snakebites poisonous?

   B: No, _____ .

6. A: _____ crocodiles lay eggs?

   B: Yes, _____ .

7. A: _____ it raining right now?

   B: No, _____ .

8. A: _____ that pen belong to you?

   B: No, _____ .

9. A: _____ you working on English grammar right now?

   B: Yes, _____ .

10. A: Mercury is a liquid metal used in thermometers. _____ mercury have a boiling

    point?

    B: Yes, _____ . It boils at 356.58°C.

◇ **PRACTICE 4. Yes/no questions and short answers. (Charts 5-1 and 5-2)**
   Directions: Answer the questions honestly. Use short answers.

   1. Do you know how to swim? ___ Yes, I do. OR No, I don't. ___

   2. Does your mother speak Chinese? _____

   3. Are you going downtown tomorrow? _____

   4. Will you be in class tomorrow? _____

   5. Can you play the guitar? _____

   6. Do you know how to play the violin? _____

   7. Are we going to have a test on grammar tomorrow? _____

   8. Can turtles swim? _____

   9. Should people smoke cigarettes? _____

   10. Did you watch TV last night? _____

   11. Do you have a bicycle? _____

   12. Will class begin on time tomorrow? _____

   13. Does class begin on time every day? _____

   14. Were all of the students in class yesterday? _____

   15. Should the teacher speak more slowly? _____

   16. Is English grammar easy? _____

   17. Was this exercise difficult? _____

◇ **PRACTICE 5. Yes/no questions and short answers. (Charts 5-1 and 5-2)**
Directions: Complete Speaker A's questions. Complete Speaker B's short answers.

1. A: _____Does Jane eat_____ lunch at the cafeteria every day?

   B: Yes, _____she does._____ (Jane eats lunch at the cafeteria every day.)

2. A: _____Do_____ your parents live nearby?

   B: No, _____ (My parents don't live nearby.)

3. A: _____ to class yesterday?

   B: No, _____ (Ann and Jim didn't come to class yesterday.)

4. A: _____ in your grammar workbook?

   B: Yes, _____ (I'm writing in my grammar workbook.)

5. A: _____ home last night?

   B: No, _____ (I wasn't home last night.)

6. A: _____ in your astronomy class?

   B: Yes, _____ (Tim Wilson is in my astronomy class.)

7. A: _____ her work before she goes to bed?

   B: Yes, _____ (Karen will finish her work before she goes to bed.)

8. A: _____ under water?

   B: Yes, _____ (Some birds can swim under water.)

9. A: _____ at your homework for tomorrow yet?

   B: No, _____ (I haven't looked at my homework for tomorrow yet.)

◇ **PRACTICE 6. Yes/no and information questions. (Charts 5-1 and 5-2)**
Directions: Complete the dialogues by writing Speaker A's questions. Write Ø if no word is needed in a space.

1.

(question word)	helping verb	subject	main verb	rest of sentence
Ø	Did	you	hear	the news yesterday?

   A:

   B: Yes, I did. (I heard the news yesterday.)

2.

(question word)	helping verb	subject	main verb	rest of sentence
When	did	you	hear	the news?

   A:

   B: Yesterday. (I heard the news yesterday.)

3.

(question word)	helping verb	subject	main verb	rest of sentence
Ø				

   A:

   B: Yes, he is. (Eric is reading today's paper.)

4.

(question word)	helping verb	subject	main verb	rest of sentence
				Ø

   A:

   B: Today's paper. (Eric is reading today's paper.)

5. | (question word) | helping verb | subject | main verb | rest of sentence |
|---|---|---|---|---|
A: _____ | _____ | _____ | _____ | _____

B: Yes, I did. (I found my wallet.)

6. | (question word) | helping verb | subject | main verb | rest of sentence |
|---|---|---|---|---|
A: _____ | _____ | _____ | _____ | _____

B: On the floor of the car. (I found my wallet on the floor of the car.)

7. | (question word) | helping verb | subject | main verb | rest of sentence |
|---|---|---|---|---|
A: _____ | _____ | _____ | _____ | _____

B: Because he enjoys the exercise. (Mr. Li walks to work because he enjoys the exercise.)

8. | (question word) | helping verb | subject | main verb | rest of sentence |
|---|---|---|---|---|
A: _____ | _____ | _____ | _____ | _____

B: Yes, he does. (Mr. Li walks to work.)

9. | (question word) | helping verb | subject | main verb | rest of sentence |
|---|---|---|---|---|
A: _____ | _____ | _____ | _____ | _____

B: Yes, she will. (Ms. Cook will return to her office at one o'clock.)

10. | (question word) | helping verb | subject | main verb | rest of sentence |
|---|---|---|---|---|
A: _____ | _____ | _____ | _____ | _____

B: At one o'clock. (Ms. Cook will return to her office at one o'clock.)

11. | (question word) | form of *be* | subject | rest of sentence |
|---|---|---|---|
A: _____ | _____ | _____ | _____

B: Yes, it is. (The orange juice is in the refrigerator.)

12. | (question word) | form of *be* | subject | rest of sentence |
|---|---|---|---|
A: _____ | _____ | _____ | _____

B: In the refrigerator. (The orange juice is in the refrigerator.)

◇ PRACTICE 7. Information questions. (Charts 5-1 → 5-3)

Directions: Create questions for the given answers. Use the information in parentheses. Use **when, what time, where,** or **why**. Pay special attention to the word order in the questions.

1. A: _____ What time (when) do the fireworks start _____ this evening?

B: 9:30. (The fireworks start at 9:30 this evening.)

2. A: _____ to see the principal?

B: Because I need to get his signature on this application form. (I'm waiting to see the principal because I need to get his signature on this application form.)

3. A: _____ her new job?

B: Next Monday morning. (Rachel starts her new job next Monday morning.)

4. A: _____ home for work?

   B: Usually around 6:00. (I usually leave home for work around 6:00.)

5. A: _____ to the meeting?

   B: Because I fell asleep after dinner and didn't wake up until 9:00. (I didn't get to the meeting because I fell asleep after dinner and didn't wake up until 9:00.)

6. A: _____ razor blades?

   B: At many different kinds of stores. (You can find razor blades at many different kinds of stores.)

7. A: _____ for home?

   B: Next Saturday. (I'm leaving for home next Saturday.)

8. A: _____ to finish this project?

   B: Next month. (I expect to finish this project next month.)

9. A: _____ ?

   B: To Mars. (The spaceship will go to Mars.)

10. A: _____ Chinese?

    B: In Germany. (I studied Chinese in Germany.)

    A: _____ Chinese in Germany?

    B: Because there is a good Chinese language school there.
    (I studied Chinese in Germany because there is a good Chinese language school there.)

    A: _____ to China to study Chinese?

    B: Because I had a scholarship to study in Germany.
    (I didn't go to China to study Chinese because I had a scholarship to study in Germany.)

◇ PRACTICE 8. Information questions. (Charts 5-1 → 5-3)
   Directions: Create information questions. Use *where, why, when,* or *what time*.

   1. A: ___When/What time did you get up___ this morning?

      B: At 7:30. (I got up at 7:30 this morning.)

   2. A: _____ today?

      B: At the cafeteria. (I ate lunch at the cafeteria today.)

   3. A: _____ lunch?

      B: At 12:15. (I ate lunch at 12:15.)

   4. A: _____ at the cafeteria?

      B: Because the food is good. (I eat lunch at the cafeteria because the food is good.)

5. A: _____ ?

   B: In Chicago. (My aunt and uncle live in Chicago.)

6. A: _____ your aunt and uncle?

   B: Next week. (I'm going to visit my aunt and uncle next week.)

7. A: _____ tonight?

   B: Around six. (I'll get home around six tonight.)

8. A: _____ tonight?

   B: At the library. (George is going to study at the library tonight.)

9. A: _____ at the library?

   B: Because it's quiet. (George studies at the library because it's quiet.)

10. A: _____ a bus?

    B: At that corner. (You can catch a bus at that corner.)

11. A: _____ ?

    B: Ten o'clock. (I have to leave at ten o'clock.)

12. A: _____ in 1998?

    B: In Japan. (I was living in Japan in 1998.)

13. A: _____ in their books?

    B: Because they're working on an exercise. (The students are writing in their books because they're working on an exercise.)

14. A: _____ you?

    B: Around seven. (You should call me around seven.)

15. A: _____ absent?

    B: Because she's flying her kite in the park. (Yoko is absent because she's flying her kite in the park.)

◇ PRACTICE 9. Information questions with WHY. (Charts 5-1 → 5-3)
Directions: Practice questions with *why*.

1. A: I was absent from class yesterday.

   B: Why _____were you_____ absent from class yesterday?

2. A: I can't come to your party this weekend.

   B: Why _____ to my party this weekend?

3. A: Tom went downtown yesterday.

   B: Why _____ downtown yesterday?

4. A: Ann won't be in class tomorrow.

   B: Why _____ in class tomorrow?

5. A: I need to go to the drugstore.

   B: Why _____ to go to the drugstore?

6. A: I'm going to buy a new dictionary.

   B: Why _____ a new dictionary?

7. A: I didn't do my homework last night.

   B: Why _____ your homework last night?

8. A: Anita is not coming to class tomorrow.

   B: Why _____ to class tomorrow?

9. A: Joe and I are going to the bank after class.

   B: Why _____ to the bank after class?

10. A: I didn't eat breakfast this morning

    B: Why _____ breakfast this morning?

11. A: Jack took a taxi to school today.

    B: Why _____ a taxi to school today?

12. A: I don't like the weather in this city.

    B: Why _____ the weather in this city?

◇ PRACTICE 10. WHO, WHO(M), and WHAT. (Chart 5-4)
   Directions: Create questions with *who, who(m),* and *what.*

	QUESTION	ANSWER
1.	Who knows Tom?	**Someone** knows Tom.
2.	Who(m) does Tom know?	Tom knows **someone.**
3.	_____	**Someone** will help us.
4.	_____	I will ask **someone.**
5.	_____	Eric is talking to **someone** on the phone.
6.	_____	**Someone** is knocking on the door.
7.	_____	**Something** surprised them.
8.	_____	Jack said **something.**
9.	_____	Sue talked about **something.**
10.	_____	Ann talked about **someone.**

Directions: Complete the dialogues by creating questions. Use the information in the long answer in parentheses to create each question.

1. A: _____Who taught_____ you to play chess?

   B: My mother. (My mother taught me to play chess.)

2. A: _____ ?

   B: A bank robbery. (Robert saw a bank robbery.)

3. A: _____ a good look at the bank robber?

   B: Robert did. (Robert got a good look at the bank robber.)

4. A: _____ ?

   B: A toy for my brother's children. (I'm making a toy for my brother's children.)

5. A: _____ to?

   B: Joe. (That calculator belongs to Joe.)

6. A: _____ in your pocket?

   B: A bag of candy. (I have a bag of candy in my pocket.)

7. A: _____ ?

   B: A mouse. (The cat killed a mouse.)

8. A: _____ ?

   B: Curiosity. (Curiosity killed the cat.*)

9. A: _____ an apple fall
   to the ground from a tree?

   B: Gravity. (Gravity makes an apple fall to the
   ground from a tree.)

10. A: _____ on the envelope?

    B: My sister. (My sister wrote a note on the
    envelope.)

11. A: _____ from?

    B: My father. (I got a letter from my father.)

Curiosity is the desire to learn about something. "Curiosity killed the cat" is an English saying that means we can get into trouble when we want to know too much about something that doesn't really concern us.

◇ **PRACTICE 12. Asking for the meaning of a word. (Charts 5-3 and 5-4)**
Directions: Ask for the meaning of the words in *italics*. Complete the dialogue.

1. Captain Cook *explored* many islands in the Pacific Ocean.
   A: ___What does "explore" mean?___
   B: It means ___"to go to a new place and find out about it."___

2. Alice put her hand *underneath* the blanket.
   A: _____
   B: It means _____

3. How many times a minute do people *blink?*
   A: _____
   B: It means _____

4. The food was absolutely *delicious!*
   A: _____
   B: It means _____

◇ **PRACTICE 13. WHAT + a form of DO. (Chart 5-6)**
Directions: Use the information in parentheses to make questions with **what** + a form of **do** to complete each dialogue. Use the same verb tense or modal that is used in the parentheses.

1. A: ___What is Alex doing___?
   B: Watching a movie on TV. (Alex is watching a movie on TV.)

2. A: ___What should I do___ if someone calls while you're out?
   B: Just take a message. (You should take a message if someone calls while I'm out.)

3. A: _____?
   B: They explore space. (Astronauts explore space.)

4. A: _____ Saturday morning?
   B: Play tennis at Waterfall Park. (I'm going to play tennis at Waterfall Park Saturday morning.)

5. A: _____ when you get sick?
   B: I see my doctor. (I see my doctor when I get sick.)

6. A: _____ to help you?
   B: Carry this suitcase. (You can carry this suitcase to help me.)

7. A: _____ when she heard the good news?
   B: She smiled. (Sara smiled when she heard the good news.)

8. A: I spilled some juice on the floor. _____?
   B: Wipe it up with a paper towel. (You should wipe it up with a paper towel.)

9. A: _____ after she graduates?

   B: I think she plans to look for a job in hotel management. (Emily <u>is going to look</u> for a job in hotel management after she graduates.)

10. A: _____ when the fire alarm sounded?

    B: Ran down the stairs and out of the building. (I <u>ran</u> down the stairs and out of the building when the fire alarm sounded.)

11. A: _____ after school today?

    B: Let's go to the shopping mall, okay? (I <u>would like to go</u> to the shopping mall after school today.)

12. A: _____?

    B: Make this coin stand on edge. (I'<u>m trying to make</u> this coin stand on edge.)

13. A: _____?

    B: He needs to hand in all of his homework. (Kevin <u>needs</u> to hand in all of his homework if he wants to pass advanced algebra.)

14. A: _____?

    B: He's an airplane mechanic. (Nick <u>repairs</u> airplanes for a living.)

15. A: Did you say something to that man over there? Why does he look angry?

    B: I accidentally ran into him and stepped on his foot.

    A: _____?

    B: Said something nasty. (He <u>said</u> something nasty when I bumped into him.)

    A: _____?

    B: Apologized. (I <u>apologized</u>.)

    A: Then _____?

    B: Walked away without saying a word. (Then he <u>walked</u> away without saying a word.)

    A: What an unpleasant person!

    B: I didn't mean to step on his foot. It was just an accident.

◇ PRACTICE 14. WHAT KIND OF. (Chart 5-7)
   Directions: Ask questions with **what kind of**.

   1. A: _____ What kind of music _____ do you like best?

      B: Rock 'n roll.

   2. A: _____ do you like to wear?

      B: Jeans and a T-shirt.

   3. A: _____ do you like best?

      B: Fresh fruit and vegetables.

4. A: _____ do you like to read?

   B: Romance novels.

5. A: _____ should I buy?

   B: A four-door sedan with good gas mileage.

6. A: _____ does your country have?

   B: It's a democratic republic.

7. A: _____ would you like to have?

   B: I'd like to have one that pays well, is interesting, and allows me to contribute to society.
   I've often thought I'd like to be a doctor or an architect.

8. A: _____ would you like to marry?

   B: Someone who is kind-hearted, loving, funny, serious, and steady.

9. A: _____ can we recycle?

   B: Paper, wood, plastic, and aluminum.

◇ PRACTICE 15. WHICH vs. WHAT. (Chart 5-8)
Directions: Complete the questions with **which** or **what**.

1. A: I have two pens. _____Which_____ one do you want?

   B: That one.

2. A: I'm hungry.

   B: So am I. _____What_____ are you going to order?

   A: I think I'll have the fish.

3. A: There are two good movies on TV tonight, a spy movie and a comedy. _____
   one do you want to watch?

   B: Let's watch the spy movie.

4. A: Did you go out last night?

   B: No. I stayed home and watched TV.

   A: _____ did you watch?

   B: A movie.

5. A: These shoes are comfortable, and so are those shoes. _____ should I buy, these
   or those? I can't decide.

   B: These.

6. A: There are flights to Atlanta at 7:30 A.M. and 8:40 A.M. _____ one are you going to take?

   B: The 7:30 flight.

7. A: _____ does "huge" mean?

   B: "Very big."

8. A: I need some help.

   B: _____ can I do to help?

   A: Please hand me that bowl.

   B: Sure.

9. A: Would you please hand me a sharp knife?

   B: I'd be happy to. There are several in this drawer. _____ one would you like?

   A: That one.

◇ **PRACTICE 16. WHO vs. WHOSE. (Chart 5-9)**
   Directions: Complete the questions with *who* or *whose*.

   1. A: _____Who_____ is driving to the game tonight?
      B: Heidi is.

   2. A: _____Whose_____ car are we taking to the game?
      B: Heidi's.

   3. A: This notebook is mine. _____ is that? Is it yours?
      B: No, it's Sara's.

   4. A: There's Ms. Adams. _____ is standing next to her?
      B: Mr. Wilson.

   5. A: _____ was the first woman doctor in the United States?
      B: Elizabeth Blackwell, in 1849.

   6. A: Okay. _____ forgot to put the ice cream back in the freezer?
      B: I don't know. Don't look at me. It wasn't me.

   7. A: _____ motorcycle ran into the telephone pole?
      B: Bill's.

   8. A: _____ suitcase did you borrow for your trip?
      B: Andy's.

◇ **PRACTICE 17. WHO vs. WHOSE. (Chart 5-9)**
Directions: Create the questions.

1. A: ___Whose house is that?___
   B: Pat's. (That's Pat's house.)

2. A: ___Who's living in that house?___
   B: Pat. (Pat is living in that house.)

3. A: _____
   B: Pedro's. (I borrowed Pedro's umbrella.)

4. A: _____
   B: Linda's. (I used Linda's book.)

5. A: _____
   B: Nick's. (Nick's book is on the table.)

6. A: _____
   B: Nick. (Nick is on the phone.)

7. A: _____
   B: Sue Smith. (That's Sue Smith.) She's a student in my class.

8. A: _____
   B: Sue's. (That's Sue's.) This one is mine.

◇ **PRACTICE 18. Using HOW. (Chart 5-10)**
Directions: Complete the sentences with any of the words in the list.

busy	*fresh*	*safe*	*soon*
expensive	✓*hot*	*serious*	*well*

1. A: How _____hot_____ does it get in Chicago in the summer?

   B: Very _____hot_____ . It can get over 100°. (100°F = 37.8°C)

2. A: How _____ will dinner be ready? I'm really hungry.

   B: In just a few more minutes.

3. A: Look at that beautiful vase! Let's get it.

   B: How _____ is it?

   A: Oh my gosh! Never mind. Never mind. We can't afford it.

4. A: Sorry to interrupt, Ted, but I need some help. How _____ are you

   today? Do you have time to read over this report?

   B: Well, I'm always _____ , but I'll make time to read it.

5. A: How _____ is Toshi about becoming an astronomer?

   B: He's very _____ . He already knows more about the stars and planets than his high school teachers.

6. A: How _____ is a car with an airbag?

   B: Well, there have been bad accidents where both drivers walked away without injuries because of airbags.

7. A: Tomatoes for sale! Hey, lady! Do you want to buy some tomatoes? Tomatoes for sale!

   B: Hmmm. They look pretty good. How _____ are they?

   A: What do you mean "How _____ are they?" Would I sell something that wasn't _____ ? They were picked from the field just this morning.

8. A: Do you know Jack Young?

   B: Yes.

   A: Oh? How _____ do you know him?

   B: Very _____ . He's one of my closest friends. Why?

   A: He's applied for a job at my store.

◇ **PRACTICE 19. Using HOW FAR, HOW LONG, and HOW OFTEN. (Charts 5-11 → 5-13)**
Directions: Complete the questions with *far*, *long*, or *often*.

1. A: How _____far_____ is it to the nearest police station?
   B: Four blocks.

2. A: How _____long_____ does it take you to get to work?
   B: Forty-five minutes.

3. A: How _____often_____ do you see your family?
   B: Once a week.

4. A: How _____ is it to your office from home?
   B: About twenty miles.

5. A: How _____ is it from here to the airport?
   B: Ten kilometers.

6. A: How _____ do you see your dentist?
   B: Every six months.

7. A: How _____ does it take to get to the airport?
   B: Fifteen minutes.

8. A: How _____ above sea level is Denver, Colorado?
   B: One mile. That's why it's called the Mile High City.

9. A: How _____ does it take to fly from Chicago to Denver?
   B: About three hours.

10. A: How _____ does your department have meetings?
    B: Twice a week.

11. A: How _____ did it take you to build your own boat?
    B: Four years.

12. A: How _____ did you walk?
    B: Two miles.

13. A: How _____ did you walk?
    B: Two hours.

14. A: How _____ does the bus come?
    B: Every two hours.

15. A: How _____ is it from here to the bus stop?
    B: About two blocks.

16. A: How _____ does the ride downtown take?
    B: About 20 minutes.

17. A: How _____ do you take the bus?
    B: Every day.

◇ **PRACTICE 20. Cumulative review. (Charts 5-1 → 5-13)**
   Directions: Complete the dialogues by writing questions for the given answers. Use the
   information in parentheses to form the questions.

1. A: _____What is Jack doing_____?
   B: He's playing tennis. (Jack is playing tennis.)

2. A: _____ with?
   B: Anna. (He is playing tennis with Anna.)

3. A: _____ ?
   B: Serving the ball. (Anna is serving the ball.)

4. A: _____ in the air?
   B: A tennis ball. (She is throwing a tennis ball in the air.)

5. A: _____ ?
   B: Rackets. (Anna and Jack are holding rackets.)

6. A: _____ between them?
   B: A net. (A net is between them.)

7. A: _____ ?
   B: On a tennis court. (They are on a tennis court.)

8. A: _____ ?
   B: For an hour and a half. (They have been playing for an hour and a half.)

9. A: _____ right now?
   B: Jack. (Jack is winning right now.)

10. A: _____ the last game?
    B: Anna. (Anna won the last game.)

◇ PRACTICE 21. Cumulative review. (Charts 5-1 → 5-13)

Directions: Complete the dialogues by writing questions for the given answers. Use the information in parentheses to form the questions.

1. A: _____ When will the clean clothes be _____ dry?
   B: In about an hour. (The clean clothes will be dry in about an hour.)

2. A: _____ Saturday afternoon?
   B: I went to a baseball game. (I went to a baseball game Saturday afternoon.)

3. A: _____ ?
   B: The small paperback. (I bought the small paperback dictionary, not the hardcover one.)

4. A: _____ to clean your apartment before your parents visited?
   B: Four hours. (It took me four hours to clean my apartment before my parents visited.)

5. A: _____ the top shelf?
   B: Stand on a chair. (You can reach the top shelf by standing on a chair.)

6. A: _____ the best?
   B: Whole wheat bread. (I like whole wheat bread the best.)

7. A: _____ the phone when it rang?
   B: Because I was in the middle of dinner with my family. (I didn't answer the phone when it rang because I was in the middle of dinner with my family.)

8. A: _____ to the show with?

B: Maria and her sister. (I'm going to the show with Maria and her sister.)

9. A: _____ the radio?

B: Eric. (Eric repaired the radio.)

10. A: _____ in your hometown in the winter?

B: It's not bad. It rarely gets below zero. (It rarely gets below zero in my hometown in the winter.)

◇ PRACTICE 22. Tag questions. (Chart 5-16)
Directions: Complete the tag questions with the correct verbs.

1. SIMPLE PRESENT

   a. You **like** strong coffee, _____*don't*_____ you?

   b. David **goes** to Ames High School, _____ he?

   c. Kate and Sara **live** on Tree Road, _____ they?

   d. Jane **has** the keys to storeroom, _____ she?

   e. Jane**'s** in her office, _____ she?

   f. You**'re** a member of this class, _____ you?

   g. Jack **doesn't** have a car, _____ he?

   h. Ann **isn't** from California, _____ she?

2. SIMPLE PAST

   a. Paul **went** to Florida, _____ he?

   b. You **didn't talk** to the boss, _____ you?

   c. Tom's parents **weren't** at home, ⸱_____ they?

   d. That **was** Pat's idea, _____ it?

3. PRESENT PROGRESSIVE, *BE GOING TO*, and PAST PROGRESSIVE

   a. You**'re studying** hard, _____ you?

   b. Tom **isn't working** at the bank, _____ he?

   c. It **isn't going to rain** today, _____ it?

   d. Susan and Kevin **were waiting** for us, _____ they?

   e. It **wasn't raining,** _____ it?

4. PRESENT PERFECT

   a. It **has been** warmer than usual, _____ it?

   b. You**'ve had** a lot of homework, _____ you?

c. We **haven't spent** much time together, _____ we?

d. Lisa **has started** her new job, _____ she?

e. Bill **hasn't finished** his sales report yet, _____ he?

5. MODAL AUXILIARIES

a. You **can answer** these questions, _____ you?

b. Kate **won't tell** anyone our secret, _____ she?

c. Sam **should come** to the meeting, _____ he?

d. Alice **would like** to come with us, _____ she?

e. I **don't have to come** to the meeting, _____ I?

f. Steve **had to leave** early, _____ he?

◇ **PRACTICE 23. Tag questions. (Chart 5-16)**
Directions: Add tag questions to the following and give the expected responses.

1. A: You've already seen that movie, ____*haven't you?*____

   B: ____*Yes, I have.*____

2. A: Alex hasn't called, ____*has he?*____

   B: ____*No, he hasn't.*____

3. A: You talked to Mike last night, ____*didn't you?*____

   B: ____*Yes, I did.*____

4. A: You usually bring your lunch to school, _____

   B: _____

5. A: Rita and Philip have been married for five years, _____

   B: _____

6. A: Kathy has already finished her work, _____

   B: _____

7. A: This isn't a hard exercise, _____

   B: _____

8. A: We have to hand in our assignments today, _____

   B: _____

9. A: Tony Wah lives in Los Angeles, _____

   B: _____

10. A: You used to live in Los Angeles, _____

    B: _____

11. A: Tomorrow isn't a holiday, _____

    B: _____

12. A: Jack doesn't have to join the army, _____

    B: _____

13. A: I don't have to be at the meeting, _____

    B: _____

14. A: This isn't your book, _____

    B: _____

15. A: Jack and Elizabeth were in class yesterday, _____

    B: _____

16. A: Jennifer won't be here for dinner tonight, _____

    B: _____

◇ PRACTICE 24. Error analysis. (Chapter 5)
Directions: Correct the errors in the sentences.

1. ~~Whom~~ *Who* saw the car accident?

2. Why you didn't say "good-bye" when you left?

3. How about ask Julie and Tim to come for dinner Friday night?

4. What time class begins today?

5. Why he have no shoes on his feet?

6. Where you can get a drink of water in this building?

7. What kind of music you like best?

8. How long it takes to get to the beach from here?

9. She is working late tonight, doesn't she?

10. Who's glasses are those?

11. How much tall your father?

12. Who you talked to about registration for next term?

13. How about we go to see the baby elephant at the zoo tomorrow?

14. How far from here to the nearest gas station?

◇ **PRACTICE 25. Review: questions. (Chapter 5)**
Directions: Using the information in parentheses, complete the questions for the given answers.

1. A: _____When are you going to buy_____ a new bicycle?

   B: Next week. (I'm going to buy a new bicycle next week.)

2. A: _____How are you going to pay_____ for it?

   B: With my credit card. (I'm going to pay for it with my credit card.)

3. A: _____ your old bike?

   B: Ten years. (I had my old bike for ten years.)

4. A: _____ your bike?

   B: Four or five times a week. (I ride my bike four or five times a week.)

5. A: _____ to work?

   B: I usually ride my bike. (I usually get to work by riding my bike.)

6. A: _____ your bike to work tomorrow?

   B: Yes. (I'm going to ride my bike to work tomorrow.)

7. A: _____ your bike to work today?

   B: I decided I would rather walk. (I didn't ride my bike to work today because I decided I would rather walk.)

8. A: _____ a comfortable seat?

   B: Yes, it does. (My bike has a comfortable seat.)

9. A: _____ ?

   B: A ten-speed. (I have a ten-speed bicycle.)

10. A: _____ his new bike?

    B: Two weeks ago. (Jason got his new bike two weeks ago.)

11. A: _____ Jason's new bike?

    B: Billy. (Billy broke Jason's new bike.)

12. A: _____ ?

    B: The front wheel on Jason's new bike. (Billy broke the front wheel on Jason's new bike.)

13. A: _____ ?

    B: Jason's new bike. (Jason's new bike is broken.)

14. A: _____ Jason's bike?

    B: He ran into a brick wall. (Billy broke Jason's bike by running into a brick wall.)

15. A: _____ yours?

    B: The blue one. (The blue bicycle is mine, not the red one.)

16. A: _____ your bicycle at night?

    B: Inside my apartment. (I keep my bicycle inside my apartment at night.)

17. A: _____ ?

    B: David. (That bike belongs to David.)

18. A: _____ ?

    B: Suzanne's. (I borrowed Suzanne's bike.)

19. A: _____ ?

    B: In the park. (Rita is in the park.)

20. A: _____ ?

    B: Riding her bike. (She's riding her bike.)

21. A: _____ her bike yesterday?

    B: 25 miles. (Rita rode her bike 25 miles* yesterday.)

22. A: _____ "bicycle"?

    B: B-I-C-Y-C-L-E. (You spell "bicycle" B-I-C-Y-C-L-E.)

---

*25 miles = approximately 40 kilometers/kilometres.

CHAPTER 6
Nouns and Pronouns

◇ PRACTICE 1. Preview: plural nouns. (Chart 6-2)
Directions: Underline each noun. Write the correct plural form if necessary. Do not change any other words.

1. <u>Airplane</u>ˢ have <u>wing</u>ˢ.

2. Child like to play on swing.

3. Some animal live in zoo.

4. Tree grow branch and leaf.

5. I saw three duck and several goose

   in a pond at the park.

6. Some baby are born with a few tooth.

7. I eat a lot of potato, bean, pea, and tomato.

8. Opinion are not the same as fact.

9. Each country has its own custom.

10. Government collect tax.

◇ PRACTICE 2. Pronunciation of -S/-ES. (Chart 6-1)
Directions: Write the correct pronunciations: /s/, /z/, or /əz/. Practice saying the words.

1. dogs = dog + / z /

2. cups = cup + /   /

3. desks = desk + /   /

4. classes = class + /   /

5. doors = door + /   /

6. radios = radio + /   /

7. pages = page + /   /

8. spoons = spoon + /   /

9. sheets = sheet + /   /

10. wishes = wish + /   /

11. collars = collar + /   /

12. shirts = shirt + /   /

◇ PRACTICE 3. Pronunciation of -S/-ES. (Chart 6-1)
Directions: Write the correct pronunciations: /s/, /z/, or /əz/. Practice saying the words.

1. ear / z /

2. cat /   /

3. dish /   /

4. disk /   /

5. table /   /

6. lie /   /

7. letter /   /

8. group /   /

9. nose /   /

10. date /   /

11. purse /   /

12. fox /   /

◇ PRACTICE 4. Pronunciation of -S/-ES. (Chart 6-1)
Directions: Write the correct pronunciations for the underlined words: /s/, /z/, or /əz/. Read the sentences aloud.

1. My friends   raise chickens   and cows.
      / z /   /   /   /   /

2. Boxes   come in many different sizes.
    /   /   /   /

3. The doctor checked the child's   eyes,   ears,   and nose.
                                /   /   /   /   /   /

4. Most businesses   need to have computers.
        /   /   /   /

5. Apples   and oranges   are my favorite fruits.
    /   /   /   /

6. Sam's   faxes   have several mistakes.
    /   /   /   /   /

7. We heard loud voices   from the houses   down the street.
                    /   /   /   /

8. Do you prefer to watch videos   or go to movies   on weekends?
                            /   /   /   /   /   /

◇ PRACTICE 5. Plural nouns. (Chart 6-2)
Directions: Write the correct singular or plural form.

SINGULAR	PLURAL
1. mouse	mice
2. pocket	pockets
3. _____	teeth
4. _____	tomatoes
5. _____	fish/fishes
6. _____	women
7. branch	_____
8. friend	_____
9. duty	_____
10. highway	_____
11. thief	thieves
12. belief	_____

13. potato _____

14. radio _____

15. offspring _____

16. _____ children

17. season _____

18. custom _____

19. business _____

20. _____ centuries

21. occurrence _____

22. _____ phenomena

23. sheep _____

24. _____ loaves

25. glass _____

26. problem _____

27. family _____

28. wife _____

29. shelf _____

30. roof _____

31. _____ feet

32. woman _____

◇ **PRACTICE 6. Plural nouns. (Chart 6-2)**
   Directions: Write the plural of each word from the box in the correct category.

✓ cow	baby	lily	husband	goose
sheep	rose	tomato	pea	child
apple	horse	daughter	cherry	
potato	daisy	strawberry	wife	
poppy	son	mouse	pear	
daffodil	grape	banana	bean	

1. Common farm animals include ____cows,_____.

2. Common vegetables include _____.

3. Common fruits include _____.

4. Common flowers include _____.

5. Family members include _____.

◇ PRACTICE 7. Subjects, verbs, and objects. (Chart 6-3)

Directions: <u>Underline</u> and identify the subject (**s**) and verb (**v**) of each sentence. Also identify the object (**o**) of the verb if the sentence has an object.

          S   V   O
1. <u>Children</u> <u>play</u> <u>games</u>.

2. Fish swim.

3. The baby doesn't like her new toys.

4. Computers process information quickly.

5. Dictionaries give definitions.

6. Teachers correct tests.

7. The cat found a mouse.

8. The sun shines brightly.

9. Water evaporates.

10. Do snakes lay eggs?

11. The child petted the dog.

12. Did the phone ring?

◇ PRACTICE 8. Objects of prepositions. (Charts 6-3 and 6-4)

Directions: <u>Underline</u> and identify the preposition (**PREP**) and object of the preposition (**O of PREP**).

                            PREP O of PREP
1. The man opened the door <u>with</u> his   <u>key</u>.

2. The little girl put her shoes on the wrong feet.

3. The student added and subtracted with a calculator.

4. My father fixes breakfast for my mother every morning.

5. Librarians work in libraries.

6. The bird flew into the window of the building.

7. I do all my homework on a computer.

8. The artist drew scenes of the beach in his notebook.

9. The children played in the backyard until dinner.

10. It rained for two weeks.

11. The painter splashed paint on the floor of his studio.

12. A man with dark glasses stood near the door.

◇ PRACTICE 9. Subjects, verbs, objects, and prepositions. (Charts 6-3 and 6-4)
   Directions: <u>Underline</u> and identify the subjects (**s**), verbs (**v**), objects (**o**), and prepositional phrases (**PP**) in these sentences.

                  S   V   O

1. <u>Bridges</u> <u>cross</u> <u>rivers</u>.

                      S   V   PP

2. <u>A terrible earthquake</u> <u>occurred</u> <u>in Turkey</u>.

3. Airplanes fly above the clouds.

4. Trucks carry large loads.

5. Rivers flow toward the sea.

6. Salespeople treat customers with courtesy.

7. Bacteria can cause diseases.

8. Clouds are floating across the sky.

9. The audience in the theater applauded the performers at the end of the show.

10. Helmets protect bicyclists from serious injuries.

◇ PRACTICE 10. Prepositions of time. (Chart 6-5)
   Directions: Complete the phrases with the correct time prepositions.

The Jacksons got married . . .

1. ___*in*___ the summer.

2. _____ June.

3. _____ June 17th.

4. _____ Saturday.

5. _____ 12:00 P.M.

6. _____ noon.

7. _____ 2000.

8. _____ Saturday afternoon.

Their baby was born . . .

9. _____ midnight.

10. _____ 12:00 A.M.

11. _____ the morning.

12. _____ April 12th.

13. _____ 2001.

14. _____ April.

15. _____ Wednesday.

◇ PRACTICE 11. Word order: object, place, and time. (Chart 6-6)

Directions: Complete each sentence by arranging the phrases in the correct order. There is only one correct solution for each sentence.

1. The dog chased

   __3__ for several minutes.

   __1__ a cat

   __2__ around the room

2. The policeman stopped

   _____ the driver

   _____ at a busy intersection

   _____ at midnight

3. My friends rented

   _____ on the lake

   _____ last summer

   _____ a houseboat

4. The children caught

   _____ in the river

   _____ several fish

   _____ last weekend

5. Our library shows

   _____ free movies

   _____ every Saturday

   _____ in the children's section

6. We ate

   _____ at noon

   _____ our lunch

   _____ in the park

7. The little girl always puts

   _____ in bed

   _____ at night

   _____ her dolls

8. The florist delivers

   _____ every Monday

   _____ fresh flowers

   _____ to our office

9. I bought

   _____ at the corner store

   _____ a newspaper

   _____ after work yesterday

◇ PRACTICE 12. Subject–verb agreement. (Chart 6-7)
Directions: Complete the sentences with *is* or *are*.

1. These magazines ____*are*____ from the library.

2. The magazines on the table _____ for you.

3. Some people _____ wise.

4. Everyone _____ here.

5. Everybody _____ on time for class.

6. Each person in class _____ ready to begin.

7. Every teacher at this school _____ patient.

8. There _____ some money on the table.

9. There _____ some bills for you to pay.

10. This information about taxes _____ helpful.

◇ PRACTICE 13. Subject–verb agreement. (Chart 6-7)
Directions: Circle the correct verb.

1. Bees (*make,*) *makes* honey.

2. Tomatoes *needs, need* lots of sunshine to grow.

3. *Do, Does* the people in your neighborhood help each other?

4. There *is, are* some people already in line for the movie.

5. The vegetables in the bowl on the table *is, are* fresh.

6. Everybody always *comes, come* to class on time.

7. Everyone in the class *is, are* paying attention.

8. The dishes on the counter *is, are* dirty.

9. Each person *needs, need* to bring identification.

10. The people next door *goes, go* hiking every weekend in the summer.

11. My father and mother *works, work* for the same company.

12. The pictures on the wall *is, are* of my father's family.

◇ PRACTICE 14. Adjectives. (Chart 6-8)
Directions: Complete each phrase with an adjective that has the opposite meaning.

1. new cars   ____*old*____ cars

2. a young man   an _____ man

3. a _____ day   a warm day

4. fast trains   _____ trains

5. sad news   _____ news

6. a good day   a _____ day

7. _____ hair   dry hair

8. _____ exercises   hard exercises

9. a soft pillow   a _____ pillow

10. a _____ street   a wide street

11. _____ plates   dirty plates

12. _____ cups   full cups

13. dangerous cities   _____ cities

14. _____ children   quiet children

15. shallow water   _____ water

16. sweet candy   _____ candy

17. _____ clothes   expensive clothes

18. a dark color   a _____ color

19. a heavy box   a _____ box

20. a _____ place   a private place

21. my left foot   my _____ foot

22. the wrong answer   the _____ answer

23. weak coffee   _____ coffee

24. a _____ walk   a short walk

◇ **PRACTICE 15. Adjectives and nouns. (Chart 6-8)**
Directions: Circle each adjective. Draw an arrow to the noun it describes.

1. Paul has a (loud) voice.

2. Sugar is (sweet.)

3. The students took an easy test.

4. Air is free.

5. We ate some delicious food at a Mexican restaurant.

6. An encyclopedia contains important facts about a wide variety of subjects.

7. The child was sick.

8. The sick child crawled into his warm bed and sipped hot tea.

9. Our camping equipment looks old and rusty.

10. The hungry bear found food in the garbage cans.

11. My elderly father needs nursing care.

12. May I offer you some fresh coffee and warm cookies?

◇ **PRACTICE 16. Nouns as adjectives. (Chart 6-9)**
Directions: Use the information in *italics* to complete the sentences. Each completion should have a noun that is used as an adjective in front of another noun.

1. *Articles in newspapers* are called _____ newspaper articles _____.

2. *Numbers on pages* are called _____.

3. *Money that is made of paper* is called _____.

4. *Buildings with apartments* are called _____.

5. *Disks for computers* are called _____.

6. *Presents for birthdays* are called _____.

7. *Gardens with roses* are called _____.

8. *Chains for keys* are called _____.

9. *Governments in cities* are called _____.

10. *Ponds for ducks* are called _____.

11. *Walls made of bricks* are called _____.

12. *Cartons that hold eggs* are called _____.

13. *Views of mountains* are called _____.

14. *Knives that people carry in their pockets* are called _____.

15. *Lights that control traffic* are called _____.

16. *Tables used for outdoor picnics* are called _____.

17. *Pies that are made with apples* are called _____.

18. *Helmets for bicycle riders* are called _____.

19. *Cabins made out of logs* are called _____.

20. *Bridges made from steel* are called _____.

◇ PRACTICE 17. Review: nouns. (Charts 6-2 → 6-9) *board dictation.*

Directions: These sentences have many mistakes in the use of nouns. Decide which nouns should be plural and add the correct plural endings to them. Do not change any other words in the sentences.

1. The mountain ^s in Chile are beautiful.

2. Cat hunt mouse.

3. Mosquito are small insect.

4. Everyone has eyelash.

5. Goose are larger than duck.

6. What are your favorite radio program?

7. Forest sometimes have fire. Forest fire endanger wild animal.

DUCK

GOOSE

8. Sharp kitchen knife can be dangerous weapon.

9. Good telephone manner are important.

10. I bought two theater ticket for the Thursday evening's performance of *A Doll's House.*

11. Our daily life have changed in many way in the past one hundred year. We no longer need to use oil lamp or candle in our house, raise our own chicken, or build daily fire for cooking.

12. There are approximately 250,000 different kind of flower in the world.

13. Newspaper reporter have high-pressure job.

14. I applied to several foreign university because I want to study abroad next year.

15. Ted lives with three other university student.

16. The offspring of animal like horse, zebra, and deer can run soon after they are born.

17. Science student do laboratory experiment in their class.

18. Housefly are troublesome pest. They carry germ.

19. I like to read magazine article about true personal experience.

20. Many modern device require battery to work. Some flashlight, pocket calculator, portable radio, tape recorder, and many kind of toy need battery.

◇ PRACTICE 18. Personal pronouns. (Chart 6-10)
     Directions: <u>Underline</u> each pronoun. Note how it is used.

  - Subject (**s**)
  - Object of a verb (**O of v**)
  - Object of a preposition (**O of PREP**)

                    O of V
 1. The teacher helped <u>me</u> with the lesson.

    S   O of PREP
 2. <u>I</u> carry a dictionary with <u>me</u> at all times.

 3. Mr. Fong has a computer. He uses it for many things. It helps him in many ways.

 4. Jessica went to Hawaii with Ann and me. We like her, and she likes us. We had a good time

    with her.

 5. Mike had dirty socks. He washed them in the kitchen sink and hung them to dry in front of

    the window. They dried quickly.

 6. Joseph and I are close friends. No bad feelings will ever come between him and me. He and I

    share a strong bond of friendship.

◇ PRACTICE 19. Personal pronouns. (Chart 6-10)
     Directions: Circle each pronoun, then draw an arrow to the noun or noun phrase it refers to.
     Enclose the noun or noun phrase in brackets.

 1. [Janet] had [a green apple.] (She) ate (it) after class.

 2. Betsy called this morning. John spoke to her.

 3. Nick and Rob are at the market. They are buying fresh vegetables.

 4. Eric took some phone messages for Karen. They're on a pad of yellow paper in the kitchen.

 5. When Louie called, Alice talked to him. He asked her for a date. She accepted.

 6. Jane wrote a letter to Mr. and Mrs. Moore. She mailed it to them yesterday. They should get

    her letter on Friday.

◇ PRACTICE 20. Personal pronouns. (Chart 6-10)

Directions: Circle the correct pronoun.

1. You can ride with Jennifer and *I,* (*me.*)

2. Did you see Mark? *He, Him* was waiting in your office to talk to you.

3. I saw Rob a few minutes ago. I passed Sara and *he, him* on the steps of the classroom

   building.

4. Nick used to work in his father's store, but his father and *he, him* had a serious

   disagreement. Nick left and started his own business.

5. When the doctor came into the room, I asked *she, her* a question.

6. The doctor was very helpful. *She, Her* answered all of my questions.

7. Prof. Molina left a message for you and *I, me. He, Him* needs to see *we, us.*

8. Emily is a good basketball player. I watch Betsy and *she, her* carefully during games.

   They, Them are the best players.

9. Once my little sister and *I, me* were home alone. When our parents returned, a valuable

   vase was broken. *They, Them* blamed *we, us* for the broken vase, but in truth the cat had

   broken *it, them. We, Us* got in trouble with *they, them* because of the cat.

10. Take these secret documents and destroy *it, them.*

11. Ron invited Mary and *I, me* to have dinner with *he, him.*

12. Maureen likes movies. Ron and *she, her* go to the movies every chance they get.

13. Tom and *I, me* both want to marry Ann. She has to choose between *he and I, him and me.*

14. I talked to Jennifer and Mike. I told *they, them* about the surprise birthday party for Lizzy.

    They, Them won't tell *she, her* about *it, them. She, Her* is really going to be surprised!

15. Ted invited *I, me* to go to the game with *he, him.*

16. Ted invited Adam and *I, me* to go to the game with Tina and *he, him.*

17. My brother always teases *I, me* and my sister when *he, him* comes home from college.

    Our parents laugh and tell *he, him* to quit picking on *we, us. We, Us* love the attention.

    We, Us miss *he, him* when *he, him* returns to school.

◇ **PRACTICE 21. Possessive nouns. (Chart 6-11)**

Directions: Use the *italicized* noun in the first sentence to write a POSSESSIVE NOUN in the second sentence. Pay special attention to where you put the apostrophe.

1. I have one *friend*. My _____friend's_____ name is Paul.

2. I have two *friends*. My _____friends'_____ names are Paul and Kevin.

3. I have one *son*. My _____ name is Ryan.

4. I have two *sons*. My _____ names are Ryan and Scott.

5. I have one *baby*. My _____ name is Joy.

6. I have two *babies*. My _____ names are Joy and Erica.

7. I have one *child*. My _____ name is Anna.

8. I have two *children*. My _____ names are Anna and Keith.

9. I know one *person*. This _____ name is Nick.

10. I know several *people*. These _____ names are Nick, Karen, and Rita.

11. I have one *teacher*. My _____ name is Ms. West.

12. I have two *teachers*. My _____ names are Ms. West and Mr. Fox.

13. I know a *man*. This _____ name is Alan Burns.

14. I know two *men*. These _____ names are Alan Burns and Joe Lee.

15. We live on the *earth*. The _____ surface is seventy percent water.

◇ **PRACTICE 22. Possessive nouns. (Chart 6-11)**

Directions: Make the nouns possessive if necessary.

1. I met ~~Dan~~ Dan's sister yesterday.

2. I met Dan and his sister yesterday. OK *(no change)*

3. I know Jack roommates.

4. I know Jack well. He's a good friend of mine.

5. I have one roommate. My roommate desk is always messy.

6. You have two roommates. Your roommates desks are always neat.

7. Jo Ann and Betty are sisters.

8. Jo Ann is Betty sister. My sister name is Sonya.

9. My name is Richard. I have two sisters. My sisters names are Jo Ann and Betty.

10. There is an old saying: "A woman work is never done."

11. I read a book about the changes in women roles and men roles in modern society.

12. Jupiter is the largest planet in our solar system. We cannot see Jupiter surface from the earth because thick clouds surround the planet.

13. Mercury is the closest planet to the sun. Mercury atmosphere is extremely hot and dry.

14. Mars* surface has some of the same characteristics as Earth surface, but Mars could not support life as we know it on Earth. The plants and animals that live on Earth could not live on any of the other planets in our solar system.

15. Venus is sometimes called Earth twin because the two planets are almost the same size. But like Mars, Venus surface is extremely hot and dry.

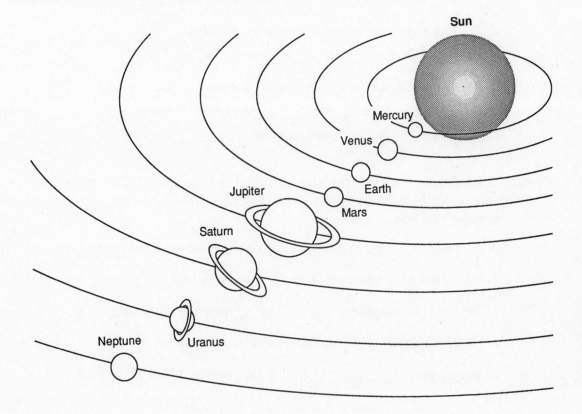

---

*When a singular noun ends in -s, there are two possible possessive forms, as in the examples below:

SINGULAR NOUNS	POSSESSIVE FORMS
James	I know *James'* brother. OR I know *James's* brother.
Chris	*Chris'* car is red. OR *Chris's* car is red.
Carlos	*Carlos'* last name is Rivera. OR *Carlos's* last name is Rivera.

16. The planets English names come from ancient Roman mythology. For example, Mars was

the name of the god of war in ancient Rome. Jupiter was the king of the gods. Mercury, who

was Jupiter son, was the messenger of the gods. Venus was the goddess of love, beauty, and

creativity. Venus son was named Cupid, the god of love and desire.

◇ **PRACTICE 23. Possessive pronouns vs. possessive adjectives. (Chart 6-12)**
Directions: Complete the sentences with possessive pronouns or possessive adjectives that refer to the words in *italics*.

1. A: Can I look at your grammar book?

   B: Why? *You* have _____**your**_____ own* book. *You* have _____**yours**_____ , and I have mine.

2. A: Anna wants to look at your grammar book.

   B: Why? *She* has _____ own book. *She* has _____ , and I have mine.

3. A: Tom wants to look at your grammar book.

   B: Why? *He* has _____ own book. *He* has _____ , and I have mine.

4. A: Tom and I want to look at your grammar book.

   B: Why? *You* have _____ own books. *You* have _____ , and I have mine.

5. A: Tom and Anna want to look at our grammar books.

   B: Why? *They* have _____ own books. *We* have _____ own books. *They*

   have _____ , and *we* have _____ .

◇ **PRACTICE 24. Possessive pronouns vs. possessive adjectives. (Chart 6-12)**
Directions: Complete the sentences with possessive pronouns or possessive adjectives that refer to the words in *italics*.

1. *Sara* asked _____**her**_____ mother for permission to go to a movie.

2. I don't need to borrow your bicycle. *Sara* loaned me _____**hers**_____ .

3. *Ted and I* are roommates. _____ apartment is small.

4. Brian and Louie have a huge apartment, but *we* don't. _____ is small.

5. *You* can find _____ keys in the top drawer of the desk.

*****Own** frequently follows a possessive adjective: e.g., *my own, your own, their own*. The word **own** emphasizes that nobody else possesses the exact same thing(s); ownership belongs **only** to me (*my own book*), to you (*your own book*), to them (*their own books*), to us (*our own books*), etc.

6. The keys in the drawer belong to you. *I* have _____ in _____ pocket.

   You should look in the drawer for _____ .

7. *Tom and Paul* talked about _____ experiences in the wilderness areas of

   Canada. I've had a lot of interesting experiences in the wilderness, but nothing to compare

   with _____ .

8. *I* know Eric well. He is a good friend of _____ . *You* know him, too, don't you?

   Isn't he a friend of _____ , too?

9. Omar, *my wife and I* would like to introduce you to a good friend of _____ .

   His name is Dan Lightfeather.

◇ **PRACTICE 25. Reflexive pronouns. (Chart 6-13)**

   Directions: Complete the sentences with reflexive pronouns that refer to the words in *italics*.

   1. *I* enjoyed _____myself_____ at Disney World.

   2. *Paul* enjoyed _____ .

   3. *Paul and I* enjoyed _____ .

   4. Hi, Emily! Did *you* enjoy _____ ?

   5. Hi, Emily and Dan! Did *you* enjoy _____ ?

   6. *Jessica* enjoyed _____ .

   7. *Jessica and Paul* enjoyed _____ .

   8. *Joe* helped _____ to more dessert.

   9. *Jane* helped _____ .

   10. *I* helped _____ .

   11. *We* helped _____ .

   12. *They* helped _____ .

   13. *The new teacher* introduced _____ to the students.

   14. *My friends and I* introduced _____ .

   15. *The assistant teacher and school nurse* introduced _____ .

   16. *Ann* introduced _____ .

17. *Jack* introduced _____ .

18. *The other teachers* introduced _____ .

19. Did *you* introduce _____ ?

◇ **PRACTICE 26. Reflexive pronouns. (Chart 6-13)**

Directions: Choose an expression and complete the sentences. Be sure to use the correct reflexive pronoun.

be proud of	help	talk to
blame	introduce	teach
✓cut	take care of	work for
enjoy		

1. Ouch! I just _____ cut myself _____ with a knife.

2. You graduated with top honors in your class. Congratulations, Anna! You must _____
_____ .

3. John often _____ . People think there is more than one person
in the room, but there isn't. It's only John.

4. When I was young, I _____ to ride a bicycle. Then I taught
the other children in the neighborhood.

5. Sheri _____ for the accident, but it wasn't her fault. There was
nothing she could have done when the car came toward her.

6. Eat! Eat! There's lots more pizza in the oven. Please, all of you, _____
_____ .

7. Adam seldom gets sick because he eats nourishing food and exercises regularly. He
_____ .

8. They went to a party last night. Let's ask them if they _____ .

9. My father never worked for anyone. He always owned his own company. He _____
_____ throughout his entire adult life.

10. At the beginning of each term, my students walk around the room and greet each other.
When they finish, they _____ to the
whole class.

◇ **PRACTICE 27. Review: pronouns. (Charts 6-10 → 6-13)**
Directions: Circle the correct pronouns.

1. Nick invited *I, (me)* to go to dinner with *he, (him.)*

2. Sam and you should be proud of *yourself, yourselves.* The two of you did a good job.

3. The room was almost empty. The only furniture was one table. The table stood by *it, itself*

   in one corner.

4. The bird returned to *its, it's*★ nest to feed *its, it's* offspring.

5. Nick has his tennis racket, and Ann has *her, hers, her's.*★

6. Where's Eric? I have some good news for Joe and *he, him, his, himself.*

7. Don't listen to Greg. You need to think for *yourself, yourselves,* Jane. It's

   you, your, your's★ life.

8. We all have *us, our, ours* own ideas about how to live *our, ours, our's*★ lives.

9. You have your beliefs, and we have *our, ours.*

10. People usually enjoy *themself, themselves, theirselves*★★ at family gatherings.

11. History repeats *himself, herself, itself.*

12. David didn't need my help. He finished the work by *him, himself, his, his self.*

◇ **PRACTICE 28. Review: pronouns. (Charts 6-10 → 6-13)**
Directions: Complete the sentences with pronouns that refer to the words in *italics*.

1. *Tom* is wearing a bandage on ____his____ arm. ____He____ hurt ____himself____
   while ____he____ was repairing the roof. I'll help ____him____ with the roof later.

2. I have *a sister.* _____ name is Kate. _____ and I share a room.

3. *My sister and I* share a room. _____ room is pretty small. _____ have
   only one desk.

4. Our desk has five drawers. *Kate* puts _____ things in the two drawers on the right.

★REMINDER: Apostrophes are NOT used with possessive pronouns. Note that *its* = possessive adjective; *it's* = *it is*. Also note that *her's, your's,* and *our's* are NOT POSSIBLE in grammatically correct English.

★★NOTE: *Themself* and *theirselves* are not really words—they are NOT POSSIBLE in grammatically correct English. Only *themselves* is the correct reflexive pronoun form.

5. *I* keep _____ stuff in the two drawers on the left. She and _____ share the middle drawer.

6. *Kate* doesn't open my two drawers, and I don't open _____ .

7. *I* don't put things in her drawers, and she doesn't put things in _____ .

8. *Ms. Lake and Mr. Ramirez* work together at the advertising company. _____ often work on projects by _____ , but I work with _____ sometimes. My office is next to _____ . _____ office has _____ names on the door, and mine has my name.

9. I have my dictionary, and *Sara* has _____ . But *Nick* doesn't have _____ .

10. My friend *James* enjoyed _____ at Mike's house yesterday. When I talked to _____ on the phone, _____ told me about _____ day with Mike. _____ and Mike played basketball, ate junk food, and played computer games. I like James a lot. I'm going to spend next Saturday with Mike and _____ at a science fair.

11. *Karen* has a bandage on _____ thumb because _____ accidentally cut _____ with a hatchet while _____ was cutting wood for _____ fireplace.

12. We don't agree with you. *You* have _____ opinion, and *we* have _____ .

◇ **PRACTICE 29. Singular forms of OTHER. (Chart 6-14)**
Directions: Write **another** or **the other** under each picture.

1. Four boxes: *one*   *another*   *another*   *the other*

2. Three circles: *one*   _____   _____

3. Five flowers: __one__ _____ _____ _____ _____

4. Two cups: __one__ _____

5. Six spoons: __one__ _____ _____ _____ _____ _____

◇ **PRACTICE 30. Singular forms of OTHER. (Chart 6-14)**
   Directions: Complete the sentences with ***another*** or ***the other***.

1. There are many kinds of animals in the world. The elephant is one kind. The tiger is

   _____another_____.

2. There are two colors on this page. One is white. _____The other_____ is black.

3. There are two women in Picture A. One is Ann. _____ is Sara.

4. There are three men in Picture B. One is Alex. _____ one is Mike.

5. In Picture B, Alex and Mike are smiling. _____ man looks sad.

6. There are three men in Picture B. All three have common first names. One is named Alex.

   a. _____ is named David.

   b. The name of _____ one is Mike.

7. There are many common English names for men. Alex is one.

    a. Mike is _____.

    b. David is _____.

    c. John is _____ common name.

    d. Joe is _____.

    e. What is _____ common English name for a man?

8. Alex's bicycle was run over by a truck and destroyed. He needs to get _____ one.

9. The Smiths have two bicycles. One belongs to Mr. Smith. _____ bike belongs to Mrs. Smith.

10. There are three books on my desk. Two of them are dictionaries. _____ one is a telephone directory.

11. The puppy chewed up my telephone directory, so I went to the telephone company to get _____ phone book.

◇ PRACTICE 31. Plural forms of OTHER. (Chart 6-15)
Directions: Complete the sentences with ***the other, the others, other,*** or ***others.***

1. There are four common nicknames for "Robert." One is "Bob." Another is "Bobby."

    ____The others____ are "Robbie" and "Rob."

2. There are five English vowels. One is "a." Another is "e." _____ are "i,"
"o," and "u."

3. There are many consonants in English. The letters "b" and "c" are consonants.

    _____ are "d," "f," and "g."

4. Some people are tall, and _____ are short. Some people are neither tall
nor short.

5. Some people are tall, and _____ people are short.

6. Some animals are huge. _____ are tiny.

7. Some animals are huge. _____ animals are tiny.

8. Some ships are fueled by petroleum. _____ are propelled by atomic
power.

9. Some boats are used for pleasure. _____ boats are used for commercial
fishing.

10. Of the twenty students in the class, eighteen passed the exam. _____ failed.

11. Out of the twenty students in the class, only two failed the exam. _____ students passed.

12. Our physical education class was divided into two groups. Half of the students stayed inside and played basketball. _____ students went outside and played soccer.

13. The telephone and the automobile are twentieth-century inventions. _____ are the computer, television, and the airplane. Can you name _____ twentieth-century inventions?

14. If you really hate your job, why don't you look for _____ one? You don't have to be a dishwasher all your life. There are lots of _____ jobs in the world.

15. An automobile consists of many parts. The motor is one, and the steering wheel is _____ . _____ parts are the brakes, the trunk, and the fuel tank.

16. The students in our class had two choices: basketball or soccer. Half of the students played basketball. _____ played soccer.

17. Here, children. I have two coins. One is for you, Tommy. _____ is for you, Jimmy.

◇ PRACTICE 32. Summary: forms of OTHER. (Charts 6-14 → 6-16)
Directions: Choose the correct completion.

Example: Copper is one kind of metal. Silver is _____ .
   (A.) another   B. the other   C. the others   D. others   E. other

1. Summer is one season. Spring is _____ .
   A. another   B. the other   C. the others   D. others   E. other

2. There are four seasons. Summer is one. _____ are winter, fall, and spring.
   A. Another   B. The other   C. The others   D. Others   E. Other

3. What's your favorite season? Some people like spring the best. _____ think fall is the nicest season.
   A. Another   B. The other   C. The others   D. Others   E. Other

4. My eyes are different colors. One eye is gray, and _____ is green.
   A. another   B. the other   C. the others   D. others   E. other

5. There are two reasons not to buy that piece of furniture. One is that it's expensive. _____ is that it's not well made.
   A. Another   B. The other   C. The others   D. Others   E. Other

6. Alex failed his English exam, but his teacher is going to give him _____ chance to pass it.
   A. another   B. the other   C. the others   D. others   E. other

7. Some people drink tea in the morning. _____ have coffee. I prefer fruit juice.
   A. Another   B. The other   C. The others   D. Others   E. Other

8. There are five digits in the number 20,000. One digit is a 2. _____ digits are all zeroes.
   A. Another   B. The other   C. The others   D. Others   E. Other

◇ PRACTICE 33. Cumulative review. (Chapter 6)
   Directions: Circle the correct answer.

1. The people at the market   *is,* *(are)* friendly.

2. How many   *potato, potatoes*   should I cook for dinner tonight?

3. I wanted to be alone, so I worked   *myself, by myself.*

4. The twins were born   *in, on*   December 25   *on, at*   midnight.

5. All the workers at our company get   *four-week, four-weeks*   vacations.

6. The bus driver waited for   *we, us*   at the bus stop.

7. Can you tell a good book by   *its, it's*   title?

8. This is   *our, ours*   dessert, and that is   *your, yours.*

9. Jack has so much confidence. He really believes in   *him, himself.*

10. These bananas are OK, but   *the other, the others*   were better.

◇ PRACTICE 34. Cumulative review. (Chapter 6)
   Directions: Correct the errors.

1. Look at those beautifuls mountains!

2. The children played on Saturday afternoon at the park a game.

3. There are two horse, several sheeps, and a cow in the farmers field.

4. The owner of the store is busy in the moment.

5. The teacher met her's students at the park after school.

6. Everyone want peace in the world.

7. I grew up in a city very large.

8. This apple tastes sour. Here's some more, so let's try the other one.

9. Some tree lose their leaf in the winter.

10. I am going to wear my shirt is brown to the party.

11. I hurt meself at work last week.

12. Our neighbors invited my friend and I to visit they.

13. My husband boss works for twelve hour every days.

14. The students couldn't find they're books.

15. I always read magazines articles while I'm in the waiting room at my dentists office.

CHAPTER 7
Modal Auxiliaries

◇ **PRACTICE 1. Preview: modal auxiliaries.** (Chapter 7)

Directions: The words in **boldfaced italics** are modal auxiliaries. Read the passage and then answer the questions.

(1)   Everyone in my family ***has to*** contribute to keeping order in our house. My parents

(2)   assign chores to my brother Joe and me. We ***must*** do these tasks every day. Sometimes if

(3)   one of us is busy and ***can't*** do a chore, the other one ***may*** take care of it.

(4)   For example, last Friday it was Joe's turn to wash the dishes after dinner. He said he

(5)   ***couldn't*** wash them because he had to hurry to school for a basketball game. Joe asked me,

(6)   "***Will*** you do the dishes for me, please? I promise to do them for you tomorrow when it's

(7)   your turn. ***I've got to*** get to school for the game." I reluctantly agreed to do Joe's chore

(8)   and washed the dishes after dinner.

(9)   But the next night, Joe "forgot" that we had traded days. When I reminded him to

(10)   wash the dishes, he said, "Who, me? It's not my turn. You ***have to*** do the dishes tonight.

(11)   It's your turn."

(12)   I think ***I'd better*** write our agreement down when I do my brother Joe's chores, and I

(13)   ***ought to*** give him a copy of the agreement. Joe has a short memory, especially if he ***has to***

(14)   wash dishes or take out the

(15)   garbage. I ***should*** write

(16)   everything down. In fact, I

(17)   ***might*** write out a weekly

(18)   schedule. Then, we ***could***

(19)   write our names in and change

(20)   assignments if necessary. That

(21)   ***ought to*** solve the problem.

(22)   I ***must*** remember to do that.

What is the meaning of these modal auxiliaries from the sentences in the passage? Circle the answer that is closest in meaning to the modal.

	MODAL AUXILIARY	MEANING			
(1)	Everyone **has to** contribute	(must)	should	is able to	might
(3)	. . . and **can't** do a chore	must not	should not	is not able to	might not
(3)	. . . the other one **may** take care of it.	must	should	is able to	might
(5)	He **couldn't** wash them	must not	should not	was not able to	might not
(7)	I've **got to** get to school	must	should	are able to	might
(10)	You **have to** do the dishes	must	should	are able to	might
(12)	I think **I'd better** write	must	should	am able to	might
(13)	. . . and I **ought to** give him	must	should	am able to	may
(13)	. . . especially if he **has to**	must	should	is able to	may
(17)	In fact, I **might** write out	must	should	am able to	may
(21)	. . . That **ought to** solve the problem.	must	should	is able to	may

◇ PRACTICE 2. The form of modal auxiliaries. (Chart 7-1)
Directions: Add the word *to* where necessary. Write Ø if *to* is not necessary.

1. Mr. Alvarez spilled tea on his shirt. He must _____Ø_____ change clothes before dinner.

2. Mr. Alvarez has _____to_____ change his shirt before dinner.

3. Tom and I might _____ play tennis after work tomorrow.

4. You had better _____ see a doctor.

5. Would you _____ speak more slowly, please?

6. The students have _____ take a test next Friday.

7. Everyone should _____ pay attention to local politics.

8. Everyone ought _____ participate in local government.

9. May I please _____ have the salt and pepper? Thanks.

10. You'd better not _____ come to the meeting late. The boss will _____ be angry if you're late.

11. I've had a lot of trouble sleeping the last few nights. I've got _____ get a good night's sleep! I can barely _____ stay awake in class.

12. We may _____ go to Argentina for our vacation.

13. Will you please _____ mail this letter for me?

◇ **PRACTICE 3. Expressing ability. (Chart 7-2)**
    Directions: Choose one of the words in parentheses to complete each sentence.

1. (*giraffe, zebra*)   A ___zebra___ **can't stretch** its neck to reach the tops of trees.

2. (*bee, cat*)   A single _____ **can kill** a thousand mice in a year.

3. (*Rabbits, Elephants*)   _____ **can crush** small trees under their huge feet.

4. (*Monkeys, Chickens*)   _____ **can climb** trees with ease.

5. (*ducks, camels*)   Did you know that _____ **can survive** seventeen days

                without any water at all?

6. (*cow, bull*)   One _____ **can produce** as much as 8,500 lbs. (3,860 kgs)

                of milk in a year.

7. (*horse, cat*)   A person **can sit** on a _____ without hurting it.

8. (*donkey, snake*)   A _____ **can carry** heavy loads on its back.

9. (*squirrel, polar bear*)   A _____ **can stay** high up in the trees for weeks,

                leaping from branch to branch.

10. (*people, ants*)   Most _____ **can lift** objects that are ten times heavier

                than their own bodies.

11. (*baby, student*)   When I was a _____, I **could sleep** most of the day.

12. (*men, women*)   One hundred years ago, _____ **couldn't vote** in many

                countries, but now they can.

◇ **PRACTICE 4. Expressing ability and possibility. (Charts 7-2 and 7-3)**
    Directions: Complete the sentences with ***can/can't, may/might,*** or ***may not/might not.***

1. Jessica hasn't made up her mind about where to go to school. She ___may/might___

    attend Duke University, or she ___may not/might not___ . She just doesn't know yet.

2. Alice is a runner. She likes to compete, but two days ago she broke her ankle when she fell.

    She ___can't___ run in the race tomorrow.

3. A: Carol's in New York now. Is she going to return to school in Chicago in September?

    B: It depends. If she _____ find a job in New York, she'll stay there

       this fall. Who knows? She _____ stay there through the winter

       and spring, too. If she likes her job, she _____ want to return to

       school in Chicago next year at all. We'll have to wait and see.

4. A: Do you remember a famous actor named Basil Rathbone? Is he still making movies?

   B: I think he _____ be dead.

5. Jodie finished law school last month, but she hasn't taken her exams yet. She

   _____ practice law until she passes them.

6. Jack and Jenny haven't decided what kind of wedding to have. They _____

   have a large, formal celebration, or they _____ have a small, quiet

   ceremony.

7. My roommate is planning to go sailing tomorrow, but he needs at least one other person to

   help him sail the boat. If no one is available, he _____ take it out.

◇ **PRACTICE 5. Expressing possibility. (Chart 7-3)**
   Directions: Rewrite the sentences using the words in parentheses.

   1. Maybe I will take a nap. *(might)* → __I might take a nap._____

   2. She might be sick. *(maybe)* → __Maybe she is sick._____

   3. There may be time later. *(maybe)* → _____

   4. Maybe our team will win. *(may)* → _____

   5. You may be right. *(might)* → _____

   6. Maybe we'll hear soon. *(may)* → _____

   7. It might rain. *(may)* → _____

   8. Maybe it will snow. *(might)* → _____

   9. She might come tomorrow. *(maybe)* → _____

   10. She might be at home right now. *(maybe)* → _____

◇ **PRACTICE 6. Expressing possibility and permission. (Chart 7-3)**
   Directions: Decide if the meaning of the modal verb is *possibility* or *permission*.

MODAL VERB	MEANING	
1. Both of my grandparents are retired. They like to travel.		
They ***may travel*** overseas next summer.	*(possibility)*	*permission*
2. They ***may take*** their two grandchildren with them.	*possibility*	*permission*
3. A: Yes, Tommy, you ***may play*** outdoors until dinner.	*possibility*	*permission*
B: Okay, Mom.		
4. A: What's wrong with the dog's foot?		
B: He ***may have*** an infection.	*possibility*	*permission*

5. The dog has an infected foot. He **might need** to go to the vet.

possibility *permission*

6. A: Susie, no, you **can't stay** overnight at your friend's house tonight.

   B: Then how about my friend staying overnight here?

   A: No.

possibility *permission*

7. It **may be** hot and humid all weekend.

possibility *permission*

8. Johnny, you **may not stay** up until midnight. Your bedtime is nine o'clock.

possibility *permission*

9. I **might not stay** up to watch the end of the game on TV. I'm sleepy.

possibility *permission*

10. Children, you **cannot go** out now. It's dark outside, and dinner is ready.

possibility *permission*

◇ **PRACTICE 7. Meanings of COULD. (Charts 7-2 and 7-4)**
   Directions: Choose the expression that has the same meaning as the *italicized* verb.

1. "How long will it take you to paint two small rooms?"
   "I'm not sure. If the job is not complicated, I *could finish* by Thursday."
   a. was able to finish   (b.) might finish

2. I think I'll take my umbrella. It *could rain* today.
   a. was able to rain   b. might rain

3. My niece *could read* by the time she was four years old.
   a. was able to read   b. might read

4. You *could see* that the little boy was unhappy because of the sad expression in his eyes.
   a. were able to see   b. might see

5. Sally is in excellent condition. I think she *could win* the 10-kilometer race on Saturday.
   a. was able to win   b. might win

6. John *couldn't drive* for a month because of a broken ankle, but now it's healed.
   a. wasn't able to drive   b. might not drive

7. Jane *could arrive* before dinner, but I don't really expect her until nine or later.
   a. was able to arrive   b. might arrive

8. John was in an accident, but he *couldn't remember* how he had hurt himself.
   a. wasn't able to remember   b. might not remember

◇ **PRACTICE 8. Polite questions. (Charts 7-5 and 7-6)**
   Directions: Circle the correct completion.

1. A: This desk is too heavy for me. *May,* (*Can*) you help me lift it?
   B: Sure. No problem.

2. A: Ms. Milano, *may, will* I be excused from class early today? I have a doctor's appointment.
   B: Yes. You may leave early. That would be fine.

3. A: I'm having trouble with this word processor. *Would, May* you show me how to set the margins one more time?
   B: Of course.

4. A: Andrew, *would, could* I speak to you for a minute?
   B: Sure. What's up?

5. A: I can't meet David's plane tonight. *Can, May* you pick him up?
   B: Sorry. I have to work tonight. Call Uncle Frank. Maybe he can pick David up.

6. A: *Could, May* you please take these letters to the post office before noon?
   B: I'd be happy to, sir. Hmmm. It's almost eleven-thirty. *May, Will* I leave for the post office now and then go to lunch early?
   A: That would be fine.

7. A: Marilyn, are you feeling okay? *Would, Can* I get you something?
   B: *May, Will* you get me a glass of water, please?
   A: Right away.

8. A: Darn these medicine bottles! I can never get the cap off!
   B: *Would, Could* I open that for you?
   A: Thanks. I'd really appreciate it.

◇ **PRACTICE 9. Polite questions. (Charts 7-5 and 7-6)**
   Directions: Check all the modal auxiliaries that correctly complete each question.

1. It's cold in here. _____ you please close the door?
   _____ May   _✓_ Could   _✓_ Can   _✓_ Would

2. Oh, my pen's out of ink. _____ I borrow yours?
   _____ Could   _____ May   _____ Will   _____ Can

3. I can't lift this box by myself. _____ you help me carry it?
   _____ Would   _____ Could   _____ May   _____ Will

4. Hello. _____ I help you find something in the store?
   _____ Can   _____ Would   _____ May   _____ Could

5. The store closes in ten minutes. _____ you please bring all your purchases to the counter?
   _____ Will   _____ May   _____ Can   _____ Could

◇ **PRACTICE 10. Expressing advice. (Chart 7-7)**

Directions: Complete the sentences. Use ***should*** or ***shouldn't*** and the expressions in the list or your own words.

be cruel to animals	give too much homework
always be on time for an appointment	miss any classes
✓drive a long distance	quit
exceed the speed limit	throw trash out of your car window

1. If you are tired, you _____ shouldn't drive a long distance _____ .

2. Cigarette smoking is dangerous to your health. You _____ .

3. A good driver _____ .

4. A teacher _____ .

5. A student _____ .

6. Animals have feelings, too. You _____
   _____ .

7. It is important to be punctual. You
   _____
   _____ .

8. Littering is against the law. You
   _____
   _____
   _____ .

NO LITTERING $300 Fine

◇ **PRACTICE 11. Expressing advice. (Chart 7-7)**

Directions: Choose the completion from the given list that seems best to you.

call the landlord and complain	✓soak it in cold water
eat it	take it back to the store
find a new girlfriend	try to fix it herself
get a job	✓wash it in hot water
send it back to the kitchen	

1. A: I cut my finger. I got blood on my shirt. My finger is okay, but I'm worried about my
   shirt. What should I do?

   B: You should _____ soak it in cold water _____ .

   You shouldn't _____ wash it in hot water _____ .

2. A: Ann bought a new tape recorder. After two days, it stopped working. What should she do?

   B: She ought to _____ .

   She shouldn't _____ .

3. A: I don't have any money. I'm broke and can't pay my rent. I don't have enough money to pay my bills. What should I do?

   B: You'd better _____ .

4. A: There's no hot water in my apartment. What should I do?

   B: You should _____ .

5. A: I asked Mary to marry me five times. She said no every time. What should I do?

   B: Maybe you should _____ .

6. A: Helen is in a restaurant. She has ordered a salad. There's a big dead fly in it. What should she do?

   B: She should _____ .

   She shouldn't _____ .

◇ PRACTICE 12. Expressing advice. (Charts 7-7 and 7-8)
   Directions: Choose the correct completion.

   1. Danny doesn't feel well. He _____ see a doctor.
      (A.) should   B. ought   C. had

   2. Danny doesn't feel well. He _____ better see a doctor.
      A. should   B. ought   C. had

   3. Danny doesn't feel well. He _____ to see a doctor.
      A. should   B. ought   C. had

   4. It's extremely warm in here. We _____ open some windows.
      A. should   B. ought   C. had

   5. It's really cold in here. We _____ to close some windows.
      A. should   B. ought   C. had

   6. There's a police car behind us. You _____ better slow down!
      A. should   B. ought   C. had

   7. People who use public parks _____ clean up after themselves.
      A. should   B. ought   C. had

   8. I have no money left in my bank account. I _____ better stop charging things on my credit card.
      A. should   B. ought   C. had

   9. It's going to be a formal dinner and dance. You _____ to change clothes.
      A. should   B. ought   C. had

   10. This library book is overdue. I _____ better return it today.
       A. should   B. ought   C. had

◇ **PRACTICE 13. Expressing necessity. (Chart 7-9)**
Directions: Choose the correct completion.

1. I _____ to wash the dishes after dinner last night. It was my turn.
   A. have   B. has   C. had   D. must

2. Bye! I'm leaving now. I _____ got to take this package to the post office.
   A. have   B. has   C. had   D. must

3. I know you didn't mean what you said. You _____ think before you speak!
   A. have   B. has   C. had   D. must

4. Yesterday everyone in the office _____ to leave the building for a fire drill. I'm glad it wasn't a real fire.
   A. have   B. has   C. had   D. must

5. Janet _____ to take an educational psychology course next semester. It's a required course.
   A. have   B. has   C. had   D. must

6. Pete, Chris, and Anna _____ to stay after class this afternoon. Professor Irwin wants them to help him grade papers.
   A. have   B. has   C. had   D. must

7. Mr. Silva, you _____ not be late today. The vice-president is coming in, and you're the only one who can answer her questions about the new project.
   A. have   B. has   C. had   D. must

8. Last year our town didn't have many tourists because of an oil spill. Business was bad. My wife and I own a small souvenir shop near the ocean. We _____ to borrow money from the bank last month to save our business.
   A. have   B. has   C. had   D. must

◇ **PRACTICE 14. Expressing necessity. (Chart 7-9)**
Directions: Complete the sentences with any appropriate forms of ***have to*** and ***must***.

1. I can't go to the movie tonight because I __*have to/must*__ study for final exams.

2. When I was in high school, I _____ work every evening at my parents' store.

3. If you want to travel to certain countries, you _____ get a visa.

4. I'm sorry I was absent from class yesterday, but I _____ go to a funeral.

5. Erica won't be in her office tomorrow afternoon because she _____ pick her brother up at the airport.

6. When I worked in my uncle's restaurant, I _____ wash dishes and clear tables.

7. If you want to enter the university, you _____ take an entrance exam.

8. We wanted to go bike riding along the river yesterday, but we _____ stay home because the weather was awful.

◇ **PRACTICE 15. Necessity: MUST, HAVE TO, HAVE GOT TO. (Chart 7-9)**
   Directions: Circle the correct verb.

1. Last week, John *must,* (*had to*) interview five people for the new management position.

2. Professor Drake *had got to, had to* cancel several lectures when she became ill.

3. Why did you *have to, had to* leave work early ?

4. I *must, had to* take my daughter to the airport yesterday.

5. Where did John *have to, had to* go for medical help yesterday?

6. We *had to, had got to* contact a lawyer last week about a problem with our neighbors.

◇ **PRACTICE 16. Necessity: MUST, HAVE TO, HAVE GOT TO. (Chart 7-9)**
   Directions: Write the past tense of the verb in *italics*.

1. I *have to study* for my medical school exams.

   PAST: I _____had to study_____ for my medical school exams.

2. We *have to turn off* our water because of a leak.

   PAST: We _____ our water because of a leak.

3. *Do* you *have to work* over the holidays?

   PAST: _____ you _____ over the holidays?

4. Jerry *has got to see* the dentist twice this week.

   PAST: Jerry _____ the dentist twice last month.

5. Who *has got to be* in early for work this week?

   PAST: Who _____ in early for work last week?

6. The bank *must close* early today.

   PAST: The bank _____ early yesterday.

◇ **PRACTICE 17. Expressing lack of necessity and prohibition. (Chart 7-10)**
   Directions: Complete the sentences with ***don't/doesn't have to*** or ***must not***.

1. The soup is too hot. You _____must not_____ eat it yet. Wait for it to cool.

2. You ____don't have to____ have soup for lunch. You can have a sandwich if you like.

3. The review class before the final exam is optional. We _____ go
   unless we want to.

4. Many vegetables can be eaten raw. You _____ cook them.

5. You _____ use a pencil to write a check because someone could
   change the amount you have written on it.

6. When the phone rings, you _____ answer it. It's up to you.

7. When you have a new job, you _____ be late the first day. In fact, it is a good idea to be a few minutes early.

8. A: I _____ forget to set my alarm for 5:30.

   B: Why do you have to get up at 5:30?

   A: I'm going to meet Ron at 6:00. We're going fishing.

9. You _____ play loud music late at night. The neighbors will call the police.

10. This box isn't as heavy as it looks. You _____ help me with it. Thanks anyway for offering to help.

11. Susan, you _____ go to the university. Your father and I think you should, but it's your choice.

12. People _____ spend their money foolishly if they want to stay out of financial trouble.

13. When you first meet someone, you _____ ask personal questions. For example, it's not polite to ask a person's age.

14. The nations of the world _____ stop trying to achieve total world peace.

15. My husband and I grow all of our own vegetables in the summer. We _____ _____ buy any vegetables at the market.

◇ PRACTICE 18. Expressing necessity, lack of necessity, and prohibition. (Charts 7-9 and 7-10)

Directions: Complete each sentence with a form of ***have to*** or ***must***. Use the negative if necessary to make a sensible sentence.

1. Smoking in this building is prohibited. You ___must/have to___ extinguish your cigar.

2. Alan's company pays all of his travel expenses. Alan ___doesn't have to___ pay for his own plane ticket to the business conference in Amman, Jordan.

3. Our company provides free advice on the use of our products. You _____ pay us for the advice.

4. Everyone here _____ leave immediately! The building is on fire!

5. Lynn _____ attend the meeting tonight because she isn't working on the project that we're going to discuss. We're going to talk about raising money for the new library. Lynn isn't involved in that.

6. The construction company _____ finish the building by the end of the month. That's the date they promised, and they will lose a lot of money if they're late.

7. Please remember, you _____ call my house between three and four this afternoon. That's when the baby sleeps, and my mother will get upset if we wake him up.

◇ PRACTICE 19. Expressing necessity, lack of necessity, and prohibition. (Charts 7-9 and 7-10)

Directions: Write the phrases in the correct columns.

✓ *fall asleep while driving*   *take other people's belongings*   *cook every meal themselves*   *pay taxes*   *say "sir" or "madam" to others*   *stay in their homes in the evening*   *eat and drink in order to live*   *stop when they see a police car's lights*   *drive without a license*   *behind them*

People have to/must . . . (necessary)	People must not . . . (DON'T!)	People don't have to . . . (not necessary)
	fall asleep while driving	

◇ PRACTICE 20. Logical conclusion or necessity. (Charts 7-9 and 7-11)

Directions: Write **1** if the modal ***must*** expresses a logical conclusion. Write **2** if the modal expresses necessity.

> **1 = logical conclusion.**
> **2 = necessity.**

1. __2__ You *must have* a passport to travel abroad.

2. __1__ You *must like* to read. You have such a large library.

3. _____ Ellen *must like* fish. She buys it several times a week.

4. _____ You *must take off* your shoes before entering this room.

5. _____ The dessert *must be* good. It's almost gone.

6. _____ You *must try* this dessert. It's wonderful.

7. _____ Children *must stay* seated during the flight.

8. _____ You *must pay* in advance if you want a guaranteed seat for the performance.

9. _____ The cat *must be* afraid. She's hiding in the flower garden again.

◇ PRACTICE 21. Imperative sentences. (Chart 7-12)

Directions: Pretend that someone says the following sentences to **you**. Which verbs give **you** instructions? Underline the imperative verbs.

1. I'll be right back. <u>Wait</u> here.

2. <u>Don't wait</u> for Rebecca. She's not going to come.

3. Read pages thirty-nine to fifty-five before class tomorrow.

4. What are you doing? Don't put those magazines in the trash. I haven't read them yet.

5. Come in and have a seat. I'll be right with you.

6.

DON'T CROSS THIS
FIELD UNLESS YOU
CAN DO IT IN
9.9 SECONDS.
THE BULL CAN
DO IT IN 10.
(NO TRESPASSING)

7. Don't just stand there! Do something!

8. A: Call me around eight, okay?

   B: Okay.

9. Here, little Mike. Take this apple to Daddy. That's good. Go ahead. Walk toward Daddy. That's great! Now give him the apple. Wonderful!

10. Capitalize the first word of each sentence. Put a period at the end of a sentence. If the sentence is a question, use a question mark at the end.

◇ **PRACTICE 22. Polite questions and imperatives. (Charts 7-5, 7-6, and 7-12)**
Directions: Number the sentences in order of politeness. **1 = most polite.**

1. _1_ Could you open the door?

   _3_ Open the door.

   _2_ Can you open the door?

2. ___ Get the phone, please.

   ___ Would you please get the phone?

   ___ Get the phone.

   ___ Can you get the phone?

3. ___ Can I borrow your eraser?

   ___ Could I borrow your eraser?

4. ___ Hand me the calculator.

   ___ Will you hand me the calculator, please?

   ___ Would you hand me the calculator, please?

   ___ Please hand me the calculator.

◇ **PRACTICE 23. LET'S and WHY DON'T. (Chart 7-13)**
Directions: Complete the sentences with verbs from the list. The verbs may be used more than once.

ask	fly	pick up	see
call	get	play	stop
fill up	go	save	take

1. A: There's a strong wind today. Let's ____go____ to the top of the hill on Cascade Avenue and ____fly____ our kite.

   B: Sounds like fun. Why don't we ____see____ if Louie wants to come with us?

   A: Okay. I'll call him.

2. A: What should we buy Mom for her birthday?

   B: I don't know. Let's _____ her some perfume or something.

   A: I have a better idea. Why don't we _____ her out for dinner and a movie?

3. A: My toe hurts. Let's not _____ dancing tonight.

   B: Okay. Why don't we _____ chess instead?

4. A: Let's _____ a taxi from the airport to the hotel.

    B: Why don't we _____ a bus and _____ ourselves some money?

5. A: We're almost out of gas. Why don't we _____ at a gas station and _____ before we drive the rest of the way to the beach?

    B: Okay. Are you hungry? I am. Let's _____ something to eat too.

    A: Great.

6. A: Let's _____ to a movie at the mall tonight.

    B: I've already seen all the good movies there. What else can we do?

    A: Well, Marika has a car. Why don't we _____ her and _____ if she wants to drive us into the city?

    B: Okay. What's her number?

◇ PRACTICE 24. Stating preferences. (Chart 7-14)
    Directions: Complete the sentences with *prefer*, *like*, or *would rather*.

1. I _____prefer_____ cold weather to hot weather.

2. A: What's your favorite fruit?

    B: I _____like_____ strawberries better than any other fruit.

3. Mary _____would rather_____ save money than enjoy herself.

4. Unfortunately, many children _____ candy to vegetables.

5. A: Why isn't your brother going with us to the movie?

    B: He _____ stay home and read than go out on a Saturday night.

6. A: Does Peter _____ football to baseball?

    B: No. I think he _____ baseball better than football.

    A: Then why didn't he go to the game yesterday?

    B: Because he _____ watch sports on TV than go to a ball park.

7. I _____ jog in the morning than after work.

8. Heidi enjoys her independence. She is struggling to start her own business, but she _____ borrow money from the bank than ask her parents for help.

9. A: Do you want to go out to the Japanese restaurant for dinner?

   B: That would be okay, but in truth I _____ Chinese food to

   Japanese food.

   A: Really? I _____ Japanese food better than Chinese food. What

   shall we do?

   B: Let's go to the Italian restaurant.

10. A: Mother, I can't believe you have another cat! Now you have four cats, two dogs, and three

   birds.

   B: I know, dear. I can't help it. I love having animals around.

   A: Honestly, Mother, I sometimes think you _____ animals to

   people.

   B: Honestly, dear, sometimes I do.

◇ PRACTICE 25. Stating preferences. (Chart 7-14)
Directions: Use the words in parentheses to create a new sentence with the same meaning.

Example: Alex would rather swim than jog. *(prefer)*
   → *Alex prefers swimming to jogging.*

Example: My son likes fish better than beef. *(would rather)*
   → *My son would rather eat/have fish than beef.*

1. Kim likes salad better than dessert. *(prefer)*

2. In general, Nicole would rather have coffee than tea. *(like)*

3. Bill prefers teaching history to working as a business executive. *(would rather)*

4. When considering a pet, Sam prefers dogs to cats. *(like)*

5. On a long trip, Susie would rather drive than ride in the back seat. *(prefer)*

6. I like studying in a noisy room better than studying in a completely quiet room. *(would rather)*

7. Alex likes soccer better than baseball. *(would rather)*

◇ PRACTICE 26. Cumulative review. (Chapter 7)
Directions: Choose the best completion.

1. "I need the milk. _____ you get it out of the refrigerator for me?"
   "Sure."
   A. May   B. Should   C. Could

2. "_____ you hand me that book, please? I can't reach it."
   "Sure. Here it is."
   A. Would   B. Should   C. Must

3. "What do you like the most about your promotion?"
   "I _____ get up at 5:30 in the morning anymore. I can sleep until 7:00."
   A. must not   B. would rather   C. don't have to

4. "Do you have a minute? I need to talk to you."
   "I _____ leave here in ten minutes. Can we make an appointment for another time?"
   A. have to   B. could   C. may

5. "Yes? _____ I help you?"
   "Yes. Do you have these sandals in a size eight?"
   A. Should   B. Can   C. Will

6. "Let's go bowling Saturday afternoon."
   "Bowling? I _____ play golf than go bowling."
   A. had better   B. should   C. would rather

7. "Diane found a library book on a bench at Central Park. Someone had left it there."
   "She _____ take it to any library in the city. I'm sure they'll be glad to have it back."
   A. will   B. should   C. would rather

8. "Beth got another speeding ticket yesterday."
   "Oh? That's not good. She _____ be more careful. She'll end up in serious trouble if she gets any more."
   A. would rather   B. will   C. ought to

9. "Are you going to take the job transfer when the company moves out of town?"
   "I _____ accept their offer if they are willing to pay all of my moving expenses."
   A. must not   B. might   C. maybe

10. "Are you going to admit your mistake to the boss?"
    "Yes. I _____ tell her about it than have her hear about it from someone else."
    A. can   B. should   C. would rather

11. "I just heard that there's an accident on the freeway. Traffic is a mess."
    "We _____ leave earlier than we planned."
    A. maybe   B. had better   C. prefer to

12. "Would you like to go with me to the Williams' wedding next month?"
    "I'm not sure. I _____ be too busy with school."
    A. will   B. might   C. maybe

13. "Do you need help washing the dishes?"

"Oh, no. You _____ help. There are enough people in the kitchen already."

    A. don't have to   B. must not   C. may not

14. "Why are you working so many evenings and weekends?"

"I _____ increase sales or I'm in danger of losing my job."

    A. may   B. can   C. have got to

15. "Are these gloves necessary?"

"Yes. You _____ use this chemical without gloves. It will burn your skin."

    A. must not   B. don't have to   C. could not

◇ **PRACTICE 27. Cumulative review. (Chapter 7)**
Directions: Correct the errors.

1. Before I left on my trip last month, I ~~must~~ get a passport. *(had to)*

2. Could you to bring us more coffee, please?

3. Ben can driving, but he prefers take the bus.

4. My roommate maybe at home this evening.

5. A few of our classmates can't to come to the school picnic.

6. May you take our picture, please?

7. Jane's eyes are red, and she is yawning. She must is sleepy.

8. Jim would rather has Fridays off in the summer than a long vacation.

9. I must reading several lengthy books for my literature class.

10. Take your warm clothes with you. It will maybe snow.

11. When the baby went to the doctor last week, she must has several shots.

12. It's very cool in here. Please you turn up the heat.

13. You had better to call us before you come over. We're often away during the day.

14. The children would rather to see the circus than a baseball game.

15. It's such a gorgeous day. Why we don't go to a park or the beach?

◇ PRACTICE 28. Cumulative review. (Chapter 7)

> *Directions:* The topic of this passage is writing a composition. Read the passage through completely to get the main ideas. Then read it again slowly and choose from the words in **boldface italics**.

Writing a Composition

(1) "What? Not another composition! I hate writing compositions. I'm not good at it." Do you ever complain about having to write compositions in English class? A lot of students do. You **may,** ~~**cannot**~~ find it difficult and time-consuming, but you are learning a useful skill. The ability to write clearly **is, must be** important. It **can, must** affect your success in school and in your job. You **may, can** learn to write effectively by practicing. One of the best ways to practice your writing skills is to prepare compositions in a thoughtful, step-by-step process.

(2) The first step in writing a composition is to choose a subject that interests you. You **maybe, should** write about a subject you already know about or **can, have to** find out about through research. Writers **might, should** never pretend to be experts. For example, if you have never bought a car and are not knowledgeable about automobiles, you **should, should not** write an essay on what to look for when buying a car—unless, of course, you plan to research the subject in books and magazines and make yourself an expert. There is one topic about which you are the most knowledgeable expert in the world, and that topic **is, may be** yourself and your experiences. Many of the most interesting and informative compositions are based simply on a writer's personal experience and observations. The questions you should ask yourself when choosing a topic are "Do I have any expertise in this subject?" and if not, "**Will, Can** I be able to find information about this subject?"

(3) After you have a topic and have researched it if necessary, start writing down your thoughts. These notes **must not, do not have to** be in any particular order. You **do not have to, could not** worry about grammar at this time. You **can, may** pay special attention to that later.

(4) Next, you **have to, may** organize your thoughts. You **cannot, might not** say everything possible about a subject in one composition. Therefore, you **may, must** carefully choose the ideas and information you want to include. Look over your notes, think hard about your topic, and find a central idea. Answer these questions: "What **am, do** I want my readers to understand? What **is, does** my main idea? How **can, am** I put this idea into one sentence?" Good writing depends on clear thinking. Writers **should, had better** spend more time thinking than actually writing. After you have a clearly formed main idea, choose relevant information from your notes to include in your composition.

(5)   Before you begin to write the actual composition, you   *ought to, can*   know exactly what you want to say and how you are going to develop your ideas. Many good writers *prepare, prepared*   an outline before they start. An outline is like a road map to keep you headed toward your destination without getting lost or sidetracked.

(6)   There   *are, ought to be*   many ways to begin a composition. For example, you *might, must*   begin with a story that leads up to your main idea. Or you   *may, ought to* start with a question that you want your reader to think about, and then suggest an answer. *Maybe, May be*   you   *could, have to*   introduce your topic by defining a key word. Simply presenting factual information   *is, will be*   another common way of beginning a composition. Your goals in your first paragraph   *is, are*   to catch your reader's attention and then state your main idea clearly and concisely. By the end of the first paragraph, your reader   *may, should* understand what you are going to cover in the composition.

(7)   If possible, write the entire first draft of your composition in a single sitting. After you have a first draft, the next step is rewriting. Every composition   *could, should*   go through several drafts. Rewriting is a natural part of the process of writing. You   *will, do not have to* find many things that you   *can change, changed*   and improve when you reread your first draft. As you revise, you   *will, should*   be careful to include connecting words such as   *then, next, for example, after,* and *therefore.* These words connect one idea to another so that your reader will not get lost. Also pay attention to grammar, punctuation, and spelling as you revise and rewrite. Your dictionary   *should, can*   be next to you, or if you are working on a computer, you   *should, must*   use the "spell checker."

(8)   Writing   *is, may be*   a skill. It improves as you gain experience with the process of choosing a subject, jotting down thoughts, organizing them into a first draft, and then rewriting and polishing. At the end of this process, you   *should,   must*   have a clear and well-written composition.

◇ PRACTICE 1. Connecting ideas with AND. (Chart 8-1)

Directions: <u>Underline</u> the words that are connected with ***and***. Label these words as nouns, verbs, or adjectives.

1. The farmer has a <u>cow</u>, a <u>goat</u>, and a black <u>horse</u>.
           noun + noun + noun

2. Danny is a <u>bright</u> and <u>happy</u> child.
        adjective + adjective

3. I <u>picked</u> up the telephone and <u>dialed</u> Steve's number.
    verb   + *verb*

4. The cook washed the vegetables and put them in boiling water.

5. My feet were cold and wet.

6. Anita is responsible, considerate, and trustworthy.

7. The three largest land animals are the elephant, the rhinoceros, and the hippopotamus.

8. A hippopotamus rests in water during the day and feeds on land at night.

◇ **PRACTICE 2. Punctuating items connected with AND. (Chart 8-1)**
   Directions: Add commas where necessary.

   1. I opened the door and walked into the room.   *(no commas)*

   2. I opened the door, walked into the room, and sat down at my desk.

   3. Their flag is green and black.

   4. Their flag is green black and yellow.

   5. Tom ate a sandwich and drank a glass of juice.

   6. Tom made a sandwich poured a glass of juice and sat down to eat his lunch.

   7. Ms. Parker is intelligent friendly and kind.

   8. Mr. Parker is grouchy and unhappy.

   9. Did you bring copies of the annual report for Sue Dan Joe and Mary?

   10. I always read the newspaper and watch the TV news in the morning.

   11. Can you watch television listen to the radio and read the newspaper at the same time?

   12. Doctors save lives and relieve suffering.

   13. Doctors save lives relieve suffering and cure diseases.

   14. The restaurant served a five-course dinner: soup fish entree salad and dessert.

   15. I had fish and a salad for dinner last night.

   16. An invitation should include your name address the date the time the purpose of the party
       and any special activities such as swimming or dancing.

◇ **PRACTICE 3. Punctuating sentences. (Chart 8-1)**
   Directions: Each of these sentences contains two independent clauses. Find the subject (**s**) and
   verb (**v**) of each clause. Add a comma or a period. Capitalize as necessary.

   ```
          S    V      S    V
   ```
   1. Birds fly, and fish swim.
   ```
          S    V   S    V
   ```
   2. Birds fly. F fish swim.

   3. Dogs bark lions roar.

   4. Dogs bark and lions roar.

   5. A week has seven days a year has 365 days.

   6. A week has seven days and a year has 365 days.

   7. Ahmed raised his hand and the teacher pointed at him.

   8. Ahmed raised his hand the teacher pointed at him.

◇ PRACTICE 4. Punctuating sentences. (Chart 8-1)
Directions: Write "**C**" if the punctuation is correct. Write "**I**" if it is incorrect.

1. __I__ Amy jogged along the road I rode my bicycle.

2. __C__ Amy stopped after 20 minutes. I continued on for an hour.

3. _____ Trained dogs can lie down and perform other tricks on command.

4. _____ My mother trained our dog to get the newspaper, my father trained it to bark at strangers.

5. _____ The river rose, it flooded the towns in the valley.

6. _____ The river and streams rose. They flooded the towns and farms in the valley.

7. _____ Astrology is the study of the planets and their effect on our lives.

8. _____ Sharon reads her horoscope every day. She believes her life is shaped by the positions of the stars and planets.

9. _____ Sharon's children don't believe in astrology, they dismiss the information she gives them.

◇ PRACTICE 5. Using AND, BUT, and OR. (Chart 8-2)
Directions: Add commas where appropriate.

1. I talked to Amy for a long time**,** but she didn't listen.

2. I talked to Tom for a long time and asked him many questions. *(no change)*

3. Please call Jane or Ted.

4. Please call Jane and Ted.

5. Please call Jane Ted or Anna.

6. Please call Jane Ted and Anna.

7. I waved at my friend but she didn't see me.

8. I waved at my friend and she waved back.

9. I waved at my friend and smiled at her.

10. Was the test hard or easy?

11. My test was short and easy but Ali's test was hard.

◇ PRACTICE 6. Using AND, BUT, OR, and SO. (Charts 8-1 → 8-3)
   Directions: Choose the correct completion.

   1. I was tired, _____ I went to bed.
      A. but   B. or   C. so

   2. I sat down on the sofa _____ opened the newspaper.
      A. but   B. and   C. so

   3. The students were on time, _____ the teacher was late.
      A. but   B. or   C. so

   4. I would like one pet. I'd like to have a dog _____ a cat.
      A. but   B. and   C. or

   5. Our children are happy _____ healthy.
      A. but   B. and   C. or

   6. I wanted a cup of tea, _____ I heated some water.
      A. but   B. and   C. so

   7. The phone rang, _____ I didn't answer it.
      A. but   B. and   C. so

   8. You can have an apple _____ an orange. Choose one.
      A. but   B. and   C. or

◇ PRACTICE 7. Using AND, BUT, OR, and SO. (Charts 8-1 → 8-3)
   Directions: Add commas where appropriate. Some sentences need no commas.

   1. I washed and dried the dishes. *(no change)*

   2. I washed the dishes, and my son dried them.

   3. I called their house but no one answered the phone.

   4. He offered me an apple or a peach.

   5. I bought some apples peaches and bananas.

   6. I was hungry so I ate an apple.

   7. Carlos was hungry and ate two apples.

   8. My sister is generous and kind-hearted.

   9. My daughter is affectionate shy independent and smart.

   10. It started to rain so we went inside and watched television.

◇ **PRACTICE 8. Using AND, BUT, OR, and SO. (Chart 8-1 → 8-3)**
Directions: Add commas where appropriate. Some sentences need no commas.

1. Gina wants a job as an air traffic controller. Every air traffic controller worldwide uses English so it is important for Gina to become fluent in the language.

2. Gina has decided to take some intensive English courses at a private language institute but she isn't sure which one to attend. There are many schools available and they offer many different kinds of classes.

3. Gina has also heard of air traffic control schools that include English as part of their coursework but she needs to have a fairly high level of English to attend.

4. Gina needs to decide soon or the classes will be full. She's planning to visit her top three choices this summer and decide on the best one for her.

◇ **PRACTICE 9. Using AND, BUT, OR, and SO. (Charts 8-1 → 8-3)**
Directions: Add periods and capital letters as necessary.

1. There are over 100,000 kinds of flies they live throughout the world.
   → *There are over 100,000 kinds of flies.* ***T****hey live throughout the world.*

2. I like to get mail from my friends and family mail is important to me.

3. We are all connected by our humanity we need to help each other we can all live in peace.

4. There was a bad flood in Hong Kong the streets became raging streams luckily no one died in the flood.

5. People have used needles since prehistoric times the first buttons appeared almost two thousand years ago zippers are a relatively recent invention the zipper was invented in 1890.

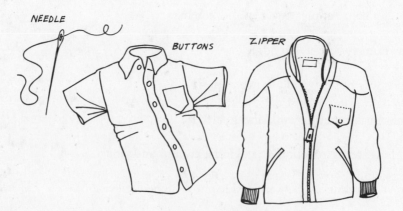

◇ PRACTICE 10. Using AND, BUT, OR, and SO. (Charts 8-1 → 8-3)
Directions: Add periods, commas, and capital letters as appropriate. Don't change any of the words or the order of the words.

1. James has a cold. ^Hʜe needs to rest and drink plenty of fluids, so he should go to bed and drink water, fruit juices, or soda pop. ^Hʜe needs to sleep a lot, so he shouldn't drink fluids with caffeine, such as tea or coffee.

2. My friend and I were tired so we went home early we wanted to stay until the end of the game but it got too late for us both of us had to get up early in the morning and go to our jobs.

3. The normal pulse for an adult is between 60 and 80 beats per minute but exercise nervousness excitement and a fever will all make a pulse beat faster the normal pulse for a child is around 80 to 90.

4. Many famous explorers throughout history set out on their hazardous journeys in search of gold silver jewels or other treasures but some explorers wanted only to discover information about their world.

5. Edward Fox was a park ranger for thirty-five years during that time, he was hit by lightning eight times the lightning never killed him but it severely burned his skin and damaged his hearing.

6. The Indian Ocean is bordered on four sides by the continents of Africa Asia Australia and Antarctica some of the important ports are Aden Bombay Calcutta and Rangoon.

7. The Indian Ocean has many fish and shellfish but it has less commercial fishing than the Atlantic or the Pacific the climate of the Indian Ocean is tropical so fish spoil quickly out of the water it is difficult and expensive for commercial fishing boats to keep fish fresh.

◇ PRACTICE 11. Using auxiliary verbs after BUT and AND. (Chart 8-4)
Directions: Practice using auxiliary verbs after *but* and *and*.

1. Dan didn't study for the test, but Amy _____did_____ .
2. Alice doesn't come to class every day, but Julie _____ .
3. Jack went to the movie last night, but I _____ .

4. I don't live in the dorm, but Rob and Jim _____ .

5. Rob lives in the dorm, and Jim _____ too.

6. I don't live in the dorm, and Carol _____ either.

7. My roommate was at home last night, but I _____ .

8. Mr. Wong isn't here today, but Miss Choki _____ .

9. Ted isn't here today, and Linda _____ either.

10. The teacher is listening to the tape, and the students _____ too.

11. Susan won't be at the meeting tonight, but I _____ .

12. Susan isn't going to go to the meeting tonight, but I _____ .

13. I'll be there, but she _____ .

14. I'll be there, and Mike _____ too.

15. I can speak French, and my wife _____ too.

16. I haven't finished my work yet, but Erica _____ .

17. I didn't finish my work last night, but Erica _____ .

18. Jane would like a cup of coffee, and I _____ too.

19. I like rock music, and my roommate _____ too.

20. My son enjoys monster movies, but I _____ .

21. Paul can't speak Spanish, and Larry _____ either.

22. My neighbor walks to work every morning, but I _____ .

23. I am exhausted from the long trip, and my mother _____ too.

24. I don't have a dimple in my chin, but my brother _____ .

25. I visited the museum yesterday, and my friend _____ too.

26. Water isn't solid, but ice _____ .

27. Clouds aren't solid, and steam _____ either.

◇ PRACTICE 12. Auxiliary verbs after BUT and AND. (Chart 8-4)
Directions: Complete the sentences by using the word in *italics* and an appropriate auxiliary.

1. *Tom*　　　　Jack has a mustache, and so ___*does Tom*___ .

　　　　　　　Jack has a mustache, and ___*Tom does*___ too.

2. *Brian*　　　Alex doesn't have a mustache, and neither _____ .

　　　　　　　Alex doesn't have a mustache, and _____ either.

3. *I*　　　　　Mary was at home last night, and so _____ .

　　　　　　　Mary was at home last night, and _____ too.

4. *Oregon*   California is on the West Coast, and so _____.

California is on the West Coast, and _____ too.

5. *Jean*   I went to a movie last night, and so _____.

I went to a movie last night, and _____ too.

6. *Jason*   I didn't study last night, and neither _____.

I didn't study last night, and _____ either.

7. *Rick*   Jim can't speak Arabic, and neither _____.

Jim can't speak Arabic, and _____ either.

8. *Laura*   I like to go to science fiction movies, and so _____.

I like to go to science fiction movies, and _____ too.

9. *Alice*   I don't like horror movies, and neither _____.

I don't like horror movies, and _____ either.

10. *porpoises*   Whales are mammals, and so _____.

Whales are mammals, and _____ too.

BLUE WHALE

PORPOISE

11. *I*   Karen hasn't seen that movie yet, and neither _____.

Karen hasn't seen that movie yet, and _____ either.

12. *my brother*   I have a car, and so _____.

I have a car, and _____ too.

13. *Erin*   Rob won't join us for lunch, and neither _____.

Rob won't join us for lunch, and _____ either.

◇ PRACTICE 13. Using TOO, SO, EITHER, or NEITHER after AND. (Chart 8-5)
Directions: Complete the sentences.

PART I. Complete the sentences with **an auxiliary** + TOO or EITHER.

1. I **can't cook**, and my roommate _____ can't either _____.

2. I **like** movies, and my wife _____.

3. I **don't like** salty food, and my wife _____.

4. Sugar **is** sweet, and honey _____.

5. Rosa Gomez **wasn't** in class yesterday, and Mr. Nazari _____.

6. Andy **didn't know** the answer to the question, and Tina _____.

7. I **couldn't understand** the substitute teacher, and Yoko _____.

8. Everyone in the room **laughed** at my foolish mistake, and I _____.

9. Fish **can't walk**, and snakes _____.

10. I **like** to fix things around the house, and Ted _____.

11. I'd **rather stay** home this evening, and my husband _____.

PART II. Complete the sentences with SO or NEITHER + **an auxiliary**.

12. Pasta **is** a famous Italian dish, and _____ so is _____ pizza.

13. Anteaters **don't have** teeth, and _____ neither do _____ most birds.

14. I **didn't go** to the bank, and _____ my husband.

15. Turtles **are** reptiles, and _____ snakes.

16. My sister **has** dark hair, and _____ I.

17. I'm **studying** English, and _____ Mr. Chu.

18. I'm **not** a native speaker of English, and _____ Mr. Chu.

19. Wood **burns,** and _____ paper.

20. Mountain climbing **is** dangerous, and _____ auto racing.

21. I've **never seen** a monkey in the wild, and _____ my children.

22. When we heard the hurricane warning, I **nailed** boards over my windows, and _____ all of my neighbors.

23. My brother and I studied chemistry together. I **didn't pass** the course, and _____ he.

◇ PRACTICE 14. Adverb clauses with BECAUSE. (Chart 8-6)
   Directions: <u>Underline</u> the adverb clauses. Find the subject (**S**) and verb (**V**) of each adverb clause.

   1. Mr. Tanaka was late for work <u>because [he] [missed] the bus</u>.
      S V

   2. I closed the door because the room was cold.

   3. Because I lost my umbrella, I got wet on the way home.

   4. Joe didn't bring his book to class because he couldn't find it.

   5. The teacher couldn't hear the question because the class was so noisy.

   6. Because the ice cream was beginning to melt, I put it back in the freezer.

◇ PRACTICE 15. Adverb clauses with BECAUSE. (Chart 8-6)
   Directions: Add periods, commas, and capital letters as necessary.

   1. I opened the window because the room was hot. We felt more comfortable then.

   2. Because his coffee was cold, Jack didn't finish it. He left it on the table and walked away.

   3. Because the weather was bad we canceled our trip into the city we stayed

      home and watched TV.

   4. Debbie is a cheerleader she woke up in the morning with a sore throat

      because she had cheered loudly at the basketball game.

   5. Francisco is an intelligent and ambitious young man because he hopes to

      get a good job later in life he is working hard to get a good education now.

◇ PRACTICE 16. Adverb clauses with BECAUSE. (Chart 8-6)
   Directions: Read each pair of phrases and circle the one that gives the reason
   (explains "why"). Then check the correct sentence.

   1. *go on a diet*
      (*lose weight*)

      ✓ ___ Eric went on a diet because he wanted to lose weight.

      ___ Because Eric went on a diet, he wanted to lose weight.

   2. *didn't have money*
      couldn't buy food

      ___ The family couldn't buy food because they didn't have money.

      ___ Because the family couldn't buy food, they didn't have money.

3. *have several children*
   be very busy

   ____ Because our neighbors are very busy, they have several children.

   ____ Our neighbors are very busy because they have several children.

4. *go to bed*
   be tired

   ____ I am tired because I am going to bed.

   ____ Because I am tired, I am going to bed.

5. *be in great shape*
   exercise every day

   ____ Because Susan exercises every day, she is in great shape.

   ____ Susan exercises every day because she is in great shape.

6. *have a high fever*
   go to the doctor

   ____ Because Jennifer has a high fever, she is going to the doctor.

   ____ Jennifer has a high fever because she is going to the doctor.

◇ **PRACTICE 17. Adverb clauses with BECAUSE. (Chart 8-6)**
   Directions: Complete the sentences with *so* or *because*. Add commas where appropriate.
   Capitalize as necessary.

   1. a. He was hungry __, so_____ he ate a sandwich.

      b. ___Because_____ he was hungry, he ate a sandwich.

      c. He ate a sandwich ____because_____ he was hungry.

   2. a. _____ my sister was tired she went to bed.

      b. My sister went to bed _____ she was tired.

      c. My sister was tired _____ she went to bed.

   3. a. _____ human beings have opposable thumbs they can easily pick

      things up and hold them.

      b. Human beings have opposable thumbs _____ they can easily pick

      things up and hold them.

      c. Human beings can easily pick things up and hold them _____ they

      have opposable thumbs.

4. a. Schoolchildren can usually identify Italy easily on a world map _____

   it is shaped like a boot.

   b. _____ Italy has the distinctive shape of a boot schoolchildren can

   usually identify it easily.

   c. Italy has the distinctive shape of a boot _____ schoolchildren can

   usually identify it easily on a map.

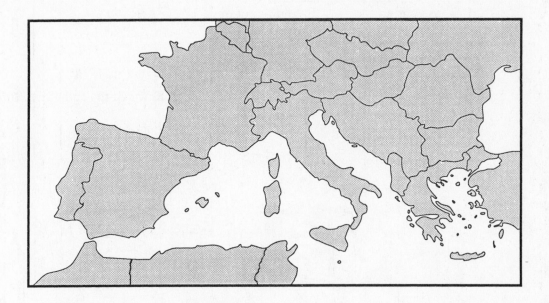

◇ PRACTICE 18. Adverb clauses with EVEN THOUGH and ALTHOUGH. (Chart 8-6)
   Directions: Complete each sentence with the correct form of the verb in *italics*. Some verbs will be
   negative.

   1. Even though I *(like)* _____ like _____ fish, I don't eat it much.

   2. Even though I *(like)* _____ don't like _____ vegetables, I eat them every day.

   3. Although my hairdresser *(be)* _____ expensive, I go to her once a week.

   4. Even though the basketball game was over, the fans *(stay)* _____ in their

   seats cheering.

   5. Although my clothes were wet from the rain, I *(change)* _____ them.

   6. Even though Po studied for weeks, he *(pass)* _____ his exams.

   7. Even though the soup was salty, everyone *(eat)* _____ it.

   8. Although the roads *(be)* _____ icy, no one got in an accident.

◇ **PRACTICE 19. Using BECAUSE and EVEN THOUGH. (Charts 8-6 and 8-7)**
Directions: Choose the correct completion.

1. Even though I was hungry, I _____ a lot at dinner.
   A. ate   (B.) didn't eat

2. Because I was hungry, I _____ a lot at dinner.
   A. ate   B. didn't eat

3. Because I was cold, I _____ my coat.
   A. put on   B. didn't put on

4. Even though I was cold, I _____ my coat.
   A. put on   B. didn't put on

5. Even though Mike _____ sleepy, he stayed up to watch the end of the game on TV.
   A. was   B. wasn't

6. Because Linda _____ sleepy, she went to bed.
   A. was   B. wasn't

7. Because Kate ran too slowly, she _____ the race.
   A. won   B. didn't win

8. Even though Jessica ran fast, she _____ the race.
   A. won   B. didn't win

9. I _____ the test for my driver's license because I wasn't prepared.
   A. failed   B. didn't fail

10. I went to my daughter's school play because she _____ me to be there.
    A. wanted   B. didn't want

11. I bought a new suit for the business trip even though I _____ it.
    A. could afford   B. couldn't afford

12. Even though I had a broken leg, I _____ to the conference in New York.
    A. went   B. didn't go

◇ **PRACTICE 20. Adverb clauses with BECAUSE. (Chart 8-6)**
   Directions: Complete the sentences by using ***even though*** or ***because***.

1. Yuko went to a dentist _____because_____ she had a toothache.

2. Colette didn't go to a dentist _____ she had a toothache.

3. Jennifer went to a dentist _____ she didn't have a toothache. She just
   wanted a checkup.

4. _____ Dan is fairly tall, he can't reach the ceiling.

5. _____ Matt is very tall, he can reach the ceiling.

6. _____ Tim isn't as tall as Matt, he can't reach the ceiling.

7. _____ Nick isn't tall, he can reach the ceiling by standing on a chair.

DAN   MATT   TIM   NICK

8. Louie didn't iron his shirt _____ it was wrinkled.

9. Eric ironed his shirt _____ it was wrinkled.

10. I would like to raise tropical fish _____ it's difficult to maintain a fish
    tank in good condition.

11. The baby shoved the pills into his mouth _____ they looked like candy.
    _____ he ingested several pills, he didn't get sick. Today many pill bottles
    have child-proof caps _____ children may think pills are candy and
    poison themselves.

◇ **PRACTICE 21. Using EVEN THOUGH/ALTHOUGH and BECAUSE. (Charts 8-6 and 8-7)**
Directions: Choose the best completion.

Example: I gave him the money because _____ .
      A. I didn't have any
      B. he had a lot of money
      Ⓒ I owed it to him

1. Although _____ , the hungry man ate every bit of it.
      A. an apple is both nutritious and delicious
      B. the cheese tasted good to him
      C. the bread was old and stale

2. The nurse didn't bring Mr. Hill a glass of water even though _____ .
      A. she was very busy
      B. she forgot
      C. he asked her three times

3. When she heard the loud crash, Marge ran outside in the snow although _____ .
      A. her mother ran out with her
      B. she wasn't wearing any shoes
      C. she ran as fast as she could

4. Even though his shoes were wet and muddy, Brian _____ .
      A. took them off at the front door
      B. walked right into the house and across the carpet
      C. wore wool socks

5. Robert ate dinner with us at our home last night. Although _____ , he left right after dinner.
    A. he washed the dishes
    B. there was a good movie at the local theater
    C. I expected him to stay and help with the dishes

6. Alex boarded the bus in front of his hotel. He was on his way to the art museum. Because he _____ , he asked the bus driver to tell him where to get off.
    A. was late for work and didn't want his boss to get mad
    B. was carrying a heavy suitcase
    C. was a tourist and didn't know the city streets very well

7. Although _____ , Eric got on the plane.
    A. he is married
    B. he is afraid of flying
    C. the flight attendant welcomed him aboard

8. Foxes can use their noses to find their dinners because _____ .
    A. they have a keen sense of smell
    B. mice and other small rodents move very quickly
    C. they have keen vision

9. Cats can't see red even though _____ .
    A. it's a bright color
    B. many animals are color-blind
    C. mice aren't red

10. When I attended my first business conference out of town, I felt very uncomfortable during the social events because _____ .
    A. we were all having a good time
    B. I didn't know anyone there
    C. I am very knowledgeable in my field

11. Although _____ , Sue drives to work every day in the middle of rush hour.
    A. her car is in good condition
    B. she isn't in a hurry
    C. traffic is always heavy

12. Everyone listened carefully to what the speaker was saying even though _____ .
    A. they had printed copies of the speech in their hands
    B. she spoke loudly and clearly
    C. the speech was very interesting

13. Talil works in the city, but once a month he visits his mother, who lives in the country. He must rent a car for these trips because _____ .
    A. he rides the local bus
    B. his mother doesn't drive
    C. he doesn't own a car

◇ PRACTICE 22. Error analysis. (Chapter 8)
   Directions: Correct the sentences.

1. I don't drink coffee **,** and my roommate ~~isn't~~ *doesn't* either.

2. The flight was overbooked, I had to fly on another airline.

3. Many people use computers for e-mail the Internet and word processing.

4. The room was stuffy and hot but I didn't close the window.

5. The baby woke up crying. Because her diaper was wet.

6. Even my father works two jobs, he always has time to play soccer or baseball on weekends with his family.

7. I saw a bad accident and my sister too.

8. Oscar always pays his bills on time but his brother wasn't.

9. Because my mother is afraid of heights, I took her up to the observation deck at the top of the building.

10. Janey doesn't like to get up early and either Joe.

11. Although it was raining quite hard, but we decided to go for a bike ride.

12. My mother and my father. They immigrated to this country 30 years ago.

13. Even though Maya is very intelligent, her parents want to put her in an advanced program at school.

CHAPTER 9
Comparisons

◇ PRACTICE 1. AS ... AS. (Chart 9-1)
   Directions: Make comparisons using *as ... as*.

   1. Rita is very busy. Jason is very busy.

      → Rita is ___(just) as busy as Jason (is)___ .

   2. Rita is not very busy at all. Jason is very, very busy.

      → Rita isn't ___(nearly) as busy as Jason (is)___ .

   3. I was tired. Susan was very tired.

      → I was _____ .

   4. Adam wasn't tired at all. Susan was very tired.

      → Adam wasn't _____ .

   5. My apartment has two rooms. Po's apartment has two rooms.

      → My apartment is _____ .

   6. My apartment has two rooms. Anna's apartment has six rooms.

      → My apartment is not _____ .

◇ PRACTICE 2. AS ... AS. (Chart 9-1)
   Directions: Using the given information and the words in parentheses, complete the comparisons using *as ... as*. Use *not* with the verbs as necessary.

   1. Dogs make more noise than cats do. *(be noisy)*

      → Cats ___aren't as noisy as___ dogs.

   2. Both Anne and her sister Amanda are lazy. *(be lazy)*

      → Anne ___is as lazy as___ her sister Amanda.

   3. Adults have more strength than children. *(be strong)*

      → Children _____ adults.

   4. Tom and Jerry are the same height. *(be tall)*

      → Tom _____ Jerry.

5. It's more comfortable to live at home than in a dormitory. *(be comfortable)*

   → Living in a dormitory _____ living at home.

6. A basketball is bigger than a soccer ball. *(be big)*

   → A soccer ball _____

   a basketball.

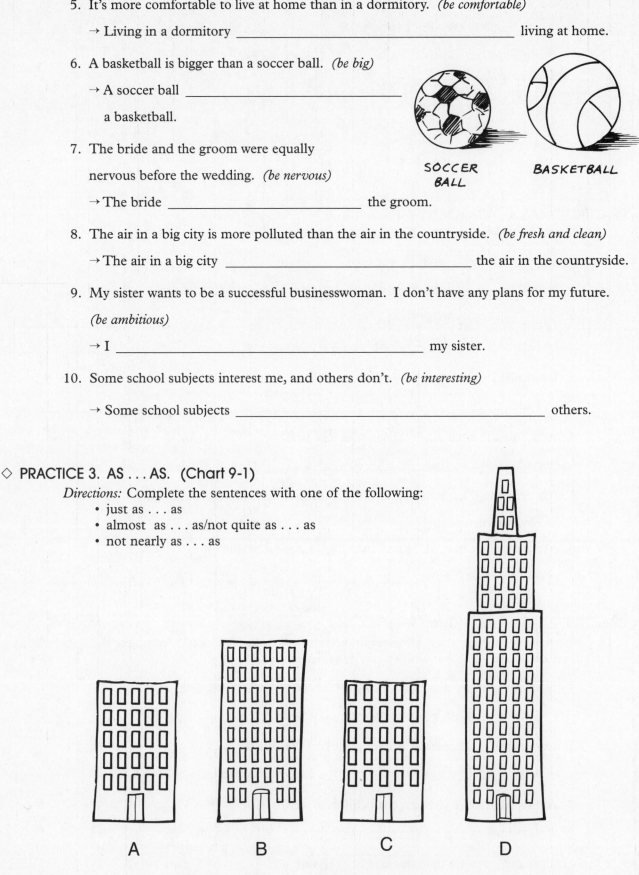

SOCCER
BALL

BASKETBALL

7. The bride and the groom were equally

   nervous before the wedding. *(be nervous)*

   → The bride _____ the groom.

8. The air in a big city is more polluted than the air in the countryside. *(be fresh and clean)*

   → The air in a big city _____ the air in the countryside.

9. My sister wants to be a successful businesswoman. I don't have any plans for my future.

   (be ambitious)

   → I _____ my sister.

10. Some school subjects interest me, and others don't. *(be interesting)*

    → Some school subjects _____ others.

◇ PRACTICE 3. AS . . . AS. (Chart 9-1)

Directions: Complete the sentences with one of the following:
- just as . . . as
- almost as . . . as/not quite as . . . as
- not nearly as . . . as

A   B   C   D

PART I.

1. Building B is ___not nearly as___ high as Building D.
2. Building A is _____ high as Building B.
3. Building C is _____ high as Building D.
4. Building A is _____ high as Building C.

PART II. Meeting time: 9:00 A.M. Compare the arrival times.

Arrival times:

David   9:01 A.M.
Julia   9:14 A.M.
Laura   9:15 A.M.
Paul   9:15 A.M.
James   9:25 A.M.

5. Paul was ___just as___ late as Laura.
6. David was _____ late as James.
7. Julia was _____ late as Laura and Paul.
8. Julia was _____ late as James.

PART III. Compare world temperatures.

Bangkok   92°F / 33°C
Cairo   85°F / 30°C
Madrid   90°F / 32°C
Moscow   68°F / 20°C
Tokyo   85°F / 30°C

9. Tokyo is _____ hot as Cairo.
10. Moscow is _____ hot as Bangkok.
11. Madrid is _____ hot as Bangkok.

PART IV. Compare world temperatures today and yesterday.

	Yesterday	Today
Bangkok	95°F / 35°C	92°F / 33°C
Cairo	95°F / 35°C	85°F / 30°C
Madrid	90°F / 32°C	90°F / 32°C
Moscow	70°F / 21°C	68°F / 20°C
Tokyo	81°F / 27°C	85°F / 30°C

12. Cairo was _____ hot as Bangkok yesterday.
13. It's _____ warm in Moscow today as yesterday.
14. Madrid is _____ hot today as yesterday.
15. It was _____ hot in Tokyo yesterday as in Bangkok.
16. It's _____ hot in Bangkok today as yesterday.

◇ PRACTICE 4. AS . . . AS. (Chart 9-1)
Directions: Choose the best sentence completion from the list.

A. as bad as she said it was	✓E. as much as possible
B. as easy as it looks	F. as often as I can
C. as fast as I could	G. as often as I used to
D. as good as they looked	H. as soon as possible

1. I have a lot of homework. I will finish __E__ before I go to bed.

2. I'm sorry I'm late. I drove _____ .

3. I saw some chocolates at the candy store. They looked delicious, so I bought some. They tasted just _____ .

4. When I was in college, I went to at least two movies every week. Now I'm very busy with my job and family, so I don't go to movies _____ .

5. It took Julie years of lessons to be able to play the piano well. She makes it look easy, but we all know that playing a musical instrument isn't _____ .

6. I need to finish working on this report, so go ahead and start the meeting without me. I'll be there _____ .

7. Even though I'm very busy, I'm usually just sitting at my desk all day. I need more exercise, so I try to walk to and from work _____ .

8. My friend told me the movie was terrible, but I went anyway. My friend was right. The movie was just _____ .

◇ PRACTICE 5. AS . . . AS. (Chart 9-1)
Directions: Write your completions in the blanks.

PART I. Complete each expression with the correct phrase.

as a bat	as ice	as a pillow
as a bird	as a mouse	✓as snow
as a bone	as a picture	as a wink
as pie		

bat

1. very white: as white ____as snow____ .

2. very cold: as cold _____ .

3. very pretty: as pretty _____ .

4. can't see anything: as blind _____ .

5. very dry: as dry _____ .

6. very soft: as soft _____ .

7. very quick: as quick _____ .

8. very quiet: as quiet _____ .

9. very free: as free _____ .

10. very easy: as easy _____ .

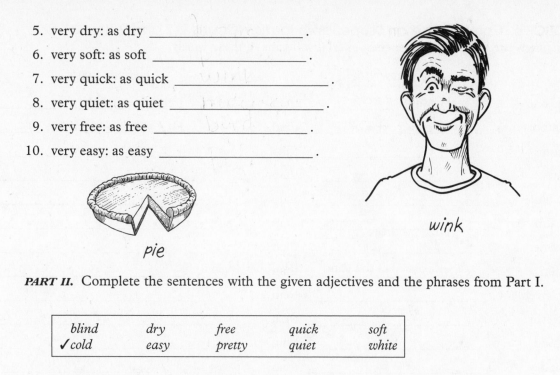

pie

wink

PART II. Complete the sentences with the given adjectives and the phrases from Part I.

blind	dry	free	quick	soft
✓cold	easy	pretty	quiet	white

11. Brrrr! Come inside. Your hands are freezing. They are as ____cold as ice____ .

12. I'm just running down to the corner store. I'll be back in a few minutes. I'll be as

_____ .

13. I can't see anything without my glasses on. I'm as _____ .

14. What laundry detergent do you use? Your white shirts were covered with dirt, and now they're

so clean and bright. They're as _____ .

15. Shhhh! Don't wake up Janet. She's sleeping on the couch. Be as _____

_____ .

16. Your little girl looks darling in that pink dress and hat. She looks as _____

_____ .

17. Don't worry. You'll pass the swimming test. It's not hard at all. It'll be as _____

_____ for you.

18. Charles looks so relaxed since he quit his job. He has no responsibilities for the next month.

He must feel as _____ .

19. I have back problems and need to sleep on a bed that has a very firm mattress. My husband

can sleep on anything, even something that is as _____ .

20. It hasn't rained in weeks. The grass is brown, and the flowers are dead. The ground is as

_____ .

◇ PRACTICE 6. Comparative and superlative forms. (Charts 9-2 and 9-3)
Directions: Write the comparative and superlative forms of these words.

	COMPARATIVE		SUPERLATIVE	
1. strong	stronger	than	the strongest	of all
2. important	more important	than	the most important	of all
3. soft	_____	than	_____	of all
4. lazy	_____	than	_____	of all
5. wonderful	_____	than	_____	of all
6. calm	_____	than	_____	of all
7. tame	_____	than	_____	of all
8. dim	_____	than	_____	of all
9. convenient	_____	than	_____	of all
10. clever	_____	than	_____	of all
11. good	_____	than	_____	of all
12. bad	_____	than	_____	of all
13. far	_____	than	_____	of all
14. slow	_____	than	_____	of all
15. slowly	_____	than	_____	of all

◇ PRACTICE 7. Comparative forms. (Charts 9-2 and 9-3)
Directions: Complete each sentence with the correct form of the word in parentheses.

1. Siberia is *(cold)* ____colder than____ South Africa.

2. My mother is a few years *(old)* _____ my father.

3. An airplane is *(expensive)* _____ a car.

4. Which is *(large)* _____ : Greenland or Iceland?

5. Red or cayenne pepper tastes *(hot)* _____ black pepper.

6. A typewriter is *(slow)* _____ a computer.

7. White chocolate is *(creamy)* _____ dark chocolate because it has
   more fat.

8. Is smoking *(bad)* _____ alcohol for your health?

9. A jaguar is *(fast)* _____ a lion.

10. Which is *(important)* _____ : happiness or wealth?

11. For long-distance trips, flying is *(quick)* _____ driving or taking
    a train.

12. Which is (heavy) _____ : a kilo of wood or a kilo of rocks?*

13. Driving in a car equipped with a seatbelt and an airbag is (safe) _____
    driving in a car with just a seatbelt.

14. Calculus is (difficult) _____ arithmetic.

◇ PRACTICE 8. Comparatives. (Charts 9-2 and 9-3)
    Directions: Complete the sentences with the correct comparative form *(more/-er)* of the given
    adjectives and adverbs.

careful	✓generous	soft
✓cold	lazy	softly
comfortable	pretty	slowly
friendly		

1. The average temperature in Moscow is _____colder_____ than the average
   temperature in Hong Kong.

2. Your father seems to give you plenty of money for living expenses. He is ____more____
   ____generous____ than mine.

3. Children seem to be able to appear out of nowhere. When I'm near a school, I always drive
   _____ than I have to.

4. In my experience, old shoes are usually a lot _____ than
   new shoes.

5. People in villages often seem to enjoy talking to strangers. They seem to be _____
   _____ than people in large cities.

6. Babies don't like loud noises. Most people speak _____ than usual when
   they're talking to a baby.

7. I like to sit on pillows. They are a lot _____ than a hardwood seat.

8. Sandy, when you drive to the airport today, you have to be _____
   than you were the last time you went. You almost had an accident because you weren't paying
   attention to your driving.

9. I like to grow flowers in my garden. They're a lot _____ than bushes.

10. I don't like to work hard, but my sister does. I'm a lot _____ than my sister.

_____

*This is a trick question. Answer: They weigh the same.

◇ **PRACTICE 9. Comparatives and superlatives. (Charts 9-2 and 9-3)**
Directions: Complete the sentences with **better, the best, worse,** or **the worst.**

1. I just finished a terrible book. It's _____the worst_____ book I've ever read.

2. The weather was bad yesterday, but it's terrible today. The weather is _____worse_____ today than it was yesterday.

3. This cake is really good. It's _____ cake I've ever eaten.

4. My grades this term are great. They're much _____ than last term.

5. Being separated from my family in time of war is one of _____ experiences I can imagine.

6. I broke my nose in a football game yesterday. Today it's very painful. For some reason, the pain is _____ today than it was yesterday.

7. The fire spread and burned down an entire city block. It was _____ fire we've ever had in our town.

8. I think my cold is almost over. I feel a lot _____ than I did yesterday. I can finally breathe again.

◇ **PRACTICE 10. FARTHER and FURTHER. (Chart 9-3)**
Directions: Choose the correct answer(s). Both answers may be correct.

1. The planet Earth is _____ from the sun than the planet Mercury is.
   (A.) farther   (B.) further

2. I have no _____ need of this equipment. I'm going to sell it.
   A. farther   (B.) further

3. I'm tired. I walked _____ than I should have.
   A. farther   B. further

4. A: Tell us more.
   B: I have no _____ comment.
      A. farther   B. further

5. I'll be available by phone if you have any _____ questions.
      A. farther   B. further

6. A: I heard that you and Tom are engaged to be married.
   B: Nothing could be _____ from the truth!
      A. farther   B. further

◇ PRACTICE 11. Adjectives vs. adverbs in the comparative. (Chart 9-3)

Directions: Complete each sentence with the comparative + the correct adjective or adverb. If it is an adjective, circle ADJ. If it is an adverb, circle ADV.

1. *slow*
   slowly
   I like to drive fast, but my brother William doesn't. As a rule, he drives ____more slowly____ than I do. ADJ (ADV)

2. *slow*
   slowly
   Alex is a ____slower____ driver than I am. (ADJ) ADV

3. *serious*
   seriously
   Some workers are _____ about their jobs than others. ADJ ADV

4. *serious*
   seriously
   Some workers approach their jobs _____ than others. ADJ ADV

5. *polite*
   politely
   Why is it that my children behave _____ at other people's houses than at home? ADJ ADV

6. *polite*
   politely
   Why are they _____ at Mrs. Miranda's house than at home? ADJ ADV

7. *careful*
   carefully
   I'm a cautious person when I express my opinions, but my sister will say anything to anyone. I'm much _____ when I speak to others than my sister is. ADJ ADV

8. *careful*
   carefully
   I always speak _____ in public than my sister does. ADJ ADV

9. *clear*
   clearly
   I can't understand Mark's father very well when he talks, but I can understand Mark. He speaks much _____ than his father. ADJ ADV

10. *clear*
    clearly
    Mark is a much _____ speaker than his father. ADJ ADV

◇ PRACTICE 12. Completing a comparative. (Chart 9-4)

Directions: Complete the comparisons with a pronoun and an appropriate auxiliary verb.

1. Bob arrived at ten. I arrived at eleven.

   → He arrived earlier than ____I did____.

2. Linda is a good painter. Steven is better.

   → He is a better painter than ____she is____.

3. Alex knows a lot of people. I don't know many people at all.

   → He knows a lot more people than _____.

4. I won the race. Anna came in second.

    → I ran faster than _____ .

5. My parents were nervous about my motorcycle ride. I was just a little nervous.

    → They were a lot more nervous than _____ .

6. My aunt will stay with us for two weeks. My uncle has to return home to his job after a couple of days.

    → She will be here with us a lot longer than _____ .

7. Ms. Ross speaks clearly. Mr. Mudd mumbles.

    → She speaks a lot more clearly than _____ .

8. I've been here for two years. Sam has been here for two months.

    → I've been here a lot longer than _____ .

9. I had a good time at the picnic yesterday. Mary didn't enjoy it.

    → I had a lot more fun at the picnic than _____ .

10. I can reach the top shelf of the bookcase. Tim can only reach the shelf next to the top.

    → I can reach higher than _____ .

◇ PRACTICE 13. Completing comparisons with pronouns. (Chart 9-4)
Directions: Complete the comparisons both formal and informal pronouns: subject pronoun + verb OR object pronoun.

1. I have a brother. His name David. He's really tall. I'm just medium height.

    → He's taller than _____ I am (formal) OR me (informal) _____ .

2. My brother is sixteen. I'm seventeen.

    → I'm older than _____ .

3. My sister is really pretty. I've never thought I was pretty.

    → She's a lot prettier than _____ .

4. I'm pretty smart, though. My sister isn't interested in school.

    → I'm smarter than _____ .

5. My mom tells me that I shouldn't compare myself to my sister. She says we are both individuals in our own right and have many fine qualities. My mom is wise. I don't think I'm wise yet.

    → My mom is much wiser than _____ .

6. My cousin Rita was born two days after I was.

    → She is two days younger than _____ .

◇ **PRACTICE 14. VERY vs. A LOT / MUCH / FAR. (Chart 9-5)**
Directions: Circle the correct answer or answers. More than one answer may be correct.

1. This watch is not _____ expensive.
   A. very   B. a lot   C. much   D. far
   (A is circled)

2. That watch is _____ more expensive than this one.
   A. very   B. a lot   C. much   D. far
   (B, C, and D are circled)

3. My nephew is _____ polite.
   A. very   B. a lot   C. much   D. far

4. My nephew is _____ more polite than my niece.
   A. very   B. a lot   C. much   D. far

5. Ted is _____ taller than his brother.
   A. very   B. a lot   C. much   D. far

6. Ted is _____ tall.
   A. very   B. a lot   C. much   D. far

7. I think astronomy is _____ more interesting than geology.
   A. very   B. a lot   C. much   D. far

8. I think astronomy is _____ interesting.
   A. very   B. a lot   C. much   D. far

9. It took me a lot longer to get over my cold than it took you to get over your cold. My cold was _____ worse than yours.
   A. very   B. a lot   C. much   D. far

◇ **PRACTICE 15. NOT AS ... AS and LESS ... THAN. (Chart 9-6)**
Directions: All of the sentences contain *not as ... as*. If possible, change them to sentences with the same meaning using *less ... than*.

1. I don't live as close to my brother as I do to my sister.
   → *(no change possible using **less**)*

2. I don't visit my brother as often as I visit my sister.
   → *I visit my brother less often than I visit my sister.*

3. Sam isn't as nice as his brother.

4. Sam isn't as generous as his brother.

5. I'm not as eager to go to the circus as the children are.

6. A notebook isn't as expensive as a textbook.

7. Wood isn't as hard as metal.

8. Some people think that life in a city isn't as peaceful as life in a small town.

9. The moon isn't nearly as far away from the earth as the sun is.

10. I don't travel to Europe on business as frequently as I used to.

◇ **PRACTICE 16. Unclear comparisons. (Chart 9-7)**
   Directions: Check the sentences that have unclear comparisons. Make the necessary corrections.

   1. ___✓___ Sam enjoys football more than his best friend_∧. *(does)*

   2. ___ok___ Andy writes better financial reports than his boss.

   3. _____ The coach helped Anna more than Nancy.

   4. _____ Sara likes tennis more than her husband.

   5. _____ Cathy leaves more generous tips at restaurants than her husband.

   6. _____ Kelly eats more organic food than his roommate.

   7. _____ Charles knows Judy better than Kevin.

◇ **PRACTICE 17. Using MORE with nouns. (Charts 9-3 and 9-8)**
   Directions: Choose from the given words to complete the sentences with the comparative
   (*more/-er*). If the word you use in the comparative is an adjective, circle ADJ. If it is an adverb,
   circle ADV. If it is a noun, circle NOUN.

books	friends	✓newspapers
carefully	homework	pleasant
easily	loud	snow

   1. My husband always wants to know everything that is going on in the world. He reads many

      ___**more newspapers**___ than I do. **ADJ** **ADV** (**NOUN**)

   2. University students study hard. They have a lot _____ than high
      school students. **ADJ** **ADV** **NOUN**

   3. There is far _____ in winter in Alaska than there is in Texas.
      ADJ **ADV** **NOUN**

   4. I'm lonely. I wish I had _____ to go places with and spend time with.
      ADJ **ADV** **NOUN**

   5. A warm, sunny day is _____ than a cold windy day.
      ADJ **ADV** **NOUN**

   6. Rob picks up languages with little difficulty. For me, learning a second language is slow and
      difficult. I guess some people just learn languages a lot _____ than
      others. **ADJ** **ADV** **NOUN**

   7. The New York City Public Library has many _____ than the public
      library in Sweetwater, Oregon. **ADJ** **ADV** **NOUN**

   8. I have been driving ___*more carefully*___ since my accident. **ADJ** **ADV** **NOUN**

   9. Karen doesn't need a microphone when she speaks to the audience. She's the only person I
      know whose voice is ___*louder*___ than mine. (**ADJ**) **ADV** **NOUN**

◇ **PRACTICE 18. Repeating a comparative. (Chart 9-9)**
   Directions: Complete the sentences with words from the list. Repeat the comparative.

angry	expensive	cold	long
sleepy	friendly	fast	
big	✓good	loud	

1. His health is improving. He's getting ___better and better___ .

2. They just had their sixth child. Their family is getting _____
   _____ .

3. As we continued traveling north, the weather got _____ .
   Eventually, everything we saw was frozen.

4. As the soccer game progressed, the crowd became _____ .
   My ears started ringing!

5. I was really mad! I got _____ until my brother touched
   my arm and told me to calm down.

6. We were so glad we had arrived early at the ticket office. As we waited for it to open, the line
   got _____ .

7. Textbooks are costly. They are getting _____
   every year.

8. We stayed up all night to work on our geology project. We became _____
   _____ as the night wore on, but we stayed awake and finally
   finished in time for class.

9. The people I met in my new job became _____ as
   we became better acquainted. Soon I began spending time with them after work.

10. When Joan was training for the marathon race, she was pretty slow in the beginning, but she
    got _____ as time went by. Eventually her time was so
    good that her coach thought she might have a chance to win.

◇ **PRACTICE 19. Double comparatives. (Chart 9-10)**
   Directions: Complete the sentences with double comparatives.

1. I exercise every day. Exercise makes me strong. ___The more___ I exercise,
   ___the stronger___ I get.

2. If butter is soft, it is easy to spread on bread. ___The___ the butter is,

___the___ it is to spread on bread.

3. I know many things now that I wasn't aware of when I was younger. It seems that

___the___ I get, ___the___ I get.

4. I'm trying to make my life simpler. It makes me feel more relaxed.

___The___ my life, ___the___ I feel.

5. I spend a long time each day looking at a computer screen. My eyes get very tired.

___The___ I look at a computer screen, ___the___

my eyes get.

6. When the wind blows hard, it whistles through the trees a lot. ___The___

the wind blows, ___the___ it whistles through the trees.

◇ **PRACTICE 20. Double comparatives. (Chart 9-10)**
Directions: Complete the sentences with double comparatives, using the ideas in parentheses.

1. *(I became bored. He talked.)*
   I met a man at a party last night. I tried to be interested in what he was saying, but the
   ___more he talked, the more bored I became___.

2. *(You understand more. You are old.)*
   There are many advantages to being young, but the _____

   _____.

3. *(I became confused. I thought about it.)*
   At first I thought I understood what she'd said, but the _____

   _____.

4. *(The air is very polluted. The chances of developing respiratory diseases are great.)*
   Pollution poses many dangers. For example, the _____

   _____.

5. *(Bill talked very fast. I became confused.)*
   Bill was trying to explain some complicated physics problems to help me prepare for an exam.

   He kept talking faster and faster. The _____

   _____.

6. *(The fans clapped and cheered. The basketball team made more shots.)*
   The fans in the stadium were excited and noisy, and it seemed to make their team play better.

   The _____

   _____.

◇ **PRACTICE 21. Using superlatives. (Chart 9-11)**
Directions: Complete the sentences with the given ideas. Use the superlative. If you don't know the right answer, guess.

✓familiar	large eyes	long necks
intelligent	large ears	

1. Kangaroos are _____the most familiar_____ of all Australian grassland animals.

2. Giraffes have _____ of all animals.

3. African elephants have _____ of all animals.

4. Horses have _____ of all four-legged animals.

5. Bottle-nosed dolphins are _____ animals that live in

   water. Apes and monkeys are _____ animals that live on

   land (besides human beings).

◇ **PRACTICE 22. Using superlatives. (Chart 9-11)**
Directions: Make comparisons.

PART I. Complete the sentences with superlatives and the appropriate word: *in*, *of*, or *ever*.

1. Physics is *(difficult)* _____the most difficult_____ course I have _____ever_____ taken.

2. Isn't my hometown *(friendly)* _____the friendliest_____ place ___of___ all the towns
   you have visited?

3. What is *(embarrassing)* _____the most embarrassing_____ experience you have had
   ___in___ your life?

4. My friends say that my grandmother is *(wise)* _____ person they have
   _____ met.

5. My wife is *(good)* _____ cook _____ the world.

6. My three children all have artistic talent, but Jimmy is *(artistic)* _____
   _____ all.

7. My bedroom on the third floor is *(hot)* _____ room _____ the
   house.

8. July is *(warm)* _____ month _____ the year.

9. Min-Sok is one of *(bright)* _____ students I've _____ taught.

10. Which is *(high)* _____ mountain _____ the world, K2 or Mt. Everest?

11. My mother found Dr. John to be *(knowledgeable)* _____

doctor _____ all the doctors she has gone to.

12. What is *(important)* _____ thing you could do _____

your life?

PART II. Complete with **least** and the appropriate word: ***in, of,*** or ***ever.***

13. Ed is not lazy, but he is certainly *(ambitious)* ____the least ambitious of____ all

the people I have worked with.

14. That painting didn't cost much. It is *(expensive)* _____

work of art we have _____ bought.

15. Antarctica is *(populated)* _____ continent _____

the world.

16. Kim seems addicted to the Internet. I think *(amount)* _____ of time

she has _____ spent on it is four hours.

◇ **PRACTICE 23. AS . . . AS, MORE/-ER, and MOST/-EST. (Charts 9-1 → 9-11)**
   Directions: Make comparisons.

   PART I. Compare the cost of the items in parentheses. Use the given expressions.

   1. *(a pencil vs.* a telephone)*

   _____A pencil_____ is less expensive than _____a telephone_____ .

   2. *(a paper clip vs. a diamond ring)*

   _____ is much more expensive than _____ .

   3. *(a cup of coffee vs. a can of coffee beans)*

   _____ is not as expensive as _____ .

   4. *(radios vs. CD players vs. big screen TVs)*

   _____ and _____ are both less expensive than

   _____ .

   5. *(a compact car vs. a house)*

   _____ is not nearly as expensive as _____ .

   6. *(footballs vs. soccer balls vs. ping-pong balls vs. basketballs)*

   _____ , _____ , and

   _____ are all more expensive than _____ .

   _____

   **vs.* is an abbreviation for *versus,* which means "as opposed to, as compared to."

PART II. Compare the waterfalls by using the given expressions.

7. _____Angel Falls_____ is much higher _____than Niagara Falls*_____ .

8. _____ is almost as high _____ .

9. _____ is the highest _____ .

10. _____ is not nearly as high _____ .

11. _____ is not quite as high _____ .

Waterfalls of the World

Niagara Falls	Giessbach Falls	Cuquenán Falls	Angel Falls
United States and Canada	Switzerland	Venezuela	Venezuela
53 meters	604 meters	610 meters	807 meters

PART III. Compare the weight of the items in parentheses. Use the given expressions.

12. *(air, iron)* _____Air_____ is lighter _____than iron_____ .

13. *(iron, wood)* _____ is heavier _____ .

14. *(water, iron, wood, air)* Of the four elements, _____ is the heaviest

_____ .

15. *(water, air)* _____ is not as heavy _____ .

16. *(water, iron, wood, air)* Of the four elements, _____ is the lightest

_____ .

17. *(water, air)* _____ is not nearly as light _____ .

18. *(water, iron, wood)* _____ and _____ are both heavier

_____ .

---

*A singular verb is used after Angel Falls because it is the name of a place. Angel Falls is in Venezuela. Similarly, the United States takes a singular verb because it is the name of a place: *The United States is a big country.*

◇ **PRACTICE 24. Using NEVER with comparatives. (Chart 9-4)**
Directions: Circle the letter of the sentence that is closest in meaning to the given sentence.

1. I've never taken a harder test in this class.
   a. The test was hard.
   b. The test wasn't hard.

2. I've never taken a hard test in this class.
   a. The tests in this class are hard.
   b. The tests in this class aren't hard.

3. Professor Jones has never given a difficult test.
   a. The test was difficult.
   b. The test wasn't difficult.

4. Professor Smith has never given a more difficult test.
   a. His tests are difficult.
   b. His tests aren't difficult.

5. I've never heard of a worse economic situation in Leadville.
   a. Leadville has a bad economic situation.
   b. Leadville doesn't have a bad economic situation.

6. I've never heard of a bad economic situation in Leadville.
   a. Leadville has bad economic situations.
   b. Leadville doesn't have bad economic situations.

7. We've never stayed in a more comfortable hotel room.
   a. The room was comfortable.
   b. The room wasn't comfortable.

8. We've never stayed in a comfortable room at that hotel.
   a. The rooms are comfortable.
   b. The rooms aren't comfortable.

◇ **PRACTICE 25. Using EVER and NEVER in comparisons. (Charts 9-4 and 9-11)**
Directions: Complete the sentences with comparatives and superlatives.

1. Pierre told a really *funny* story. It is _____the funniest_____ story I've ever heard

   (in my life). I've never heard a _____funnier_____ story (than that one).

2. John felt very *sad* when he saw the child begging for money. In fact, he has never felt

   _____ (than he did then). That is _____ he has

   ever felt (in his life).

3. Jan just finished a really *good* book. She thinks it was _____ book she has

   ever read. She says that she has never read a _____ .

4. The villagers fought the rising flood all through the night. They were *exhausted* when the river finally crested. They have never had a _____ experience. That was _____ experience they have ever had.

5. When her daughter was born, Rachel felt extremely *happy*. In fact, she has never felt _____ (than she did then). That was _____ she has ever felt (in her life).

6. Oscar told a very *entertaining* story after dinner. In fact, he has never told a _____ _____ story. It is one of _____ stories I have ever heard in my life.

7. Mari studied very *hard* for her college entrance exams. In fact, she has never studied _____ . That was _____ she has ever studied in her life.

8. The weather is really *hot* today! In fact, so far this year the weather has never been _____ . This is _____ weather we've had so far this year.

◇ **PRACTICE 26. Review of comparatives and superlatives. (Charts 9-1 → 9-11)**

Directions: Complete the sentences. Use any appropriate form of the words in parentheses and add any other necessary words.

1. Sometimes I feel like all of my friends are *(intelligent)* ___more intelligent than___ I am, and yet, sometimes they tell me that they think I am *(smart)* ___the smartest___ person ___in___ the class.

2. One of *(popular)* _____ holidays _____ Japan is New Year's.

3. A mouse is *(small)* _____ a rat.

4. Europe is first in agricultural production of potatoes. *(potatoes)* _____ are grown in Europe _____ on any other continent.

5. Mercury is *(close)* _____ planet to the sun. It moves around the sun *(fast)* _____ any other planet in the solar system.

6. In terms of area, *(large)* _____ state _____ the United States is Alaska, but it has one of *(small)* _____ populations _____ all the states.

7. Nothing is *(important)* _____ good health. Certainly, gaining wealth is much *(important)* _____ enjoying good health.

8. I need more facts. I can't make my decision until I get *(information)* _____

_____ .

9. Rebecca is a wonderful person. I don't think I've ever met a *(kind)* _____ and *(generous)* _____ person.

10. You can trust her. You will never meet a *(honest)* _____ person _____ she is.

11. I'm leaving! This is *(bad)* _____ movie I've ever seen! I won't sit through another second of it.

12. One of *(safe)* _____ places to be during a lightning storm is inside a car.

13. Small birds have a much *(fast)* _____ heartbeat _____ large birds.

14. Are your feet exactly the same size? Almost everyone's left foot is *(big)* _____

_____ their right foot.★

15. Both Bangkok and Venice are famous for their waterways, but Bangkok has *(extensive)*

_____ canals _____ Venice has.

◇ **PRACTICE 27. Review of comparatives and superlatives. (Charts 9-1 → 9-11)**
Directions: Complete the sentences. Use any appropriate form of the words in parentheses and add any other necessary words.

1. I feel *(safe)* ___**safer**___ in a plane ___**than**___ I do in a car.

2. Jakarta is *(large)* _____ city _____ Indonesia.

3. Mountain climbing takes *(strength)* _____ walking on a level path.

4. Cheese usually tastes *(good)* _____ at room temperature than it does just after you take it out of the refrigerator.

5. The *(short)* _____ distance between two points is a straight line.

6. The *(thin)* _____ a lemon's rind is, the *(juicy)* _____ the lemon is.

7. Mr. Hochingnauong feels *(comfortable)* _____ speaking his native language _____ he does speaking English.

_____

★Grammar note: In formal English, a singular pronoun is used to refer to *everyone*:
   Almost **everyone**'s left foot is bigger than **his or her** right foot.
In everyday informal usage, a plural pronoun is frequently used:
   Almost **everyone**'s left foot is bigger than **their** right foot.

8. My friend has studied many languages. He thinks Japanese is *(difficult)* _____ _____ all the languages he has studied.

9. One of the *(bad)* _____ nuclear accidents _____ the world occurred at Chernobyl in 1986.

10. I think learning a second language is *(hard)* _____ learning chemistry or mathematics.

11. The *(low)* _____ temperature ever recorded in Alaska was minus 80°F (−27°C) in 1971.

12. Computers are complicated machines, but probably *(complex)* _____ _____ thing _____ the universe is the human brain.

13. I've seen a lot of funny movies over the years, but the one I saw last night was *(funny)* _____ all.

14. Riding a bicycle can be dangerous. *(people)* _____ were killed in bicycle accidents last year _____ have been killed in airplane accidents in the last four years.

15. Some people build their own boats from parts that they order from a manufacturer. They save money that way. It is *(expensive)* _____ to build your own boat _____ to buy a boat.

◇ PRACTICE 28. LIKE, ALIKE. (Chart 9-12)
   Directions: Complete the sentences with *like* or *alike*.

1. My mother and my father rarely argue because they think _____*alike*_____.

2. The Browns designed their summer cabin to look _____*like*_____ the inside of a boat.

3. Joe and John are twins, but they don't look _____.

4. They dress _____ because they have the same taste in clothes.

5. This lamp doesn't look _____ the one I ordered.

6. Mike is 30, but he continually acts _____ a child.

7. Professor Miller's lectures are all _____ : repetitive and boring.

8. This coffee doesn't taste _____ the coffee we sampled at the store.

9. The clouds to the east look _____ rain clouds.

10. My grandmother and mother sound _____ on the phone.

◇ **PRACTICE 29. THE SAME AS, SIMILAR TO, DIFFERENT FROM. (Chart 9-12)**
    Directions: Complete the sentences with the correct preposition: *as, to,* or *from*.

1. My coat is different __from__ yours.

2. Our apartment is similar __to__ my cousin's.

3. The news report was the same __as__ the report we heard on Channel Six last night.

4. How is the North Pole different _____ the South Pole?

5. Your jacket is exactly the same _____ mine.

6. I enjoyed reading your letters from China. My experiences in Beijing were similar _____ yours.

7. For many students, their grades in college are similar _____ their grades in high school.

8. The movie on our flight to London was the same _____ the movie on our flight to Paris.

9. Some herbal teas are somewhat similar _____ green tea.

10. Courtship and dating patterns in Europe are very different _____ those in many Middle Eastern and Asian countries.

11. Except for a few minor differences in grammar, spelling, and vocabulary, American English is the same _____ British English.

12. The English spoken in the United States is only slightly different _____ the English spoken in Britain, Canada, and Australia.

◇ **PRACTICE 30. LIKE, ALIKE, SIMILAR (TO), DIFFERENT (FROM). (Chart 9-12)**
    Directions: Make comparisons.

PART I. Compare the figures. Use the words in parentheses.

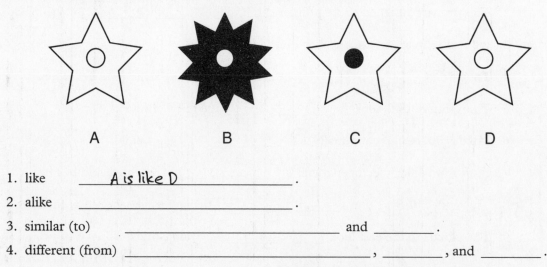

1. like   _____A is like D_____.
2. alike   _____.
3. similar (to) _____ and _____.
4. different (from) _____, _____, and _____.

PART II. Compare the figures. Use *the same (as)*, *similar (to)*, or *different (from)*.

A   B   C   D

5. All of the triangles are _____ each other.

6. A and D are _____ each other.

7. A and C are _____ .

8. A isn't _____ C.

9. B and C are _____ D.

◇ PRACTICE 31. THE SAME, SIMILAR, DIFFERENT, LIKE, ALIKE. (Chart 9-12)
  Directions: Complete the sentences with *the same, similar, different, like,* or *alike*.

1. Dana swims _____like_____ a fish. She never wants to come out of the water.

2. The lake doesn't have a ripple on it. It looks _____ glass.

3. There are six girls in our family, but none of us look _____ . Our brothers also look different.

4. A: Some people can tell we're sisters. Do you think we look _____ ?

   B: Somewhat. The color of your hair is not _____ , but your eyes are exactly _____ color. You also have _____ shaped face.

5. A: I'm sorry, but I believe you have my umbrella.

   B: Oh? Yes, I see. It looks almost exactly _____ mine, doesn't it?

6. A: How do you like the spaghetti sauce I made? I tried to make it exactly _____ yours.

   B: I can tell. Your sauce is very _____ the one I make, but I think it's missing one spice.
   A: Oh? What's that?
   B: That's a secret! But I'll tell if you promise to keep it a secret.

7. Some people think my sister and I are twins. We look _____ and talk _____ , but our personalities are quite _____ .

8. Homonyms are words that have _____ pronunciation but different spelling, such as "pair" and "pear" or "sea" and "see." For many people, "been" and "bean" are homonyms and have _____ pronunciation. For other people, however, "been" and "bean" are _____ words with different pronunciations. These people pronounce "been" like "bin" or "ben."

◇ **PRACTICE 32. Error analysis. (Chapter 9)**
Directions: Correct the errors.

than
1. My brother is older ~~from~~ me.

2. A sea is more deeper than a lake.

3. A donkey isn't as big to a horse.

4. Ellen is happiest person I've ever met.

5. When I feel embarrassed, my face gets red and more red.

6. One of a largest animal in the world is the hippopotamus.

7. The traffic on the highway is more bad from than it was a few months ago.

8. Jack is the same old from Jerry.

9. Peas are similar from beans, but they have several differences.

10. Last winter was pretty mild. This winter is cold and rainy. It's much rain than last winter.

11. Mrs. Peters, the substitute teacher, is very friendly than the regular instructor.

12. Although alligators and crocodiles are similar, alligators are less big than crocodiles.

13. Mohammed and Tarek come from different countries, but they became friends easily because

    they speak a same language, Arabic.

14. Mothers of young children are busyier than mothers of teenagers.

15. We'd like to go sailing, but the wind is not as strong today that it was yesterday.

16. We asked for a non-smoking room, but the air and furniture in our hotel room smelled

    cigarette smoke.

CHAPTER 10
The Passive

◇ PRACTICE 1. Active vs. passive. (Chart 10-1)

Directions: Circle ACTIVE if the given sentence is active; circle PASSIVE if it is passive. <u>Underline</u> the verb.

1. (ACTIVE) PASSIVE Farmers <u>grow</u> rice.

2. ACTIVE (PASSIVE) Rice <u>is grown</u> by farmers.

3. ACTIVE PASSIVE Sara wrote the letter.

4. ACTIVE PASSIVE The letter was written by Sara.

5. ACTIVE PASSIVE The teacher explained the lesson.

6. ACTIVE PASSIVE The lesson was explained by the teacher.

7. ACTIVE PASSIVE Bridges are designed by engineers.

8. ACTIVE PASSIVE Engineers design bridges.

◇ PRACTICE 2. Active vs. passive. (Chart 10-1)

Directions: Change the active verbs in *italics* to passive.

1. Mr. Catt *delivers* our mail.

   Our mail ____is____ ____delivered____ by Mr. Catt.

2. The children *have eaten* the cake.

   The cake _____ _____ by the children.

3. Linda *wrote* that letter.

   That letter _____ _____ by Linda.

4. The jeweler *is going to fix* my watch.

   My watch _____ _____ by the jeweler.

5. Ms. Bond *will teach* our class.

   Our class _____ _____ by Ms. Bond.

6. Anne *is going to bring* dinner.

   Dinner _____ _____ by Anne.

193

7. Our team *won* the final game.

The final game _____ _____ by our team.

8. Dr. Pitt *will treat* the patient.

The patient _____ _____ by Dr. Pitt.

9. Ms. Davis *has planted* several trees.

Several trees _____ _____ by Ms. Davis.

10. The police *catch* criminals.

Criminals _____ _____ by the police.

◇ PRACTICE 3. Review of past participles. (Charts 2-6 and 2-7)
Directions: Write the past participles of the verbs. The list contains both regular and irregular verbs.

Simple Form	Simple Past	Past Participle	Simple Form	Simple Past	Past Participle
1. bring	brought	brought	14. play	played	_____
2. build	built	_____	15. read	read*	_____
3. buy	bought	_____	16. save	saved	_____
4. eat	ate	_____	17. send	sent	_____
5. plan	planned	_____	18. speak	spoke	_____
6. give	gave	_____	19. spend	spent	_____
7. grow	grew	_____	20. take	took	_____
8. hit	hit	_____	21. teach	taught	_____
9. hurt	hurt	_____	22. go	went	_____
10. leave	left	_____	23. visit	visited	_____
11. lose	lost	_____	24. wear	wore	_____
12. make	made	_____	25. write	wrote	_____
13. find	found	_____	26. do	did	_____

◇ PRACTICE 4. Passive form. (Charts 10-1, 10-2, and 10-5)
Directions: Use the given form of *be (was, is, going to be, etc.)* and complete the sentences with the past participles of any verbs in the list in Practice 3.

1. *was*   There's no more candy. All the candy _____ was eaten _____ by the children.

2. *is*   Arabic _____ by the people of Syria and Iraq.

_____

*The simple past and past participle of *read* are pronounced "red," as the color red.

3. *are*   Books _____ by authors.

4. *was*   My friend _____ in an accident. He broke his nose.

5. *is going to be*   Bombay, India, _____ by thousands of tourists this year.

6. *has been*   *War and Peace* is a famous book. It _____ by millions of people.

7. *will be*   The championship game _____ in Milan next week.

8. *can be*   Everyone _____ to read. I'll teach you if you'd like.

9. *are going to be*   Our pictures _____ by a professional photographer at the wedding.

10. *have been*   Oranges _____ by farmers in Jordan since ancient times.

11. *is*   Special fire-resistant clothing _____ by firefighters.

12. *will be*   A new bridge across the White River _____ by the city government next year.

◇ **PRACTICE 5. Passive vs. active meaning. (Charts 10-1 and 10-2)**
Directions: Circle the letter of the sentence that has the same meaning as the given sentence.

1. My grandmother makes her own bread.

    (a.) This bread is made by my grandmother.

    b. Someone makes my grandmother's bread.

2. Bob was taken to the hospital by car.

    a. Bob drove to the hospital.

    b. Someone drove Bob to the hospital.

3. Suzanne has just been asked to her first dance.

    a. Suzanne has asked someone to the dance.

    b. Someone has asked Suzanne to the dance.

4. You will be informed of the test results.

    a. You will inform someone of the test results.

    b. Someone will inform you of the test results.

5. You are not allowed to enter.

    a. You do not allow people to enter.

    b. Someone says you cannot enter.

6. The child was saved after five minutes in the water.

    a. Someone saved the child.

    b. The child saved herself.

◇ **PRACTICE 6. Tense forms of the passive. (Charts 10-1 and 10-2)**
    Directions: Complete the sentences with the passive form of the given verbs.

PART I. Use the SIMPLE PRESENT with:

✓collect	grow	understand
eat	pay	write

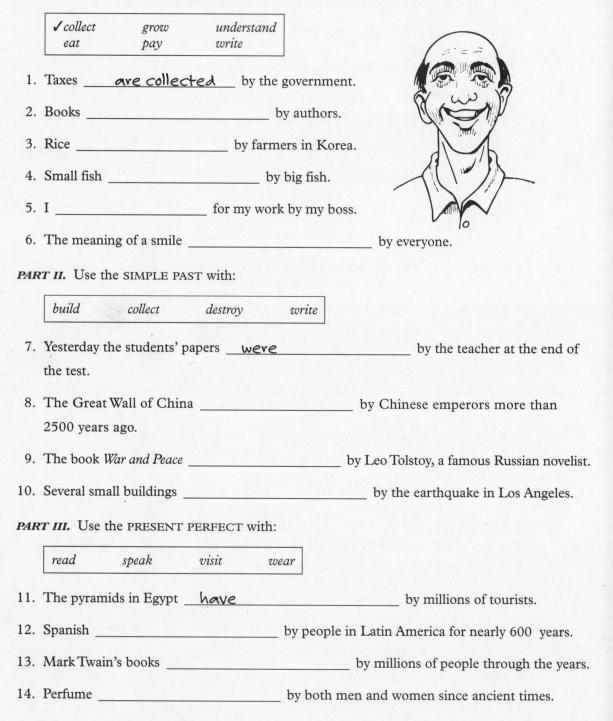

1. Taxes ___are collected___ by the government.

2. Books _____ by authors.

3. Rice _____ by farmers in Korea.

4. Small fish _____ by big fish.

5. I _____ for my work by my boss.

6. The meaning of a smile _____ by everyone.

PART II. Use the SIMPLE PAST with:

build	collect	destroy	write

7. Yesterday the students' papers __were_____ by the teacher at the end of the test.

8. The Great Wall of China _____ by Chinese emperors more than 2500 years ago.

9. The book *War and Peace* _____ by Leo Tolstoy, a famous Russian novelist.

10. Several small buildings _____ by the earthquake in Los Angeles.

PART III. Use the PRESENT PERFECT with:

read	speak	visit	wear

11. The pyramids in Egypt __have_____ by millions of tourists.

12. Spanish _____ by people in Latin America for nearly 600 years.

13. Mark Twain's books _____ by millions of people through the years.

14. Perfume _____ by both men and women since ancient times.

PART IV. Use ***will*** with:

discover	visit	save

15. New information about the universe ___will_____ by scientists in the twenty-first century.

16. Hawaii _____ by thousands of tourists this year.

17. Tigers _____ from extinction by people who care.

PART V. Use ***be going to*** with:

elect	hurt	offer

18. Your friend ___is going_____ by your unkind remark when she hears about it.

19. New computer courses _____ by the university next year.

20. A new leader _____ by the people in my country next month.

◇ PRACTICE 7. Passive to active. (Charts 10-1 and 10-2)
Directions: Change the passive sentences to active. Keep the same verb tense.

1. Taxes are collected by the government.
   → *The government collects taxes.*

2. Small fish are eaten by big fish.

3. The meaning of a smile is understood by everyone.

4. *War and Peace* was written by Leo Tolstoy.

5. The cat was chased by the dog.

6. ABC Corporation is going to be bought by XYZ Inc.

7. The pyramids in Egypt have been visited by millions of tourists.

8. New information about the universe will be discovered by scientists in the twenty-first century.

◇ PRACTICE 8. Passive to active. (Charts 5-2, 10-1, and 10-2)
Directions: Change the passive sentences to active. Keep the same tense. Some of the sentences are questions.

1. The letter was signed by Mr. Rice.
   → *Mr. Rice signed the letter.*

2. Was the letter signed by Mr. Foster?
   → *Did Mr. Foster sign the letter?*

3. The fax was sent by Ms. Owens.

4. Was the other fax sent by Mr. Chu?

5. Will Adam be met at the airport by Mr. Berg?

6. Have you been invited to the reception by Mrs. Jordan?

7. I have been invited to the reception by Mr. Lee.

8. Is the homework going to be collected by the teacher?

◇ **PRACTICE 9. Transitive vs. intransitive. (Chart 10-3)**

Directions: Circle TRANSITIVE if the verb takes an object; circle INTRANSITIVE if it does not. Underline the object of the verb.

1. (TRANSITIVE) INTRANSITIVE   Alex wrote <u>a letter</u>.

2. TRANSITIVE (INTRANSITIVE)   Alex waited for Amy. *(There is no object of the verb.)*

3. TRANSITIVE   INTRANSITIVE   Rita lives in Mexico.

4. TRANSITIVE   INTRANSITIVE   Sam walked to his office.

5. TRANSITIVE   INTRANSITIVE   Kate caught the ball.

6. TRANSITIVE   INTRANSITIVE   My plane arrived at six-thirty.

7. TRANSITIVE   INTRANSITIVE   Emily is crying.

8. TRANSITIVE   INTRANSITIVE   A falling tree hit my car.

9. TRANSITIVE   INTRANSITIVE   I returned the book to the library yesterday.

10. TRANSITIVE   INTRANSITIVE   A bolt of lightning appeared in the sky last night.

◇ **PRACTICE 10. Active and passive. (Charts 10-1 → 10-3)**

Directions: Underline the object of the verb if the given sentence has one. Then change the sentence to the passive. Some sentences cannot be changed to the passive.

ACTIVE	PASSIVE
1. A noise awakened <u>me</u>.	*I was awakened by a noise.*
2. It rained hard yesterday.	*(no change)*
3. Alice discovered the mistake.	
4. We stayed at a hotel last night.	

ACTIVE	PASSIVE

5. I slept only four hours last night. _____

6. Anita fixed the chair. _____

7. Did Susan agree with Prof. Hill? _____

8. Ann's cat died last week. _____

9. That book belongs to me. _____

10. The airplane arrived twenty minutes late. _____

11. The teacher announced a quiz. _____

12. I agree with Larry. _____

13. Do you agree with me? _____

14. Jack went to the doctor's office. _____

◇ PRACTICE 11. Review: identifying passives with transitive and intransitive verbs. (Charts 10-1 → 10-3)

Directions: Check the sentences that are passive.

1. _____ I came by plane.

2. __✓__ I was invited to the party by Alex.

3. _____ Many people died during the earthquake.

4. _____ Many people were killed by collapsing buildings.

5. _____ The earthquake has killed many people.

6. _____ The game will be won by the Bulls.

7. _____ The Bulls will win the game.

8. _____ Gina's baby cried for more than an hour.

9. _____ Most of the fresh fruit at the market was bought by customers.

10. _____ Some customers bought boxes full of fresh fruit.

11. _____ Accidents always occur at that intersection.

◇ PRACTICE 12. The BY-phrase. (Chart 10-4)

Directions: <u>Underline</u> the passive verbs. Answer the questions. If you don't know the exact person or people who performed the action, write "unknown."

1. Soft duck feathers <u>are used</u> to make pillows.

   Who uses duck feathers to make pillows? ____unknown____

2. The mail <u>was opened</u> by Shelley.

   Who opened the mail? ____Shelley____

3. Eric Wong's new book will be translated into many languages.

   Who will translate Eric Wong's new book? _____

4. Rebecca's bicycle was stolen yesterday from in front of the library.

   Who stole Rebecca's bicycle? _____

5. Our wedding photos were taken by a professional photographer.

   Who took our wedding photos? _____

6. Malawi is a small country in southeastern Africa. A new highway is going to be built in Malawi next year.

   Who is going to build the new highway? _____

7. There are no more empty apartments in our building. The apartment next to ours has been rented by a young family with two small children.

   Who rented the apartment next to ours? _____

8. The apartment directly above ours was empty for two months, but now it has also been rented.

   Who rented the apartment directly above ours? _____

◇ PRACTICE 13. The BY-phrase. (Chart 10-4)
   Directions: Cross out the unnecessary *by*-phrases (those that do not give important information).

   1. We were helped right away at the appliance store ~~by someone~~.

   2. We were helped at the appliance store by a friendly and knowledgeable salesperson.

      (no change)

   3. Our mail was delivered early today by someone.

   4. My favorite lamp was broken by the children when they were playing ball in the house.

   5. Our house was built just last year by Baker Construction Company.

   6. Our neighbors' house was built ten years ago by someone who builds houses.

   7. The child will be operated on tomorrow by three specialists at Hope Hospital.

   8. The child will be operated on tomorrow by someone.

◇ PRACTICE 14. Active to passive. (Charts 10-1 → 10-4)
   Directions: Change the active sentences to passive. Use the *by*-phrase only if necessary.

   1. Someone has canceled the soccer game.
      → *The soccer game has been canceled.*

   2. The president has canceled the meeting.
      → *The meeting has been canceled by the president.*

   3. Someone serves beer and wine at that restaurant.

   4. Something confused me in class yesterday.

5. The teacher's directions confused me.

6. No one has washed the dishes yet.

7. Someone should wash them soon.

8. Did someone wash this sweater in hot water?

9. No one should wash wool sweaters in hot water.

10. Luis invited me to the party.

11. Has anyone invited you to the party?

◇ PRACTICE 15. Review: active vs. passive. (Charts 10-1 → 10-4)
Directions: Create sentences with the given words. Use the present tense. Some are passive. Some are not.

1. Sometimes keys / hide / under cars
   → *Sometimes keys are hidden under cars.*

2. Cats / hide / under cars
   → *Cats hide under cars.*

3. Students / teach / by teachers

4. Students / study / a lot

5. Cereal / often eat / at breakfast

6. Cats / eat / cat food

7. Mice / eat / by cats

8. Songs / sing / to children / by their mothers

9. Children / sing / songs / in school

10. Thai food / cook / in Thai restaurants

11. Chefs / cook / in restaurants

◇ PRACTICE 16. Progressive tenses in passive. (Chart 10-5)
Directions: <u>Underline</u> the progressive verb. Then complete each sentence with the correct passive form.

1. Some people <u>are considering</u> a new plan.

   → A new plan _____is being considered_____ .

2. The grandparents are watching the children.

   → The children _____ by their grandparents.

3. Some painters are painting Mr. Rivera's apartment this week.

   → Mr. Rivera's apartment _____ this week.

4. We can't use the language lab today because someone is fixing the equipment.

   → We can't use the language lab today because the equipment _____

   _____ .

5. We couldn't use the language lab yesterday because someone was fixing the equipment.

   → We couldn't use the language lab yesterday because the equipment _____

   _____ .

6. Eric's cousins are meeting him at the airport this afternoon.

   → Eric _____ by his cousins at the airport this afternoon.

7. I watched while the movers were moving the furniture from my apartment to a truck.

   → I watched while the furniture _____ from my apartment to a truck.

8. Everyone looked at the flag while they were singing the national anthem.

   → Everyone looked at the flag while the national anthem _____ .

9. Scientists are still discovering new species of plants and animals.

   → New species of plants and animals _____ .

◇ PRACTICE 17. Passive forms of progressive verbs. (Chart 10-5)
   Directions: Complete the sentences with the given verbs. Use the present progressive or the past progressive. All the sentences are passive.

build	clean	fly	✓play	read	watch

1. A soccer game _____is being played_____ in Wellstone Arena today.

2. The office __was_____ by the janitor when I got there early this morning.

3. A new house _____ in our neighborhood right now.

4. The book _____ aloud to the children by the teacher in the first grade class right now.

5. The protestors _____ by the police during the anti-war demonstration.

6. The small plane _____ by the co-pilot when it crashed.

◇ PRACTICE 18. Passive forms of progressive verbs. (Chart 10-5)
Directions: Circle the letter of the sentence with the same meaning as the given sentence.

1. A mouse is being chased.
    a. A mouse is trying to catch something.
    (b.) Something is trying to catch a mouse.

2. The soldiers are being trained.
    a. The soldiers are training someone.
    b. Someone is training the soldiers.

3. The earthquake victims are being helped by the medics.
    a. The medics are receiving help.
    b. The victims are receiving help.

4. The children were trying to find their parents after the school play.
    a. The children were looking for their parents.
    b. The parents were looking for their children.

5. The airline passengers were being asked to wait while the plane was cleaned.
    a. The passengers made a request.
    b. Someone asked the passengers to wait.

◇ PRACTICE 19. Review: active vs. passive. (Chart 10-1 → 10-5)
Directions: Write "C" if the sentence is correct. Write "I" if it is incorrect. Make any necessary corrections.

1. __I__ It ~~was~~ happened many years ago.

2. __C__ Rice is grown in California.

3. _____ I was go to school yesterday.

4. _____ Two firefighters have injured while they were fighting the fire.

5. _____ Sara was accidentally broken the window.

6. _____ Kara was eaten a snack when she got home from school.

7. _____ Timmy was eating when the phone rang.

8. _____ I am agree with you.

9. _____ The little boy was fallen down while he was running in the park.

10. _____ The swimmer was died from a shark attack.

11. _____ The swimmer was killed by a shark.

12. _____ I was slept for nine hours last night.

◇ **PRACTICE 20. Passive modals. (Chart 10-6)**

Directions: Change the sentences from active to passive. Include the *by*-phrase only if it contains important information.

1. Someone might cancel class.
   → *Class might be canceled.*

2. A doctor can prescribe medicine.

3. Mr. Hook must sign this report.

4. Someone may build a new post office on First Street.

5. People have to place stamps in the upper right-hand corner of an envelope.

6. Someone ought to paint that fence.

7. All of the students must do the assignment.

◇ **PRACTICE 21. Passive modals. (Chart 10-6)**

Directions: Complete the sentences by using the words in the list with the modals in parentheses. All of the completions are passive.

build	kill	✓ put off	teach	write
divide	know	sell	tear down	

1. Don't postpone things you need to do. Important work _____shouldn't be put off_____ until the last minute. *(should not)*

2. Your application letter _____ in ink, not pencil. *(must)*

3. Dogs _____ to do tricks. *(can)*

4. Mrs. Papadopolous didn't want her son to go to war because he _____
   _____ . *(could)*

5. My son's class is too big. It _____ into two classes.
   (ought to)

6. A: Hey, Tony. These bananas are getting too ripe. They _____
      today. Reduce the price. *(must)*
   B: Right away, Mr. Rice.

7. It takes time to correct an examination that is taken by ten thousand students nationwide.

   The test results _____ for at least four weeks. *(will not)*

8. The big bank building on Main Street was severely damaged in the earthquake. The structure

   is no longer safe. The building _____ . *(has to)* Then a

   new bank _____ in the same place. *(can)*

◇ **PRACTICE 22. Passive modals. (Chart 10-6)**
   Directions: Complete the sentences by changing the active modals to passive modals.

   1. This book *(have to return)* ___**has to be returned**___ to the library today.

   2. That book *(should return)* _____ tomorrow.

   3. This letter *(must send)* _____ today.

   4. This package *(could send)* _____ tomorrow.

   5. That package *(should send)* _____ by express mail.

   6. That box *(can put away)* _____ now.

   7. These boxes *(may throw away)* _____ soon.

   8. Those boxes *(might pick up)* _____ this afternoon.

   9. This room *(will clean up)* _____ soon.

◇ **PRACTICE 23. Summary: active vs. passive. (Charts 10-1 → 10-6)**
   Directions: Circle ACTIVE if the given sentence is active; circle PASSIVE if it is passive. <u>Underline</u> the verb.

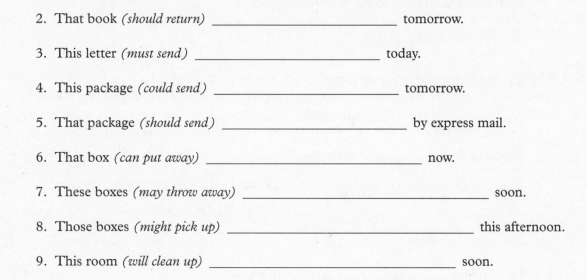

   1. (ACTIVE) PASSIVE   People <u>have used</u> sundials since ancient times.

   2. ACTIVE (PASSIVE)   Sundials <u>have been used</u> for almost three thousand years.

   3. ACTIVE   PASSIVE   Sundials, clocks, and watches are used to tell time.

   4. ACTIVE   PASSIVE   Some watches show the date as well as the time.

   5. ACTIVE   PASSIVE   On digital watches, the time is shown by lighted numbers.

   6. ACTIVE   PASSIVE   The first watches were made in Europe six hundred years ago.

   7. ACTIVE   PASSIVE   The earliest watches were worn around a person's neck.

   8. ACTIVE   PASSIVE   Pocket watches became popular in the 1600s.

   9. ACTIVE   PASSIVE   Today most people wear wristwatches.

   10. ACTIVE   PASSIVE   Close to seventy million watches are sold in the United States each year.

   11. ACTIVE   PASSIVE   How many watches are made and sold throughout the world in one year?

12. ACTIVE PASSIVE   Somewhere in the world, a watch is being sold at this very moment.

13. ACTIVE PASSIVE   Many different styles of watches can be bought today.

14. ACTIVE PASSIVE   Do you own a watch?

15. ACTIVE PASSIVE   Where was it made?

◇ **PRACTICE 24. Summary: active vs. passive. (Charts 10-1 → 10-6)**
  Directions: Complete the sentences with the verbs in parentheses; use active or passive.

1. I don't have my car today. It's in the garage. It *(repair)* ___is being___
   ___repaired___ right now.

2. Kate didn't have her car last week because it was in the garage. While it *(repair)*
   _____ , she took the bus to work.

3. The mechanic *(repair)* _____ Tina's car last week.

4. Glass *(make)* _____ from sand.

5. You *(should carry, not)* _____ large sums of money with you.

6. Large sums of money *(ought to keep)* _____ in a bank, don't
   you think?

7. At our high school, the students' grades *(send)* _____ to their parents
   four times each year.

8. I'm sorry, but the computer job is no longer available. A new computer programmer
   (hire, already) _____ .

9. Household cleaning agents *(must use)* _____ with care. For
   example, mixing chlorine bleach with ammonium *(can produce)* _____
   toxic gases.

10. What products *(manufacture)* _____ in your country?

11. Aluminum* is a valuable metal that *(can use)* _____ again and again.
    Because this metal *(can recycle)* _____ , aluminum cans
    (should throw away, not) _____ .

12. Endangered wildlife *(must protect)* _____ from extinction.

13. People with the moral courage to fight against injustices *(can find)* _____
    in every corner of the world.

———————————
Aluminum in American English = *aluminium* in British English.

◇ PRACTICE 25. Summary: active vs. passive. (Charts 10-1 → 10-6)
Directions: Complete the sentences with the verbs in parentheses; use active or passive.

1. Flowers (love) ___are loved___ throughout the world. Their beauty (bring)
___brings___ joy to people's lives. Flowers (use, often) _____
_____ to decorate homes or tables in restaurants. Public gardens
(can find) _____ in almost every country in the world.

2. Around 250,000 different kinds of flowers (exist) _____ in the world. The
majority of these species (find) _____ only in the tropics. Nontropical
areas (have) _____ many fewer kinds of flowering plants than tropical regions.

3. Flowers may spread from their native region to other similar regions. Sometimes seeds
(carry) _____ by birds or animals. The wind also (carry) _____
some seeds. In many cases throughout history, flowering plants (introduce) _____
_____ into new areas by humans.

4. Flowers (appreciate) _____ mostly for their beauty, but they can
also be a source of food. For example, honey (make) _____ from the
nectar which (gather) _____ from flowers by bees. And some flower
buds (eat) _____ as food; for example, broccoli and cauliflower are
actually flower buds.

5. Some very expensive perfumes (make) _____ from the petals of flowers.
Most perfumes today, however, (come, not) _____ from natural
fragrances. Instead, they are synthetic; they (make) _____ from
chemicals in a laboratory.

6. Some kinds of flowers (may plant) _____ in pots and (grow)
_____ indoors. Most flowers, however, (survive) _____
best outdoors in their usual environment.

◇ PRACTICE 26. Using past participles as adjectives. (Chart 10-7)
Directions: Complete the sentences with the correct prepositions.

PART I. Jack is . . .
1. married ___to___ Katie.
2. excited _____ vacation.
3. exhausted _____ work.
4. frightened _____ heights.
5. disappointed _____ his new car.

6. tired _____ rain.

7. pleased _____ his new boss.

8. involved _____ charity work.

9. worried _____ his elderly parents.

10. acquainted _____ a famous movie star.

PART II. Jack's friend is . . .

11. interested _____ sports.

12. done _____ final exams.

13. terrified _____ spiders.

14. related _____ a famous movie star.

15. opposed _____ private gun ownership.

16. pleased _____ his part-time job.

17. divorced _____ his wife.

PART III. Jack's house is . . .

18. made _____ wood.

19. located _____ the suburbs.

20. crowded _____ antique furniture.

21. prepared _____ emergencies.

◇ **PRACTICE 27. Using past participles as adjectives. (Chart 10-7)**
Directions: Each sentence has errors with the adjectives used as past participles. Correct the errors.

1. The little girl is ~~excite in~~ *excited about* her coming birthday party.

2. Mr. and Mrs. Rose devoted each other.

3. Could you please help me? I need directions. I lost.

4. The students are boring in their chemistry project.

5. The paper bags at this store is composed in recycled products.

6. Your friend needs a doctor. He hurt.

7. How well are you prepare the driver's license test?

8. Mary has been engaging with Paul for five years. Will they ever get married?

◇ **PRACTICE 28. -ED vs. -ING. (Chart 10-8)**
Directions: Complete the sentences with the appropriate *-ed* or *-ing* form of the words in parentheses.

Ben is reading a book. He really likes it. He can't put it down. He has to keep reading.

1. The book is really ___interesting___ . (*interest*)

2. Ben is really _____ . (*interest*)

3. The story is _____ . (*excite*)

4. Ben is _____ about the story. (*excite*)

5. Ben is _____ by the characters in the book. (*fascinate*)

6. The people in the story are _____ . (*fascinate*)

7. Ben doesn't like to read books when he is _____ and
   _____ . (*bore, confuse*)

8. Ben didn't finish the last book he started because it was _____ and
   _____ . (*bore, confuse*)

9. What is the most _____ book you've read lately? (*interest*)

10. I just finished a _____ mystery story that had a very
    _____ ending. (*fascinate, surprise*)

◇ **PRACTICE 29. -ED vs. -ING. (Chart 10-8)**
Directions: Choose the correct adjective.

1. Don't bother to read that book. It's (*boring,*) *bored*.

2. The students are *interesting, interested* in learning more about the subject.

3. Ms. Green doesn't explain things well. The students are *confusing, confused*.

4. Have you heard the latest news? It's really *exciting, excited.*

5. I don't understand these directions. I'm *confusing, confused.*

6. I read an *interesting, interested* article in the newspaper this morning.

7. I heard some *surprising, surprised* news on the radio.

8. I'm *boring, bored.* Let's do something. How about going to a movie?

9. Mr. Sawyer bores me. I think he is a *boring, bored* person.

10. Mr. Ball fascinates me. I think he is a *fascinating, fascinated* person.

11. Most young children are *fascinating, fascinated* by animals.

12. Young children think that animals are *fascinating, fascinated.*

13. That was an *embarrassing, embarrassed* experience.

14. I read a *shocking, shocked* report yesterday on the number of children who die from starvation in the world every day. I was really *shocking, shocked.*

15. The children went to a circus. For them, the circus was *exciting, excited.* The *exciting, excited* children jumped up and down.

◇ PRACTICE 30. -ED vs. -ING. (Chart 10-8)
Directions: Choose the correct adjective.

1. The street signs in our city are *confused,* *(confusing.)*

2. The drivers are *frustrated,* *frustrating.*

3. The professor's lecture on anatomy was *confused,* *confusing* for the students.

4. The student was very *embarrassed,* *embarrassing* by all the attention she got for her high test scores.

5. Sophie said it was *embarrassed,* *embarrassing* to have so many people congratulate her.

6. I am really *interested,* *interesting* in eighteenth-century art.

7. Eighteenth-century art is really *interested,* *interesting.*

8. What an *exhausted,* *exhausting* day! I am so *tired,* *tiring* from picking strawberries.

9. Some of the new horror movies are *frightened,* *frightening* because they are so realistic.

10. Young children shouldn't see them. They would become too *frightened,* *frightening.*

◇ PRACTICE 31. -ED vs. -ING. (Chart 10-8)
Directions: In each group, one sentence is incorrect. Write "I" beside the incorrect sentence.

1. a. _____ Science fascinates me.
   b. _____ Science is fascinating to me.
   c. __I__ Science is fascinated to me.

2. a. _____ The baby is exciting about her new toy.
   b. _____ The baby is excited about her new toy.
   c. _____ The new toy is exciting to the baby.

3. a. _____ The book is really interesting.
   b. _____ The book is really interested.
   c. _____ The book interests me.

4. a. _____ I am exhausting from working in the fields.
   b. _____ I am exhausted from working in the fields.
   c. _____ Working in the fields exhausts me.
   d. _____ Working in the fields is exhausting.

5. a. _____ Your grandmother is amazing to me.
   b. _____ Your grandmother amazes me.
   c. _____ Your grandmother is amazed to me.
   d. _____ I am amazed by your grandmother.

◇ **PRACTICE 32. GET + adjective and past participle. (Chart 10-9)**
Directions: Complete the sentences using words from the list.

arrested	dressed	invited	lost	stolen
bored	hungry	late	rich	wet
✓ sick	dizzy			

1. Just a few days before the Jensens were going to leave for a family reunion in Hawaii, everyone got _____sick_____ with the flu. They had to cancel their trip.

2. When Jane gave us directions to her house, I got _____ . So I asked her to explain again how to get there.

3. Some people are afraid of heights. They get _____ and have trouble keeping their balance.

4. I didn't like the movie last night. It wasn't interesting. I got _____ and wanted to leave early.

5. When's dinner? I'm getting _____ .

6. We should leave for the concert soon. It's getting _____ . We should leave in the next five minutes if we want to be on time.

7. I want to make a lot of money. Do you know a good way to get _____ quick?

8. Jake got _____ for stealing a car yesterday. He's in jail now.

9. I overslept this morning. When I finally woke up, I jumped out of bed, got _____ , picked up my books, and ran to class.

10. Anita got _____ when she stood near the pool of dolphins. They splashed her more than once.

11. Yes, I have an invitation to Joan and Paul's wedding. Don't worry. You'll get _____ to the wedding, too.

12. Tarik was afraid his important papers or his wife's jewelry might get _____ , so he had a wall safe installed in his home.

◇ **PRACTICE 33. GET + adjective and past participle. (Chart 10-9)**
   Directions: Complete the sentences with an appropriate form of ***get***.

   1. Shake a leg! Step on it! _____Get_____ busy. There's no time to waste.

   2. Tom and Sue _____got_____ married last month.

   3. Let's stop working for a while. I _____am getting_____ tired.

   4. I don't want _____to get_____ old, but I guess it happens to everybody.

   5. I _____ interested in biology when I was in high school, so I decided to major
      in it in college.

   6. My father started _____ bald when he was in his twenties. I'm in my twenties,
      and I'm starting _____ bald. It must be in the genes.

   7. Brrr. It _____ cold in here. Maybe we should turn on the furnace.

   8. When I was in the hospital, I got a card from my aunt and uncle. It said, "_____
      well soon."

   9. When I went downtown yesterday, I _____ lost. I didn't remember to take my map
      of the city with me.

  10. A: Why did you leave the party early?
      B: I _____ bored.

  11. A: I _____ hungry. Let's eat soon.
      B: Okay.

  12. A: What happened?
      B: I don't know. Suddenly I _____ dizzy, but I'm okay now.

  13. A: Do you want to go for a walk?
      B: Well, I don't know. It _____ dark outside right now. Let's wait and
         go for a walk tomorrow.

  14. I always _____ nervous when I have to give a speech.

  15. A: Where's Bud? He was supposed to be home two hours ago. He always calls when he's
         late. I _____ worried. Maybe we should call the police.
      B: Relax. He'll be home soon.

  16. A: Hurry up and _____ dressed. We have to leave in ten minutes.
      B: I'm almost ready.

17. A: I'm going on a diet.

    B: Oh?

    A: See? This shirt is too tight. I _____ fat.

18. A: Janice and I are thinking about _____ married in June.

    B: That's a nice month for a wedding.

◇ PRACTICE 34. BE USED/ACCUSTOMED TO. (Charts 2-11 and 10-10)
   Directions: Choose the correct completion. More than one completion may be correct.

1. Frank has lived alone for twenty years. He _____ alone.
   A. used to live   (B.) is used to living   (C.) is accustomed to living

2. I _____ with my family, but now I live alone.
   (A.) used to live   B. am used to living   C. am accustomed to living

3. Rita rides her bike to work every day. She _____ her bike to work.
   A. used to ride   B. is used to riding   C. is accustomed to riding

4. Tom rode his bike to work for many years, but now he takes the bus. Tom _____ his bike to work.
   A. used to ride   B. is used to riding   C. is accustomed to riding

5. Carl showers every day. He _____ a shower every day.
   A. used to take   B. is used to taking   C. is accustomed to taking

6. Carl _____ a bath only once a week, but now he showers every day.
   A. used to take   B. is used to taking   C. is accustomed to taking

7. Ari _____ a small breakfast every day because he was always in a hurry.
   A. used to eat   B. is used to eating   C. is accustomed to eating

8. Maria _____ a large breakfast because she likes to take her time in the morning.
   A. used to eat   B. is used to eating   C. is accustomed to eating

◇ PRACTICE 35. USED TO vs. BE USED TO. (Chart 10-11)
   Directions: Add an appropriate form of **be** if necessary. If no form of **be** is needed, write **Ø** in the blank.

1. Trains ____Ø____ used to be the main means of cross-continental travel. Today, most people take airplanes for long-distance travel.

2. Ms. Stanton's job requires her to travel extensively throughout the world. She ____is____ used to traveling by plane.

3. You and I are from different cultures. You _____ used to having fish for breakfast. I _____ used to having cheese and bread for breakfast.

4. People _____ used to throw away or burn their newspapers after reading them, but now many people recycle them.

5. Jeremy wakes up at 5:00 every morning for work. After a year of doing this, he _____ used to getting up early, even on weekends.

6. Mrs. Hansen _____ used to do all of the laundry and cooking for her family. Now the children are older and Mrs. Hansen has gone back to teaching, so the whole family shares these household chores.

7. Before modern dentistry, people _____ used to pull painful teeth.

8. Cindy swims only in swimming pools. She _____ used to swim in lakes and rivers, but now she finds them too cold.

◇ PRACTICE 36. USED TO vs. BE USED TO. (Chart 10-11)
Directions: Complete the sentences with **used to** or **be used to** and the correct form of the verb in parentheses.

1. Kate grew up on a farm. She *(get)* _____*used to get*_____ up at dawn and go to bed as soon as the sun went down. Now she works in the city at an advertising agency and has different sleeping hours.

2. Hiroki's workweek is seven days long. He *(work)* _____ on Saturdays and Sundays.

3. Luis spends weekends with his family now. He *(attend)* _____ soccer games before he was married, but now he enjoys staying home with his young children.

4. Sally went back to school to become a computer programmer. She *(work)* _____ _____ as a typist, but now she has a job that she likes better.

5. Joan has taught kindergarten for eight years. She *(teach)* _____ small children and uses many creative techniques with them.

6. Before I went overseas, I had a very simple, uninteresting diet. After visiting many different countries, however, I *(eat)* _____ much spicier, tastier dishes now.

◇ PRACTICE 37. BE SUPPOSED TO. (Chart 10-12)
Directions: Create sentences with a similar meaning by using **be supposed to**.

1. Someone expected me to return this book to the library yesterday, but I didn't.
   → *I was supposed to return this book to the library.*

2. Our professor expects us to read Chapter 9 before class tomorrow.

3. Someone expected me to go to a party last night, but I stayed home.

4. The teacher expects us to do Exercise 10 for homework.

5. The weather bureau has predicted rain for tomorrow. According to the weather bureau, it . . . .

6. The directions on the pill bottle say, "Take one pill every six hours." According to the directions on the bottle, I . . . .

7. My mother expects me to dust the furniture and (to) vacuum the carpet.

◇ **PRACTICE 38. BE SUPPOSED TO. (Chart 10-12)**
Directions: Complete the sentences with *be supposed to* and any appropriate verb from the list.

take off	register	sweep	give
be	clean	cook	send

1. A: What are you doing home? You _____ *are supposed to be* _____ at work.
   B: I called in sick.

2. A: The floor is still dirty. You _____ it this morning before you left for school, weren't you?
   B: I know. I forgot.

3. Sarah's late paying her taxes. She _____ her check to the government last month.

4. When you eat in a restaurant, you _____ your order to the waitress or waiter.

5. I know you'd rather be playing tennis, but you _____ the house today. The house is dirty, and it's your turn.

6. A: Where _____ I _____ for my English class? I'm new here.
   B: Down the hall to your right.

7. Jack _____ dinner tonight, but he didn't get home until 9:00 P.M.

8. A: You're tracking mud all over the house.
   B: Sorry. We _____ our shoes at the door, aren't we?

◇ PRACTICE 39. Error analysis. (Chapter 10)
  Directions: Correct the errors.

1. The moving boxes ⌄ packed by Pierre.
   were

2. My uncle was died in the war.

3. Miami located in Florida.

4. I was very worried about my son.

5. Mr. Rivera interested in finding a new career.

6. Did you tell everyone the shocked news?

7. After ten years, I finally used to this wet and rainy climate.

8. The newspaper suppose to come every morning before eight.

9. The Millers have been marry with each other for 60 years.

10. I am use to drink coffee with cream, but now I drink it black.

11. What was happen at the party last night?

12. Several people almost get kill when the fireworks exploded over them.

13. A new parking garage being build for our office.

14. I have been living in England for several years, so I accustom driving on the left side of the road.

CHAPTER **11**

Count/Noncount Nouns and Articles

◇ PRACTICE 1. A vs. AN: singular count nouns. (Chart 11-1)
Directions: Write **a** or **an** in the blanks.

1. __a__ game
2. __an__ office
3. _____ car
4. _____ friend
5. _____ mountain
6. _____ rock
7. _____ army
8. _____ egg
9. _____ island
10. _____ ocean
11. _____ umbrella
12. _____ university
13. _____ horse

14. _____ hour
15. _____ star
16. _____ eye
17. _____ new car
18. _____ old car
19. _____ used car
20. _____ uncle
21. _____ house
22. _____ honest mistake
23. _____ hospital
24. _____ hand
25. _____ ant
26. _____ neighbor

◇ PRACTICE 2. Preview: count and noncount nouns. (Charts 11-2 → 11-5)
Directions: Draw a line through the expressions of quantity that **cannot** be used to complete the sentences.

NONCOUNT NOUNS: *fruit, mail, traffic*
COUNT NOUNS: *apples, letters, cars*

1. I ate _____ **fruit**.
   a. some
   b. several
   c. a little
   d. a few
   e. too many
   f. too much
   g. a lot of
   h. two

2. I ate _____ **apples**.
   a. some
   b. several
   c. a little
   d. a few
   e. too many
   f. too much
   g. a lot of
   h. two

3. I get _____ **mail** every day.
   - a. a lot of
   - b. some
   - c. a little
   - d. a few
   - e. too much
   - f. too many
   - g. several
   - h. three

4. I get _____ **letters** every day.
   - a. a lot of
   - b. some
   - c. a little
   - d. a few
   - e. too much
   - f. too many
   - g. several
   - h. three

5. There is _____ **traffic** in the street.
   - a. several
   - b. some
   - c. too many
   - d. a little
   - e. a lot of
   - f. a few
   - g. too much
   - h. five

6. There are _____ **cars** in the street.
   - a. several
   - b. some
   - c. too many
   - d. a little
   - e. a lot of
   - f. a few
   - g. too much
   - h. five

◇ **PRACTICE 3. Count and noncount nouns. (Charts 11-2 → 11-4)**

Directions: Which of the words can follow *one* and which can follow *some?* Write the correct form of the noun in the blanks. If the noun does not have a singular form, write Ø.

	one . . .	some . . .
1. word	word	words
2. vocabulary	Ø	vocabulary
3. slang		
4. homework		
5. assignment		
6. grammar		
7. dress		
8. clothes		
9. clothing		
10. parent		
11. family		
12. knowledge		
13. information		
14. fact		
15. luck		
16. garbage		

◇ **PRACTICE 4. Count and noncount nouns. (Charts 11-2 → 11-4)**
 Directions: Complete the sentences with the words below. Use the plural form as necessary.

✓ apple trees	grass	machine	rice
✓ bracelets	hardware	machinery	ring
✓ bread	jewel	mountain	sandwich
✓ corn	jewelry	pea	scenery
equipment	lake	plant	tool

1. I went to the grocery store and bought some ___ bread, corn, ___

   _____

2. I stood on a hill in the countryside and saw some ___ apple trees, ___

   _____

3. I went to a jewelry store and saw some ___ bracelets, ___

   _____

4. At the auto repair shop, I saw some _____

   _____

◇ **PRACTICE 5. Count and noncount nouns. (Charts 11-2 → 11-5)**
 Directions: Fill in the blanks with *one, much,* or *many*.

1. ___one___ chair		14. _____ games
2. ___much___ furniture		15. _____ water
3. ___many___ vegetables		16. _____ parent
4. _____ clothing		17. _____ sand
5. _____ vegetable		18. _____ professors
6. _____ clothes		19. _____ dust
7. _____ fruit		20. _____ money
8. _____ facts		21. _____ stuff
9. _____ grammar		22. _____ thing
10. _____ word		23. _____ things
11. _____ idioms		24. _____ English
12. _____ vocabulary		25. _____ toast
13. _____ cars		

◇ **PRACTICE 6. Count and noncount nouns. (Charts 11-2 → 11-4)**

Directions: Complete the sentences with the correct form, singular or plural, of the given nouns. If a verb is needed, circle the correct one in the parentheses.

1. *snow*　　　In Alaska in the winter, there ((is,) are) a lot of _____snow_____ on the ground.

2. *weather*　　There *(is, are)* a lot of cold _____ in Alaska.

3. *sunshine*　　_____ *(is, are)* a source of vitamin D.

4. *knowledge*　Prof. Nash has a lot of _____ about that subject.

5. *fun*　　　　We had a lot of _____ on the picnic.

6. *factory,**　Sometimes _____ cause _____ .
   pollution

7. *pride,*　　　Parents take _____ in the success of their _____ .
   *child****

8. *people,*　　I admire _____ who use their _____ to the
   intelligence　fullest extent.

9. *peace*　　　There have been many conflicts and wars throughout the history of the world, but almost all people prefer _____ .

10. *hospitality*　Thank you for your _____ .

11. *beef*　　　The _____ we had for dinner last night *(was, were)* very good.

12. *fog*　　　　During the winter months along the coast, there *(is, are)* usually a lot of _____ in the morning.

---

*See Chart 6-1, p. 157, in the student book for variations in the pronunciation of words with a final -*s*.

**Some nouns have irregular plurals. See Chart 6-2, p. 158.

◇ PRACTICE 7. MANY vs. MUCH. (Chart 11-5)
Directions: Complete the sentences with **much** or **many** and the singular or plural form of the noun. If a verb is needed, circle the correct one in the parentheses.

1. *apple*   How ___many apples___ did you buy?

2. *fruit*   How ___much fruit___ did you buy?

3. *mail*   How _____ did you get yesterday?

4. *letter*   How _____ did you get yesterday?

5. *English*   Anna's husband doesn't know _____ .

6. *slang*   Sometimes I can't understand my roommate because he uses too

            _____ .

7. *word*   How _____ (*is, are*) there in your dictionary?

8. *coffee*   Louise drinks too _____ .

9. *sandwich*   Billy has a stomach ache. He ate too _____ .

10. *sugar*   You shouldn't eat too _____ .

11. *course*   How _____ are you taking this semester?

12. *homework*   How _____ do you have to do tonight?

13. *news*   There (*isn't, aren't*) _____ in the paper today.

14. *article*   How _____ (*is, are*) there on the front

            page of today's paper?

15. *fun*   I didn't have _____ at the party. It was boring.

16. *star*   How _____ (*is, are*) there in the universe?

17. *sunshine*   There (*isn't, aren't*) _____ in Seattle in winter.

18. *pollution*   (*Is, Are*) there _____ in Miami?

19. *luck*   We didn't have _____ when we went fishing.

20. *kind*   There (*is, are*) _____ of flowers.

21. *violence*   I think there (*is, are*) too _____ on television.

22. *makeup*   I think that Mary wears too _____ .

23. *car*   How _____ pass in front of this building in 30 seconds?

24. *traffic*   (*Is, Are*) there _____ in front of your apartment building?

Directions: Complete the questions with **many** or **much.** Add final *-s/-es* if necessary to make a noun plural. (Some of the count nouns have irregular plural forms.) If a verb is needed, circle the correct one in the parentheses. If final *-s/-es* is not necessary, put a slash (/) in the blank.

1. How ____many____ letter __s__ *(is, (are))* there in the English alphabet?*

2. How ____much____ mail __/__ did you get yesterday?

3. How ____many____ ~~man~~ men *(has, (have))* a full beard at least once in their life?

4. How ____many____ family̶ ies *(is, (are))* there in your apartment building?

5. How _____ sentence _____ *(is, are)* there in this exercise?

6. How _____ chalk _____ *(is, are)* there in the classroom?

7. How _____ English _____ does Stefan know?

8. How _____ English **literature** _____ have you studied?

9. How _____ English **word** _____ do you know?

10. How _____ **gasoline** _____ does it take to fill the tank in your car?

    (British: How _____ **petrol** _____ does it take to fill the tank?)

11. How _____ **homework** _____ did the teacher assign?

12. How _____ **grandchild** _____ does Mrs. Cunningham have?

13. How _____ **page** _____ *(is, are)* there in this book?

14. How _____ **library** _____ *(is, are)* there in the United States?†

15. How _____ **glass** _____ of water do you drink every day?

16. How _____ **fun** _____ did you have at the amusement park?

17. How _____ **education** _____ does Ms. Martinez have?

18. How _____ **soap** _____ should I use in the dishwasher?

19. How _____ **island** _____ *(is, are)* there in Indonesia?**

20. How _____ **people** _____ will there be by the year 2050?††

21. How _____ **zero** _____ *(is, are)* there in a billion?***

---

*Answer: twenty-six (26). There are twenty-six letters in the English alphabet.

†Answer: approximately fifteen thousand (15,000).

**Answer: more than thirteen thousand seven hundred (13,700).

††Answer: estimated at more than thirteen billion (13,000,000,000).

***Answer: nine (9).

◇ **PRACTICE 9. Review: count and noncount nouns.** (Charts 11-1 → 11-5)
Directions: Circle all the words that can be used with each given noun.

1. flower	(a)	an	some	much	many
2. flowers	a	an	(some)	much	(many)
3. coin	a	an	some	much	many
4. money	a	an	some	much	many
5. coins	a	an	some	much	many
6. salt	a	an	some	much	many
7. error	a	an	some	much	many
8. mistake	a	an	some	much	many
9. honest mistake	a	an	some	much	many
10. mistakes	a	an	some	much	many
11. dream	a	an	some	much	many
12. interesting dream	a	an	some	much	many
13. questions	a	an	some	much	many
14. soap	a	an	some	much	many
15. bar of soap	a	an	some	much	many
16. beauty	a	an	some	much	many
17. cup of tea	a	an	some	much	many
18. unsafe place	a	an	some	much	many
19. fruit	a	an	some	much	many
20. pieces of fruit	a	an	some	much	many

◇ **PRACTICE 10. A FEW vs. A LITTLE.** (Chart 11-5)
Directions: Complete the sentences with *a few* or *a little*. Add a final *-s* to the noun if necessary. Otherwise, write a slash (/) in the blank.

1. Let's listen to _____*a little*_____ **music** _/_ during dinner.

2. Let's sing _____*a few*_____ **song** _s_ around the campfire.

3. We all need _____ **help** _____ at times.

4. Ingrid is from Sweden, but she knows _____ **English** _____ .

5. I need _____ more **apple** _____ to make a pie.

6. I like _____ **honey** _____ in my coffee.

7. I have a problem. Could you give me _____ **advice** _____ ?

8. I need _____ **suggestion** _____ .

9. He asked _____ **question** _____ .

10. We talked to _____ **people** _____ on the plane.

11. Please give me _____ more **minute** _____ .

12. Ann opened the curtains to let in _____ **light** _____ from outdoors.

13. I have _____ **homework** _____ to do tonight.

14. Pedro already knew _____ English **grammar** _____ before he took this course.

15. I picked _____ **flower** _____ from my garden.

16. I've made _____ **progress** _____ in the last couple of weeks.

◇ PRACTICE 11. Error analysis. (Charts 11-1 → 11-5)
Directions: Correct the errors.

1. Kim has applied to ~~an~~ university in England.
   (a written above "an")

2. For Anita's wedding anniversary, her husband gave her a jewelry and a poetry he wrote.

3. The politician wanted specific suggestion for her speech on the economy.

4. Some of the homeworks for my English class was easy, but many of the assignment were unclear.

5. Diane has been to Rome several time recently. She always has wonderful time.

6. Many parents need advices about raising children.

7. The boys played together in the sands and dirts for hours.

8. A person doesn't need many equipment to play baseball: just ball and a bat.

9. Many happiness can come from enjoying the simple thing in life.

◇ PRACTICE 12. Count and noncount nouns. (Charts 6-2 and 11-1 → 11-6)
Directions: Add final *-s/-es* as necessary. Do not make any other changes. The number in parentheses at the end of each item is the number of nouns that need final *-s/-es*.

1. Plant^s are the oldest living thing^s on earth. (2) = [2 nouns need final *-s/-es*.]

2. Scientist divide living thing into two group: plant and animal. Generally speaking, plant stay in one place, but animal move around. (7)

3. Flower, grass, and tree grow every place where people live. Plant also grow in desert, in ocean, on mountaintop, and in polar region. (7)

4. Plant are useful to people. We eat them. We use them for clothing. We build house from them. Plant are also important to our health. We get many kind of beneficial drug from plant. In addition, plant provide beauty and enjoyment to all our lives. (7)

5. Crop are plant that people grow for food. Nature can ruin crop. Bad weather—such as too much rain or too little rain—can destroy field of corn or wheat. Natural disaster such as flood and storm have caused farmer many problem since people first began to grow their own food. (9)

6. Food is a necessity for all living thing. All animal and plant need to eat. Most plant take what they need through their root and their leaf. The majority of insect live solely on plant. Many bird have a diet of worm and insect. Reptile eat small animal, egg, and insect. (15)

◇ **PRACTICE 13. Units of measure with noncount nouns. (Chart 11-7)**
Directions: Use the words in the list to complete the sentences. Use the plural form if necessary. Some sentences have more than one possible completion.

bar	gallon	piece	sheet
bottle	glass	pound	spoonful
bowl	loaf	quart	tube
cup	kilo		

1. I drank a _____cup_____ of coffee.
2. I bought two _____pounds_____ of cheese.
3. I had a _____ of soup for lunch.
4. I drank a _____ of orange juice.
5. I had a _____ of toast and an egg for breakfast.
6. I put ten _____ of gas in my car.
7. I bought a _____ of milk at the supermarket.
8. I need a _____ of chalk.
9. I drank a _____ of beer.
10. I used two _____ of bread to make a sandwich.
11. There is a _____ of fruit on the table.
12. There are 200 _____ of lined paper in my notebook.

13. I bought one _____ of bread at the store.

14. I put a _____ of honey in my tea.

15. I need to buy a new _____ of toothpaste.

16. There is a _____ of soap in the bathroom.

17. Let me give you a _____ of advice.

18. I just learned an interesting _____ of information.

19. There were a dozen* _____ of mail in my mailbox today.

20. A three-piece suit is made up of three _____ of clothing: slacks, a jacket, and a vest.

◇ PRACTICE 14. Units of measure with noncount nouns. (Chart 11-7)
   Directions: What units of measure are usually used with the following nouns? More than one unit of measure can be used with some of the nouns.

bag	bottle	box	can/tin**	jar

1. a ___*jar*___ of pickles.

2. a _____ of aspirin.

3. a _____ of laundry detergent

4. a _____ of instant coffee

5. a _____ of sardines

6. a _____ of sugar

7. a _____ of peanut butter

8. a _____ of soy sauce

9. a _____ of uncooked noodles

10. a _____ of refried beans

◇ PRACTICE 15. MUCH vs. MANY. (Charts 11-5 → 11-7)
   Directions: Complete the questions with **much** or **many**.

1. A: How ___*many suitcases*___ did you take with you on the plane to Tahiti?
   B: Three. (I took three suitcases on the plane to Tahiti.)

2. A: How ___*much suntan oil*___ did you take with you?
   B: A lot. (I took a lot of suntan oil with me.)

3. A: How _____ did you take?
   B: Two pairs. (I took two pairs of sandals.)

4. A: How _____ did you take?
   B: One tube. (I took one tube of toothpaste.)

---
*A dozen = twelve. It is followed by a plural noun: *a dozen eggs.*
**a can = a tin* in British English.

5. A: How _____ did you have?

    B: Twenty. (I had twenty kilos of luggage.)

6. A: How _____ did you pay in overweight baggage charges?

    B: A lot. (I paid of lot of money for overweight baggage.)

◇ PRACTICE 16. A/AN vs. SOME. (Chart 11-8)
Directions: Complete the sentences with *a/an* or *some*.

1. I wrote ___*a*___ **letter**.

2. I got ___*some*___ **mail**.

3. We bought _____ **equipment** for our camping trip.

4. You need _____ **tool** to cut wood.

5. I ate _____ **food**.

6. I had _____ **apple**.

7. I wore _____ old **clothing**.

8. I wore _____ old **shirt**.

9. Jim asked me for _____ **advice**.

10. I gave Jim _____ **suggestion**.

11. I read _____ interesting **story** in the paper.

12. The paper has _____ interesting **news** today.

13. I read _____ **poem** after dinner.

14. I read _____ **poetry** after dinner.

15. I know _____ **song** from India.

16. I know _____ Indian **music**.

17. I learned _____ new **word**.

18. I learned _____ new **slang**.

◇ PRACTICE 17. A vs. SOME. (Chart 11-8)
Directions: Write *a* or *some* in the blank before each singular noun. Then write a sentence with the plural form of the noun if possible.

Singular Objects	**Plural Objects**
1. I saw ___*a*___ bird.	I saw some birds.
2. I ate ___*some*___ corn.	∅ (none possible)
3. Would you like _____ tea?	
4. I picked _____ flower.	

5. I drank _____ water. _____

6. I fed grass to _____ horse. _____

7. Pat is wearing _____ jewelry. _____

8. I bought _____ honey. _____

9. Tom bought _____ new shirt. _____

10. I need _____ soap to wash the dishes. _____

◇ PRACTICE 18. A/AN vs. THE: singular count nouns. (Chart 11-8)
   Directions: Complete the sentences with ***a/an*** or ***the***.

1. A: _____A_____ dog makes a good pet.
   B: I agree.

2. A: Did you feed ___the___ dog?
   B: Yes, I did.

3. My dorm room has _____ desk, _____ bed, _____ chest of drawers, and two chairs.

4. A: Jessica, where's the stapler?
   B: On _____ desk. If it's not there, look in _____ top drawer.

5. A: Sara, put your bike in _____ basement before dark.
   B: Okay, Dad.

6. Our apartment building has _____ basement. Sara keeps her bike there at night.

7. Almost every sentence has _____ subject and _____ verb.

8. Look at this sentence: *Jack lives in Miami.* What is _____ subject, and what is _____ verb?

9. A: I can't see you at four. I'll be in _____ meeting then. How about four-thirty?
   B: Fine.

10. A: What time does _____ meeting start Tuesday?
    B: Eight.

11. Jack's car ran out of gas. He had to walk _____ long distance to find _____ telephone and call his brother for help.

12. _____ distance from _____ sun to _____ earth is 93,000,000 miles.

13. A: Jake, _____ telephone is ringing. Can you get it?
    B: Sure.

14. A: Did you feed _____ cat?
    B: Yes. I fed him a couple of hours ago.

15. A: Does Jane have _____ cat?

    B: No, she has _____ dog. She doesn't like cats.

16. A: I wrote _____ poem. Would you like to read it?

    B: Sure. What's it about?

17. A: Was _____ lecture interesting?

    B: Yes. _____ speaker gave _____ interesting talk.

18. A: Where should we go for _____ cup of coffee after class?

    B: Let's go to _____ cafe around _____ corner from the First National Bank.

19. A: Where do you live?

    B: We live on _____ quiet street in the suburbs.

20. A: I'm hungry, and I'm tired of walking. How much farther is it to _____ restaurant?

    B: Just a couple of blocks. Let's cross _____ street here.

    A: Are you sure you know where you're going?

21. A: Did Bob find _____ job?

    B: Yes. He's working at _____ restaurant.

    A: Oh? Which one?

◇ PRACTICE 19. Ø vs. THE. (Chart 11-8)
   Directions: Write **Ø** or ***the*** in the blanks. Add capital letters as necessary.

1. A: _____Ø_____ D̸ogs make good pets.

   B: I agree.

2. A: Did you feed __the__ dogs?

   B: Yes, I did.

3. A: _____Ø_____ F̸ruit is good for you.

   B: I agree.

4. A: __The__ fruit in this bowl is ripe.

   B: Good. I think I'll have a piece.

5. John, where's _____ milk? Is it in _____ refrigerator or on _____ table?

6. _____ milk comes from cows and goats.

7. Tom usually has _____ wine with dinner.

8. Dinner's ready. Shall I pour _____ wine?

9. We usually have _____ meat for dinner.

10. _____ meat we had for dinner last night was tough.

11. A: Mom, please pass _____ potatoes.

B: Here you are. Anything else? Want some more chicken, too?

12. _____ potatoes are _____ vegetables.

13. _____ frogs are _____ small animals without _____ tails that live on land or in water. _____ turtles also live on land or in water, but they have _____ tails and _____ hard shells.

14. A: Nicole, what are those animals doing in here!?

B: We're playing. _____ frogs belong to Jason. _____ turtles are mine.

15. Do you like _____ weather in this city?

16. _____ copper is used in electrical wiring.

17. People used to use _____ candles for _____ light, but now they use _____ electricity.

18. There are many kinds of _____ books. We use _____ textbooks and _____ workbooks in school. We use _____ dictionaries and _____ encyclopedias for reference. For _____ entertainment, we read _____ novels and _____ poetry.

19. _____ books on this desk are mine.

◇ **PRACTICE 20. Using THE for second mention. (Charts 11-6 → 11-8)**
Directions: Use *a/an*, *some*, or *the* in the sentences. REMINDER: Use *the* when a noun is mentioned for the second time.

1. I drank __some__ coffee and __some__ milk. __The__ coffee was hot. __The__ milk was cold.

2. I had _____ soup and _____ sandwich for lunch. _____ soup was too salty, but _____ sandwich was pretty good.

3. Yesterday I bought _____ clothes. I bought _____ suit, _____ shirt, and _____ tie. _____ suit is gray and comes with a vest. _____ shirt is pale blue, and _____ tie has black and gray stripes.

4. A: I saw _____ accident yesterday.

   B: Oh? Where?

   A: On Grand Avenue. _____ man in _____ Volkswagen drove through a stop sign and hit _____ bus.

   B: Was anyone hurt in _____ accident?

   A: I don't think so. _____ man who was driving _____ Volkswagen got out of his car and seemed to be okay. His car was only slightly damaged. No one in _____ bus was hurt.

5. Yesterday I saw _____ man and _____ woman. They were having _____ argument. _____ man was yelling at _____ woman, and _____ woman was shouting at _____ man. I don't know what _____ argument was about.

6. Yesterday while I was walking to work, I saw _____ birds in _____ tree. I also saw _____ cat under _____ tree. _____ birds didn't pay any attention to _____ cat, but _____ cat was watching _____ birds intently.

◇ **PRACTICE 21. Using THE for second mention. (Charts 11-6 → 11-8)**
Directions: Write *a/an, some,* or *the* in the blanks.

One day last month while I was driving through the countryside, I saw _____a_____ man and
                                                                    1

_____ truck next to _____ covered bridge. _____ bridge crossed _____ small
    2   3   4   5

river. I stopped and asked _____ man, "What's the matter? Can I be of help?"
                               6

"Well," said _____ man, "my truck is about a half-inch* too tall. Or _____ top of
                 7   8

_____ bridge is a half-inch too short. Either way, my truck won't fit under _____
    9   10

bridge."

"Hmmm. There must be _____ solution to this problem," I said.
                         11

"I don't know. I guess I'll have to turn around and take another route," he replied.

After a few moments of thought, I said, "Aha! I have _____ solution!"
                                                         12

"What is it?" asked the man.

"Let a little air out of your tires. Then _____ truck won't be too tall and you can cross
                                              13

_____ bridge over _____ river."
    14   15

"Hey, that's _____ great idea. Let's try it!" So _____ man let a little air out of
                 16   17

_____ tires and was able to cross _____ river and go on his way.
    18   19

---

*One-half inch = 1.2 centimeters.

◇ **PRACTICE 22. Summary: A/AN vs. THE vs. Ø.** (Chart 11-8)
Directions: Complete the sentences with *a/an*, *the*, or **Ø**. Add capital letters as necessary.

1. A: What would you like for breakfast?

   B: ___An___ egg and some toast.

   A: How would you like ___the___ egg?

   B: Fried, sunny side up.

2. ___Ø___ eggs are nutritious.

3. It is _____ scientific fact: _____ steam rises when _____ water boils.

4. _____ gas is expensive nowadays.

5. _____ gas I got yesterday cost more than I've ever paid.

6. _____ newspapers are _____ important source of _____ information.

7. _____ sun is _____ star. We need _____ sun for _____ heat, _____
   light, and _____ energy.

8. _____ ducks are my favorite farm animals.

9. _____ pizza originated in Italy. It is a pie with _____ cheese, _____ tomatoes,
   and other things on top. _____ "pizza" means "pie" in _____ Italian.

10. A: Hey, Nick. Pass _____ pizza. I want another piece.

    B: There are only two pieces left. You take _____ big piece, and I'll take _____
       small one.

11. _____ gold is _____ excellent conductor of _____ electricity. It is used in many
    of the electrical circuits on _____ spaceship.

12. A: Where's Alice?

    B: She's in _____ kitchen making _____ sandwich.

13. A: Where'd _____ plumber go? _____ sink's still leaking!

    B: Relax. He went to shut off _____ water supply to _____ house. He'll fix
       _____ leak when he gets back.

14. A: Do you see _____ man who is standing next to Janet?

    B: Yes. Who is he?

    A: He's _____ president of this university.

15. A one-dollar bill has a picture of _____ president of the United States. It's a picture of George Washington.

16. A: What did you buy when you went shopping?

    B: I bought _____ blouse and _____ jewelry.

    A: What color is _____ blouse?

    B: Red.

17. A: Where's my bookbag?

    B: It's on _____ floor over there, in _____ corner next to _____ sofa.

18. We need to buy _____ furniture. I'd like to get _____ sofa and _____ easy chair.

19. _____ furniture is expensive these days.

20. _____ vegetarian doesn't eat _____ meat.

21. Only one of _____ continents in _____ world is uninhabited. Which one?

22. Last week, I took _____ easy exam. It was in my economics class. I had _____ right answers for all of _____ questions on _____ exam. My score was 100%.

23. Anyone who goes to _____ job interview should wear _____ nice clothes.

24. A mouse has _____ long, thin, almost hairless tail. _____ rats also have _____ long, skinny tails.

25. Years ago, people used _____ wood or _____ coal for _____ heat, but now most people use _____ gas, _____ oil, or _____ electricity.

26. I had _____ interesting experience yesterday. _____ man in _____ blue suit came into my office and handed me _____ bouquet of _____ flowers. I had never seen _____ man before in my life, but I thanked him for _____ flowers. Then he walked out _____ door.

27. A: What is your favorite food?

    B: _____ ice cream—it's cold, sweet, and smooth.

28. We had _____ steamed rice, _____ fish, and _____ vegetables for lunch yesterday. _____ rice was cooked just right. _____ fish was very tasty. _____ vegetables were fresh.

29. Karen is _____ exceptionally talented person.

30. A: Where's _____ letter I wrote to Ted?

B: It's gone. _____ strong wind blew it on _____ floor, and _____ dog tore it up. I threw _____ scraps in _____ wastebasket.

31. A: I'm looking for _____ tape player. Where is it?

B: It's on one of _____ shelves next to my desk.

A: Ah! There it is. Thanks.

B: You're welcome.

A: Hmmm. I don't think it works. Maybe _____ batteries are dead.

32. _____ chalk is _____ necessity in a classroom.

33. _____ efficient transportation system is _____ essential part of a healthy economy.

◇ **PRACTICE 23. Using THE or Ø with names. (Chart 11-9)**
Directions: Complete the sentences with ***the*** or **Ø**.

1. Although Ingrid has been to Orly Airport several times, she has never visited ___Ø___ Paris.

2. ___The___ Atlantic Ocean is smaller than ___the___ Pacific.

3. _____ Dr. James was the youngest person at her university to get a Ph.D.

4. _____ Mt. Rainier in Washington State is in _____ Cascade Mountain Range.

5. _____ Nile is the longest river in _____ Africa.

6. Is _____ Toronto or _____ Montreal the largest city in Canada?

7. During her tour of Africa, Helen climbed _____ Mt. Kilimanjaro and visited several national parks in _____ Kenya.

8. _____ New Zealand is made up of two islands: North Island and South Island.

9. _____ Himalayas extend through several countries: _____ Pakistan, _____ India, _____ Tibet, and _____ Nepal.

10. _____ President Davis was surprised to be elected to a fourth term.

11. _____ Ho Chi Minh City in _____ Vietnam was formerly called _____ Saigon.

12. _____ Andes Mountains in South America extend for 5000 miles.

◇ **PRACTICE 24. Using THE or Ø with names. (Chart 11-9)**

Directions: Answer the questions. Choose from the list below. Use *the* if necessary. (Not all names on the list will be used.)

Africa	*Europe*	*Mont Blanc*	*Shanghai*
Alps	*Gobi Desert*	*Mt. Vesuvius*	*South America*
Amazon River	*Indian Ocean*	*Netherlands*	*Taipei*
Beijing	*Lagos*	*Nile River*	*Thames River*
Black Sea	*Lake Baikal*	*North America*	*Tibet*
Dead Sea	*Lake Tanganyika*	*Sahara Desert*	*United Arab Emirates*
Elbe River	*Lake Titicaca*	*Saudi Arabia*	*Urals*

GEOGRAPHY TRIVIA

Question	Answer
1. What is the lowest point on Earth?	the Dead Sea
2. What is the second-longest river in the world?	
3. What is the most populated city in China?	
4. What is the largest desert in the world?	
5. What river runs through London?	
6. On what continent is the Volga River?	
7. What mountains border France and Italy?	
8. What lake is in East Central Africa?	
9. On what continent is Mexico?	
10. What is the third-largest ocean in the world?	
11. What country is also known as Holland?	
12. What is the third-largest continent in the world?	
13. What country is located in the Himalayas?	
14. What mountains are part of the boundary between Europe and Asia?	
15. What is the capital of Nigeria?	
16. What country consists of seven kingdoms?	

◇ PRACTICE 25. Capitalization. (Chart 11-10)
    Directions: Add capital letters where necessary.

                     B
    1. I'm taking ~~b~~iology 101 this semester.

    2. I'm taking history, biology, english, and calculus this semester.

    3. Some lab classes meet on saturday.

    4. Marta lives on a busy street. Marta lives at 2358 olive street.

    5. We went to canada last summer. we went to montreal in july.

    6. My roommate likes vietnamese food, and i like thai food.

    7. The religion of saudi arabia is islam.

    8. Shelia works for the xerox corporation. it is a very large corporation.

    9. Pedro is from latin america.

    10. My uncle lives in st. louis. I'm going to visit uncle bill next spring.

    11. We went to a park. we went to waterfall park.

    12. Are you going to the university of oregon or oregon state university?

    13. Alice goes to a university in oregon.

    14. The next assignment in literature class is to read *the adventures of tom sawyer.*

    15. Many countries have holidays to celebrate the date they became independent. In france, they

        call it "bastille day."

◇ PRACTICE 26. Capitalization. (Chart 11-10)
    Directions: Add capital letters where necessary.

                 R   J
    1. Do you know ~~r~~obert ~~j~~ones?

    2. Do you know my uncle? *(no change)*

    3. I like uncle joe and aunt sara.

    4. I'd like you to meet my aunt.

    5. susan w. miller is a professor.

    6. I am in prof. miller's class.

    7. The weather is cold in january.

    8. The weather is cold in winter.

    9. I have three classes on monday.

10. I would like to visit los angeles.

11. It's the largest city in california.

12. I like to visit large cities in foreign countries.

13. There are fifty states in the united states of america.

14. It used to take weeks or months to cross an ocean.

15. Today we can fly across the atlantic ocean in hours.

16. Mark lives on a busy street near the local high school.

17. Mark lives on market street near washington high school.

18. Our family stayed at a very comfortable hotel.

19. Our family stayed at the hilton hotel in bangkok.

20. Yoko is japanese, but she can also speak german.

◇ PRACTICE 27. Error analysis. (Chapter 11)
Directions: Correct the errors.

1. The mail carrier brought only one ~~mail~~ letter today.

2. Mr. Dale gave his class long history assignment for the weekend.

3. Tariq speaks several language, including Arabic and Spanish.

4. Dr. kim gives all her patients toothbrush and toothpaste at their dental appointments.

5. I usually have glass water with my lunch.

6. A helpful policeman gave us an information about the city.

7. This cookie recipe calls for two cup of nut.

8. Much vegetable are believed to have cancer-fighting ingredients.

9. Only applicants with the necessary experiences should apply for the computer position.

10. When Vicki likes a movie, she sees it several time.

11. A popular children's story is *Snow White And The Seven Dwarfs*.

12. Is it possible to stop all violences in the world?

◇ **PRACTICE 1. Using WHO in adjective clauses. (Charts 12-1 and 12-2)**

Directions: Underline the adjective clause in the long sentence. Then change the long sentence into two short sentences.*

1. *Long sentence:*   I thanked the man <u>who helped me move the refrigerator</u>.

   Short sentence 1: _____I thanked_____ the man.

   Short sentence 2: _____He helped_____ me move the refrigerator.

2. *Long sentence:*   A woman who was wearing a gray suit asked me for directions.

   Short sentence 1: _____ me for directions.

   Short sentence 2: _____ a gray suit.

3. *Long sentence:*   The woman who aided the rebels put her life in danger.

   Short sentence 1: _____ her life in danger.

   Short sentence 2: _____ the rebels.

4. *Long sentence:*   I saw a man who was wearing a blue coat.

   Short sentence 1: _____ a man.

   Short sentence 2: _____ a blue coat.

5. *Long sentence:*   The girl who broke the vase apologized to Mrs. Cook.

   Short sentence 1: _____ to Mrs. Cook.

   Short sentence 2: _____ the vase.

---

*In grammar terminology, the "long sentence" is called a **complex sentence**, and the "short sentence" is called a **simple sentence**.
  • A complex sentence has an independent clause and one or more dependent clauses. For example:
      I thanked the man who helped me. = a complex sentence consisting of one independent clause *(I thanked the man)* and one dependent clause *(who helped me)*.
  • A simple sentence has only an independent clause. For example:
      I thanked the man. = a simple sentence consisting of one independent clause.
      He helped me. = a simple sentence consisting of one independent clause.

◇ **PRACTICE 2. Using WHO in adjective clauses. (Chart 12-2)**

Directions: Combine the two short sentences into one long sentence using "short sentence 2" as an adjective clause. Use **who**. Underline the adjective clause.

1. *Short sentence 1:* The woman was polite.
   Short sentence 2: She answered the phone.
   Long sentence: The woman <u>who answered the phone</u> was polite.

2. *Short sentence 1:* The man has a good voice.
   Short sentence 2: He sang at the concert.

   Long sentence:

3. *Short sentence 1:* We enjoyed the actors.
   Short sentence 2: They played the leading roles.

   Long sentence:

4. *Short sentence 1:* The girl is hurt.
   Short sentence 2: She fell down the stairs.

   Long sentence:

5. *Short sentence 1:* I read about the soccer player.
   Short sentence 2: He was injured in the game yesterday.

   Long sentence:

◇ **PRACTICE 3. Using WHO and WHOM in adjective clauses. (Chart 12-2)**

Directions: Underline the adjective clause. Identify the subject and verb of the adjective clause. Then complete the change from one long sentence to two short sentences, and identify the subject and verb of the second short sentence.

1. *Long sentence:*   The people <u>who live next to me</u> are nice.
   Short sentence 1: The people are nice.
   Short sentence 2: They live next to me.

2. *Long sentence:*   The people <u>whom Kate visited yesterday</u> were French.
   Short sentence 1: The people were French.
   Short sentence 2: Kate visited them yesterday.

3. *Long sentence:*   The people whom I saw at the park were having a picnic.
   Short sentence 1: The people were having a picnic.

   Short sentence 2:

4. *Long sentence:*   The students who go to this school are friendly.
   Short sentence 1: The students are friendly.

   Short sentence 2:

5. *Long sentence:*   The woman whom you met last week lives in Mexico.
   Short sentence 1: The woman lives in Mexico.

   Short sentence 2:

◇ PRACTICE 4. Using WHO and WHOM in adjective clauses. (Chart 12-2)
Directions: Change the two short sentences into one long sentence with an adjective clause.
Use **who** or **whom**. <u>Underline</u> the adjective clause.

1. *Short sentence 1:* The woman was polite.
   Short sentence 2: Jack met her.
   Long sentence: The woman <u>whom Jack met</u> was polite.

2. *Short sentence 1:* I like the woman.
   Short sentence 2: She manages my uncle's store.
   Long sentence: I like the woman <u>who manages my uncle's store.</u>

3. *Short sentence 1:* The singer was wonderful.
   Short sentence 2: We heard him at the concert.

   Long sentence:

4. *Short sentence 1:* The people brought a small gift.
   Short sentence 2: They came to dinner.

   Long sentence:

5. *Short sentence 1:* What is the name of the woman?
   Short sentence 2: Tom invited her to the dance.

   Long sentence:

◇ PRACTICE 5. Using WHO and WHO(M) in adjective clauses. (Chart 12-2)
Directions: Complete the sentences with **who** or **who(m)**.*

1. I know a man _____who_____ works at the post office.

2. One of the people ___who(m)___ I watched at the race track lost a huge amount of money.

3. My neighbor is a kind person _____ is always willing to help people in trouble.

4. My mother is a woman _____ I admire tremendously.

5. I thanked the man _____ helped me.

6. The woman _____ I helped thanked me.

7. The doctor _____ lives on my street is a surgeon.

8. I talked to the people _____ were sitting next to me.

_____

*There are parentheses around the "m" in *who(m)* to show that, in everyday informal English, *who* may be used as an object pronoun instead of *whom*.

9. I saw the woman _____ was walking her dog.

10. Do you like the mechanic _____ fixed your car?

11. Mr. Polanski is a mechanic _____ you can trust.

12. There are many good people in the world _____ you can trust to be honest and honorable.

13. The children _____ live down the street in the yellow house are always polite.

14. The children _____ I watched at the park were feeding ducks in a pond.

15. My husband is a person _____ enjoys good food and good friends.

◇ **PRACTICE 6. Using THAT or Ø in adjective clauses. (Chart 12-3)**
Directions: Write **S** if *who* or *that* is the subject of the adjective clause. Write **O** if *who* or *that* is the object of the adjective clause. Cross out the words *who* or *that* where possible.

1. ___O___ The secretary ~~that~~ I hired is very efficient.

2. ___S___ The secretary **who** works in the office next door is interviewing for my old job.

3. _____ The students **who** worked together in study groups got the highest scores on the test.

4. _____ The students **who** the teacher helped did very well on the test.

5. _____ The man **that** lives next door is a famous scientist.

6. _____ The children **that** came to the party wore animal costumes.

7. _____ The teachers **who** went to the workshop felt encouraged to try new techniques.

8. _____ The teachers **that** I had for science were very well trained.

9. _____ The policeman **who** caught the thief had been watching him for days.

10. _____ The policeman **that** we met on the street told us about several interesting tourist spots.

◇ **PRACTICE 7. Using THAT or Ø in adjective clauses. (Chart 12-3)**
Directions: Cross out the word *that* if possible.

1. That man ~~that~~ I saw was wearing a black hat.

2. The people that visited us stayed too long. *(no change)*

3. The fruit that I bought today at the market is fresh.

4. My high school English teacher is a person that I will never forget.

5. The puppy that barked the loudest got the most attention in the pet store.

6. The girl that sits in front of Richard has long black hair that she wears in a ponytail.

7. The forest that lies below my house provides a home for deer and other wildlife.

8. The animals that live in our neighborhood behaved strangely before the earthquake.

◇ **PRACTICE 8. Using WHO, WHO(M), THAT, or Ø in adjective clauses.** (Chart 12-3)
Directions: In the box, write every possible pronoun that can be used to connect the adjective clause to the main clause: *who, who(m),* or *that.* Also, write **Ø** if the pronoun can be omitted.

1. The woman ⎡who / that⎤ sat next to me on the plane was very nice.

2. The woman ⎡who(m) / that / Ø⎤ I met on the plane was very nice.

3. Two people ⎡ ⎤ I didn't know walked into the classroom.

4. The people ⎡ ⎤ walked into the classroom were strangers.

5. My cousin's wife is the woman ⎡ ⎤ is talking to Mr. Horn.

6. I like the woman ⎡ ⎤ my brother and I visited.

◇ **PRACTICE 9. WHO and WHO(M) vs. WHICH. (Charts 12-2 → 12-4)**
    Directions: Choose the correct answer.

1. The magazine _____ I read on the plane was interesting.
   A. who   B. who(m)   Ⓒ. which

2. The artist _____ drew my picture is very good.
   A. who   B. who(m)   C. which

3. I really enjoyed the experiences _____ I had on my trip to Nigeria.
   A. who   B. who(m)   C. which

4. Most of the games _____ we played as children no longer amuse us.
   A. who   B. who(m)   C. which

5. All of the people _____ I called yesterday can come to the meeting on Monday.
   A. who   B. who(m)   C. which

6. The teacher _____ was ill canceled her math class.
   A. who   B. who(m)   C. which

7. The flight _____ I took to Singapore was on time.
   A. who   B. who(m)   C. which

8. I read an article _____ discussed the current political crisis.
   A. who   B. who(m)   C. which

◇ **PRACTICE 10. Adjective clauses. (Charts 12-2 → 12-4)**
    Directions: Complete the definitions with the given information. Use adjective clauses in the definitions.

> *S/he leaves society and lives completely alone.*
> *It has a hard shell and can live in water or on land.*
> ✓*S/he designs buildings.*
> *It forms when water boils.*
> *S/he doesn't eat meat.*
> *It grows in hot climates and produces large bunches of yellow fruit.*
> *It cannot be understood or explained.*
> *It can be shaped and hardened to form many useful things.*

1. An architect is someone _____who/that designs buildings._____

2. A vegetarian is a person _____

3. Steam is a gas _____

4. A turtle is an animal _____

5. A hermit is a person _____

6. A banana tree is a plant _____

7. Plastic is a synthetic material _____

8. A mystery is something _____

◇ PRACTICE 11. WHICH and THAT. (Chart 12-4)

Directions: Write **S** if *which* or *that* is the subject of the adjective clause. Write **O** if *which* or *that* is the object of the adjective clause. Cross out the words *which* or *that* where possible.

1. __O__ The medicine ~~which~~ the doctor prescribed for me was very expensive.

2. __S__ The medicine **which** is on the shelf is no longer good.

3. _____ The computer **that** I bought recently has already crashed several times.

4. _____ The car **which** my husband drives is very reliable.

5. _____ The house **which** sits on top of the hill has won several architecture awards.

6. _____ The restaurant **that** offered low-cost dinners to senior citizens has recently closed.

7. _____ The baseball **which** all the players autographed will be donated to charity.

8. _____ The windstorm **that** is moving toward us is very powerful.

9. _____ The trees **that** shade our house are over 300 years old.

10. _____ The trees **that** we planted last year have doubled in size.

◇ PRACTICE 12. Using WHICH, THAT, and Ø in adjective clauses. (Chart 12-4)

Directions: Write the pronouns that can be used to connect the adjective clause to the main clause: *which* or *that*. Also write **Ø** if the pronoun can be omitted.

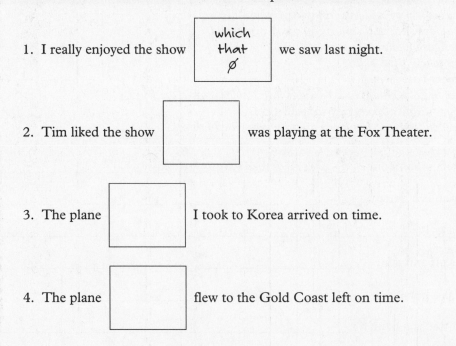

1. I really enjoyed the show [which / that / Ø] we saw last night.

2. Tim liked the show [ ] was playing at the Fox Theater.

3. The plane [ ] I took to Korea arrived on time.

4. The plane [ ] flew to the Gold Coast left on time.

5. The books ☐ Jane ordered came in the mail today.

6. Jane was glad to get the books ☐ came in the mail today.

◇ PRACTICE 13. Error analysis: object pronouns in adjective clauses. (Charts 12-3 and 12-4)
Directions: Cross out the incorrect pronouns in the adjective clauses.

1. I enjoy the relatives I visited ~~them~~ in Mexico City last year.

2. The coffee that I drank it was cold and tasteless.

3. The tennis shoes I was wearing them in the garden got wet and muddy.

4. My cousin Ahmed is a person I've known and loved him since he was born.

5. I have a great deal of respect for the wonderful woman I married her eleven years ago.

6. The dog which we have had him for several years is very gentle with young children.

◇ PRACTICE 14. Pronoun usage in adjective clauses. (Charts 12-2 → 12-4)
Directions: Choose the correct answers. NOTE: There is more than one correct answer for each sentence.

1. I liked the teacher _____ I had for chemistry in high school.
   Ⓐ whom   B. which   Ⓒ that   Ⓓ Ø

2. The university scientist _____ did research in the Amazon River basin found many previously unknown species of plants.
   A. who   B. whom   C. which   D. that   E. Ø

3. The children enjoyed the sandwiches _____ Mr. Rice made for them.
   A. who   B. whom   C. which   D. that   E. Ø

4. Have you ever read any books by the author _____ the teacher mentioned in class this morning?
   A. whom   B. which   C. that   D. Ø

5. The fans _____ crowded the ballpark roared their approval.
   A. who   B. whom   C. which   D. that   E. Ø

6. Have you been to the Clayton Art Gallery? It has a new exhibit _____ includes the work of several local artists.
   A. who   B. whom   C. which   D. that   E. Ø

7. The operation _____ the surgeon performed on my uncle was very dangerous.
   A. who   B. whom   C. which   D. that   E. Ø

8. Bricks are made of soil _____ has been placed in molds, pounded down, and dried.
   A. who   B. whom   C. which   D. that   E. Ø

9. The actors _____ we saw at Stratford performed out-of-doors.
   A. whom   B. which   C. that   D. Ø

10. Many of the games _____ children play teach them about the adult world.
    A. who   B. whom   C. which   D. that   E. Ø

11. When Jason arrived at the reunion, the first person _____ he encountered was Sally Sellers, one of his best friends when he was in high school.
    A. whom   B. which   C. that   D. Ø

12. Fire swept through an old apartment building in the center of town. I know some of the people _____ the firefighters rescued. The people lost all their possessions. They were grateful simply to be alive.
    A. whom   B. which   C. that   D. Ø

13. Most of the islands in the Pacific are the tops of volcanic mountains _____ rise from the floor of the ocean.
    A. who   B. whom   C. which   D. that   E. Ø

◇ **PRACTICE 15. Subject–verb agreement in adjective clauses. (Chart 12-5)**
   Directions: In each sentence, choose the correct form of the verb in *italics*. Use the simple present. <u>Underline</u> the noun that determines whether the verb in the adjective clause is singular or plural.

   1. The <u>students</u> who *is,* (*are*) in my class come from many countries.

   2. The people who *is, are* standing in line to get into the theater are cold and wet.

   3. Water is a chemical compound that *consists, consist* of oxygen and hydrogen.

   4. There are two students in my class who *speaks, speak* Portuguese.

   5. I met some people who *knows, know* my brother.

   6. The student who *is, are* talking to the teacher is from Peru.

7. Do you know the people that *lives, live* in that house?

8. A carpenter is a person who *makes, make* things out of wood.

9. Sculptors are artists who *make, makes* things from clay or other materials.

◇ **PRACTICE 16. Prepositions in adjective clauses. (Chart 12-6)**

Directions: The adjective clauses in the following sentences need prepositions. Add the prepositions and give all the possible patterns for the adjective clause. Write Ø if nothing is needed.

1. The bus _____that_____ we were waiting __for__ was an hour late.

   The bus _____which_____ we were waiting __for__ was an hour late.

   The bus _____Ø_____ we were waiting __for__ was an hour late.

   The bus ___for which___ we were waiting __Ø__ was an hour late.

2. The music _____ I listened _____ was pleasant.

   The music _____ I listened _____ was pleasant.

   The music _____ I listened _____ was pleasant.

   The music _____ I listened _____ was pleasant.

3. Ecology is one of the subjects _____ I am very interested _____.

   Ecology is one of the subjects _____ I am very interested _____.

   Ecology is one of the subjects _____ I am very interested _____.

   Ecology is one of the subjects _____ I am very interested _____.

4. The man _____ Maria was arguing _____ was very angry.

   The man _____ Maria was arguing _____ was very angry.

   The man _____ Maria was arguing _____ was very angry.

   The man _____ Maria was arguing _____ was very angry.

◇ **PRACTICE 17. Prepositions in adjective clauses. (Chart 12-6 and Appendix 2)**

Directions: Complete the sentences with pronouns and prepositions as necessary. Give all possible patterns for the adjective clauses.

Example: The movie . . . we went . . . was good.
   → *The movie that we went to was good.*
   The movie which we went to was good.
   The movie Ø we went to was good.
   The movie to which we went was good.

1. I enjoyed meeting the people . . . you introduced me . . . yesterday.
2. English grammar is a subject . . . I am quite familiar . . . .
3. The woman . . . Mr. Low told us . . . works for the government.
4. The people . . . I work . . . are very creative.
5. The train . . . you are waiting . . . is usually late.
6. The job . . . I am interested . . . requires several years of computer experience.

◇ **PRACTICE 18. Prepositions in adjective clauses. (Chart 12-6 and Appendix 2)**

Directions: Supply appropriate prepositions in the blanks. Write Ø if no preposition is necessary. Draw brackets around the adjective clause.

1. I enjoyed the CD ⌈we listened __to__ at Sara's apartment.⌉

2. I paid the shopkeeper for the glass cup ⌈I accidentally broke __Ø__ .⌉

3. The bus we were waiting _____ was only three minutes late.

4. Mrs. Chan is someone I always enjoy talking _____ about politics.

5. I showed my roommate the letter I had just written _____ .

6. One of the subjects I've been interested _____ for a long time is astronomy.

7. The people I talked _____ at the reception were interesting.

8. One of the places I want to visit _____ next year is Mexico City.

9. The book catalogue I was looking _____ had hundreds of interesting titles.

10. The book I wanted _____ wasn't available at the library.

11. I really enjoyed the music we were listening _____ at Jim's yesterday.

12. Botany is a subject I'm not familiar _____ .

13. The bags I was carrying _____ were really heavy.

14. My parents are people I can always rely _____ for support and help.

15. Taking out the garbage is one of the chores our fourteen-year-old is responsible _____ .

16. The newspaper I was reading _____ had the latest news about the election.

17. The furniture I bought _____ was expensive.

18. English grammar is one of the subjects _____ which I enjoy studying the most.

19. The friend I waved _____ didn't wave back. Maybe he just didn't see me.

20. The people _____ whom Alex was waiting were over an hour late.

◇ PRACTICE 19. Adjective clauses with WHOSE. (Chart 12-7)
Directions: Underline the adjective clause in each long sentence. Then change the long sentence into two short sentences.

1. *Long sentence:* I know a man <u>whose daughter is a pilot.</u>

   Short sentence 1: _____ I know a man. _____

   Short sentence 2: _____ His daughter is a pilot. _____

2. *Long sentence:* The woman whose husband is out of work found a job at Mel's Diner.

   Short sentence 1: _____

   Short sentence 2: _____

3. *Long sentence:* The man whose wallet I found gave me a reward.

   Short sentence 1: _____

   Short sentence 2: _____

◇ PRACTICE 20. Adjective clauses with WHOSE. (Chart 12-7)
Directions: Follow these steps:
   1. Underline the possessive pronoun.
   2. Draw an arrow to the noun it refers to.
   3. Replace the possessive pronoun with *whose*.
   4. Combine the two sentences into one.

1. The firefighters are very brave. <u>Their</u> department has won many awards.
   → *The firefighters whose department has won many awards are very brave.*

2. I talked to the boy. <u>His</u> kite was caught in a tree.
   → *I talked to the boy whose kite was caught in a tree.*

3. The family is staying in a motel. Their house burned down.

4. I watched a little girl. Her dog was chasing a ball in the park.

5. The reporter won an award. Her articles explained global warming.

6. I know a man. His daughter entered college at the age of fourteen.

7. We observed a language teacher. Her teaching methods included role-playing.

8. The teachers are very popular. Their methods include role-playing.

◇ **PRACTICE 21. Meaning of adjective clauses. (Charts 12-1 → 12-7)**
   Directions: Check all the sentences that are true.

1. The policeman who gave Henry a ticket seemed very nervous.

   a. __✓__ Henry received a ticket.

   b. _____ Henry seemed nervous.

   c. __✓__ The policeman seemed nervous.

2. A co-worker of mine whose wife is a pilot is afraid of flying.

   a. _____ My co-worker is a pilot.

   b. _____ My co-worker's wife is afraid of flying.

   c. __✓__ The pilot is a woman.

3. The man that delivers office supplies to our company bought a Ferrari.

   a. _____ Our company bought a Ferrari.

   b. __✓__ A man delivers office supplies.

   c. __✓__ A man bought a Ferrari.

4. The doctor who took care of my father had a heart attack recently.

   a. _____ My father had a heart attack.

   b. _____ The doctor treated a heart attack patient.

   c. __✓__ The doctor had a heart attack.

5. The forest fire which destroyed two homes in Woodville burned for two weeks across a wide area.

   a. __✓__ The forest fire burned for two weeks.

   b. _____ Two homes burned for two weeks.

   c. _____ The forest fire destroyed Woodville.

6. The salesman who sold my friend a used car was arrested for changing the mileage on cars.

   a. __✓__ My friend bought a car.

   b. _____ My friend was arrested.

   c. __✓__ The salesman changed the mileage on cars.

7. The waiter who took Julie's order is her best friend's cousin.

   a. _____ The waiter is Julie's cousin.

   b. __✓__ Julie's best friend is the waiter's cousin.

   c. _____ Julie's best friend is a waiter.

◇ **PRACTICE 22. Adjective clauses. (Charts 12-1 → 12-7)**

Directions: Use the given information to complete the sentences with adjective clauses. Omit the pronoun from the adjective clause if possible.

I share their views.
Their children were doing poorly in her class.
They disrupted the global climate and caused mass extinctions of animal life.
Ted bought them for his wife on their anniversary.
I slept on it at the hotel last night.
They had backbones.
✓*It is used to carry boats with goods and/or passengers.*

---

1. A waterway is a river or stream ___which/that is used to carry boats with goods___
   ___and/or passengers___ .

2. The second grade teacher talked to all the parents _____
   _____ .

3. The flowers _____
   wilted in the heat before he got home.

4. The candidates _____ will get my votes.

5. According to scientists, the first animals _____
   _____ were fish. They appeared on the
   earth about 500 million years ago.

6. Approximately 370 million years ago, seventy percent of Earth's
   marine species mysteriously vanished. Approximately 65 million
   years ago, the dinosaurs and two-thirds of all marine animal species
   became extinct. According to some scientific researchers, Earth was
   struck by speeding objects from space _____
   _____ .

◇ **PRACTICE 23. Adjective clauses. (Charts 12-1 → 12-7)**

Directions: Which of the following can be used in the blanks: **who, who(m), which, that, whose,** or **Ø**?

1. What do you say to people _____who/that_____ ask you personal questions that you don't
   want to answer?

2. In my country, any person _____ is twenty-one years old or older can vote. I
   turned twenty-one last year. The person I voted for in the national election lost. I hope the
   next candidate for _____ I vote has better luck. I'd like to vote for a winning
   candidate.

3. Vegetarians are people _____ do not eat meat. True vegetarians do not eat flesh _____ comes from any living creature, including fish. Some vegetarians even exclude any food _____ is made from animal products, such as milk and eggs.

4. People _____ live in New York City are called New Yorkers.

5. Tina likes the present _____ I gave her for her birthday.

6. George Washington is the president _____ picture is on a one-dollar bill.

7. Have you seen the movie _____ is playing at the Fox Theater?

8. Do you know the woman _____ Michael is engaged to?

9. That's Tom Jenkins. He's the boy _____ parents live in Switzerland.

10. A thermometer is an instrument _____ measures temperature.

11. A high-strung person is someone _____ is always nervous.

12. The man _____ I told you about is standing over there.

◇ **PRACTICE 24. Error analysis. (Chapter 12)**
Directions: Correct the errors.

1. A movie that look͜ₛ interesting opens tomorrow.

2. My family lived in a house which it was built in 1900.

3. The little boy was lost who asked for directions.

4. I don't know people who their lives are carefree.

5. It is important to help people who has no money.

6. At the airport, I was waiting for friends which I hadn't seen them for a long time.

7. The woman live next door likes to relax by doing crossword puzzles every evening.

8. My teacher has two cats who their names are Ping and Pong.

9. A beautiful garden that separates my house from the street.

10. I asked the children who was sitting on the bench to help us.

11. The school that my children attend it is very good academically.

12. I enjoyed the songs which we sang them.

13. One of the places that I like to visit Central Park.

14. The movie we saw it last evening was very exciting.

15. I sent the parents who I hiked with their son a picture of us on Mt. Fuji.

16. Do you know the man who work in that office?

17. A mother who's daughter is in my class often brings cookies for the children.

18. The CD player who I bought can hold several CDs at once.

19. The bed which I sleep is very comfortable.

20. I would like to tell you about several problems which I have had them since I came here.

CHAPTER 13

Gerunds and Infinitives

◇ **PRACTICE 1. Verb + gerund. (Chart 13-1)**
    Directions: Complete the sentences with the correct form of the verbs in parentheses.

1. Joan often talks about *(move)* ____moving____ overseas.

2. The Browns sometimes discuss *(live)* _____ in a smaller town.

3. Christine enjoys *(take)* _____ care of her young niece.

4. Nathan keeps *(buy)* _____ lottery tickets, but he never wins.

5. My manager considered *(give)* _____ pay raises but decided not to.

6. I always put off *(do)* _____ my math homework.

7. The students finished *(review)* _____ for the test at 3:00 A.M.

8. Ann stopped *(run)* _____ and walked the rest of the way home.

9. Dana quit *(drive)* _____ after she had a serious car accident.

10. My dentist thinks about *(retire)* _____ , but he enjoys his work too much.

11. Last week, Joan and David postponed *(get married)* _____ for the
    second time.

12. Do you mind *(work)* _____ another shift tonight?

◇ **PRACTICE 2. GO + gerund. (Chart 13-2)**
    Directions: Complete the sentences with a form of *go* and one of the given words.

camp	*fish*	*sail*	*sightsee*	*skydive*
✓*dance*	*hike*	*shop*	*ski*	*swim*

1. I love to dance. Last night, my husband and I danced for hours.

    → Last night, my husband and I ____went dancing____ .

2. Later this afternoon, Ted is going to take a long walk in the woods.

    → Ted _____ later today.

3. Yesterday, Alice visited many stores and bought some clothes and makeup.

    → Yesterday, Alice _____ .

4. Let's go to the beach and jump in the water.

   → Let's _____ .

5. My grandfather takes his fishing pole to a farm pond every Sunday.

   → My grandfather _____ every Sunday.

6. When I visit a new city, I like to look around at the sights.

   → When I visit a new city, I like to _____ .

7. I love to put up a small tent by a stream, make a fire, and listen to the sounds of the forest during the night.

   → I love to _____ .

8. I want to take the sailboat out on the water this afternoon.

   → I want to _____ this afternoon.

9. Once a year, we take our skis to our favorite mountain resort and enjoy an exciting weekend.

   → Once a year, we _____ at our favorite mountain resort.

10. Last year on my birthday, my friends and I went up in an airplane, put on parachutes, and jumped out of the plane at a very high altitude.

    → Last year on my birthday, my friends and I

    _____ .

◇ **PRACTICE 3. Identifying gerunds and infinitives. (Charts 13-1 and 13-3)**
Directions: Underline the gerunds and infinitives in the sentences. Circle GER for gerunds. Circle INF for infinitives.

1. GER (INF)   Ann promised <u>to wait</u> for me.
2. (GER) INF   I kept <u>walking</u> even though I was tired.
3. GER INF   Alex offered to help me.
4. GER INF   Karen finished writing a letter and went to bed.
5. GER INF   Don't forget to call me tomorrow.
6. GER INF   David discussed quitting his job several times.
7. GER INF   The police officers planned to work overtime during the conference.
8. GER INF   Kevin would like to grow organic vegetables in his garden.

◇ PRACTICE 4. Gerunds and infinitives. (Charts 13-1, 13-3, and 13-4)
    Directions: Complete the sentences with the gerund or infinitive form of the verb.

   PART I. Complete the sentences with **work**.

   1. I agreed ___to work___.   7. I decided ___to___.
   2. I put off ___working___.   8. I offered ___to___.
   3. I would love ___to work___.   9. I quit ___ing___.
   4. I thought about ___working___.   10. I refused ___to___.
   5. I promised ___to___.   11. I stopped ___ing___.
   6. I began ___to / ing___.   12. I finished ___ing___.

   PART II. Complete the sentences with **leave**.

   13. She expected ___to___.   18. She put off ___i___.
   14. She wanted ___to___.   19. She refused ___to___.
   15. She considered ___i___.   20. She needed ___to___.
   16. She talked about ___i___.   21. She thought about ___i___.
   17. She postponed ___i___.   22. She hoped ___to___.

   PART III. Complete the sentences with **know**.

   23. They seemed ___to___.   28. They want ___to___.
   24. They expected ___to___.   29. They can't stand ___i___.
   25. They would like ___to___.   30. They needed ___to___.
   26. They don't mind ___i___.   31. They appeared ___to___.
   27. They would love ___to___.   32. They hated ___to / i___.

◇ PRACTICE 5. Verb + gerund vs. infinitive. (Charts 13-1 → 13-3)
    Directions: Choose the correct completion.

   1. I would like _____ you and some of my other friends for dinner sometime.
      A. inviting   (B.) to invite

   2. I enjoyed _____ with my family at the lake last summer.
      A. being   B. to be

   3. Ron agreed _____ me move out of my apartment this weekend.
      A. helping   B. to help

   4. My parents can't afford _____ all of my college expenses.
      A. paying   B. to pay

   5. Liang-Siok, would you mind _____ this letter on your way home?
      A. mailing   B. to mail

   6. Do you expect _____ this course? If so, you'd better work harder.
      A. passing   B. to pass

7. Adam offered _____ for me tonight because I feel awful.
   A. working   B. to work

8. I refuse _____ your proposal. I've made up my mind.
   A. considering   B. to consider

9. I wish you would consider _____ my proposal. I know I can do the job.
   A. accepting   B. to accept

10. I don't think I'll ever finish _____ this report. It just goes on and on.
    A. reading   B. to read

11. I would enjoy _____ you in Cairo while you're studying there.
    A. visiting   B. to visit

12. The children seem _____ why they have to stay home tonight.
    A. understanding   B. to understand

13. Don't forget _____ all of the doors before you go to bed.
    A. locking   B. to lock

14. I'm really sorry. I didn't mean _____ your feelings.
    A. hurting   B. to hurt

15. Why do you keep _____ me the same question over and over again?
    A. asking   B. to ask

16. I've decided _____ for another job. I'll never be happy here.
    A. looking   B. to look

17. You need _____ harder if you want to get a promotion.
    A. trying   B. to try

18. Why do you pretend _____ his company? I know you don't like him.
    A. enjoying   B. to enjoy

19. Let's get together tonight. I want to talk about _____ a new business.
    A. opening   B. to open

20. I have a secret. Do you promise _____ no one?
    A. telling   B. to tell

21. The president plans _____ everyone a bonus at the end of the year.
    A. giving   B. to give

22. I have a good job, and I hope _____ myself all through school.
    A. supporting   B. to support

23. I can't wait _____ work today. I'm taking off on vacation tonight.
    A. finishing   B. to finish

24. My neighbor and I get up at six every morning and go _____ .
    A. jogging   B. to jog

◇ **PRACTICE 6. Verb + gerund or infinitive. (Charts 13-1 → 13-4)**
Directions: Choose the correct answer(s). Both answers may be correct.

1. I want _____ the comedy special on TV tonight.
   A. watching   (B.) to watch

2. I'm a people-watcher. I like _____ people in public places.
   (A.) watching   (B.) to watch

3. I've already begun _____ ideas for my new novel.
   A. collecting   B. to collect

4. A group of Chinese scientists plan _____ their discovery at the conference next spring.
   A. presenting   B. to present

5. Whenever I wash my car, it starts _____.
   A. raining   B. to rain

6. Angela and I continued _____ for several hours.
   A. talking   B. to talk

7. I love _____ on the beach during a storm.
   A. walking   B. to walk

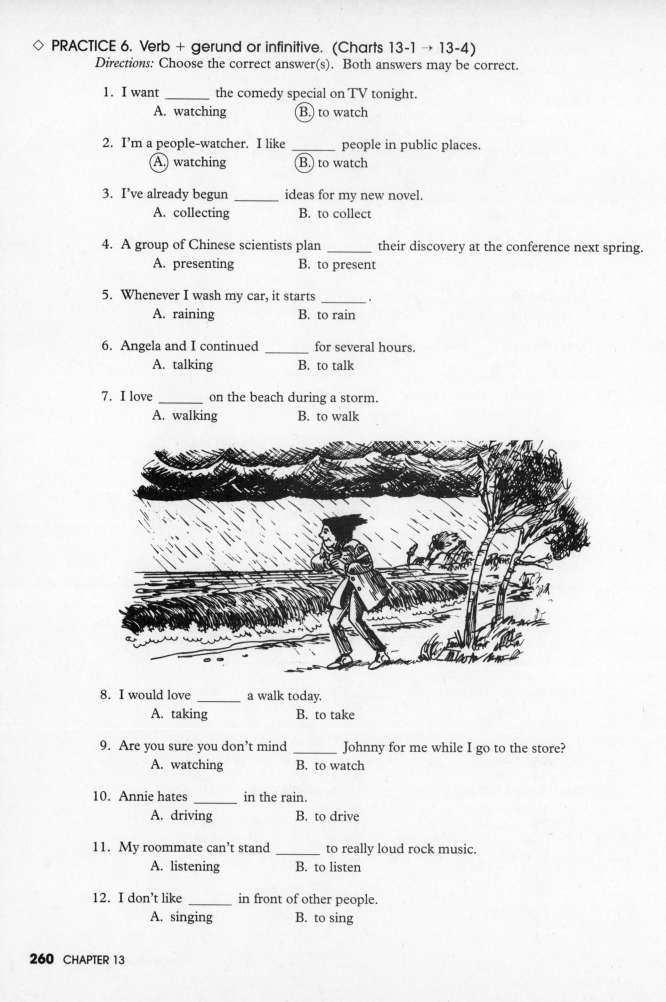

8. I would love _____ a walk today.
   A. taking   B. to take

9. Are you sure you don't mind _____ Johnny for me while I go to the store?
   A. watching   B. to watch

10. Annie hates _____ in the rain.
    A. driving   B. to drive

11. My roommate can't stand _____ to really loud rock music.
    A. listening   B. to listen

12. I don't like _____ in front of other people.
    A. singing   B. to sing

13. Would you like _____ to the concert with us?
    A. going   B. to go

14. Charlie likes to go _____ when the weather is very windy.
    A. sailing   B. to sail

15. Most children can't wait _____ their presents on their birthday.
    A. opening   B. to open

◇ **PRACTICE 7. Verb + gerund or infinitive. (Charts 13-1, 13-3, and 13-4)**
    Directions: Complete the sentences with the infinitive or gerund form of the words in parentheses.

1. Cindy intends *(go)* _____**to go**_____ to graduate school next year.

2. Pierre can't afford *(buy)* _____ a new car.

3. Janice is thinking about *(look)* _____ for a new job.

4. I'm planning *(go)* _____ *(shop)* _____ tomorrow.

5. Would you mind *(pass)* _____ this note to Joanna? Thanks.

6. Tim expects *(go)* _____ *(fish)* _____ this weekend.

7. When Tommy broke his toy, he started *(cry)* _____ .

8. Oscar likes *(go)* _____ to professional conferences.

9. Would you like *(go)* _____ to Sharon's house next Saturday?

10. Mr. Blake appears *(have)* _____ a lot of money.

11. Eric agreed *(meet)* _____ us at the restaurant at seven.

12. Have you discussed *(change)* _____ your major with your academic advisor?

13. The Wilsons went *(camp)* _____ in Yellowstone National Park last summer.

14. What time do you expect *(arrive)* _____ in Denver?

15. Don't put off *(write)* _____ your composition until the last minute.

16. Ken had to quit *(jog)* _____ because he hurt his knee.

17. Don't forget *(call)* _____ the dentist's office this afternoon.

18. How do you expect *(pass)* _____ your courses if you don't study?

19. I haven't heard from Stacy in a long time. I keep *(hope)* _____ that I'll get a

    letter from her soon.

20. Shhh. I'm trying *(concentrate)* _____. I'm doing a problem for my accounting class, and I can't afford *(make)* _____ any mistakes.

21. I'm sleepy. I'd like *(go)* _____ home and take a nap.

22. When are you going to start *(do)* _____ the research for your term paper?

23. Why did Marcia refuse *(help)* _____ us?

24. Khalid tries *(learn)* _____ at least 25 new words every day.

25. I considered *(drive)* _____ to Minneapolis. Finally I decided *(fly)* _____ .

26. Our teacher agreed *(postpone)* _____ the test until Friday.

27. I expect *(be)* _____ in class tomorrow.

28. I enjoy *(teach)* _____ .

29. Mr. Carter continued *(read)* _____ his book even though the children were making a lot of noise.

30. Would you like *(go)* _____ *(dance)* _____ tonight?

31. The Knickerbockers talked about *(build)* _____ a new house.

32. Children like *(play)* _____ make-believe games. Yesterday Tommy pretended *(be)* _____ a doctor, and Bobby pretended *(be)* _____ a patient.

33. My cousin offered *(take)* _____ me to the airport.

◇ **PRACTICE 8. Preposition + gerund. (Chart 13-5)**
Directions: Complete the sentences with the correct preposition and <u>underline</u> the gerund.

PART I. Liz . . .

   1. is afraid ____of____ flying.

   2. apologized _____ hurting her friend's feelings.

   3. believes _____ helping others.

   4. is good _____ listening to her friends' concerns.

   5. is tired _____ working weekends.

   6. is nervous _____ walking home from work late at night.

   7. dreams _____ owning a farm with horses, cows, and sheep.

PART II. Leonard . . .

    8. is responsible _____ closing the restaurant where he works at night.

    9. thanked his father _____ lending him some money.

   10. plans _____ becoming an accountant.

   11. forgave his roommate _____ taking his car without asking.

   12. insists _____ eating only fresh fruits and vegetables.

   13. is looking forward _____ finishing school.

   14. stopped his best friend _____ making a bad decision.

   15. is worried _____ not having enough time for family and friends.

◇ **PRACTICE 9. Preposition + gerund. (Chart 13-5 and Appendix 2)**
    Directions: Complete the sentences. Use prepositions and gerunds.

    1. Bill interrupted me. He apologized ___*for*___ that.

      → Bill apologized ___*for interrupting*___ me.

    2. I like to learn about other countries and cultures. I'm interested _____ that.

      → I'm interested _____ about other countries and cultures.

    3. I helped Ann. She thanked me _____ that.

      → Ann thanked me _____ her.

    4. Nadia wanted to walk to work. She insisted _____ that.

      → We offered Nadia a ride, but she insisted _____ to work.

    5. Nick lost my car keys. I forgave him _____ that.

      → I forgave Nick _____ my car keys when he borrowed my car.

    6. Sara wants to go out to eat just because she feels _____ it.

      → She feels _____ out to eat.

    7. I'm not a good artist. I try to draw faces, but I'm not very good _____ it.

      → I'm not good _____ faces.

    8. Mr. and Mrs. Reed have always saved for a rainy day. They believe _____ that.

      → Mr. and Mrs. Reed believe _____ for a rainy day.

    9. I may fall on my face and make a fool of myself. I'm worried _____ that.

      → I'm worried _____ on my face and _____ a fool

      of myself when I walk up the steps to receive my diploma.

10. The children are going to go to Disneyland. They're excited _____ that.

→ The children are excited _____ to Disneyland.

11. Their parents are going to Disneyland, too. They are looking forward _____ that.

→ Their parents are looking forward _____ there too.

12. Max doesn't like to stay in hotels because he is scared of heights. He is afraid _____ that.

→ Max is afraid _____ in hotels.

◇ PRACTICE 10. Review: gerund vs. infinitive. (Charts 13-1 → 13-5)
Directions: Complete the sentences with the gerund or infinitive form of the verb. Some verbs may require a preposition.

PART I. Use the verb *ask*.

1. Marie is thinking ____*about asking*____ the Petersons over for dinner.

2. Yoko intends ____*to ask*____ for a day off from work this week.

3. Mika insists _____ questions that have already been answered.

4. Chris is excited _____ the new girl in his class to the first school dance.

5. Tarik is new at school. He is nervous _____ anyone to the dance.

6. My father promised _____ the doctor for more information on his illness.

7. Mrs. Kim is responsible _____ parents to help in their children's classroom.

8. Jody would love _____ her former boyfriend to her wedding, but her fiance has said "no."

9. Jerry hates _____ for directions when he's lost.

10. Mansour is very independent and doesn't like _____ others for help with anything.

PART II. Use the verb *fix*.

11. Hiro agreed _____ the window after he broke it.

12. Hiro began _____ it, but he soon needed more parts.

13. Janet intends _____ her bicycle herself.

14. Janet learned how _____ her bicycle from her mother.

15. Her mother learned _____ bicycles from her father.

16. My parents talk _____ their sailboat before summer.

17. The little boy tried _____ his parent's leaky faucet.

18. His father attempted _____ his son's repairs, but couldn't.

19. A plumber promised _____ the faucet the next day.

20. The plumber finished _____ the faucet in ten minutes.

◇ PRACTICE 11. Review. (Charts 13-1 → 13-5)
Directions: Complete the sentences with verbs from the list. Use each verb only once.

adopt	cash	install	stay	use
be	go	lower	take	✓write

1. Ruth puts off _____*writing*_____ thank-you notes for gifts because she doesn't know what to say.

2. The city intends _____ a new traffic light at its most dangerous intersection.

3. I meant _____ my paycheck on the way home, but I forgot.

4. Would you mind _____ at the office late tonight so we can finish our budget review?

5. The bus drivers are on strike. They refuse _____ back to work until they get a new contract.

6. The Adamses want another child. They are discussing _____ a baby from another country.

7. Sue can't afford _____ a vacation this year because she didn't get a pay raise.

8. My mother is an old-fashioned cook. She doesn't believe _____ frozen or canned foods.

9. Little Daniel pretends _____ a monster whenever someone comes to the door.

10. Politicians always promise _____ taxes, but my taxes keep rising.

◇ PRACTICE 12. Review. (Charts 13-1 → 13-5)
Directions: Complete the sentences with the appropriate gerund or infinitive of the word in *italics*. (Some sentences can take either a gerund or an infinitive.) Some sentences require a preposition as well.

1. Matthew wanted to *go* to a different doctor for his back pain. He considered

_____*going*_____ to a specialist.

2. Jim would rather walk than *drive* to work. Instead _____*of driving*_____ , Jim walks along bike trails to his office.

3. I need to drive to the airport, but I don't want to *park* there. I'm not planning _____ there because it's too expensive.

4. I never *watch* commercials on TV. In fact, I can't stand _____ TV commercials, so I generally watch videotaped shows.

5. Joanne's hobby is *cooking*. She loves _____ gourmet meals for friends and relatives.

6. Here's some fresh bread I just *baked*. I enjoy _____ a variety of breads. They're so much better than store-bought.

7. Martina is nervous about *going* to the dentist for a filling. She has been afraid _____ _____ the dentist since she was a little girl.

8. Walter's dream is to *become* a doctor in a rural area. He has dreamed _____ _____ a doctor since he was hospitalized as a child.

9. Nathan *has* a chocolate milkshake every afternoon for a snack. He often feels like _____ two, but he doesn't.

10. Every morning, rain or shine, Debbie rises early and stretches. Then she goes outside and *runs* for 30 minutes. Every morning, Debbie goes _____ for half an hour.

11. Marta's neighbors *watered* her plants while she was out of town, and she thanked them with a bouquet of flowers when she returned. Marta thanked her neighbors _____ _____ her flowers while she was gone.

12. Sandy *spoke* harshly to her secretary one morning without meaning to. She immediately apologized _____ harshly.

13. Mark *washes* all his clothes in hot water. Although his roommates tell him hot water could damage some clothes, he doesn't listen. He insists _____ all his clothes in hot water.

14. The little girl didn't see the car rolling slowly toward her. No one was in it, and fortunately a neighbor jumped into the car and stopped it before it could *hit* her. The neighbor stopped the car _____ the girl.

15. When Rita came to work, her eyes *were* red and she appeared upset, but she said everything was OK. Later, she was laughing and looked more relaxed. Rita seemed _____ better.

16. If the construction company doesn't complete the highway repairs on time, it will have to pay a fine for every day it is late. Crews are working around the clock to *repair* the highway. They believe they will finish _____ it on time.

17. Richard's company is reorganizing. Some people will lose their jobs, and others will *get* new positions. Richard really likes this firm and hopes _____ a new position.

18. Christine grew up in a family of ten children. She enjoys her brothers and sisters, but doesn't want to *have* such a large family herself. She plans _____ a smaller family.

19. Noelle started her own company and hasn't had a vacation in three years. She doesn't feel she can *take* a vacation until the company is financially stable. She is looking forward _____ a vacation when the company is more financially secure.

20. Tang has been studying medicine abroad for two years and hasn't *seen* his family in all that time. He is going home next week and is very excited _____ his family.

◇ PRACTICE 13. BY + gerund. (Chart 13-6)
Directions: Describe what the people did by using *by* + a gerund.

1.   MARY: How did you comfort the child?
      SUE: I held him in my arms.

      → Sue comforted the child ____*by holding*____ him in her arms.

2.   PAT: How did you improve your vocabulary?
      NADIA: I read a lot of books.

      → Nadia improved her vocabulary _____ a lot of books.

3.   KIRK: How did Grandma amuse the children?
      SALLY: She read them a story.

      → Grandma amused the children _____ them a story.

4. MASAKO: How did you improve your English?
      PEDRO: I watched TV a lot.

      → Pedro improved his English _____ TV a lot.

5. JEFFREY: How did you catch up with the bus?
      JIM: I ran as fast as I could.

      → Jim caught up with the bus _____ as fast as he could.

6. MR. LEE: How did you earn your children's respect?
   MR. FOX: I treated them with respect at all times.

      → Mr. Smith earned his children's respect _____ them with respect at all times.

◇ **PRACTICE 14. BY + gerund. (Chart 13-6)**
   Directions: Complete the sentences in Column A with *by* + an appropriate idea from Column B.

   Example: I arrived on time
      → *I arrived on time by taking a taxi instead of a bus.*

Column A	**Column B**
1. I arrived on time	A. tighten the loose screws
2. I put out the fire	B. count its rings
3. Giraffes can reach the leaves at the tops of trees	C. read the directions on the package
4. I fixed the chair	D. walk on the bottom of the riverbed
5. Sylvia was able to buy an expensive stereo system	E. pour water on it
6. A hippopotamus can cross a river	F. work all through the night
7. I figured out how to cook the noodles	G. stretch their long necks
8. Pam finished her project on time	H. save her money for two years
9. You can figure out how old a tree is	✓I. take a taxi instead of a bus

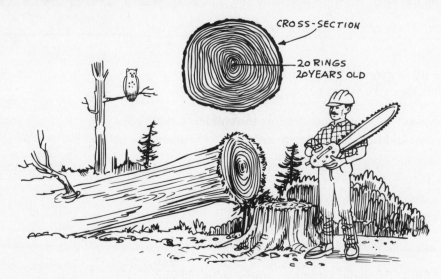

◇ **PRACTICE 15. BY vs. WITH. (Chart 13-6)**
   Directions: Complete the sentences with *by* or *with*.

   1. Alice greeted me _____with_____ a smile.

   2. Ms. Williams goes to work every day _____by_____ bus.

   3. I pounded the nail into the wood _____ a hammer.

   4. Tom went to the next city _____ train.

   5. I got in touch with Bill _____ phone.

   6. Po eats _____ chopsticks.

   7. I didn't notice that the envelope wasn't addressed to me. I opened it _____ mistake.

   8. I sent a message to Ann _____ fax.

   9. Jack protected his eyes from the sun _____ his hand.

10. Janice put out the fire _____ a bucket of water.

11. I pay my bills _____ mail.

12. I solved the math problem _____ a calculator.

13. We traveled to Boston _____ car.

14. The rider kicked the sides of the horse _____ her heels.

15. Jim was extremely angry. He hit the wall _____ his fist.

16. At the beach, Julie wrote her name in the sand _____ her finger.

◇ PRACTICE 16. Gerund as subject; IT + infinitive. (Chart 13-7)

Directions: Complete the sentences by using *a gerund as the subject* or *it* + infinitive. Add the word *is* where appropriate. Use the verbs in the list.

complete	eat	live
drive	✓learn	swim

1. a. _____It is_____ easy for anyone _____to learn_____ how to cook an egg.

   b. _____Learning_____ how to cook an egg _____is_____ easy for anyone.

2. a. _____ nutritious food _____ important for your health.

   b. _____ important for your health _____ nutritious food.

3. a. _____ on the wrong side of the road _____ against the law.

   b. _____ against the law _____ on the wrong side of the road.

4. a. _____ fun for both children and adults _____ in the ocean.

   b. _____ in the ocean _____ fun for both children and adults.

5. a. _____ expensive _____ in a dormitory?

   b. _____ in a dormitory expensive?

6. a. _____ difficult _____ these sentences correctly?

   b. _____ these sentences correctly difficult?

◇ PRACTICE 17. Purpose: TO vs. FOR. (Chart 13-8)

Directions: Rewrite the sentences. Use *it ... for someone* + *an infinitive phrase.* Use the adjective in parentheses.

1. Shy people have a hard time meeting others at social events. *(difficult)*

   _____It is difficult for shy people to meet_____ others at social events.

2. Babies enjoy looking at black-and-white objects. *(interesting)*

   _____ at black-and-white objects.

3. In many cultures, young children sleep in the same room as their parents. *(customary)*

   In many cultures, _____ in the same

   room as their parents.

4. Airline pilots need to have good eyesight. *(necessary)*

   _____ good eyesight.

5. Many teenagers can't wake up early. *(hard)*

   _____ early.

6. Elderly people need to keep their minds active. *(important)*

   _____ their minds active.

7. People don't like listening to monotone speakers. *(boring)*

   _____ to monotone speakers.

8. Students need to have strategies to remember new information. *(necessary)*

   _____ strategies to remember new

   information.

9. Scientists will never know the origin of every disease in the world. *(impossible)*

   _____ the origin of every disease in

   the world.

10. Parents should teach their children by modeling good behavior. *(important)*

    _____ their children by modeling

    good behavior.

11. People are often more critical of others than of themselves. *(easy)*

    _____ more critical of others than of

    themselves.

12. Small children shouldn't cross a busy street without help *(dangerous)*

    _____ a busy street without help.

◇ PRACTICE 18. Purpose: TO vs. FOR. (Chart 13-9)
Directions: Complete the sentences with *to* or *for*.

PART I. Yesterday, I called the doctor's office . . .

1. _____for_____ an appointment.
2. _____to_____ make an appointment.
3. _____ get a prescription.
4. _____ a prescription.
5. _____ ask a question.
6. _____ get some advice.
7. _____ some advice.

PART II. Yesterday, Chuck stayed after class . . .

8. _____ get help from the teacher.
9. _____ talk with the teacher.
10. _____ a talk with the teacher.
11. _____ extra help.
12. _____ finish a project.
13. _____ work with other students.
14. _____ a meeting with other students.
15. _____ help plan a class party.

◇ PRACTICE 19. Purpose: TO vs. FOR. (Chart 13-9)
Directions: Complete the sentences with *to* or *for*.

1. We wear coats in the winter _____to_____ keep warm.
2. We wear coats in the winter _____for_____ warmth.
3. Mark contacted a lawyer _____ legal advice.
4. Mark contacted a lawyer _____ discuss a legal problem.
5. Sam went to the hospital _____ an operation.
6. I hired a cab _____ take me to the boat dock.
7. Frank went to the library _____ review for the test.
8. I play tennis twice a week _____ exercise and relaxation.
9. Jennifer used some medicine _____ cure an infection on her arm.
10. I lent Yvette money _____ her school expenses.
11. I went to my manager _____ permission to take the rest of the day off.

◇ PRACTICE 20. (IN ORDER) TO. (Chart 13-9)
Directions: Combine the given phrases in *italics* to create sentences using *(in order) to*.

1. *watch the news + turn on the TV*

   After he got home from work, Jack _____turned on the TV (in order) to watch_____
   _____the news._____

2. *wash his clothes + go to the laundromat*

   Every weekend Martin _____
   _____

3. *run + get to class on time*

Every morning Jeannette _____

_____

4. *let in some fresh air + open the bedroom windows*

Every night I _____

5. *ask them for some money + write a letter to his parents*

Sometimes Pierre _____

6. *listen to a baseball game + have the radio on*

Some afternoons at work, my co-workers _____

_____

7. *study in peace and quiet + go to the library*

Some evenings, I _____

◇ **PRACTICE 21. TOO vs. ENOUGH. (Chart 13-10)**

Directions: Complete the sentences with the words in parentheses and ***too*** or ***enough***.

1. I have a tight schedule tomorrow, so I can't go to the park.

    a. *(time)* I don't have _____enough time to go_____ to the park.

    b. *(busy)* I'm _____too busy to go_____ to the park.

2. I'm pretty short. I can't touch the ceiling.

    a. *(tall)* I'm not _____ to touch the ceiling.

    b. *(short)* I'm _____ to touch the ceiling.

3. Tom has been out of work for months. He can't pay any of his bills.

    a. *(money)* Tom doesn't have _____ to pay his bills.

    b. *(poor)* Tom is _____ to pay his bills.

4. This tea is very hot. I need to wait a while until I can drink it.

    a. *(hot)* This tea is _____ to drink.

    b. *(cool)* This tea isn't _____ to drink.

5. I feel sick. I don't want to eat anything.

    a. *(sick)* I feel _____.

    b. *(well)* I don't feel _____.

6. Susie is only six years old. She can't stay home by herself.

    a. *(old)* _____.

    b. *(young)* _____.

◇ PRACTICE 22. TOO vs. ENOUGH. (Chart 13-10)
    Directions: Complete the sentences with ***too, enough,*** or **Ø**.

1. I think this problem is ____*Ø*____ important __*enough*__ to require our immediate
   attention.

2. Nora is not ____*too*____ tired ____*Ø*____ to finish the project before she goes home.

3. I can't take the citizenship test next week. I haven't had _____ time _____
   to study for it.

4. The sun is _____ bright _____ to look at directly.

5. You can do this math problem by yourself. You're _____ smart _____ to
   figure it out.

6. Our company is _____ successful _____ to start several new branches
   overseas.

7. My niece doesn't drive yet. She's _____ young _____ to get a driver's
   license.

8. Robert is an amazing runner. His coach thinks he is _____ good _____
   to begin training for an Olympic marathon.

9. Only one person volunteered to help us. We don't have _____ help _____
   to finish this task.

10. Look at the children watching the clowns. They can't sit still. They're _____
    excited _____ to stay in their chairs.

11. I would love to go hiking with you in the mountains, but I don't think I have _____
    energy or strength _____ to hike for two days.

12. The heat outside is terrible! It's _____ hot _____ to fry an egg on the
    sidewalk!

◇ PRACTICE 23. Gerund vs. infinitive. (Chapter 13)
    Directions: <u>Underline</u> the gerunds and infinitives.

1. Do you enjoy <u>being</u> alone sometimes, or do you prefer <u>to be</u> with other people all the time?

2. My son isn't old enough to stay home alone.

3. Jim offered to help me with my work.

4. I called my friend to thank her for the lovely gift.

5. Mary talked about going downtown tomorrow, but I'd like to stay home.

6. It is interesting to learn about earthquakes.

7. Approximately one million earthquakes occur around the world in a year's time. Six thousand can be felt by humans. Of those, one hundred and twenty are strong enough to cause serious damage to buildings, and twenty are violent enough to destroy a city.

8. It's important to recognize the power of nature. A recent earthquake destroyed a bridge in California. It took five years for humans to build the bridge. It took nature fifteen seconds to knock it down.

9. Predicting earthquakes is difficult. I read about one scientist who tries to predict earthquakes by reading the daily newspaper's lost-and-found ads for lost pets. He believes that animals can sense an earthquake before it comes. He thinks they then begin to act strangely. Dogs and cats respond to the threat by running away to a safer place. By counting the number of ads for lost pets, he expects to be able to predict when an earthquake will occur.

◇ **PRACTICE 24. Gerund vs. infinitive. (Chapter 13)**
    Directions: Complete the sentences with the words in parentheses: gerund or infinitive.

1. *(study)* _____Studying_____ English is fun.

2. My boss makes a habit of *(jot)*★ _____ quick notes to her employees when they've done a good job.

3. From the earth, the sun and the moon appear *(be)* _____ almost the same size.

4. A: I don't like airplanes.

   B: Why? Are you afraid of *(fly)* _____?

   A: No, I'm afraid of *(crash)* _____ .

5. A: Let's quit *(argue)* _____ . We're getting nowhere. Let's just agree *(disagree)* _____ and still *(be)* _____ friends.

   B: Sounds good to me. And I apologize for *(raise)* _____ my voice. I didn't mean *(yell)* _____ at you.

   A: That's okay. I didn't intend *(get)* _____ angry at you either.

6. A: David, why did you want *(sneak)* _____ into the movie theater without *(pay)* _____?

   B: I don't know, Mom. My friends talked me into *(do)* _____ it, I guess.

★*Jot* = write quickly and briefly.

A: That's not a very good reason. <u>You</u> are responsible for your actions, not your friends.

B: I know. I'm sorry.

A: How does this make you feel? Do you like yourself for *(try)* _____ *(sneak)* _____ into the theater?

B: No. It doesn't make me feel good about myself.

A: You're young. We all have lessons like this to learn as we grow up. Just remember: It's essential for you *(have)* _____ a good opinion of yourself. It's very important for all of us *(like)* _____ ourselves. When we do something wrong, we stop *(like)* _____ ourselves, and that doesn't feel good. Do you promise never *(do)* _____ anything like that again?

B: Yes. I promise! I'm really sorry, Mom.

7. People in the modern world are wasteful of natural resources. For example, every three months, people in North America throw away enough aluminum *(build)* _____ an entire airplane.

8. I am so busy! I have just enough time *(do)* _____ what I need *(do)* _____, but not enough time *(do)* _____ what I'd like *(do)* _____.

9. A: What do you feel like *(do)* _____ this afternoon?

B: I feel like *(go)* _____ *(shop)* _____ at the mall.

A: I feel like *(go)* _____ to a used car lot and *(pretend)* _____ *(be)* _____ interested in *(buy)* _____ a car.

B: You're kidding. Why would you want *(do)* _____ that?

A: I like cars. Maybe we could even take one out for a test drive. You know I'm planning *(get)* _____ a car as soon as I can afford *(buy)* _____ one. I can't wait *(have)* _____ my own car. Maybe we'll find the car of my dreams at a used car lot. Come on. It sounds like fun.

B: Nah. Not me. You go ahead. *(pretend)* _____ *(be)* _____ interested in *(buy)* _____ a used car isn't my idea of fun.

10. A: Have you called Amanda yet?

B: No. I keep *(put)* _____ it off.

A: Why?

B: She's mad at me for *(forget)* _____ *(send)* _____ her a card on her birthday.

A: It's silly for her *(get)* _____ mad about something like that. Just call her and say you are sorry about *(remember, not)* _____ to wish her a happy birthday. She can't stay mad at you forever.

11. One of my good friends, Larry, has the bad habit of *(interrupt)* _____ others while they're talking.

12. In days of old, it was customary for a servant *(taste)* _____ the king's food before the king ate *(make)* _____ sure it was not poisoned.

◇ **PRACTICE 25. Error analysis. (Chapter 13)**
Directions: Correct the errors.

1. I decided not ~~buying~~ ^{to buy} a new car.

2. The Johnsons are considering to sell their antique store.

3. Sam finally finished build his vacation home in the mountains.

4. My wife and I go to dancing at the community center every Saturday night.

5. Suddenly, it began to raining and the wind started to blew.

6. The baby is afraid be away from her mother for any length of time.

7. I am excited for start college this September.

8. You can send your application fax.

9. My country is too beautiful.

10. Is exciting a sports car to drive.

11. My grandparents enjoy to traveling across the country in a motor home.

12. Elena made this sweater with her hands.

13. Swimming it is one of the sports we can participate in at school.

14. That was very good, but I'm too full no eat any more.

15. My mother-in-law went to a tourist shop for buying a disposable camera.

16. Instead to get her degree in four years, Michelle decided traveling abroad first.

17. Swim with a group of people is more enjoyable than swim alone.

18. Is interesting meet new people.

19. Is hard me to stay up past 9:00.

20. The professor thanked his students do well on the test.

CHAPTER 14
Noun Clauses

◇ **PRACTICE 1. Information questions and noun clauses. (Charts 5-2 and 14-2)**

Directions: If the sentence contains a noun clause, underline it and circle NOUN CLAUSE. If the question word introduces a question, circle QUESTION. Add appropriate final punctuation: a period (**.**) or a question mark (**?**).

1.	I don't know <u>where Jack bought his boots</u>**.**	(NOUN CLAUSE)	QUESTION
2.	Where did Jack buy his boots**?**	NOUN CLAUSE	(QUESTION)
3.	I don't understand why Ann left	NOUN CLAUSE	QUESTION
4.	Why did Ann leave	NOUN CLAUSE	QUESTION
5.	I don't know where your book is	NOUN CLAUSE	QUESTION
6.	Where is your book	NOUN CLAUSE	QUESTION
7.	When did Bob come	NOUN CLAUSE	QUESTION
8.	I don't know when Bob came	NOUN CLAUSE	QUESTION
9.	What does "calm" mean	NOUN CLAUSE	QUESTION
10.	Tarik knows what "calm" means	NOUN CLAUSE	QUESTION
11.	I don't know how long the earth has existed	NOUN CLAUSE	QUESTION
12.	How long has the earth existed	NOUN CLAUSE	QUESTION

◇ **PRACTICE 2. Noun clauses. (Chart 14-2)**

Directions: <u>Underline</u> the noun clause in each sentence. Draw brackets around and identify the subject (**s**) and verb (**v**) of the noun clause.

1. I don't know <u>where [Patty] [went]</u> last night.
   (s over Patty, v over went)

2. Do you know <u>where [Joe's parents] [live]</u>?*
   (s over Joe's parents, v over live)

---

*A question mark is used at the end of this noun clause because the main subject and verb of the sentence (*Do you know*) are a question. *Do you know* asks a question; *where Joe lives* is a noun clause.

278

3. I know where Joe lives.

4. Do you know what time the movie begins?

5. She explained where Brazil is.

6. I don't believe what Estefan said.

7. I don't know when the packages will arrive.

8. Please tell me how far it is to the post office.

9. I don't know who knocked on the door.

10. I wonder what happened at the party last night.

◇ PRACTICE 3. Information questions and noun clauses. (Charts 5-2 and 14-2)
    Directions: Underline the noun clause. Change the underlined noun clause to a question.

1.   QUESTION: _Why did Tim leave?_
      NOUN CLAUSE: I don't know <u>why Tim left</u>.

2.   QUESTION: _Where_
      NOUN CLAUSE: I don't know <u>where he went</u>.

3.   QUESTION: _____
      NOUN CLAUSE: I don't know where he lives.

4.   QUESTION: _____
      NOUN CLAUSE: I don't know where he is now.

5.   QUESTION: _____
      NOUN CLAUSE: I don't know what time he will return.

6.   QUESTION: _____
      NOUN CLAUSE: I don't know how far it is to his house.

7.   QUESTION: _____
      NOUN CLAUSE: I don't know who lives next door to him.

8.   QUESTION: _____
      NOUN CLAUSE: I don't know what happened to him.

◇ PRACTICE 4. Information questions and noun clauses. (Charts 5-2 and 14-2)
    Directions: Complete the question and noun clause forms of the given sentences.

1. Marcos left at 11:00.

   When _did Marcos leave?_

   Could you tell me _when Marcos left?_

2. He said good-bye.

   What _____

   I didn't hear _____

3. The post office is on Second Street.

   Where _____

   Could you please tell me _____

4. It's half-past six.

   What time _____

   Could you please tell me _____

5. David arrived two days ago.

   When _____

   I don't know _____

6. Anna is from Peru.

   What country _____

   I'd like to know _____

7. Kathy was absent because she was ill.

   Why _____ absent?

   Do you know _____ absent?

8. Pedro lives next door.

   Who _____ next door?

   Do you know _____ next door?

9. Eric invited Sonya to the party.

   Who(m) _____ to the party?

   Do you know _____ to the party?

10. The Bakers borrowed our camping equipment.

    Who _____ our camping equipment?

    Do you remember _____ our camping equipment?

11. The restrooms are located down the hall.

    Where _____

    Could you please tell me _____

◇ **PRACTICE 5. Noun clauses. (Chart 14-2)**
   Directions: Complete the sentences by changing the given questions to noun clauses.

1. *Who(m) did Helen talk to?* Do you know _____who (m) Helen talked to?_____

2. *Who lives in that apartment?* Do you know _____

3. *What did he say?* Tell me _____

4. *What kind of car does Pat have?* I can't remember _____

5. *How old are their children?* I can't ever remember _____

6. *Why did you say that?* I don't understand _____

7. *Where can I catch the bus?* Could you please tell me _____

8. *Who did Sara talk to?* I don't know _____

9. *How long has Ted been living here?* Do you know _____

10. *What does this word mean?* Could you please tell me _____

◇ **PRACTICE 6. Information questions and noun clauses. (Charts 5-2 and 14-2)**
   Directions: Complete the sentences using the words in parentheses.

1. A: Why *(you, were)* _____were you_____ late?
   B: What?
   A: I want to know why *(you, were)* _____you were_____ late.

2. A: Where *(Tom, go)* _____ last night?
   B: I'm sorry. I didn't hear what *(you, say)* _____ .
   A: I want to know where *(Tom, go)* _____ last night.

3. A: What *(a bumblebee, is)* _____ ?
   B: Excuse me?
   A: I want to know what *(a bumblebee, is)* _____

      _____ .

   B: It's a big bee.

4. A: Whose car *(Oscar, borrow)* _____

      yesterday?
   B: I don't know whose car *(Oscar, borrow)* _____

      _____ yesterday.

5. A: Could you please tell me where *(Mr. Gow's office, is)* _____ ?
   B: I'm sorry. I didn't understand.
   A: Where *(Mr. Gow's office, is)* _____ ?
   B: Ah. Down the hall on the right.

6. A: Rachel left the hospital two weeks ago. When *(she, come)* _____

   back to work?

   B: I have no idea. I don't know when *(she, come)* _____ back to work.

   A: Why *(she, be)* _____ in the hospital?

   B: I don't know that either. I haven't heard. I'll ask Tom. Maybe he knows why *(she, be)*

   _____ in the hospital.

◇ **PRACTICE 7. Noun clauses with WHO, WHAT, WHOSE + BE. (Chart 14-3)**
   Directions: Draw brackets around and identify the subject (**s**) and verb (**v**) of each noun clause.

   1. I don't know who [that man] [is].
             s   v

   2. I don't know [who] [called].
               s   v

   3. I don't know who those people are.

   4. I don't know who that person is.

   5. I don't know who lives next door to me.

   6. I don't know who my teacher will be next semester.

   7. I don't know who will teach us next semester.

   8. I don't know what a lizard is.

   9. I don't know what happened in class yesterday.

   10. I don't know whose hat this is.

   11. I don't know whose hat is on the table.

◇ **PRACTICE 8. Noun clauses with WHO, WHAT, WHOSE + BE. (Chart 14-3)**
   Directions: Add the word *is* to each sentence in the correct place. If nothing is needed, write a slash (/) in the blank.

   1. I don't know who ____/____ that man ___is___ .

   2. I don't know who ___is___ in that room ____/____ .

   3. I don't know what _____ a crow _____ .

   4. I don't know who _____ in the doctor's office _____ .

5. I don't know who _____ that person _____ .

6. I don't know what _____ our new address _____ .

7. I don't know what _____ on the carpet _____ .

8. I don't know what _____ the date _____ today.

9. I don't know what _____ day it _____ .

10. I don't know whose office _____ at the end of the hall _____ .

◇ PRACTICE 9. Noun clauses with WHO, WHAT, WHOSE + BE. (Chart 14-3)
Directions: Complete the sentences by changing the questions to noun clauses.

1. *Who is she?* I don't know _____

2. *Who are they?* I don't know _____

3. *Whose book is that?* I don't know _____

4. *Whose glasses are those?* Could you tell me _____

5. *What is a wrench?* Do you know _____

6. *Who is that woman?* I wonder _____

7. *What is a clause?* Don't you know _____

8. *What is in that drawer?* I don't know _____

9. *Who is in that room?* I don't know _____

10. *What is on TV tonight?* I wonder _____

11. *What is a carrot?* Do you know _____

12. *Who am I?* He doesn't know _____

◇ PRACTICE 10. Noun clauses with WHO, WHAT, WHOSE + BE. (Chart 14-3)
Directions: Complete the dialogues by changing the questions to noun clauses.

1. A: Whose car is that?

   B: I don't know _____whose car that is_____ .

2. A: Whose car is in front of Sam's house?

   B: I don't know _____whose car is in front of Sam's house_____ .

3. A: Who are the best students?

   B: Ask the teacher _____ .

4. A: What time is dinner?

   B: I'm not sure _____ .

5. A: Who's next in line?

B: I don't know _____.

6. A: Whose purse is this?

B: Ask the woman in black _____.

7. A: What are the main ideas of the story?

B: Ask a student _____.

8. A: Whose shoes are those under the chair?

B: I don't know _____.

9. A: What causes tornadoes?

B: I'm not sure _____.

◇ PRACTICE 11. Noun clauses and yes/no questions. (Charts 5-2 and 14-4)
Directions: Change each yes/no question to a noun clause.

1. YES/NO QUESTION: Is Tom coming?

   NOUN CLAUSE: I wonder _____*if (whether) Tom is coming*_____.

2. YES/NO QUESTION: Has Jin finished medical school yet?

   NOUN CLAUSE: I don't know _____.

3. YES/NO QUESTION: Does Daniel have any time off soon?

   NOUN CLAUSE: I don't know _____.

4. YES/NO QUESTION: Is the flight on time?

   NOUN CLAUSE: Can you tell me _____?

5. YES/NO QUESTION: Is there enough gas in the car?

   NOUN CLAUSE: Do you know _____?

6. YES/NO QUESTION: Is Yuki married?

   NOUN CLAUSE: I can't remember _____.

7. YES/NO QUESTION: Are the Petersons going to move?

   NOUN CLAUSE: I wonder _____.

8. YES/NO QUESTION: Did Khaled change jobs?

   NOUN CLAUSE: I don't know _____.

Directions: Complete the sentences using noun clauses. Use *if*.

1. A: Are you going to need help moving furniture to your new apartment?

   B: I don't know ____if I'm going to need____ help. Thanks for asking. I'll let you know.

2. A: Is chicken okay for dinner tonight?

   B: I'm sorry. I couldn't hear you with the TV on.

   A: I want to know _____ okay for dinner tonight.

3. A: Does the new teaching position include health insurance?

   B: Oh, I'm sorry. Were you talking to me? I wasn't listening.

   A: Yes. I'd like to know _____ health insurance.

4. A: Will there be a movie on this flight?

   B: I'll ask the flight attendant. Excuse me, we're wondering _____

   _____ on this flight.

5. A: Does Greg have to come with us?

   B: Shhh. Don't ask _____ with us. Of course he does.

   He's your brother!

6. A: Do penguins ever get cold?

   B: That's an interesting question. I don't know _____

   cold.

7. A: Can I drive the car to the store, Dad?

   B: Are you serious? Of course not! Why do you ask _____ the car

   to the store? You haven't passed your driver's test.

8. A: Has Nasser already left the party?

   B: Sorry, it's so noisy here. I didn't catch that.

   A: I need to know _____ the party.

◇ PRACTICE 13. Noun clauses. (Charts 5-2, 14-2, and 14-4)

Directions: Change the questions to noun clauses.

1. *Is Karen at home?* Do you know ____if (whether) Karen is____ at home?

2. *Where did Karen go?* Do you know ____where Karen went?____

3. *How is Pat feeling today?* I wonder _____ today.

4. *Is Pat feeling better today?* I wonder _____ better today.

5. *Does the bus stop here?* Do you know _____ here?

6. *Where does the bus stop?* I wonder _____

7. *Why is Elena absent today?* The teacher wants to know _____ today.

8. *Is Elena going to be absent again tomorrow?* I wonder _____ _____ again tomorrow.

9. *Should I buy that book?* I wonder _____ that book.

10. *Which book should I buy?* I wonder _____

11. *Are we going to have a test tomorrow?* Let's ask the teacher _____ _____ a test tomorrow.

12. *Is there a Santa Claus?* The little boy wants to know _____ a Santa Claus.

◇ **PRACTICE 14. Noun clauses. (Charts 14-2 and 14-4)**

Directions: Complete the sentences with the correct form of the verbs. Pay special attention to the use of final **-s/-es**.

1. Does it rain a lot here?

   Could you tell me if it ____rains____ a lot here?

2. How hot does it get in the summer?

   Could you tell me how hot it _____ in the summer?

3. What do people like to do here?

   Could you tell me what people _____ to do here?

4. Does Bus #10 run on holidays?

   Could you tell me if Bus #10 _____ on holidays?

5. Do the buses run on holidays?

   Could you tell me if the buses _____ on holidays?

6. How long does it take to get to the city?

   Could you tell me how long it _____ to get to the city?

7. What do people enjoy most about this area?

   Could you tell me what people _____ most about this area?

8. Does it seem like an expensive place to live?

   Could you tell me if it _____ like an expensive place to live?

◇ **PRACTICE 15. THAT-clauses. (Charts 14-5 and 14-6)**

Directions: Add the word ***that*** to the sentences at the appropriate places to mark the beginning of a noun clause.

1. I'm sorry ∧ you won't be here for Joe's party.
   (handwritten: that)

2. I predict Jim and Sue will get married before the end of the year.

3. I'm surprised you sold your bicycle.

4. Are you certain Mr. McVay won't be here tomorrow?

5. Did you notice Marco shaved off his mustache?

6. John is pleased Claudio will be here for the meeting.

7. Anna was convinced I was angry with her, but I wasn't.

8. It's a fact the Nile River flows north.

9. A: Guido is delighted you can speak Italian.

   B: I'm surprised he can understand my Italian. It's not very good.

10. A: How do you know it's going to be nice tomorrow?

    B: I heard the weather report.

    A: So? The weather report is often wrong, you know. I'm still worried it'll rain on our picnic.

11. A: Mrs. Lane hopes we can go with her to the museum tomorrow.

    B: I don't think I can go. I'm supposed to babysit my little brother tomorrow.

    A: Oh, too bad. I wish you could join us.

12. A: Do you think technology benefits humankind?

B: Of course. Everyone knows modern inventions make our lives better.

A: I'm not sure that's true. For example, cars and buses provide faster transportation, but

they pollute our air. Air pollution can cause lung disease and other illnesses.

◇ **PRACTICE 16. THAT-clauses. (Charts 14-5 and 14-6)**
   Directions: Complete the sentences with clauses from the list.

> All people are equal.
> Flying in an airplane is safer than riding in a car.
> He always twirls his mustache when he's nervous.
> High school students in the United States don't study as hard as the students in my country do.
> A huge monster was chasing me.
> I should study tonight.
> I will get married someday.
> ✓I will have a peanut butter sandwich.
> John "Cat Man" Smith stole Mrs. Adams' jewelry.
> More than half of the people in the world go hungry every day.
> People are pretty much the same everywhere.
> Plastic trash kills thousands of marine animals every year.

1. I'm hungry. I guess _____(that) I will have a peanut butter sandwich._____

2. I have a test tomorrow. I suppose _____ , but I'd rather

   go to a movie.

3. Why are you afraid to fly in an airplane? Read this report. It proves _____

   _____

4. Right now I'm single. I can't predict my future exactly, but I assume _____

   _____

5. Last night I had a bad dream. In fact, it was a nightmare. I dreamed _____

   _____

6. The police are investigating the burglary. They don't have much evidence, but they suspect

_____

7. My cousin feels that people in the United States are unfriendly, but I disagree with him. I've

discovered _____

8. I've learned many things about life in the United States since I came here. For example, I've

learned _____

_____

9. I always know when Paul is nervous. Have you ever noticed _____

_____

10. I believe that it is wrong to judge another person on the basis of race, religion, or sex. I

believe _____

11. World hunger is a serious problem. Do you realize _____

_____

12. Don't throw that plastic bag into the sea! Don't you know _____

_____

◇ **PRACTICE 17. THAT-clauses. (Charts 14-5 and 14-6)**
Directions: Write sentences with the given information. Combine one of the verbs in parentheses with a noun clause.

1. Smoking in public places should be prohibited. *(feel / don't feel)*
   → *I feel (don't feel) that smoking in public places should be prohibited.*

2. I'm living in this country. *(regret / don't regret)*

3. When will I die? *(would like to know / wouldn't like to know)*

4. There will be peace in the world soon. *(doubt / don't doubt)*

5. What was I like as a child? *(remember / can't remember)*

6. Why does the world exist? *(wonder / don't wonder)*

7. Someone may make unwise decisions about my future. *(am afraid / am not afraid)*

8. What do I want to do with my life? *(know / don't know)*

◇ **PRACTICE 18. THAT-clauses. (Chart 14-6)**

Directions: Write two sentences for each situation. Use the words in parentheses with a noun clause.

1. The Jensens celebrated the graduation of their granddaughter Alice from the university. After graduation, she was offered a good job in chemical research in a nearby town. *(be pleased)*
   → *The Jensens are pleased that their granddaughter graduated from the university. They are pleased that she was offered a good job.*

2. Po was asleep. Around one in the morning the smoke alarm in his apartment rang. He woke up and discovered that his apartment building was on fire. *(be lucky)*

3. Ming Soo didn't study for her math exam. Afterward, she thought she had failed, but got one of the highest grades in the class. Her teacher had known she would do well and praised her for earning such a high grade. *(be surprised)*

4. Karen lent her cousin Mark some money. She heard that he left town. He owed a lot of people money. She needs the money she gave her cousin. Her children need new shoes, but she can't afford to buy them. *(be sorry)*

◇ **PRACTICE 19. THAT-clauses. (Chart 14-7)**

Directions: Give the meaning of *so* by writing a *that*-clause.

1. A: Does Alice have a car?

   B: I don't think *so*. (= *I don't think* ____that Alice has a car____ .)

2. A: Is the library open on Sunday?

   B: I believe *so*. (= *I believe* _____ .)

3. A: Does Ann speak Spanish?

   B: I don't think *so*. (= *I don't think* _____ .)

4. A: Did Alex pass his French course?

   B: I think *so*. (= *I think* _____ .)

5. A: Is Mr. Kozari going to be at the meeting?

   B: I hope *so*. (= *I hope* _____ .)

6. A: Are the photos ready to be picked up at the photo shop?

   B: I believe *so*. (= *I believe* _____

   _____ .)

◇ **PRACTICE 20. Quoted speech. (Chart 14-8)**

Directions: All of the sentences contain quoted speech. Punctuate them by adding quotation marks ("..."), commas (,), periods (.), and question marks (?). Also use capital letters as necessary.

Example: My roommate said the door is open could you close it
→ *My roommate said,* **"T**he door is open. **C**ould you close it?"

1. Alex said do you smell smoke

2. Something is burning he said

3. He said do you smell smoke something is burning

4. Do you smell smoke he said something is burning

5. Rachel said the game starts at seven

6. The game starts at seven we should leave here at six she said

7. She said the game starts at seven we should leave here at six can you be ready to leave then

◇ **PRACTICE 21. Quoted speech. (Chart 14-8)**

Directions: All of the sentences contain quoted speech. Punctuate them by adding quotation marks ("..."), commas (,), periods (.), and question marks (?). Also use capital letters as necessary.

Example: Jack said please wait for me
→ *Jack said,* **"P**please wait for me."

1. Mrs. Hill said my children used to take the bus to school

2. She said we moved closer to the school

3. Now my children can walk to school Mrs. Hill said

4. Do you live near the school she asked

5. Yes, we live two blocks away I replied

6. How long have you lived here Mrs. Hill wanted to know

7. I said we've lived here for five years how long have you lived here

8. We've lived here for two years Mrs. Hill said how do you like living here

9. It's a nice community I said it's a good place to raise children

◇ **PRACTICE 22. Quoted speech. (Chart 14-8)**
Directions: Punctuate the quoted passage. Add quotation marks (" . . . "), commas (,), periods (.), and question marks (?). Also use capital letters as necessary.

"Why weren't you in class yesterday?" Mr. Garcia asked me.

I had to stay home and take care of my pet bird I said. He wasn't feeling well.

What? Did you miss class because of your pet bird Mr. Garcia demanded to know.

I replied yes, sir. That's correct. I couldn't leave him alone. He looked so miserable.

Now I've heard every excuse in the world Mr. Garcia said.

Then he threw his arms in the air and walked away.

Directions: Punctuate the quoted passage. Add quotation marks ("..."), commas (,), periods (.), and question marks (?). Also use capital letters as necessary.

One day my friend Laura and I were sitting in her apartment. We were having a cup of tea together and talking about the terrible earthquake that had just occurred in Iran. Laura asked me, "Have you ever been in an earthquake?"

Yes, I have I replied.

Was it a big earthquake she asked.

I've been in several earthquakes, and they've all been small ones I answered. Have you ever been in an earthquake?

There was an earthquake in my village five years ago Laura said. I was in my house. Suddenly the ground started shaking. I grabbed my little brother and ran outside. Everything was moving. I was scared to death. And then suddenly it was over.

I'm glad you and your brother weren't hurt I said.

Yes, we were very lucky. Has everyone in the world felt an earthquake sometime in their lives Laura wondered. Do earthquakes occur everywhere on the earth?

Those are interesting questions I said but I don't know the answers.

◇ PRACTICE 24. Reported speech: changing pronouns. (Chart 14-9)

Directions: Complete the sentences with the correct pronouns.

1. Mr. Lee said, "I'm not happy with my new assistant."

   Mr. Lee said that ____he____ wasn't happy with ____his____ new assistant.

2. Tom said to his wife, "My parents invited us over for dinner next weekend."

   Tom said that _____ parents had invited _____ over for dinner next weekend.

3. The little girl said, "I don't want to wear my raincoat outside."

   The little girl said that _____ didn't want to wear _____ raincoat outside.

4. Jim said, "A policeman gave Anna and me tickets for jaywalking and told us to cross the street at the pedestrian crosswalk."

Jim said that a policeman had given Anna and _____ tickets for jaywalking and told _____ to cross the street at the pedestrian crosswalk.

5. The Johnsons said to me, "We will send you an e-mail when we arrive in Nepal."

The Johnsons said that _____ would send _____ an e-mail when _____ arrived in Nepal.

6. Jane said, "I want my daughter to feel good about herself."

Jane said that _____ wanted _____ daughter to feel good about herself.

7. Mary and Jack said to me, "We are going to be out of town on the day of your party."

Mary and Jack said that _____ were going to be out of town on the day of _____ party.

8. Bob said to us, "I will join you after I help my neighbors move some furniture."

Bob told us that _____ would join _____ after _____ helped _____ neighbors move some furniture.

◇ PRACTICE 25. Reported speech: changing verbs. (Chart 14-10)
Directions: Complete each sentence with the correct form of the verb.

1. Juan said, "I will meet you at the corner of 5th and Broadway."

   Formal: Juan said (that) he ___would meet___

   Informal: Juan said (that) he ___will meet___ > us at the corner of 5th and Broadway.

2. Maria said, "I'm going to be about 15 minutes late for work."

   Formal: Maria said she _____

   Informal: Maria said she _____ > about 15 minutes late for work.

3. Bob said, "My new car has a dent."

   Formal: Bob said his new car _____

   Informal: Bob said his new car _____ > a dent.

4. Phil said, "I need to borrow some money."

   Formal: Phil said he _____

   Informal: Phil said he _____ > to borrow some money.

5. Sandy said, "I have flown on an airplane only once."

    Formal: Sandy said she _____

    Informal: Sandy said she _____   on an airplane only once.

6. Sami and Jun said, "We are planning a surprise party for Naoko."

    Formal: Sami and Jun said they _____

    Informal: Sami and Jun said they _____ a surprise party for Naoko.

7. Naoko said, "I don't want any gifts for my birthday."

    Formal: Naoko said she _____

    Informal: Naoko said she _____ any gifts for her birthday.

8. Ms. Wall said, "I can babysit next weekend."

    Formal: Ms. Wall said she _____

    Informal: Ms. Wall said she _____ next weekend.

◇ **PRACTICE 26. Reported speech. (Charts 14-9 and 14-10)**

Directions: Complete the sentences. Write the opposite of the quoted speech. Use formal sequence of tenses.

1. A: I have a lot of time.

   B: Oh? I misunderstood you. I heard you say ____(that) you didn't have____ a lot of time.

2. A: I found my credit cards.

   B: I misunderstood you. I heard you say _____ your credit cards.

3. A: The Smiths canceled their party.

   B: I misunderstood you. I heard you say _____ their party.

4. A: It will rain tomorrow.

   B: I misunderstood you. I heard you say _____ tomorrow.

5. A: The Whites got a new dog.

   B: I misunderstood you. I heard you say _____ a new dog.

6. A: Mei exercises every day.

   B: I misunderstood you. I heard you say _____ every day.

7. A: My computer is working.

   B: I misunderstood you. I heard you say _____ .

8. A: Ali isn't coming on Friday.

   B: I misunderstood you. I heard you say _____ on Friday.

◇ PRACTICE 27. Reporting questions. (Charts 14-9 → 14-11)
   Directions: Change the quoted questions to reported questions. Use formal tense sequences.

   1. Eric said to me, "How old are you?"

      → Eric asked me ____how old I was____ .

   2. Ms. Rush said to Mr. Long, "Are you going to be at the meeting?"

      → Ms. Rush asked Mr. Long ____if he was going to be____ at the meeting.

   3. Larry said to Ms. Ho, "Do you have time to help me?"

      → Larry asked Ms. Ho _____ time to help him.

   4. Don said to Robert, "Did you change your mind about going to Reed College?"

      → Don asked Robert _____ mind about going to Reed College.

   5. Igor said to me, "How long have you been a teacher?"

      → Igor asked me _____ a teacher.

   6. I said to Tina, "Can you speak Swahili?"

      → I asked Tina _____ Swahili.

   7. Kathy said to Mr. May, "Will you be in your office around three?"

      → Kathy asked Mr. May _____ around three.

   8. The teacher said to Ms. Chang, "Why are you laughing?"

      → The teacher asked Ms. Chang _____ .

   9. My uncle said to me, "Have you ever considered a career in business?"

      → My uncle asked me _____ a career in business.

◇ PRACTICE 28. Quoting questions. (Charts 14-8 → 14-11)
   Directions: Change the reported speech to quotations. Use quotation marks.

   1. Eric asked me if I had ever gone skydiving.

      → Eric said, ____"Have you ever gone skydiving?"____

   2. Chris wanted to know if I would be at the meeting.

      → Chris said, _____

   3. Kate wondered whether I was going to quit my job.

      → Kate said, _____

4. Anna asked her friend where his car was.

→ Anna said, _____

5. Brian asked me what I had done after class yesterday.

→ Brian said, _____

6. Luigi asked me if I knew Italian.

→ Luigi said, _____

7. Debra wanted to know if I could guess what she had in her pocket.

→ Debra asked, _____

8. My boss wanted to know why I wasn't working at my desk.

→ My boss angrily asked me, _____

◇ PRACTICE 29. Reporting questions. (Charts 14-9 → 14-11)

Directions: Look at the picture and complete the sentences with noun clauses. Use verbs that are appropriate for later reporting (rather than immediate reporting).

A new student, Mr. Sheko, joined an English class. The teacher asked the students to interview him. Later, Mr. Sheko told his friend about the interview.

1. They asked me ___where I was from.___

2. They asked me _____

3. They asked me _____

4. They asked me _____

5. They asked me _____

6. They asked me _____

7. They asked me _____

8. They asked me _____

9. They asked me _____

◇ **PRACTICE 30. Reported speech. (Charts 14-9 → 14-11)**
   Directions: Complete the reported speech sentences. Use the formal sequence of tenses.

1. David said to me, "I'm going to call you on Friday."

   → David said (that) ___he was going to call me___

   on Friday.

2. John said to Ann, "I have to talk to you."

   → John told Ann _____

   to _____ .

3. Diane said to me, "I can meet you after work."

   → Diane said _____ after work.

4. Maria said to Bob, "I wrote you a note."

   → Maria told Bob _____

   a note.

5. I said to David, "I need your help to prepare for the exam."

   → I told David _____ help to

   prepare for the exam.

6. Anna asked Mike, "When will I see you again?"

   → Anna asked Mike when _____

   _____ again.

7. Mr. Fox said to me, "I'm going to meet Jack and you
   at the restaurant."

   → Mr. Fox said _____

   _____ Jack and _____ at the restaurant.

8. Laura said to George, "What are you doing?"

   → Laura asked George _____

   _____ .

9. A strange man looked at me and said, "I'm sure I've met you before."

   → A strange man looked at me and said _____

   before. I was sure I'd never seen him before in my entire life.

◇ **PRACTICE 31. SAY vs. TELL vs. ASK. (Chart 14-11)**
   Directions: Complete the sentences with *said*, *told*, or *asked*.

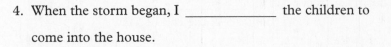

1. Ann _____*told*_____ me that she was hungry.

2. Ann _____*said*_____ that she was hungry.

3. Ann _____ me if I wanted to go out to lunch with her.

4. When the storm began, I _____ the children to
   come into the house.

5. When I talked to Mr. Grant, he _____ he would be at the meeting.

6. Ali _____ his friends that he had won a scholarship to college. His friends
   _____ they weren't surprised.

7. My supervisor _____ me if I could postpone my vacation. I _____ him
   what the reason was. He _____ that our sales department needed me for a project.

8. My neighbor and I had a disagreement. I _____ my neighbor that he was wrong.
   My neighbor _____ me that I was wrong.

9. Fumiko _____ the teacher that Fatima
   wasn't going to be in class.

10. Ellen _____ if I could join her for a movie.
    I _____ I wasn't feeling well, but I
    _____ her what movie she was going to. The
    next day, Ellen _____ me she had enjoyed the movie.

◇ **PRACTICE 32. Reported speech. (Chapter 14)**
Directions: Complete the dialogues by changing the quoted speech to reported speech. Use *said*, *told*,
asked, or *replied*. Practice using the formal sequence of tenses.

1. Bob said, "Where do you live?"   Bob ___*asked me where I lived.*___

2. He said, "Do you live in the dorm?"   He _____ in the dorm.

3. I said, "I have my own apartment."   I _____ my own apartment.

4. He said, "I'm looking for a new   He _____ for a new
   apartment."   apartment.

5. He said, "I don't like living in the dorm."   He _____ in the dorm.

6. I said, "Do you want to move in with me?"   I _____

7. He said, "Where is your apartment?"

He _____

8. I said, "I live on Seventh Avenue."

I _____ on Seventh Avenue.

9. He said, "I can't move until the end of May."

He _____ until the end of May.

10. He said, "I will cancel my dorm contract at the end of May."

He _____ dorm contract at the end of May.

11. He said, "Is that okay?"

He _____

12. I said, "I'm looking forward to having you as a roommate."

I _____ as a roommate.

◇ PRACTICE 33. Reported speech. (Chapter 14)
Directions: Check **all** the sentences that are correct.

1. ____ The teacher asked are you finished?
   ✓ The teacher asked if I was finished.
   ____ The teacher asked if was I finished?
   ____ The teacher asked that I was finished?
   ✓ The teacher asked, "Are you finished?"

2. ✓ Aki said he was finished.
   ✓ Aki said that he was finished.
   ✓ Aki replied that he was finished.
   ✓ Aki answered that he was finished.
   ____ Aki said whether was he finished.

3. ____ Ann told Tom, she needed more time.
   ✓ Ann told Tom she needed more time.
   ____ Ann told to Tom she needed more time.
   ____ Ann told she needed more time.
   ____ Ann said Tom she needed more time.
   ✓ Ann said she needed more time.

4. ✓ Donna answered that she was ready.
   ____ Donna answered was she ready.
   ____ Donna replied she was ready.
   ✓ Donna answered, "I am ready."
   ____ Donna answered if she was ready.

5. ✓ Mr. Wong wanted to know if Ted was coming.
   ____ Mr. Wong wanted to know is Ted coming?
   ✓ Mr. Wong wondered if Ted was coming.
   ____ Mr. Wong wondered was Ted coming.
   ✓ Mr. Wong wondered, "Is Ted coming?"

◇ PRACTICE 34. Reported speech. (Chapter 14)
Directions: Read the dialogues and complete the sentences. Use the formal sequence of tenses.

1. A: *Oh no! I forgot my briefcase! What am I going to do?*
   B: *I don't know.*
   → When Bill got on the bus, he realized _____(that) he had forgotten_____ his briefcase.

2. A: *Where's your bicycle, Jimmy?*
   B: *I sold it to a friend of mine.*
   A: *You what?!*

   → Yesterday I asked my fourteen-year-old son _____.

   He _____ it to a friend. I was flabbergasted.

3. A: *The bus is supposed to be here in three minutes. Hurry up! I'm afraid we'll miss it.*
   B: *I'm ready. Let's go.*

   → I told my friend to hurry because I was afraid _____ the bus.

4. A: *Can you swim?*
   B: *Yes.*
   A: *Thank heaven.*

   → When the canoe tipped over, I asked my friend _____.

5. A: *Do you want to go downtown?*
   B: *I can't. I have to study.*

   → When I asked Kathy _____ to go downtown, she said

   _____ because she _____.

6. A: *Ow! My finger really hurts! I'm sure I broke it.*
   B: *Let me see.*

   → When Nancy fell down, she was sure _____ her finger.

7. A: *Where's Jack? I'm surprised he isn't here.*
   B: *He went to Chicago to visit his sister.*

   → When I got to the party, I asked my friend where Jack _____ .

   I was surprised _____ there. My friend told me

   _____ to Chicago to visit his sister.

8. A: *Will you be home in time for dinner?*
   B: *I'll be home around 5:30.*

   → My wife asked me _____ home in time for dinner. I told her

   _____ home around 5:30.

9. A: *Have you ever been to Mexico?*
   B: *Yes, I have. Several times.*

   → I asked George _____ ever _____ to Mexico. He said

   _____ there several times.

10. A: *Where's my cane?*
    B: *I don't know. Do you need it?*
    A: *I want to walk to the mailbox.*
    B: *I'll find it for you.*

→ Grandfather asked me _____ . I told him

_____ . Then I asked him _____

it. He said _____ to the mailbox. I told him

_____ for him.

◇ **PRACTICE 35. Reported speech. (Charts 14-9 → 14-11)**

Directions: Write a report on the people in the pictures and what they say. Use the formal sequence of tenses.

BEFORE SCHOOL IN THE MORNING

Directions: Correct the errors.

1. Excuse me. May I ask if how old are you?

2. I wonder did Rashed pick up something for dinner?

3. I'm unsure what does Lawrence do for a living.

4. Fernando said, "the best time for me to meet would be Thursday morning.

5. Eriko said to me was I coming to the graduation party. I say her that I wasn't.

6. I hope so that I will do well on my final exams.

7. Antonio asked his mother what does she want for her birthday?

8. I'm not sure if the price include sales tax.

9. My mother said to me that: "How many hours you spent on your homework?

10. Pedro asked is that okay? (*2 answers: direct and indirect speech*)

11. Mika told she would going to stay home today.

12. I'd like to know how do you do that.

13. My parents knew what did Sam and I do.

14. Beth said she had working hard all week but now had some time off.

15. Is a fact that life always changes.

APPENDIX 1
Phrasal Verbs

◇ **PRACTICE 1. Phrasal verbs: separable. (Group A)**
Directions: Complete each sentence with a correct particle from the list. Particles may be used more than once or not at all.

away	*in*	*on*	*up*
down	*off*	*out*	

1. I'd like to listen to some music. Would you please *turn* the radio _____*on*_____?

2. My husband *makes* _____ bedtime stories for our children.

3. My arms hurt, so I *put* the baby _____ for a minute. But he started crying right away, so I *picked* him _____ again.

4. A: We need a plumber to fix our leaky water faucet. You need to call one today.
   B: I will.
   A: Don't *put* it _____ .
   B: I won't. I'll call today. I promise.

5. A: Why are you wearing your new suit?
   B: I just *put* it _____ to see what it looks like.
   A: It looks fine. *Take* it _____ and hang it up before it gets wrinkled.

6. A: I found this notebook in the wastebasket. It's yours, isn't it?
   B: Yes. I *threw* it _____ . I don't need it anymore.
   A: Okay. I thought maybe it had fallen in the wastebasket accidentally.

7. A: I need Jan's address again.
   B: I gave you her address just yesterday.
   A: I'm afraid I've lost it. Tell me again, and I'll *write* it _____ .
   B: Just a minute. I have to *look* it _____ in my address book.

8. A: You'll never believe what happened in physics class today!

   B: What happened?

   A: We had a big test. When I first looked it over, I realized that I couldn't *figure* _____ any of the answers. Our teacher had *handed* _____ the wrong test! We hadn't covered that material yet.

9. A: You're all wet!

   B: I know. A passing truck went through a big puddle and splashed me.

   A: You'd better *take* those clothes _____ and *put* _____ something clean and dry before you go to work.

10. A: *Wake* _____! It's seven o'clock! Rise and shine!

    B: What are you doing!? *Turn* the light _____ and close the window curtain!

    A: My goodness but we're grumpy this morning. Come on. It's time to get up, dear. You don't want to be late.

◇ PRACTICE 2. Phrasal verbs: separable. (Group A)
   Directions: Circle all the correct completions for each sentence.

   1. Lisa took off   *her toys*   *her socks*   *her notebooks.*

   2. Akiko turned off   *the TV*   *the butter*   *the stove.*

   3. Jonas put on   *his new shoes*   *a fire*   *the dishes.*

   4. Benjamin made up   *a story*   *a fairy tale*   *an excuse.*

5. Susanna threw out   *some air*   *some rotten food*   *an old shirt.*

6. Antonio put off   *a doctor's appointment*   *a meeting*   *a trip.*

7. Max figured out   *a puzzle*   *a math problem*   *a riddle.*

8. Kyong handed in   *some candy*   *a report*   *some late homework.*

9. The secretary wrote down   *a message*   *a pencil*   *a phone number.*

10. The mail carrier put down   *a box*   *the mail truck*   *a sack of mail.*

11. I took off   *my coat*   *my bicycle*   *my wedding ring.*

12. Mustafa turned off   *the light*   *the computer*   *the car engine.*

◇ PRACTICE 3. Phrasal verbs: nonseparable. (Group B)
Directions: Complete each sentence with a correct particle from the list. Particles may be used more than once.

from	*into*	*on*	*over*
in	*off*	*out of*	

1. A: Why are your pants so dirty?

   B: I lost my balance when I got ___out of___ the car, and I fell in the mud.

2. A: I was so embarrassed in class today.

   B: What happened?

   A: The teacher called _____ me, and I didn't know the answer.

3. A: The bus is coming. When do I pay?

   B: Don't pay when you get on. Pay the driver when you get _____ .

4. A: You look great! I thought you had the flu.

   B: I did, but I got _____ it very quickly.

5. A: Why haven't we gotten a reply to our letter to the telephone company?

   B: I don't know. I'll look _____ it.

6. A: Guess who I ran _____ today?

   B: Who?

   A: Melanie Nelson, from high school. She's married now and has seven children.

7. A: Mommy, where do butterflies come _____ ?

   B: Well, first they are caterpillars. Then, when the caterpillars become large, they turn into butterflies.

8. A: Hurry! Get _____ the car. We've got to be at the train station in ten minutes.

   B: OK. I'm ready. Let's go.

9. A: I went downtown by mistake today.

   B: How on earth did that happen?

   A: I got _____ the wrong bus. It didn't stop until we were in the city.

◇ **PRACTICE 4. Phrasal verbs: nonseparable. (Group B)**
   Directions: Complete each sentence in Column A with the correct phrase from Column B.

   Example: Annette speaks both French and English because she comes . . .
   → *Annette speaks both French and English because she comes from Quebec.*

   Column A

   1. Annette speaks both French and English because she comes . . .

   2. When Sylvia lost her job, it took her several weeks to get . . .

   3. Our office will need several days to look . . .

   4. When a plane lands, the first-class passengers get . . .

   5. While I was walking in the mall, I ran . . .

   6. When he left the hotel, David got . . .

   7. Mrs. Riley, our math teacher, often calls . . .

   Column B

   A. into your request for medical records.

   ✓B. from Quebec.

   C. over the shock.

   D. in a taxi and went to the airport.

   E. on unprepared students.

   F. into several friends from high school.

   G. off first.

◇ **PRACTICE 5. Phrasal verbs: separable. (Group C)**
   Directions: Complete each sentence with a correct particle from the list. Particles may be used more than once.

away	*down*	*on*	*up*
back	*off*	*out*	

   1. You still owe me the money I lent you. When are you going to *pay* me ____back____ ?

   2. *Turn* _____ the radio! It's too loud! I can't hear myself think.

   3. Debra *put* _____ the fire in the wastebasket with a fire extinguisher.

   4. After I wash and dry the dishes, I *put* them _____ . I put them in the cupboard where they belong.

   5. Before you buy shoes, you should *try* them _____ to see if they fit.

   6. I can't hear the TV. Could you please *turn* it _____ ? No, don't shut it _____ ! I wanted you to make it louder, not turn it off. I want to hear the news.

7. A: That's mine! *Give* it _____ !

   B: No, it's not. It's mine!

   C: Now children, don't fight.

8. A: I don't hear anyone on the other end of the phone.

   B: Just *hang* _____ . It's probably a wrong number.

9. A: I hear that Tom *asked* you _____ for next Saturday night.

   B: Yes, he did. He *called* me _____ a couple of hours ago and invited me to the symphony concert.

   A: The concert's been *called* _____ because the musicians are on strike. Didn't you hear about it?

   B: No, I didn't. I'd better *call* Tom _____ and ask him what he wants to do instead.

10. I don't mind if you look at these maps, but please *put* them _____ in the drawer when you're finished.

◇ PRACTICE 6. Phrasal verbs: separable. (Groups A, B, C)
Directions: Complete the sentences with a given particle where possible. If not possible, write "X."

1. *out*   a. Paulo asked _____out_____ one of his classmates.

   b. Paulo asked one of his classmates _____out_____ .

2. *on*   a. The teacher called _____on_____ Ted for the answer.

   b. The teacher called Ted _____X_____ for the answer.

3. *into*   a. The police are looking _____ the murder, but need help from the public to solve it.

   b. The police are looking the murder _____ , but need help from the public to solve it.

4. *into*   a. Khalifa ran _____ his cousin at the store.

   b. Khalifa ran his cousin _____ at the store.

5. *up*   a. Claire turned _____ the ringer on the phone.

   b. Claire turned the ringer on the phone _____ .

6. *away*   a. Dr. Benson threw _____ a valuable coin by mistake.

   b. Dr. Benson threw a valuable coin _____ by mistake.

7. *down*   a. Yumi's baby cries whenever she puts him _____ .

   b. Yumi's baby cries whenever she puts _____ him.

8. *up*   a. Would you please wake _____ me in one hour?

   b. Would you please wake me _____ in one hour?

9. *away*   a. You can leave the dishes. I'll put them _____ later.

b. You can leave the dishes. I'll put _____ them later.

10. *up*   a. When Joan feels lonely, she calls _____ a friend and talks for a while.

b. When Joan feels lonely, she calls a friend _____ and talks for a while.

11. *off*   a. The hill was so steep that I had to get _____ my bicycle and walk.

b. The hill was so steep that I had to get my bicycle _____ and walk.

12. *from*   a. This fruit is very fresh. It came _____ my garden.

b. This fruit is very fresh. It came my garden _____ .

◇ **PRACTICE 7. Phrasal verbs: separable. (Group D)**
  Directions: Complete each sentence with a correct particle from the list. Particles may be used more than once or not at all.

around	down	in	out	up
back	from	off	over	

1. When I finish writing on one side of the paper, I *turn* it ____over____ and write on the back.

2. When the teacher finds a mistake in our writing, she *points* it _____ so we can correct it.

3. When I write words in this practice, I am *filling* _____ the blanks.

4. When I discover new information, I *find* something _____ .

5. When I need to see information from my computer on paper, I *print* it _____ .

6. When buildings are old and dangerous, we *tear* them _____ .

7. When I turn and go in the opposite direction, I *turn* _____ .

8. When I remove a piece of paper from a spiral notebook, I *tear* the paper _____ of my notebook.

9. When I write something that I don't want anybody else to see, I tear the paper into tiny pieces. I *tear* _____ the paper.

10. When I write information on an application form, I *fill* the form _____ .

11. When I make a mistake in something I write, I erase the mistake if I'm using a pencil. If I'm using a pen, I *cross* the mistake _____ by drawing a line through it.

12. When my teacup is empty, I *fill* it _____ again if I'm still thirsty.

13. When I check my homework carefully before I give it to the teacher, I *look* it _____ .

◇ **PRACTICE 8. Phrasal verbs: separable and nonseparable. (Groups A, B, C, D)**
Directions: Complete the sentences with the particles in *italics*. The particles may be used more than once or not at all.

1. *out, away, back, down, off, on*

   Carol . . .

   a. put ____off____ her vacation because she was sick.

   b. put _____ her boots to go out in the rain.

   c. put the phone _____ when she saw a spider crawling toward her.

   d. put her things _____ in her suitcase after the customs officer checked them.

   e. put _____ the stovetop fire with a small fire extinguisher.

   f. put _____ all the groceries she bought before she started dinner.

2. *out, in, up*

   James . . .

   a. handed _____ his financial report before the due date.

   b. handed _____ cigars when his son was born.

3. *into, off, on, up, over, out of*

   Linda . . .

   a. got _____ the flu in three days and felt wonderful.

   b. got _____ the bus and walked home.

   c. got _____ the bus and sat down behind the driver.

   d. got _____ a taxi to go to the airport.

   e. got _____ the taxi, paid the driver, and left a nice tip.

4. *in, down, up, out*

   a. This book has a few pages missing. The baby tore them _____ .

   b. Before I throw my credit card receipts away, I tear them _____ . I don't want anyone to read them.

   c. The building across the street will be torn _____ to make room for a parking garage.

5. *over, into, up*

   a. The neighbors asked the sheriff to look _____ a crime in their neighborhood.

   b. The sheriff looked _____ a suspect's address on the computer.

   c. The sheriff took the suspect's I.D., looked it _____ , and decided it was fake.

6. *off, down, up, back*

   a. I called Rita _____ several times, but got no answer. I'm a little worried.

   b. The meeting was called _____ because the chairperson was sick.

   c. Jack called and left a message. I'll call him _____ after dinner.

7. *over, up, in, off, back*

    a. My ears are ringing! Please turn _____ the music.

    b. It's cold, and I'm tired. Let's turn _____ and go home.

    c. Could I turn _____ the TV? I can't hear the news.

    d. Joe, the meat needs to be cooked on the other side. Would you turn it _____, please?

8. *in, out, up*

    a. I forgot to fill _____ a couple of blanks on the test. I hope I passed.

    b. Can I take this application home and fill it _____? I don't have much time now.

    c. Jack carries a thermos bottle to work. He fills _____ his cup when he gets thirsty.

◇ **PRACTICE 9. Phrasal verbs: separable. (Group E)**

Directions: Complete each sentence with a correct particle from the list. Particles may be used more than once or not at all.

away	back	off	on	out	over	up

1. It's pretty chilly in here. You might want to leave your jacket ____on____ .

2. Mrs. Jefferson became a widow at a young age. She had to bring _____ six children by herself.

3. Give us a few hours. We'll work this problem _____ and let you know our solution.

4. Those are trick birthday candles. Every time you blow them _____, they light again.

5. My roommate gives homeless people his old clothes. He tries to help them _____ as often as possible.

6. A: Robert has taken Diane _____ several times. They go to restaurants and movies, but he doesn't seem serious about her.

    B: I know. Diane keeps trying to talk _____ their future, but he isn't interested in doing that.

7. A: It's hard to understand our company's policies. All the senior managers are getting large bonuses while the company is laying _____ people in every department.

   B: I know. I need to think _____ whether I want to continue with this job.

8. A: What is your store's return policy?

   B: You can bring clothes _____ within two weeks, and you need your receipt.

9. A: Are you going to meet with your supervisor this morning?

   B: Yes. I'm going to try to bring _____ the idea of a raise.

10. A: What time are you coming home?

    B: Around midnight.

    A: OK. I'll leave some lights _____ .

11. A: We did something that will cheer you _____ .

    B: What's that?

    A: We cleaned _____ your yard and garden while you were in the hospital. You'll see as soon as we get there.

    B: Thanks! What a wonderful surprise.

◇ PRACTICE 10. Phrasal verbs: separable. (Group E)
Directions: Complete the sentences with a phrasal verb from the list.

blow out	cheer up	give away	take back	think over
bring up	clean up	✓lay off	take out	work out

1. Michael is worried. His company is planning to ___lay___ 20% of its workforce ___off___ , and he doesn't have much seniority.

2. If you decide these shoes won't work for you, you can _____ them _____ within seven days.

3. That was so nice of you to water my plants while I was gone. I'd like to _____ you _____ to dinner to thank you.

4. There are ten candles on this cake, Jenny. Can you _____ them all _____ ?

5. Pauline has many clothes in her closet that she doesn't wear. Why doesn't she _____ them _____ ?

6. I have some news that will _____ you _____ . We're getting two weeks additional vacation!

7. Let's set aside some time this weekend and finally _____ this place _____ . This apartment is a mess.

8. The Smiths had a lot of arguments during the first year of their marriage, but I think they've finally _____ their differences _____ . They seem pretty happy now.

9. Buying this house is a huge decision. We really need more time to _____ it _____ .

10. You'd better not _____ the subject of politics _____ with Ron. He becomes very upset when someone disagrees with his point of view.

◇ PRACTICE 11. Phrasal verbs: intransitive. (Group F)
Directions: Complete each sentence with a correct particle from the list. The particles may be used more than once or not al all.

back	in	off	out	to
down	of	on	over	up

1. The plane shook a little when it *took* ____off____ . It made me nervous.

2. Emily's parents are upset because she *goes* _____ with friends every night and doesn't seem to have enough time for her studies.

3. Ken *grew* _____ in a small town and isn't used to the fast pace of the city.

4. I'm afraid we can't hear you in the back of the room. Could you please *speak* _____ ?

5. The computer teacher was so confusing. I didn't learn a thing! I think I'll just *start* _____ with a new teacher next term.

6. I'm exhausted. All week long I've been *getting* _____ between 4:00 and 5:00 A.M. for work.

7. A: Professor Wilson, do you have a minute?
   B: Sure. *Come* _____ and *sit* _____ .

8. A: I don't feel like cooking tonight.
   B: Me neither. Let's *eat* _____ .

9. A: Sorry I'm late. The bus *broke* _____ on the highway, and we had to wait for another.

   B: No problem. The meeting just started.

10. A: Mrs. Taylor is in the hospital again.

    B: What happened?

    A: She *fell* _____ and broke her hip.

11. A: The children are all *dressed* _____ . They look so nice.

    B: Yes. They're having their school pictures taken today.

12. A: I'm really excited about Victoria and Nathan's wedding next month. They're such a great couple.

    B: I'm afraid I have bad news. They *broke* _____ two days ago.

13. A: Ever since I *gave* _____ smoking, I want to eat all the time.

    B: Try chewing gum. It helped me when I quit.

14. A: Look who just *showed* _____ .

    B: Rover, what are you doing here? Dogs were not invited to this party!

15. A: Our new house will be finished April 1.

    B: We can help you *move* _____ _____ your old apartment.

    A: That would be wonderful.

16. A: Where's Julia?

    B: At the doctor's. She *broke* _____ in a rash last night, and she doesn't know what it is.

17. A: Don't stop now. Finish the story for us. Please!

    B: Okay, children. I'll *go* _____ if you promise to listen quietly.

18. A: Buddy, if you get all ready for bed, you can *stay* _____ and watch your favorite cartoon.

    B: O.K., Mom.

19. A: How was your dental appointment?

    B: I tried to *sit* _____ and relax. Even though it didn't hurt, I was nervous the whole time.

20. A: I feel very dizzy. I think I *stood* _____ too fast.

    B: Keep your head down and rest for a minute.

21. A: Someone keeps calling and *hanging* _____ .

    B: Call the phone company. They have a way for you to find out who it is.

◇ PRACTICE 12. Phrasal verbs: intransitive. (Group F)

Directions: Complete each sentence with a correct particle from the list. Particles may be used more than once.

of	out	up

1. *Lazy Leo . . .*

   a. broke ___up___ with his girlfriend because she didn't want to wash his clothes.

   b. stayed _____ all night and didn't come home until morning.

   c. showed _____ late for class without his homework.

   d. goes _____ with friends to parties on school nights.

   e. eats _____ at restaurants because he doesn't like to cook.

   f. moved _____ _____ his apartment without telling the manager.

2. *Serious Sally . . .*

   a. goes to bed very early. She never stays _____ past 9:00.

   b. gets _____ at 5:00 every morning.

   c. speaks _____ in class when no one will answer.

   d. dresses _____ for school.

   e. never gives _____ when she gets frustrated.

   f. grew _____ as an only child.

◇ PRACTICE 13. Phrasal verbs: three-word. (Group G)

Directions: Complete each sentence with **two** particles.

1. When I cross a busy street, I'm careful. I *look* ___out___ ___for___ cars and trucks.

2. Some friends visited me last night. I hadn't expected them. They just *dropped* _____ _____ me.

3. When I put my name on a list for a class, I *sign* _____ _____ it.

4. If I like people and enjoy their company, that means that I *get* _____ _____ them.

5. My cousin never does anything useful. He just *fools* _____ _____ his friends all day, wasting time.

6. When somebody uses the last spoonful of sugar in the kitchen, we don't have any more sugar. That means we have *run* _____ _____ sugar and need to go to the market.

7. I'm glad when I finish my homework. When I *get* _____ _____ my homework, I can go out and play tennis or do whatever else I feel like doing.

8. In some places, it's important to be careful about pickpockets. There are places where tourists have to *watch* _____ _____ pickpockets.

9. If you return from a trip, that means you *get* _____ _____ a trip.

10. Sometimes students have to quit school because they need to get a job, fail their courses, or lose interest in their education. There are various reasons why students *drop* _____ _____ school.

11. Maria was born and raised in Brazil. In other words, she *grew* _____ _____ Brazil.

◇ PRACTICE 14. Phrasal verbs: three-word. (Group G)
   Directions: Complete each sentence with the correct word from the list.

| assignment | ✓gymnastics class | paint | snakes |
| cord | Hawaii | rocks | their neighbors |

1. Martin signed up for a __gymnastics class__ . It starts next week.

2. The Hansens get along well with _____ . They even take vacations together.

3. I can't finish the living room walls because I've run out of _____ .

4. The highway sign said to watch out for _____ . They roll down the hills and sometimes hit cars.

5. As soon as I get through with this _____ , we can go to lunch. I have just one more problem to figure out.

6. Don't fool around with that _____ . You might get an electric shock.

7. You look very rested and relaxed. When did you get back from _____ ?

8. Look out for _____ on the path. They're not poisonous, but they might startle you.

◇ PRACTICE 15. Phrasal verbs: three-word. (Group H)
   Directions: Complete each sentence with **two** particles.

1. Before we consider buying a home in this area, we'd like to *find* __out__ more __about__ the schools.

2. The mountain climbers *set* _____ _____ the summit at dawn and reached it by lunchtime.

3. A: Marty is 43 tomorrow, and she's decided to *go* _____ _____ school.

B: Good for her! It's never too late.

4. A: What do teenagers like to do around here for fun?

B: Some like to *hang* _____ _____ friends at the mall, but I wouldn't recommend it. The management doesn't approve.

5. A: Please *keep* Susie _____ _____ the dog.

B: Is she afraid?

A: No, that's the problem. She'll try to kiss him.

6. A: I'm going grocery shopping. Do you want to *come* _____ _____ me?

B: No, thanks. I've got too much to do. But wait a minute. I *cut* some coupons _____ _____ the paper for you. Let me get them.

7. A: Let's invite the Tangs to *come* _____ _____ our beach house on Saturday.

B: Good idea. I'll call them now.

8. A: We're going out for pizza at Little Italy. Do you want to come along?

B: Sure. I wasn't going to do anything except *sit* _____ _____ my cat tonight!

9. A: Let's *go* _____ _____ Brian's tonight.

B: Shall we call first or surprise him?

10. A: Why don't we *get* _____ _____ Eriko next week?

B: Great! We can talk to her about our new plans for the company.

◇ **PRACTICE 16. Phrasal verbs: three-word. (Group H)**
Directions: Complete the sentences with words from the list that will give the same meanings as the underlined words.

along with	*back to*	*out for*	*over to*
around	✓*out about*	*out of*	*together with*

1. I'd like to <u>get information</u> about the company before I apply for a job there.

I'd like to find ___**out about**___ the company before I apply for a job there.

2. The two brothers <u>left for</u> the lake before sunrise. They wanted to be the first ones there.

The two brothers set _____ the lake before sunrise. They wanted to be the first ones to arrive.

3. After Maria had her first child, she took a year off before she <u>returned to</u> work.

   After Maria had her first child, she took a year off before she went _____ work.

4. Jimmy really needs to find a job. He spends his days <u>sitting</u> at home <u>doing nothing</u>.

   Jimmy really needs to find a job. He spends his days sitting _____ at home.

5. Mark won't be home for dinner. He plans to <u>join</u> his co-workers for a party.

   Mark won't be home for dinner. He plans to get _____ his co-workers for a party.

6. Who wants to <u>accompany</u> me to the doctor's?

   Who will go _____ me to my doctor's appointment?

7. The dog was growling, so the dog catcher <u>approached</u> him very carefully.

   The dog was growling, so the dog catcher went _____ him very carefully.

8. Here's the article I told you about. I <u>removed</u> it from this morning's paper.

   I cut it _____ this morning's paper.

◇ **PRACTICE 17. Review: phrasal verbs. (Appendix 1)**
   Directions: Choose the correct particle.

1. Professor Brown always *calls* _____ the students who sit in the back of the class to answer.
   A. on   B. off   C. out   D. back

2. Tommy takes other children's toys and doesn't want to *give* them _____ .
   A. away   B. back   C. in   D. to

3. Laurie needs to *wake* her roommate _____ every morning because she sleeps through her alarm.
   A. in   B. on   C. up   D. over

4. Bobby, let's take a few minutes and *pick* _____ the toys in your room. They're all over the floor.
   A. over   B. on   C. up   D. away

5. Not enough people *signed up* _____ the gardening class, so it had to be canceled.
   A. for   B. in   C. into   D. with

6. This cold has lasted too long. I feel like I'll never *get* _____ it.
   A. with   B. over   C. away   D. back

7. Aren't you going to *try* _____ these shoes before you buy them?
   A. in   B. on   C. up   D. of

8. *Keep away* _____ the stove! It's still hot.
   A. off   B. from   C. out   D. of

9. We'll feel more confident about the success of our new business after we *pay* _____ our loan.
   A. back   B. up   C. in   D. together

10. Look how nice Jenny's bedroom looks! She spent all morning *cleaning* it _____ .
    A. over   B. back   C. up   D. away

11. Steven had problems early in his career, but he seems to have *worked* them _____ .
    A. up   B. over   C. off   D. out

12. *Watch out* _____ the cat. She might scratch you.
    A. for   B. in   C. on   D. of

13. The fire department recommends keeping a fire extinguisher in your house to *put* _____ fires.
    A. off   B. out   C. back   D. down

14. It took Tim only 20 minutes to *figure* _____ the entire crossword puzzle.
    A. on   B. in   C. up   D. out

15. Although Mrs. Warren had been very wealthy, the size of her estate was quite small when she died. She had *given* _____ most of her money to charities.
    A. away   B. in   C. into   D. from

16. I *cut* your picture *out* _____ the newspaper today. Did you know you were going to be in it?
    A. in   B. off   C. of   D. from

17. Even though Kimberly's been home from the hospital for a week, she doesn't want anyone to *come* _____ to her house. She's still quite weak.
    A. over   B. about   C. into   D. from

18. This hike is pretty exhausting. I don't think I can *go* _____ any farther. I need to rest.
    A. out   B. in   C. to   D. on

19. There's a gas station. I'll wash the windows while you *fill* _____ the tank.
    A. on   B. in   C. out   D. up

20. A fight *broke* _____ among students after school. Fortunately, no one was injured.
    A. out   B. down   C. in   D. off

21. Sometimes when I recite a poem, I forget a line. So I go back to the beginning and *start* _____ .
    A. over   B. to   C. with   D. back

22. The school administrators have started new programs to prevent students from *dropping out* _____ high school.
    A. in   B. off   C. of   D. for

23. Mr. Robinson is happy to lend his adult children money as long as they *pay* it _____ .
    A. up   B. back   C. down   D. for

24. My computer printer isn't working. I can't *print* _____ any of my work.
    A. out   B. in   C. over   D. back

APPENDIX 2
Preposition Combinations

◇ **PRACTICE 1. Preposition combinations. (Group A)**

Directions: Complete the sentences with prepositions.

1. My eight-year-old son Mark is afraid __*of*__ thunder and lightning.

2. My mother really likes my friend Ahmed because he is always polite _____ her.

3. Fifty miles is equal _____ eighty kilometers.

4. A: How do I get to your house?

   B: Are you familiar _____ the red barn on Coles Road? My house is just past that and

   on the left.

   A: Oh, sure. I know where it is.

5. It's so hot! I'm thirsty _____ a big glass of ice water.

6. My boss was nice _____ me after I made that mistake, but I could tell she wasn't pleased.

7. Mr. Watts is often angry _____ some silly little thing that isn't important.

8. A: Harry, try some of this pasta. It's delicious.

   B: No, thanks. My plate is already full _____ food.

9. Four council members were absent _____ the meeting last night.

10. A: Why are you friendly with Mr. Parsons? He's always so mean to everybody.

    B: He's always been very kind _____ me, so I have no reason to treat him otherwise.

11. My sister is very angry _____ me. She won't even speak to me.

12. Is everybody ready _____ dinner? Let's eat before the food gets cold.

13. Ben's wife got a promotion at work. He is really happy _____ her.

◇ **PRACTICE 2. Preposition combinations. (Group A)**
   Directions: Create a sentence by matching each phrase in Column A with a phrase in Column B.
   Use each phrase only once.

Column A	Column B
1. Our dog is afraid __B__	A. about his team's win.
2. The class is curious _____	✓B. of cats.
3. Mr. White is angry _____	C. for a glass of lemonade.
4. Several nurses have been absent _____	D. for the start of school.
5. After gardening all day, Helen was thirsty _____	E. from work due to illness.
6. The workers are angry _____	F. about the snake in the cage.
7. The baseball coach was happy _____	G. to everyone.
8. The kitchen cupboard is full _____	H. of canned foods.
9. I'm not ready _____	I. about their low pay.
10. It's important to be kind _____	J. at his dog for chewing his slippers.

◇ **PRACTICE 3. Preposition combinations. (Group B)**
   Directions: Complete the sentences with prepositions.

1. What are you laughing __at__ ?

2. I can't stop staring _____ Tom's necktie. The colors are wild!

3. A: I don't believe _____ flying saucers. Do you?
   B: I don't know. I think anything is possible.

4. Ted is going to help me _____ my homework tonight.

5. Do you mind if I apply _____ your job after you quit?

6. Kyong is excited about going back home to see her family. She leaves _____ Korea next Monday.

7. I admire Carmen _____ her courage and honesty in admitting that mistake.

8. A: Where did you get that new car?
   B: I borrowed it _____ my neighbor.

9. A: What are you two arguing _____ ?
   B: Modern art.

10. A: Where will you go to school next year?
    B: Well, I applied _____ admission at five different universities, but I'm worried that none of them will accept me.

11. I hate to argue _____ my older sister. I hardly ever win.

12. I'll introduce you _____ my cousins when they come to my wedding next week.

13. Ivan discussed his calculus problems _____ his college advisor.

◇ PRACTICE 4. Preposition combinations. (Group B)
   Directions: Choose the correct preposition.

   1. You're shivering. Would you like to borrow a jacket _____ me?
      (A.) from   B. for   C. with

   2. I'm applying _____ a new management position in my company.
      A. to   B. in   C. for

   3. It's unfortunate that the Bakers are always arguing _____ something.
      A. with   B. about   C. at

   4. Russ believes _____ his ability to succeed under difficult conditions.
      A. in   B. on   C. at

   5. Poor Mr. Miller. No one laughed _____ his story even though it was supposed to be funny.
      A. over   B. at   C. from

   6. It's rather amazing. Gail and Brian plan to get married soon, but they were just introduced
      _____ each other a month ago.
      A. to   B. with   C. at

   7. Please wake me up at 5:00 A.M. tomorrow. I need to leave _____ work early.
      A. from   B. to   C. for

   8. People say they admire me _____ my truthfulness, but sometimes I wonder if I may be too
      honest.
      A. about   B. with   C. for

   9. It's very difficult to discuss serious matters _____ Mark. He always tries to make jokes.
      A. with   B. about   C. at

   10. I'm trying not to stare _____ that man, but his toupee keeps falling off.
      A. at   B. with   C. to

◇ PRACTICE 5. Preposition combinations. (Group C)
   Directions: Complete the sentences with prepositions.

   1. A: Why are you friendly __with/to__ George? I thought you didn't like him.

      B: I'm not crazy _____ his attitude, but I'm his supervisor, so I have to encourage
         him to do better work.

   2. A: Do you think it's bad that I drink so much coffee every day?

      B: I believe too much of almost anything is bad _____ you.

3. I don't know why they fired me. It certainly isn't clear _____ me.

4. A: Dad, I got ninety-five percent on my algebra exam!

   B: I'm proud _____ you. I knew you could do it.

5. A: You seem to be interested _____ aerobic exercise and jogging.

   B: I think regular physical exercise is good _____ everyone.

6. That sweater is very similar _____ mine. Did you buy it at the mall?

7. A: You were up awfully late last night.

   B: I couldn't sleep. I was hungry _____ something sweet, but I couldn't find anything in the kitchen.

8. I have no doubt that I'm doing the right thing. I'm sure _____ it.

9. George Gershwin, an American composer, is most famous _____ his *Rhapsody in Blue*, an orchestral piece that combines jazz with classical music.

10. A: Why is Gary avoiding you? Is he angry about something?

    B: I don't know. I'm not aware _____ anything I did that would upset him.

11. A: Who is responsible _____ this dog? We don't allow dogs in this office!

    B: He belongs to the boss's wife.

    A: Oh.

12. My car is a lot like yours, but different _____ Margaret's.

13. Don't be nervous _____ your job interview. Just be yourself.

14. Teachers need to be patient _____ their students.

15. Ken carelessly dropped the football before he could score, so his team lost. He was very sad _____ that.

◇ PRACTICE 6. Review: preposition combinations. (Groups A and C)
Directions: Complete the sentences with prepositions.

1. Dr. Nelson, a heart specialist, is . . .

   a. proud _____ her work.

   b. famous _____ her medical expertise.

   c. sure _____ her skills.

   d. familiar _____ the latest techniques.

   e. patient _____ her patients.

   f. aware _____ the stresses of her job.

g. interested _____ her patients' lives.

h. nice _____ her patients' families.

2. Her patient, Mrs. Green, is . . .

a. sad _____ her illness.

b. nervous _____ an upcoming surgery.

c. aware _____ her chances for survival.

d. full _____ hope.

e. not afraid _____ dying.

f. curious _____ alternative medicines.

g. ready _____ unexpected side-effects.

h. hungry _____ a home-cooked meal.

◇ PRACTICE 7. Preposition combinations. (Group D)
Directions: Complete the sentences with prepositions.

1. How much did you pay ___*for*___ that beautiful table?

2. A: Did you talk _____ the manager _____ returning that dress?

   B: No. She didn't arrive _____ the store while I was there. I waited _____ her for
   a half an hour and then left.

3. I listened _____ you very carefully, but I didn't understand anything you said.

4. When I graduated _____ college, my mother and father told everyone we knew that
   I had graduated.

5. A: We don't have all day! How long is it going to take for someone to wait _____ us?
   I'm hungry.

   B: We just got here. Be patient. Do you have to complain _____ everything?

6. When did you arrive _____ Mexico City?

7. A: This sauce is delicious!

   B: Well, it consists _____ tomatoes, garlic, olive oil, and lemon juice all blended together.

8. There were ten people at the meeting and ten different opinions. No one agreed _____
   anyone else _____ the best way to solve the club's financial problems.

9. I have to complain _____ the manager. Both the food and the service are terrible.

10. We've invited only family members _____ our wedding. I hope our friends aren't offended.

11. The soccer coaches disagree _____ one another _____ the best way to get their
    team mentally prepared for a game.

◇ PRACTICE 8. Preposition combinations. (Groups B and D)
   Directions: Complete the sentences with the verb in parentheses and the correct preposition.

   1. Margo **got to** the airport early so she wouldn't miss her flight.

      (arrive) Margo _____ **arrived at** _____ the airport early so she wouldn't miss her flight.

   2. The store manager had time to **help** a few customers.

      (wait) The store manager had time to _____ a few customers.

   3. Sigrid **asked me to go** to the symphony with her.

      (invite) Sigrid _____ me _____ the symphony.

   4. Water **is made of** hydrogen and oxygen.

      (consist) Water _____ hydrogen and oxygen.

   5. Sara **stood at the bus stop** for 20 minutes before the bus came.

      (wait) Sara _____ the bus for 20 minutes.

   6. The restaurant owner **discussed** the management changes with her staff.

      (talk) The restaurant owner _____ the management changes with
      her staff.

   7. Joseph **is going to** Athens for graduate work in archeology.

      (leave) Joseph _____ Athens for graduate work in archeology.

   8. Why is that man **continuing to look at** me?

      (stare) Why _____ that man _____ me?

   9. Barb **assisted** her friend **with** her finances.

      (help) Barb _____ her friend _____ her finances.

   10. I **checked** ten books **out of** the library. I'll return them next week.

      (borrow) I _____ ten books _____ the library.

◇ PRACTICE 9. Preposition combinations. (Group E)
   Directions: Complete the sentences with prepositions.

   1. Molly is always looking _____ **for** _____ her keys. She seems so disorganized.

   2. Something's the matter _____ Dan. He's crying.

   3. Do whatever you want. It doesn't matter _____ me.

   4. Look _____ those clouds. It's going to rain.

   5. Are you looking forward _____ your trip to Mexico?

   6. A: Does this watch belong _____ you?

      B: Yes. Where did you find it? I searched _____ it everywhere.

7. I woke up frightened after I dreamed _____ falling off the roof of a building.

8. Tomorrow I'm going to ask my father _____ a ride to school.

9. Tomorrow I'm going to ask my father _____ his work. I don't know much _____ his new job.

10. Please empty that bowl of fruit and separate the fresh apples _____ the old apples.

11. Mr. Sanchez looks a lot _____ a famous movie actor I've seen.

12. My brother Ben warned me _____ taking a shortcut through the back streets. I got lost and was late for a job interview.

◇ PRACTICE 10. Preposition combinations. (Group E)
Directions: Create sentences by matching each phrase in Column A with a phrase in Column B. Use each phrase only once.

Column A

1. The sheriff is searching ___G___
2. The baby keeps looking _____
3. Once again, Rita is looking _____
4. In this picture, Paula looks _____
5. The Browns are looking forward _____
6. Before you do the wash, you need to separate the darks _____
7. Sometimes Joey is afraid to sleep. He often dreams _____
8. Something's the matter _____
9. The sign on the highway warned drivers _____
10. Do you know much _____

Column B

A. about monsters and dragons.
B. to their 20th wedding anniversary.
C. for her glasses. She always misplaces them.
D. about housing prices in this area?
E. about high winds on the bridge.
F. with this car. It's making strange noises.
✓G. for the escaped prisoner.
H. from the whites.
I. at the TV screen. The picture is fuzzy.
J. like her maternal grandmother. The resemblance is very strong.

◇ PRACTICE 11. Preposition combinations. (Group F)
Directions: Complete the sentences with prepositions.

1. Please don't argue. I insist ___on___ lending you the money for your vacation.

2. That thin coat you're wearing won't protect you _____ the bitter, cold wind.

3. A: What's the matter? Don't you approve _____ my behavior?

   B: No, I don't. I think you're rude.

4. A: Can I depend _____ you to pick up my mother at the airport tomorrow?

   B: Of course you can!

5. A: The police arrested a thief in my uncle's store yesterday.

   B: What's going to happen _____ him? Will he go to jail?

6. My friend Ken apologized _____ me _____ forgetting to pick me up in his car after the movie last night. I forgave him _____ leaving me outside the theater in the rain, but I'm not going to rely _____ him for transportation in the future.

7. A: Thank you _____ helping me move to my new apartment last weekend.
   B: You're welcome.

8. It isn't fair to compare Mr. Wong _____ Ms. Chang. They're both good teachers, but they have different teaching methods.

9. I've had a bad cold for a week and just can't get rid _____ it.

10. Excuse me _____ interrupting you, but I have a call on the other line. Could I get back to you in a second?

11. A: I need to be excused _____ the office meeting tomorrow morning.
    B: I was going to announce your promotion at the meeting. Can you change your plans?
    A: I'd love to. It's a dental appointment.

12. People don't die _____ embarrassment, but sometimes they wish they could.

13. I'm sorry. The office staff is very busy right now. It will be a half hour before someone can take care _____ your request.

◇ **PRACTICE 12. Preposition combinations. (Group F)**
Directions: Write "C" beside the correct sentences. Write "X" beside those that are incorrect. In some cases, both may be correct.

1. a. __C__ John needs to be excused from the meeting.
   b. __C__ John excused his associate for the accounting error.

2. a. __C__ Do you approve of your government's international policies?
   b. __X__ Do you approve on the new seat-belt law?

3. a. _____ I apologized for the car accident.
   b. _____ I apologized to Mary's parents.

4. a. _____ Why did you get rid over your truck? It was in great condition.
   b. _____ I got rid of several boxes of old magazines.

5. a. _____ Pierre died of a heart attack.
   b. _____ Pierre's father also died from heart problems.

6. a. _____ It's not a good idea to compare one student to another.
   b. _____ I wish my parents wouldn't compare me with my brother.

7. a. _____ We can rely on Lesley to keep a secret.

   b. _____ There are several people whom my elderly parents rely in for assistance.

8. a. _____ You can relax. I took care about your problem.

   b. _____ The nurses take wonderful care of their patients at Valley Hospital.

◇ **PRACTICE 13. Preposition combinations. (Group G)**
   Directions: Complete the sentences with prepositions.

   1. Please try to concentrate ___on___ my explanation. I can't repeat it.

   2. I spoke _____ my brother _____ your problem, and he said that there was nothing he could do to help you.

   3. All right, children, here is your math problem: add ten _____ twelve, subtract two _____ that total; divide ten _____ that answer; and multiply the result _____ five. What is the final answer?*

   4. I feel pretty good about my final examination in English. I'm hoping _____ a good grade.

   5. A: Did you hear _____ the plans to build a new hotel in the middle of town? It's wonderful!

      B: Yes, I heard, but I disagree _____ you. I think it's terrible! It means the town will be full of tourists all the time.

   6. A: Have you heard _____ your friend in Thailand recently?

      B: Yes. She's having a difficult time. She's not accustomed _____ hot weather.

   7. A: I must tell you _____ a crazy thing that happened last night. Have you heard?

      B: What? What happened?

      A: A hundred monkeys escaped _____ the zoo.

      B: You've got to be kidding! How did that happen?

   8. A: Do you ever wonder _____ the future of our natural environment?

      B: Yes, especially when I read about the deforestation of the rainforests.

   9. A: Is Carol hiding _____ me? Is she afraid of me?

      B: No, but since she turned two years old, she loves to play hide-and-seek. She hides _____ everyone now.

   _____

   *Answer: 10

10. A: Can I tell you _____ the new preschool later? Someone's at the door.

B: Sure.

◇ **PRACTICE 14. Preposition combinations. (Group G)**
Directions: Complete the sentences with the verb in parentheses and the correct preposition.

1. The skiers **wanted** snow for the holiday weekend, but it rained instead.

   (hope)   The skiers _____*hoped for*_____ snow for the holiday weekend.

2. Jenny often **thinks about** people she went to high school with. She's curious about what happened to them.

   (wonder)   Jenny often _____ people she went to high school with.

3. I **cut** the pie **into** eight equal pieces.

   (divide)   I _____ the pie _____ eight equal pieces.

4. Could you **put** another egg **in** the mixture? It's a little dry.

   (add)   Could you _____ another egg _____ the mixture? It's a little dry.

5. An artist **focuses on** the way light strikes his subject.

   (concentrate)   An artist _____ the way light strikes his subject.

6. The prisoners **got away from** their guards and ran into the woods.

   (escape)   The prisoners _____ their guards and ran into the woods.

7. I **am used to** humid weather in the summer.

   (accustom)   I _____ humid weather in the summer.

8. Ben **got the news about** his father's death from his secretary.

   (hear)   Ben _____ the news _____ his father's death from his secretary.

◇ PRACTICE 15. Review: preposition combinations. (Appendix 2)
Directions: Circle the correct preposition in each sentence. In some cases, both prepositions are correct.

1. The taxi driver apologized (to,) for   Ann for the accident.

2. My mother died (from, of)   cancer.

3. Jack was excused from, for   school for several days so he could travel with his father.

4. Mary always compares her country with, to   this country.

5. Susie dreamed of, about   winning the lottery.

6. The mountain climbers were warned of, about   the avalanche danger.

7. Maria needed ten dollars immediately. She asked her sister about, for   some money.

8. Beth looks like, for   her sister. They could almost be twins.

9. Dennis tried talking to, about   Roman, but the noise in the restaurant was so loud that neither he nor Roman could hear each other.

10. This dish tastes like it has meat in it, but it consists only in, of   vegetables.

11. Mary and Joe argue about, with   everything. They always disagree with, about   each other.

12. Are you sure of, about   your data?

13. Our dentist is very patient to, with   children.

14. Professor Case always seems angry at, with   his students, but maybe he's upset about something else.

15. We discussed our house plans with, about   several architects.

16. The apartment owner spoke to, with   several tenants about a possible rent increase.

17. We heard about, from   the plane crash on the radio.

18. If you multiply any number from, by   zero, the answer is always zero.

19. Shhh! I'm concentrating in, on   my homework.

◇ PRACTICE 16. Review: preposition combinations. (Appendix 2)
Directions: Choose the correct preposition.

1. What time do you need to be ready _____ work?
   A. at   B. about   C. on   (D.) for

2. One pound is equal _____ 2.2 kilos.
   A. for   B. to   C. in   D. on

3. Too many vitamins may be bad _____ your health.
   A. in   B. about   C. for   D. with

4. That box looks very heavy. Can I help you _____ it?
   A. with   B. in   C. about   D. on

5. Our cat got rid _____ all the mice in our basement.
   A. about   B. of   C. in   D. off

6. Everyone admires Mr. Kim _____ his generosity with his time and money.
   A. for   B. from   C. with   D. about

7. I need to hide this chocolate _____ the children or they will eat it in one day.
   A. with   B. from   C. to   D. at

8. Billy, stop that! It's not polite to stare _____ people.
   A. to   B. at   C. in   D. on

9. Angela has applied _____ several jobs in the airline industry, but she hasn't gotten an interview yet.
   A. to   B. with   C. of   D. for

10. This car can't belong _____ Mike. It's too nice!
    A. about   B. with   C. to   D. at

11. Monica loves vegetables, but she's not crazy _____ fruit.
    A. over   B. of   C. at   D. about

12. Jack paid _____ my dinner.
    A. with   B. for   C. on   D. in

13. I tried to tell Jessica _____ my trip, but she didn't seem interested. I wonder if she was jealous.
    A. to   B. about   C. with   D. off

14. We're really happy _____ Professor James. He just received an award for excellence in teaching.
    A. for   B. to   C. over   D. in

15. People say I shouldn't care what other students think, but their opinions matter _____ me.
    A. to   B. for   C. with   D. on

16. Annie eats vegetables only if they are separated _____ the other foods on her plate.
    A. between   B. from   C. with   D. to

17. Kristi forgave her twin sister _____ taking her cell phone without asking.
    A. about   B. from   C. for   D. with

18. Doctors say that even ten minutes of exercise a day is good _____ you.
    A. at   B. for   C. with   D. about

19. I'm sorry. Your explanation still isn't clear _____ me.
    A. about   B. with   C. to   D. in

20. My sister complained _____ the manager.
    A. to   B. with   C. at   D. for

21. She complained _____ the slow service in the restaurant.
    A. for   B. about   C. over   D. by

22. What happened _____ your hand? It's swollen.
    A. on   B. to   C. in   D. about

23. The problem with your answer is that you multiplied six _____ eight instead of subtracting it.
    A. by   B. from   C. to   D. over

24. Paul is so smart. He graduated _____ the university in just three years.
    A. of   B. at   C. from   D. to

Index

V

Verbs:
  reporting, 293–302
  vs. subjects and objects, 111–112, 198–199
  transitive/intransitive, 198–199
  (SEE ALSO Auxilary verbs; Modal auxiliaries; Passive;
      Phrasal verbs; Tenses; individual items)
Very, 179

W

Was, were, 21, 34–35
  + *-ing (was eating),* 34–35
What, 93–95
  in noun clauses, 282–283
  what + a form of *do,* 95
  what kind of, 96
  what vs. *which,* 97
  what time vs. *when,* 90–91
When:
  in questions, 89–95
  in time clauses, 34–37, 54
Where, 279
Whether, 284–286
Which:
  in adjective clauses, 245–246
  in questions, 97
While, 34–37, 54

Will, 132–133
  vs. *be going to,* 43–46, 49–50
  forms, 44–46
  future, 43–44
  in polite questions, 137
  with *probably,* 46–47
With vs. *by,* 268
Who/who(m):
  in adjective clauses, 240–242, 244–245
  in noun clauses, 282–283
  in questions, 93–94
  who's vs. *whose,* 98–99
Whose:
  in adjective clauses, 251
  in noun clauses, 282–283
  in questions (vs. *who's*), 98–99
Why, 92, 279
Why don't, 145
Word order (S-V-O-P-T), 113
Worse, worst, 176
Would, 133
  in polite questions, 137, 145
Would rather, 146–147

Y

Yes/no questions, 19–20, 86–89, 284–285
Yet, 77–78

Answer Key

To the student: To make it easy to correct your answers, remove this answer key along the perforations and make a separate answer key booklet for yourself.

Chapter 1: PRESENT TIME

◇ **PRACTICE 1, p. 1.**

A: Hi. My name ____**is**____ Kunio.

B: Hi. My ____**name is**____ Maria. I ____**'m**____ glad to meet you.

KUNIO: I ____**am**____ glad to ____**meet**____ you, too. Where ____**are you from**____?

MARIA: I ____**am**____ from Mexico. Where ____**are you from**____?

KUNIO: I ____**am from**____ Japan.

MARIA: Where ____**are you**____ living now?

KUNIO: On Fifth Avenue in an apartment. And you?

MARIA: I ____**am**____ living in a dorm.

KUNIO: What ____**are**____ you studying?

MARIA: Business. After I study English, I am going to attend the School of Business Administration. How ____**about**____ you? What ____**is**____ your major?

KUNIO: Engineering.

MARIA: What ____**do**____ you like to do in your free time?

KUNIO: I read a lot. How ____**about**____ you?

MARIA: I like to get on the Internet.

KUNIO: Really? What ____**do**____ you do when you're online?

MARIA: I visit many different Web sites. It ____**is**____ a good way to practice my English.

KUNIO: That's interesting. I ____**like**____ to get on the Internet, too.

MARIA: I have to ____**write**____ your full name on the board when I introduce you to the class. How ____**do you**____ spell your name?

KUNIO: My first name ____**is**____ Kunio. K-U-N-I-O. My family name ____**is**____ Akiwa.

MARIA: Kunio Akiwa. ____**Is**____ that right?

KUNIO: Yes, it ____**is**____. And what ____**is**____ your name again?

MARIA: My first name ____**is**____ Maria. M-A-R-I-A. My last name ____**is**____ Lopez.

KUNIO: Thanks. It's been nice talking to you.

MARIA: I enjoyed it, too.

◇ **PRACTICE 2, p. 2.**

1. am sitting
2. am reading
3. am looking
4. am writing
5. am doing
6. sit . . . am sitting
7. read . . . am reading
8. look . . . am looking
9. write . . . am writing
10. do . . . am doing

◇ **PRACTICE 3, p. 2.**

PART I.

1. speak
2. speak
3. speaks
4. speak
5. speaks

PART II.

6. do not (don't) speak
7. do not (don't) speak
8. does not (doesn't) speak
9. do not (don't) speak
10. does not (doesn't) speak

PART III.

11. Do you speak
12. Do they speak
13. Does he speak
14. Do we speak
15. Does she speak

◇ **PRACTICE 4, p. 3.**

PART I.

1. am speaking
2. are speaking
3. is speaking
4. are speaking
5. is speaking

PART II.

6. am not speaking
7. are not speaking
8. is not speaking
9. are not speaking
10. is not speaking

PART III.

11. Are you speaking
12. Is he speaking
13. Are they speaking
14. Are we speaking
15. Is she speaking

◇ **PRACTICE 5, p. 3.**

1. Is he
2. Does he
3. Does he
4. Is he
5. Does he
6. Is he
7. Is he
8. Does he
9. Does he
10. Is he

◇ PRACTICE 6, p. 4.

1. Is she	6. Does she
2. Does she	7. Is she
3. Is she	8. Is she
4. Is she	9. Does she
5. Does she	10. Is she

◇ PRACTICE 7, p. 4.

1. does	7. do
2. Do	8. Ø . . . Ø
3. Ø	9. does
4. Does	10. Ø
5. Ø	11. Do
6. Ø	

◇ PRACTICE 8, p. 5.

1. is	7. Ø	13. am
2. are	8. is	14. are
3. is	9. Are	15. Ø
4. Is	10. Do	16. am
5. does	11. Ø	17. Do
6. Ø	12. are	

◇ PRACTICE 9, p. 5.

1. Ø	5. Are	9. Ø
2. Do	6. are	10. is
3. Does	7. Ø	11. Do
4. Is	8. are	

◇ PRACTICE 10, p. 6.

1. is	7. Ø	13. is
2. are	8. do	14. Ø . . . Ø
3. Ø	9. Ø	15. is
4. Does	10. does	16. Ø . . . are
5. do	11. does	17. Do
6. Ø	12. Ø	18. Does

◇ PRACTICE 11, p. 7.

1. usually . . . Ø	7. sometimes . . . Ø
2. Ø . . . usually	8. never . . . Ø
3. always . . . Ø	9. Ø . . . never
4. Ø . . . always	10. Ø . . . usually . . . Ø
5. usually . . . Ø	11. Ø . . . always . . . Ø
6. Ø . . . always	12. Ø . . . always

◇ PRACTICE 12, p. 7.

1. a. usually doesn't come	2. a. usually isn't
b. doesn't ever come	b. is rarely
c. seldom comes	c. isn't always
d. sometimes comes	d. frequently isn't
e. always comes	e. is never
f. occasionally comes	f. isn't ever
g. never comes	g. is seldom
h. hardly ever comes	

◇ PRACTICE 13, p. 8.

1. always wakes	5. seldom surfs
2. sometimes skips	6. usually talks
3. frequently visits	7. rarely does
4. is usually	8. is never

◇ PRACTICE 14, p. 8.

1. often OR usually	7. seldom OR rarely
2. seldom OR rarely	8. seldom OR rarely
3. always	9. never
4. often OR usually	10. always
5. sometimes	11. often OR usually
6. usually	12. seldom

◇ PRACTICE 15, p. 9.

1. always chooses	7. often OR usually gets
2. seldom OR rarely go	8. sometimes gets
3. sometimes ride	9. seldom OR rarely finishes
4. seldom OR rarely exercises	10. never play
5. never eat	11. usually arrives
6. is always	12. always take

◇ PRACTICE 16, p. 10.

1. likes	11. Ø
2. watches	12. Does . . . Ø
3. doesn't . . . Ø	13. doesn't
4. Ø	14. carries
5. Ø . . . Ø	15. plays
6. Does . . . Ø	16. lives
7. likes	17. Ø
8. washes	18. visits
9. goes	19. catches
10. gets	20. Ø

◇ PRACTICE 17, p. 11.

Sam **leaves** his apartment at 8:00 every morning. **He walks** to the bus stop and **catches** the 8:10 bus. It takes him downtown. Then he **transfers** to another bus, and it takes him to his part-time job. **He arrives** at work at 8:50. **He stays** until 1:00, and then **he leaves** for school. **He attends** classes until 5:00. **He** usually **studies** in the library and **tries** to finish his homework. Then **he goes** home around 8:00. **He has** a long day.

◇ PRACTICE 18, p. 11.

/s/	/z/	/əz/
cooks	stays	promises
invites	seems	watches
hates	travels	misses
picks	draws	introduces

◇ PRACTICE 19, p. 12.

1. /z/	6. /z/	11. /əz/
2. /s/	7. /əz/	12. /z/
3. /əz/	8. /s/	13. /s/
4. /z/	9. /z/	14. /z/
5. /z/	10. /əz/	15. /s/

◇ PRACTICE 20, p. 12.

	simple pres.	pres. prog.
1.	buys	is buying
2.	comes	is coming
3.	opens	is opening
4.	begins	is beginning
5.	stops	is stopping
6.	dies	is dying

simple pres.	pres. prog.
7. rains	is raining
8. dreams	is dreaming
9. eats	is eating
10. enjoys	is enjoying
11. writes	is writing
12. tries	is trying
13. stays	is staying
14. hopes	is hoping
15. studies	is studying
16. lies	is lying
17. flies	is flying
18. sits	is sitting

◇ PRACTICE 21, p. 12.

1. a	5. a	9. b
2. a	6. a	10. b
3. a	7. b	11. b
4. b	8. a	12. a

◇ PRACTICE 22, p. 13.

1. is snowing
2. takes
3. drive
4. am watching
5. prefer
6. need
7. are playing
8. is looking . . . sees
9. sings
10. bite
11. writes
12. understand
13. belongs
14. is shining . . . is raining

◇ PRACTICE 23, p. 14.

1. usually doesn't take
2. needs
3. is enjoying
4. are
5. are eating
6. are drinking
7. (are) reading
8. is working
9. is hugging
10. are playing
11. is waving
12. is walking
13. (is) entertaining
14. is smiling
15. usually takes
16. is

◇ PRACTICE 24, p. 15.

1. My friend **doesn't** speak English well.
2. I **don't** believe you.
3. My sister's dog **doesn't** bark.
4. Our teacher **always starts** class on time.
5. Look! The cat **is getting** up on the counter.
6. **Does** Marie **have** enough money?
7. We **don't like** this rainy weather.
8. Mrs. Gray is **worrying** about her daughter. OR
   Mrs. Gray **worries** about her daughter.
9. My brother **doesn't have** enough free time.
10. **Does** Jim drive to school every day?
11. He always **hurries** in the morning. He **doesn't want**
   to be late.
12. Anna **usually has** dinner at eight.

◇ PRACTICE 25, p. 15.

1. A: Are
   B: I am OR I'm not
2. A: Do
   B: they do OR they don't
3. A: Do
   B: I do OR I don't

4. A: Does
   B: she does OR she doesn't
5. A: Are
   B: they are OR they aren't
6. A: Do
   B: they do OR they don't
7. A: Is
   B: he is OR he isn't
8. A: Are
   B: I am OR I'm not
9. A: Is
   B: it is OR it isn't
10. A: Do
    B: we do OR we don't

◇ PRACTICE 26, p. 16.

1. A: are you doing
   B: am watching . . . want
   A: enjoy . . . go . . . is . . . run
   B: are making
2. A: Do you read
   B: do . . . read . . . subscribe . . . always look
3. am I studying . . . do I want . . . need
4. A: am leaving . . . Do you want
   B: am waiting
5. B: Is the baby sleeping
   A: is taking
   B: don't want
6. goes . . . likes . . . is preparing
7. is . . . is blowing . . . are falling
8. eats . . . don't eat . . . do you eat
9. A: Do you shop
   B: don't . . . usually shop
   A: are you shopping
   B: am trying
10. lose . . . rest . . . grow . . . keep . . . stay . . . don't grow
    . . . don't have . . . is . . . grow

Chapter 2: PAST TIME

◇ PRACTICE 1, p. 18.

1. walked . . . yesterday
2. talked . . . last
3. opened . . . yesterday
4. went . . . last
5. met . . . last
6. Yesterday . . . made . . . took
7. paid . . . last
8. Yesterday . . . fell
9. left . . . last

◇ PRACTICE 2, p. 19.

1. started	11. fell	21. took
2. went	12. heard	22. paid
3. saw	13. sang	23. left
4. stood	14. explored	24. wore
5. arrived	15. asked	25. opened
6. won	16. brought	26. decided
7. had	17. broke	27. planned
8. made	18. ate	28. wrote
9. finished	19. watched	29. taught
10. felt	20. built	30. held

◇ PRACTICE 3, p. 19.

1. A: Did you answer
   B: I did. I answered OR I didn't. I didn't answer
2. A: Did he see
   B: he did. He saw OR he didn't. He didn't see
3. A: Did they watch
   B: they did. They watched OR they didn't. They didn't watch
4. A: Did you understand
   B: I did. I understood OR I didn't. I didn't understand
5. A: Were you
   B: I was. I was OR I wasn't. I wasn't

◇ PRACTICE 4, p. 20.

1. didn't fly . . . walked/took the bus
2. aren't . . . are sour
3. didn't walk . . . walked on the moon
4. wasn't a baby . . . was (number of years old)
5. didn't come . . . came
6. doesn't come . . . comes from coffee beans
7. didn't sleep . . . slept inside
8. isn't . . . is cold
9. didn't disappear . . . disappeared millions of years

◇ PRACTICE 5, p. 21.

1. Did he study
2. Was he sick
3. Was she sad
4. Did they eat
5. Were they hungry
6. Did you go
7. Did she understand
8. Did he forget

◇ PRACTICE 6, p. 21.

1. Did
2. Were
3. Did
4. Did
5. Was
6. Did
7. Was
8. Did

◇ PRACTICE 7, p. 22.

1. shook
2. stayed
3. swam
4. jumped
5. held
6. fought
7. taught
8. froze
9. thought
10. called
11. rode
12. sold

◇ PRACTICE 9, p. 23.

1. /t/
2. /d/
3. /əd/
4. /d/
5. /əd/
6. /əd/
7. /d/
8. /t/
9. /d/
10. /əd/
11. /d/
12. /t/
13. /t/
14. /əd/
15. /t/
16. /d/
17. /t/
18. /əd/
19. /d/
20. /t/

◇ PRACTICE 10, p. 23.

	spelling	pron.
1.	walk**ed**	/t/
2.	pat**ted**	/əd/
3.	wor**ried**	/d/
4.	stay**ed**	/d/
5.	visit**ed**	/əd/
6.	die**d**	/d/
7.	trade**d**	/əd/
8.	plan**ned**	/d/
9.	open**ed**	/d/

10.	hur**ried**	/d/
11.	rent**ed**	/əd/
12.	tr**ied**	/d/
13.	enjoy**ed**	/d/
14.	stop**ped**	/t/
15.	need**ed**	/əd/

◇ PRACTICE 12 p. 24.

double consonant?	-ING	-ED
no	exciting	excited
no	existing	existed
no	shouting	shouted
yes	patting	patted
no	visiting	visited
yes	admitting	admitted
no	praying	prayed
no	prying	pried
no	tying	tied

◇ PRACTICE 13, p. 25.

double consonant	drop -E	add -ING
hitting	coming	learning
cutting	taking	listening
hopping	hoping	raining
beginning	smiling	staying
winning	writing	studying

◇ PRACTICE 14, p. 25.

	-ING	-ED
1.	riding	(ridden)
2.	starting	started
3.	coming	(came)
4.	happening	happened
5.	trying	tried
6.	buying	(bought)
7.	hoping	hoped
8.	keeping	(kept)
9.	tipping	tipped
10.	failing	failed
11.	filling	filled
12.	feeling	(felt)
13.	dining	dined
14.	meaning	(meant)
15.	winning	(won)
16.	learning	learned
17.	listening	listened
18.	beginning	(began)

◇ PRACTICE 15, p. 26.

	-ing	simple form
1.	waiting	wait
2.	petting	pet
3.	biting	bite
4.	sitting	sit
5.	writing	write
6.	fighting	fight
7.	waiting	wait
8.	getting	get
9.	starting	start
10.	permitting	permit
11.	lifting	lift
12.	eating	eat

	-ing	simple form
13.	tasting	taste
14.	cutting	cut
15.	meeting	meet
16.	visiting	visit

◇ PRACTICE 16, p. 27.

PART I.
bought
brought
taught
caught
fought
thought
found

PART II.
swam
drank
sang
rang

PART III.
blew
drew
flew
grew
knew
threw

PART IV.
broke
wrote
froze
rode
sold
stole

PART V.
hit
hurt
read
shut
cost
put
quit

PART VI.
paid
said

◇ PRACTICE 17, p. 28.

1. drank/had
2. ate
3. began . . . shut
4. rang
5. came
6. built
7. fell . . . hurt
8. stole/took
9. shut
10. drove
11. ran
12. led
13. paid
14. froze
15. did
16. rose
17. thought
18. wrote
19. kept
20. built

◇ PRACTICE 18, p. 29.

1. spoke
2. dug
3. chose
4. lost
5. quit
6. slept
7. found
8. cut
9. met
10. taught
11. gave . . . spoke
12. grew
13. forgot
14. bought/read
15. shook
16. stole
17. felt
18. drew
19. heard
20. fell . . . broke

◇ PRACTICE 19, p. 30.

question	*negative*
1. Did I ride	I didn't ride
2. Did she sit	She didn't sit
3. Were we	We weren't
4. Did they try	They didn't try
5. Was he	He wasn't
6. Did they cut	They didn't cut
7. Did she throw	She didn't throw
8. Did we do	We didn't do

◇ PRACTICE 20, p. 31.

1. What did you do last night?
2. What is your friend's name?
3. Is he nice?
4. How was your evening?
5. Where did you go?
6. Did you enjoy it?
7. Was the music loud?
8. What time did you get home?
9. What did you wear?
10. What is he like?
11. What does he look like?
12. Do you want to go out with him again?

◇ PRACTICE 21, p. 32.

	every day	*now*	*yesterday*
1.	is	is	was
2.	think	am thinking	thought
3.	play	are playing	played
4.	drink	am drinking	drank
5.	teaches	is teaching	taught
6.	swims	is swimming	swam
7.	sleep	are sleeping	slept
8.	reads	is reading	read
9.	try	are trying	tried
10.	eat	are eating	ate

◇ PRACTICE 22, p. 32.

1. A: Did you hear
   B: didn't . . . didn't hear . . . was
2. A: Do you hear
   B: don't . . . don't hear
3. A: Did you build
   B: didn't . . . built
4. A: Is a fish
   B: it is
   A: Are they
   B: they are . . . don't know
5. A: want . . . Do you want
   B: have . . . bought . . . don't need
6. offer . . . is . . . offered . . . didn't accept
7. took . . . found . . . didn't know . . . isn't . . . didn't want
   . . . went . . . made . . . heated . . . seemed . . . am not
8. likes . . . worry . . . is . . . trust . . . graduated . . . went
   . . . didn't travel . . . rented . . . rode . . . was . . . worried
   . . . were . . . saw . . . knew

◇ PRACTICE 23, p. 34.

1. were hiding
2. were singing
3. was watching
4. were talking
5. were reading . . . were sitting . . . (were) looking

◇ PRACTICE 24, p. 34.

1. was playing . . . broke
2. scored . . . was playing
3. hurt . . . was playing
4. was hiking . . . found
5. saw . . . was hiking
6. picked up . . . was hiking
7. tripped . . . fell . . .
   was dancing
8. was dancing . . . met
9. was dancing . . . got

1. began . . . were walking
2. was washing . . . dropped . . . broke
3. saw . . . was eating . . . (was) talking . . . joined
4. was walking . . . fell . . . hit
5. was singing . . . didn't hear
6. was walking . . . heard . . . was
7. A: Did your lights go out
   B: was . . . was taking . . . found . . . ate . . . tried . . . went . . . slept
8. went . . . saw . . . had . . . were walking . . . began . . . dried . . . were passing . . . lowered . . . started . . . stretched . . . tried . . . didn't let . . . was standing . . . pointed . . . said

◇ PRACTICE 26, p. 36.

1. I gave Alan his allowance <u>after he finished his chores.</u>
   OR
   <u>After Alan finished his chores,</u> I gave him his allowance.
2. The doorbell rang <u>while I was climbing the stairs.</u> OR
   <u>While I was climbing the stairs,</u> the doorbell rang.
3. The firefighters checked the ashes one last time <u>before they went home.</u> OR
   <u>Before they went home,</u> the firefighters checked the ashes one last time.
4. <u>When the Novaks stopped by our table at the restaurant,</u> they showed us their new baby. OR
   The Novaks showed us their new baby <u>when they stopped by our table at the restaurant.</u>
5. We started to dance <u>as soon as the music began.</u> OR
   <u>As soon as the music began,</u> we started to dance.
6. We stayed in our seats <u>until the game ended.</u> OR
   <u>Until the game ended,</u> we stayed in our seats.
7. <u>While my father was listening to a baseball game on the radio,</u> he was watching a basketball game on television.
   OR
   My father was watching a basketball game on television <u>while he was listening to a baseball game on the radio.</u>

◇ PRACTICE 27, p. 37.

1. was	17. comes	33. is
2. slept	18. sat	34. drew
3. came	19. spoke	35. played
4. packed	20. ate	36. won
5. took	21. took	37. won
6. spent	22. was sleeping	38. taught
7. got	23. bit	39. were playing
8. found	24. woke	40. fell
9. fed	25. heard	41. found
10. threw	26. looked	42. joined
11. swam	27. saw	43. were
12. caught	28. flew	44. were
13. hit	29. did	45. hurt
14. stole	30. took	46. was
15. were feeding	31. got	47. left
16. met	32. read	48. was

◇ PRACTICE 28, p. 39.

1. used to hate school
2. used to be a secretary
3. used to have a rat
4. used to go bowling
5. used to have fresh eggs
6. used to crawl under his bed . . . put his hands over his ears
7. used to go
8. didn't use/used to wear
9. used to hate . . . didn't use/used to have
10. did you use/used to do

◇ PRACTICE 29, p. 40.

1. They **didn't stay** at the park very long last Saturday
2. They ~~are~~ walked to school yesterday.
3. I ~~was~~ **understood** all the teacher's questions yesterday.
4. We didn't **know** what to do when the fire alarm **rang** yesterday.
5. I ~~was~~ really enjoyed the baseball game last week.
6. Mr. Rice didn't **die** in the accident.
7. I **used** to live with my parents**,** but now I have my own apartment.
8. My friends ~~were~~ went on vacation together last month.
9. I **wasn't** afraid of anything when I **was** a child.
10. The teacher ~~was~~ changed his mind yesterday.
11. Sally **loved** Jim, but he didn't **love** her.
12. Carmen **didn't use/used** to eat fish, but now she does.

◇ PRACTICE 30, p. 41.

1. was preparing	11. excused	21. yelled
2. rang	12. reached	22. shooed
3. put	13. was trying	23. sat
4. rushed	14. ran	24. stayed
5. opened	15. was trying	25. began
6. found	16. were swimming	26. felt
7. was holding	17. said	27. rang
8. needed	18. hung	28. rang
9. was dealing	19. thanked	
10. rang	20. shut	

Chapter 3: FUTURE TIME

◇ PRACTICE 1, p. 43.

1. a. arrives
   b. arrived
   c. is going to arrive OR will arrive
2. a. eats
   b. ate
   c. is going to eat OR will eat
3. a. doesn't arrive
   b. didn't arrive
   c. isn't going to arrive OR will not/won't arrive
4. a. Do . . . eat
   b. Did . . . eat
   c. Are . . . going to eat OR Will . . . eat
5. a. don't eat
   b. didn't eat
   c. 'm/am not going to eat OR will not/won't eat

◇ PRACTICE 2, p. 44.

be going to	*will*
am going to	will
are going to	will
is going to	will
are going to	will
are going to	will
are not going to	will not
is not going to	will not
am not going to	will not

PRACTICE 3, p. 44.
1. I'm going to eat
2. he isn't going to be
3. they're going to take
4. she's going to walk
5. it isn't going to rain
6. we're going to be
7. you aren't going to hitchhike
8. I'm not going to get
9. he isn't going to wear

PRACTICE 4, p. 44.
The Smiths **will** celebrate their 50th wedding anniversary on December 1 of this year. Their children are planning a party for them at a local hotel. Their family and friends **will** join them for the celebration.

Mr. and Mrs. Smith have three children and five grandchildren. The Smiths know that two of their children **will** be at the party, but the third child, their youngest daughter, is far away in Africa, where she is doing medical research. They believe she **will** not come home for the party.

The Smiths don't know it, but their youngest daughter **will** be at the party. She is planning to surprise them. It **will** be a wonderful surprise for them! They **will** be very happy to see her. The whole family **will** enjoy being together for this special occasion.

PRACTICE 5, p. 45.
1. Will Nick start
   Is Nick going to start
2. Will Mr. Jones give
   Is Mr. Jones going to give
3. Will Jacob quit
   Is Jacob going to quit
4. Will Mr. and Mrs. Kono adopt
   Are Mr. and Mrs. Kono going to adopt
5. Will the Johnsons move
   Are the Johnsons going to move
6. Will Dr. Johnson retire
   Is Dr. Johnson going to retire

PRACTICE 6, p. 46.
1. A: Will you help
   B: I will OR I won't
2. A: Will Paul lend
   B: he will OR he won't
3. A: Will Jane graduate
   B: she will OR she won't
4. A: Will her parents be
   B: they will OR they won't
5. A: Will I benefit
   B: you will OR you won't

PRACTICE 7, p. 46.
1. probably won't
2. will probably
3. will probably
4. probably won't
5. will probably
6. probably won't
7. will probably
8. will probably

PRACTICE 8, p. 47.
PART I.
1. I'll probably go
2. she probably won't come
3. he will probably go
4. he probably won't hand
5. they will probably have

PART II.
6. I'm probably going to watch
7. I'm probably not going to be
8. it's probably going to be
9. they probably aren't going to come
10. she probably isn't going to ride

PRACTICE 9, p. 47.
1. 90%
2. 50%
3. 100%
4. 90%
5. 50%
6. 90%
7. 100%
8. 50%

PRACTICE 10, p. 48.
1. are probably going to have
2. are probably not going to invite
3. may get married . . . Maybe . . . will get married
4. may rent
5. will probably decide
6. may not be . . . may be
7. will go
8. probably won't go

PRACTICE 11, p. 49.
1. 'll answer it
2. 'll hold
3. 'll take
4. 'll move
5. 'll turn . . . off
6. 'll leave
7. 'll get
8. 'll read

PRACTICE 12, p. 49.
1. 'm going to
2. 'll
3. 'm going to
4. 'll
5. 'm going to
6. 'll
7. 'm going to . . . 'll

PRACTICE 13, p. 50.
1. 'll
2. 'm going to
3. 'm going to
4. 'm going to
5. A: are . . . going to
   B: 'm going to
6. 'll
7. 'm going to
8. 'll
9. 's going to
10. 'll put
11. 'm going to
12. 'll

PRACTICE 14, p. 52.
Time clauses:
1. After I did my homework last night
2. after I do my homework tonight
3. Before Bob left for work this morning
4. Before Bob leaves for work this morning
5. after I get home this evening

Time clauses:
6. after I got home last night
7. as soon as the teacher arrives
8. As soon as the teacher arrived
9. When the rain stops
10. when the rain stopped

◇ PRACTICE 15, p. 52.
1. After I finish . . . I'm going to go
2. I'm not going to go . . . until I finish
3. Before Ann watches . . . she will (she'll) finish
4. Jim is going to read . . . after he gets
5. When I call . . . I'll ask
6. Mrs. Fox will stay . . . until she finishes
7. As soon as I get . . . I'm going to take
8. While I am . . . I'm going to go

◇ PRACTICE 16, p. 53.
1. If it rains tomorrow,
2. If it's hot tomorrow,
3. if he has enough time
4. If I don't get a check tomorrow,
5. if the weather is nice tomorrow
6. If Gina doesn't study for her test,
7. if I have enough money
8. If I don't study tonight,

◇ PRACTICE 17, p. 54.
1. When I see you Sunday afternoon, I'll give you my answer OR
   I'll give you my answer when I see you Sunday afternoon.
2. Before my friends come over, I'm going to clean up my apartment. OR
   I'm going to clean up my apartment before my friends come over.
3. When the storm is over, I'm going to do some errands. OR
   I'm going to do some errands when the storm is over.
4. If you don't learn how to use a computer, you will have trouble finding a job. OR
   You will have trouble finding a job if you don't learn how to use a computer.
5. As soon as Joe finishes his report, he'll meet us at the coffee shop. OR
   Joe will meet us at the coffee shop as soon as he finishes his report.
6. After Sue washes and dries the dishes, she will put them away. OR
   Sue will put the dishes away after she washes and dries them.
7. If they don't leave at seven, they won't get to the theater on time. OR
   They won't get to the theater on time if they don't leave at seven.

◇ PRACTICE 18, p. 54.
PART II.
(1) Tomorrow morning **will be** an ordinary morning. I **'ll get** up at 6:30. I **'ll wash** my face and **brush** my teeth. Then I **'ll** probably put on my jeans and a sweater. I **'ll** go to the kitchen and **start** the electric coffee maker.

(2) Then I **'ll walk** down my driveway to get the morning newspaper. If I **see** a deer in my garden, I **'ll** watch it for a while and then **make** some noise to chase it away before it **destroys** my flowers.

(3) As soon as I **get** back to the kitchen, I'll **pour** myself a cup of coffee and **open** the morning paper. While I'm reading the paper, my teenage daughter **will come** downstairs. We **'ll talk** about her plans for the day. I **'ll help** her with her breakfast and **make** a lunch for her to take to school. After we **say** goodbye, I **'ll eat** some fruit and cereal and **finish** reading the paper.

(4) Then I **'ll go** to my office. My office **is** in my home. My office **has** a desk, a computer, a radio, a fax, a copy machine, and a lot of bookshelves. I **'ll work** all morning. While I'm working, the phone **will ring** many times. I **'ll talk** to many people. At 11:30, I **'ll go** to the kitchen and **make** a sandwich for lunch. As I said, it **will be** an ordinary morning.

◇ PRACTICE 19, p. 56.
1. I'm going to stay . . . I'm staying
2. They're going to travel . . . They're traveling
3. We're going to get . . . We're getting
4. He's going to start . . . He's starting
5. She's going to go . . . She's going
6. My neighbors are going to build . . . My neighbors are building

◇ PRACTICE 20, p. 56.
1. is traveling
2. are arriving
3. 'm/am meeting
4. 'm/am getting
5. is . . . taking
6. 'm/am studying
7. 'm/am leaving
8. is attending . . . 'm/am seeing
9. is speaking
10. are coming . . . 'm/am planning . . . 'm/am preparing
11. 'm/am calling

◇ PRACTICE 21, p. 58.
1. A: does . . . begin/start
   B: begins/starts
2. opens
3. arrives/gets in
4. begins
5. A: does . . . close
   B: closes
6. open . . . starts/begins . . . arrive . . . ends/finishes
7. A: does . . . depart/leave
   B: leaves
   A: does . . . arrive/land

◇ PRACTICE 22, p. 59.
1. is about to rain
2. is about to leave
3. is about to write
4. is about to ring
5. is . . . about to break

1. study
2. set
3. doing
4. go
5. fell
6. is writing . . . waiting
7. takes . . . buys
8. go . . . tell
9. 'm/am taking . . . forgetting
10. will discover . . . (will) apologize

◇ PRACTICE 24, p. 60.

1. My friends will ~~to~~ join us after work.
2. Maybe the rain **will stop / is going to stop** soon.
3. On Friday, our school **is closing / will close / is going to close** early so teachers can go to a workshop.
4. My husband and I ~~will~~ intend to be at your graduation.
5. Our company is going to **sell** computer equipment to schools.
6. Give grandpa a hug. He's about to **leave**.
7. Mr. Scott is going to retire and **move** to a warmer climate.
8. If your soccer team ~~will~~ **wins** the championship tomorrow, we'll have a big celebration for you.
9. **Maybe I** won't be able to meet you for coffee. OR **I may not** be able to meet you for coffee. OR I ~~maybe~~ won't be able to meet you for coffee.
10. I bought this cloth because I **am going to** make some curtains for my bedroom.
11. I **am** (I'm) moving / **will move** / **am going to move** to London when I ~~will~~ finish my education here.
12. Are you going **to** go to the meeting?
13. I opened the door and **walked** to the front of the room.
14. When will you ~~be going to~~ move into your new apartment? OR
When **are** you going to move into your new apartment? OR
When **are** you **moving** into your new apartment?

◇ PRACTICE 25, p. 61.

1. go . . . am going to finish / will finish . . . write
2. was making . . . spilled . . . caught . . . started . . . ran . . . thought
3. plays . . . cuts . . . is not doing . . . doesn't study . . . go . . . will flunk / is going to flunk
4. cries . . . stomps . . . gets . . . got . . . picked . . . threw . . . didn't hit . . . felt . . . apologized . . . kissed
5. is beginning . . . begins . . . don't like . . . think . . . are going to take / will take . . . is . . . are going to drive / will drive . . . enjoy
6. is going to meet / will meet . . . arrives
7. see . . . am going to tell / will tell
8. am . . . see
9. am . . . will stay
10. are going to go / will go . . . is
11. is watching . . . is . . . is going to mow / will mow
12. was . . . left
13. get . . . run
14. don't need
15. is planning / plans . . . Are you going to come / Are you coming
16. A: do you usually get
    B: take
17. was combing . . . broke . . . finished . . . rushed
18. get . . . 'm/am going to read / I will read . . . watch . . . 'm/am not going to do / won't do

19. saw . . . ran . . . caught . . . knocked . . . went . . . sat . . . waited . . . got . . . understood . . . put . . . took
20. A: has . . . has
    B: does she have
    B: Do you have
    A: 'm/am not going to get . . . don't have

Chapter 4: THE PRESENT PERFECT AND THE PAST PERFECT

◇ PRACTICE 1, p. 64.

1. A: Have you ever eaten
   B: have . . . have eaten OR haven't . . . have never eaten
2. A: Have you ever talked
   B: have . . . have talked OR haven't . . . have never talked
3. A: Has Erica ever rented
   B: has . . . has rented OR hasn't . . . has never rented
4. A: Have you ever seen
   B: have . . . have seen OR haven't . . . have never seen
5. A: Has Joe ever caught
   B: has . . . has caught OR hasn't . . . has never caught
6. A: Have you ever had
   B: have . . . have had OR haven't . . . have never had

◇ PRACTICE 2, p. 65.

1. have wanted
2. have been
3. has been
4. have flown
5. have not picked up
6. has changed
7. has already corrected . . . hasn't returned
8. hasn't talked
9. have needed . . . have looked
10. A: Have you had
    B: have gotten

◇ PRACTICE 3, p. 66.

GROUP I.

simple form	simple past	past participle
hurt	hurt	hurt
put	put	put
quit	quit	quit
upset	upset	upset
cut	cut	cut
shut	shut	shut
let	let	let
set	set	set

GROUP II.

simple form	simple past	past participle
ring	rang	rung
drink	drank	drunk
swim	swam	swum
sing	sang	sung
sink	sank	sunk

GROUP III.

simple form	simple past	past participle
win	won	won
feed	fed	fed
weep	wept	wept
stand	stood	stood
keep	kept	kept
sit	sat	sat
stick	stuck	stuck
meet	met	met
have	had	had
find	found	found
buy	bought	bought
catch	caught	caught
fight	fought	fought
teach	taught	taught
pay	paid	paid
bring	brought	brought
think	thought	thought

◇ PRACTICE 4, p. 67.

1. have used
2. has risen
3. have never played
4. have won
5. hasn't spoken
6. hasn't eaten
7. has given
8. haven't saved
9. Have you ever slept
10. have never worn
11. has improved
12. have looked

◇ PRACTICE 5, p. 68.

1. C	6. F	11. F
2. F	7. F	12. F
3. F	8. F	13. F
4. F	9. C	14. C
5. C	10. C	

◇ PRACTICE 6, p. 68.

1. began . . . have begun
2. bent . . . have bent
3. broadcast . . . has broadcast
4. caught . . . have caught
5. came . . . have come
6. cut . . . have cut
7. dug . . . have dug
8. drew . . . has drawn
9. fed . . . have fed
10. fought . . . have fought
11. forgot . . . have forgotten
12. hid . . . have hidden
13. hit . . . has hit
14. held . . . has held
15. kept . . . have kept
16. led . . . has led
17. lost . . . has lost
18. met . . . have met
19. rode . . . have ridden
20. rang . . . has rung
21. saw . . . have seen
22. stole . . . has stolen
23. stuck . . . have stuck
24. swept . . . have swept
25. took . . . have taken
26. upset . . . have upset
27. withdrew . . . have withdrawn
28. wrote . . . have written

◇ PRACTICE 7, p. 70.

1. went . . . have gone
2. lived
3. has lived
4. moved . . . worked
5. roomed . . . returned
6. was . . . died
7. has played
8. has not/hasn't slept
9. made
10. have enjoyed
11. collected

◇ PRACTICE 8, p. 71.

1. a. have gone
   b. went
2. a. gave
   b. Has she ever given
3. a. have fallen
   b. fell
4. a. Have you ever broken
   b. broke
5. a. have never shaken
   b. shook
6. a. heard
   b. have heard
7. a. flew
   b. has flown
8. a. has worn
   b. wore
9. a. Have you ever built
   b. built
10. a. has taught
    b. taught
11. a. have you ever found
    b. found
12. a. drove
    b. have never driven
13. a. sang
    b. have sung
14. a. have never run
    b. ran
15. a. told
    b. has told
16. a. stood
    b. have stood
17. a. spent
    b. have already spent
18. a. have made
    b. made
19. a. has risen
    b. rose
20. a. felt
    b. have felt

◇ PRACTICE 9, p. 73.

1. since	6. since	11. for
2. for	7. since	12. for
3. since	8. for	13. since
4. for	9. since	14. for
5. for	10. since	

◇ PRACTICE 10, p. 74.

1. I have been in this class **for** a month.
2. I have known my teacher **since** September.
3. Sam has wanted a dog **for** two years.
4. Sara has needed a new car **since** last year / **for** a year.
5. Our professor has been sick **for** a week / **since** last week.
6. They have lived in Canada **since** December.
7. I have known Mrs. Brown **since** 1999.
8. Tom has worked at a fast-food restaurant **for** three weeks.

◇ PRACTICE 11, p. 74.

Checked phrases:

1. two weeks ago
   yesterday
   last year
   several months ago
   the day before yesterday
   in March

2. since Friday
   since last week
   for several weeks

◇ PRACTICE 12, p. 75.

1. have known . . . was
2. has had . . . came
3. have not experienced . . . came
4. began . . . has given
5. has been . . . was
6. has not been . . . graduated
7. started . . . have completed
8. began . . . has not had
9. have become . . . changed
10. has risen . . . bought

1. A: has Eric been studying
   B: 's been studying . . . for two hours
2. A: has Kathy been working at the computer
   B: 's been working . . . two o'clock
3. A: has it been raining
   B: 's been raining . . . two days
4. A: has Liz been reading
   B: 's been reading . . . 30 minutes/half an hour
5. A: has Boris been studying English
   B: 's been studying English . . . 2001
6. A: has Nicole been working at the Silk Road Clothing Store
   B: 's been working . . . three months
7. A: has Ms. Rice been teaching at this school
   B: 's been teaching . . . 2001
8. A: has Mr. Fisher been driving a Chevy
   B: 's been driving a Chevy . . . twelve years
9. A: has Mrs. Taylor been waiting to see her doctor
   B: 's been waiting . . . one and a half hours
10. A: have Ted and Erica been playing tennis
    B: have been playing tennis . . . two o'clock

◇ PRACTICE 14, p. 76.

1. B	4. B	7. B
2. B	5. A	8. A
3. A	6. A	

◇ PRACTICE 15, p. 77.

1. B	5. C	9. B
2. D	6. A	10. C
3. A	7. C	
4. D	8. D	

◇ PRACTICE 16, p. 78.

1. yet	11. A: yet
2. yet	B: still
3. still	12. yet . . . still
4. yet	13. already
5. still	14. still
6. still	15. anymore
7. yet	16. still
8. still	17. already
9. anymore	18. yet . . . still
10. still	

◇ PRACTICE 17, p. 79.

1. need	13. don't have
2. is	14. haven't had
3. Have you ever worked	15. quit
4. have worked	16. Are you looking
5. had	17. 'm/am going
6. did you work	18. is looking
7. have worked	19. 'll/will do
8. have never had	20. have never looked
9. did you like	21. 'll/will be (*also possible:* is)
10. didn't like	22. don't know
11. was	23. 'll/will find
12. are you working	24. go

◇ PRACTICE 18, p. 80.

1. have already eaten	5. had already finished
2. had already eaten	6. had already started
3. have already finished	7. has already started
4. had already finished	8. had already left

◇ PRACTICE 19, p. 81.
1. was raining
2. had stopped
3. was studying
4. had finished
5. was washing
6. had already washed . . . (had) put

◇ PRACTICE 20, p. 82.

Past perfect verbs:
(1) had always watched
(2) had always read
(3) had never let . . . had always listened
(4) had always left
(5) 'd/had never put
(6) had never shared

1. had always watched
2. had always read
3. had never let
4. had always left
5. had never put
6. had never shared

◇ PRACTICE 21, p. 83.
1. A: Did you enjoy
   B: hadn't gone
2. A: Did you see
   B: was . . . hadn't seen
3. A: haven't seen
   B: is . . . haven't seen
4. A: Did you get
   B: got . . . had already begun
5. had already gone
6. have painted
7. A: was watching
   B: did you do
   A: ran
8. A: Did you go
   B: got . . . had already made
   A: was
   B: had . . . were eating . . . stopped . . . invited

◇ PRACTICE 22, p. 84.
1. Where have you been? I've **been** waiting for you for an hour.
2. Anna **has** been a soccer fan **for** a long time.
3. Since I **was** a child, I **have** liked to solve puzzles.
4. Have you ever **wanted** to travel around the world?
5. The family **has been** at the hospital since they **heard** about the accident.
6. My sister is only 30 years old, but her hair has **begun** to turn gray.
7. Jake has **worked** as a volunteer at the children's hospital several times.

8. Steve has worn his black suit only once since he ~~has~~ bought it.
9. My cousin **has been** studying for medical school exams since last month.
10. The students **have been** hearing rumors about their teacher's engagement for a week.
11. I don't know the results of my medical tests **yet**. I'll find out soon.
12. Jean has been **trying** to get online to go Internet shopping for an hour.
13. By the time Michelle unlocked the door and got into her apartment, the phone **had** already stopped ringing.

Chapter 5: ASKING QUESTIONS

◇ PRACTICE 1, p. 85.

1. (your name)
2. what is your name
3. Is that your first name?
4. What's your last name?
5. How do you spell it?
6. Where are you from?
7. What is your hometown?
8. When did you come here?
9. Why did you come here?
10. What are you studying? (OR What is your major?)
11. How long are you going to stay here?
12. Where are you living?
13. Is it far from school?
14. How far is it?
15. How do you get to school?
16. Do you like it?

◇ PRACTICE 2, p. 86.

helping verb	subject	main verb	rest of sentence
1. Do	you	like	coffee?
2. Does	Tom	like	coffee?
3. Is	Ann	watching	TV?
4. Are	you	having	lunch with Rob?
5. Did	Sara	walk	to school?
6. Was	Ann	taking	a nap?
7. Will	Ted	come	to the meeting?
8. Can	Rita	ride	a bicycle?

form of **be**	subject	rest of sentence
9. Is	Ann	a good artist?
10. Were	you	at the wedding?

◇ PRACTICE 3, p. 87.

1. A: Do
   B: I don't
2. A: Is
   B: it isn't
3. A: Do
   B: they do
4. A: Are
   B: I am
5. A: Are
   B: they aren't
6. A: Do
   B: they do
7. A: Is
   B: it isn't
8. A: Does
   B: it doesn't
9. A: Are
   B: I am
10. A: Does
    B: it does

◇ PRACTICE 4, p. 88.

1. Yes, I do. OR No, I don't.
2. Yes, she does. OR No she doesn't.
3. Yes, I am. OR No, I'm not.
4. Yes, I will. OR No, I won't.
5. Yes, I can. OR No, I can't.
6. Yes, I do. OR No, I don't.
7. Yes, we are. OR No, we aren't.
8. Yes, they can. OR No, they can't.
9. Yes, they should. OR No, they shouldn't.
10. Yes, I did. OR No, I didn't.
11. Yes, I do. OR No, I don't.
12. Yes, it will. OR No, it won't.
13. Yes, it does. OR No, it doesn't.
14. Yes, they were. OR No, they weren't.
15. Yes, he/she should. OR No, he/she shouldn't.
16. Yes, it is. OR No, it isn't.
17. Yes, it was. OR No, it wasn't.

◇ PRACTICE 5, p. 89.

1. A: Does Jane eat
   B: she does.
2. A: Do
   B: they don't.
3. A: Did Ann and Jim come
   B: they didn't.
4. A: Are you writing
   B: I am.
5. A: Were you
   B: I wasn't.
6. A: Is Tim Wilson
   B: he is.
7. A: Will Karen finish
   B: she will.
8. A: Can birds swim
   B: they can.
9. A: Have you looked
   B: I haven't.

◇ PRACTICE 6, p. 89.

question word	helping verb	subject	main verb	rest of sentence
1. Ø	Did	you	hear	the news yesterday?
2. When	did	you	hear	the news?
3. Ø	Is	Eric	reading	today's paper?
4. What	is	Eric	reading?	Ø
5. Ø	Did	you	find	your wallet?
6. Where	did	you	find	your wallet?
7. Why	does	Mr. Li	walk	to work?
8. Ø	Does	Mr. Li	walk	to work?
9. Ø	Will	Ms. Cook	return	to her office?
10. When	will	Ms. Cook	return	to her office?
11. Ø	Is	the orange juice		in the refrigerator?
12. Where	is	the orange juice?		Ø

◇ PRACTICE 7, p. 90.

1. What time/When do the fireworks start
2. Why are you waiting
3. When does Rachel start
4. What time/When do you leave
5. Why didn't you get
6. Where can I find
7. When are you leaving
8. When do you expect
9. Where will the spaceship go
10. Where did you study . . . Why did you study . . . Why didn't you go

◇ PRACTICE 8, p. 91.

1. When/What time did you get up
2. Where did you eat lunch
3. When/What time did you eat
4. Why do you eat lunch
5. Where do your aunt and uncle live
6. When are you going to visit
7. When/What time will you get home
8. Where is George going to study
9. Why does George study
10. Where can I catch
11. When/What time do you have to leave
12. Where were you living
13. Why are the students writing
14. What time should I call
15. Why is Yoko

◇ PRACTICE 9, p. 92.

1. were you
2. can't you come
3. did Tom go
4. won't Ann be
5. do you need
6. are you going to buy
7. didn't you do
8. isn't Anita coming
9. are you and Joe going
10. didn't you eat
11. did Jack take
12. don't you like

◇ PRACTICE 10, p. 93.

1. Who knows Tom?
2. Who(m) does Tom know?
3. Who will help us?
4. Who(m) will you ask?
5. Who(m) is Eric talking to on the phone? OR (formal: To whom is Eric talking on the phone?)
6. Who is knocking on the door?
7. What surprised them?
8. What did Jack say?
9. What did Sue talk about?
10. Who(m) did Ann talk about? OR (formal: About whom did Ann talk?)

◇ PRACTICE 11, p. 94.

1. Who taught
2. What did Robert see
3. Who got
4. What are you making
5. Who does that calculator belong
6. What do you have
7. What did the cat kill
8. What killed the cat
9. What makes
10. Who wrote a note
11. Who(m) did you get a letter

◇ PRACTICE 12, p. 95.

1. A: What does "explore" mean?
   B: "to go to a new place and find out about it."
2. A: What does "underneath" mean?
   B: "under."
3. A: What does "blink" mean?
   B: "to open and close your eyes quickly."
4. A: What does "delicious" mean?
   B: "it tastes very, very, good."

◇ PRACTICE 13, p. 95.

1. What is Alex doing?
2. What should I do
3. What do astronauts do?
4. What are you going to do
5. What do you do
6. What can I do
7. What did Sara do
8. What should I do?
9. What is Emily going to do
10. What did you do
11. What would you like to do (*also possible:* Where would you like to go)
12. What are you trying to do?
13. What does Kevin need to do?
14. What does Nick do?
15. What did he do? . . . What did you do? . . . what did he do?

◇ PRACTICE 14, p. 96.

1. What kind of music
2. What kind of clothes/clothing
3. What kind of food
4. What kind of books
5. What kind of car
6. What kind of government
7. What kind of job
8. What kind of person/man/woman
9. What kind of products/things

◇ PRACTICE 15, p. 97.

1. Which
2. What
3. Which
4. What
5. Which
6. Which
7. What
8. What
9. Which

◇ PRACTICE 16, p. 98.

1. Who
2. Whose
3. Whose
4. Who
5. Who
6. Who
7. Whose
8. Whose

◇ PRACTICE 17, p. 99.

1. Whose house is that?
2. Who's living in that house?
3. Whose umbrella did you borrow?
4. Whose book did you use?
5. Whose book is on the table?
6. Who is on the phone?
7. Who's that?
8. Whose is that?

1. A: hot
   B: hot
2. soon
3. expensive
4. A: busy
   B: busy
5. A: serious
   B: serious
6. safe
7. B: fresh
   A: fresh . . . fresh
8. A: well
   B: well

◇ PRACTICE 19, p. 100.

1. far	7. long	13. long
2. long	8. far	14. often
3. often	9. long	15. far
4. far	10. often	16. long
5. far	11. long	17. often
6. often	12. far	

◇ PRACTICE 20, p. 101.

1. What is Jack doing
2. Who is he playing
3. What is Anna doing
4. What is she throwing
5. What are Anna and Jack holding
6. What is
7. Where are they
8. How long have they been playing
9. Who is winning
10. Who won

◇ PRACTICE 21, p. 102.

1. When will the clean clothes be
2. Where did you go
3. Which dictionary did you buy
4. How long did it take you
5. How can I reach
6. What kind of bread do you like
7. Why didn't you answer
8. Who are you going
9. Who repaired
10. How is the weather

◇ PRACTICE 22, p. 103.

1. a. don't
   b. doesn't
   c. don't
   d. doesn't
   e. isn't
   f. aren't
   g. does
   h. is
2. a. didn't
   b. did
   c. were
   d. wasn't
3. a. aren't
   b. is
   c. is
   d. weren't
   e. was
4. a. hasn't
   b. haven't
   c. have
   d. hasn't
   e. has
5. a. can't
   b. will
   c. shouldn't
   d. wouldn't
   e. do
   f. didn't

◇ PRACTICE 23, p. 104.

1. A: haven't you?
   B: Yes, I have.
2. A: has he?
   B: No, he hasn't.
3. A: didn't you?
   B: Yes, I did.
4. A: don't you?
   B: Yes, I do.
5. A: haven't they?
   B: Yes, they have.
6. A: hasn't she?
   B: Yes, she has.
7. A: is it?
   B: No, it isn't.
8. A: don't we?
   B: Yes, we do.
9. A: doesn't he?
   B: Yes, he does.
10. A: didn't you?
    B: Yes, I did.
11. A: is it?
    B: No, it isn't.
12. A: does he?
    B: No, he doesn't.
13. A: do I?
    B: No, you don't.
14. A: is it?
    B: No, it isn't.
15. A: weren't they?
    B: Yes, they were.
16. A: will she?
    B: No, she won't.

◇ PRACTICE 24, p. 105.

1. **Who** saw the car accident?
2. Why **didn't you** say "good-bye" when you left?
3. How about **asking** Julie and Tim to come for dinner Friday night?
4. What time **does** class **begin** today?
5. Why **does** he have no shoes on his feet?
   (*also possible:* Why **doesn't** he have **any** shoes on his feet?)
6. Where **can you** get a drink of water in this building?
7. What kind of music **do** you like best?
8. How long **does** it **take** to get to the beach from here?
9. She is working late tonight, **isn't** she?
10. **Whose** glasses are those?
11. How ~~much~~ tall **is** your father?
12. Who **did** you **talk** to about registration for next term?
13. How about ~~we~~ **going** to see the baby elephant at the zoo tomorrow?
14. How far **is it** from here to the nearest gas station?

◇ PRACTICE 25, p. 106.

1. When are you going to buy
2. How are you going to pay
3. How long did you have
4. How often do you ride
5. How do you get
6. Are you going to ride
7. Why didn't you ride
8. Does your bike have
9. What kind of bike do you have
10. When did Jason get
11. Who broke
12. What did Billy break
13. Whose new bike is broken
14. How did Billy break
15. Which bicycle is
16. Where do you keep
17. Who does that bike belong to
18. Whose bike did you borrow
19. Where is Rita
20. What is she doing
21. How far did Rita ride
22. How do you spell

Chapter 6: NOUNS AND PRONOUNS

◇ **PRACTICE 1, p. 108.**

1. Airplanes . . . wings
2. Child**ren** . . . swings
3. animals . . . zoos
4. Trees . . . branch**es** . . . lea**ves**
5. ducks . . . **gee**se . . . pond . . . park
6. bab**ies** . . . t**eeth**
7. potato**es** . . . beans . . . peas . . . tomato**es**
8. Opinions . . . facts
9. country . . . customs
10. Governments . . . taxes

◇ **PRACTICE 2, p. 108.**

1. /z/	7. /əz/
2. /s/	8. /z/
3. /s/	9. /s/
4. /əz/	10. /əz/
5. /z/	11. /z/
6. /z/	12. /s/

◇ **PRACTICE 3, p. 108.**

1. /z/	7. /z/
2. /s/	8. /s/
3. /əz/	9. /əz/
4. /s/	10. /s/
5. /z/	11. /əz/
6. /z/	12. /əz/

◇ **PRACTICE 4, p. 109.**

1. /z/ . . . /z/ . . . /z/
2. /əz/ . . . /əz/
3. /z/ . . . /z/ . . . /z/
4. /əz/ . . . /z/
5. /z/ . . . /əz/
6. /z/ . . . /əz/ . . . /s/
7. /əz/ . . . /əz/
8. /z/ . . . /z/ . . . /z/

◇ **PRACTICE 5, p. 109.**

1. mouse	12. beliefs	23. sheep
2. pockets	13. potatoes	24. loaf
3. tooth	14. radios	25. glasses
4. tomato	15. offspring	26. problems
5. fish	16. child	27. families
6. woman	17. seasons	28. wives
7. branches	18. customs	29. shelves
8. friends	19. businesses	30. roofs
9. duties	20. century	31. foot
10. highways	21. occurrences	32. women
11. thieves	22. phenomenon	

◇ **PRACTICE 6, p. 110.**

1. cows, sheep, horses, mice, geese
2. potatoes, tomatoes, peas, beans
3. apples, grapes, strawberries, bananas, cherries, pears
4. poppies, daffodils, roses, daisies, lilies
5. babies, sons, daughters, husbands, wives, children

◇ **PRACTICE 7, p. 111.**

1. <u>Children</u> <u>play</u> <u>games</u>. (S V O)
2. <u>Fish</u> <u>swim</u>. (S V)
3. The <u>baby</u> <u>doesn't like</u> her new <u>toys</u>. (S V O)
4. <u>Computers</u> <u>process</u> <u>information</u> quickly. (S V O)
5. <u>Dictionaries</u> <u>give</u> <u>definitions</u>. (S V O)
6. <u>Teachers</u> <u>correct</u> <u>tests</u>. (S V O)
7. The <u>cat</u> <u>found</u> a <u>mouse</u>. (S V O)
8. The <u>sun</u> <u>shines</u> brightly. (S V)
9. <u>Water</u> <u>evaporates</u>. (S V)
10. <u>Do</u> <u>snakes</u> <u>lay</u> <u>eggs</u>? (V S V O)
11. The <u>child</u> <u>petted</u> the <u>dog</u>. (S V O)
12. <u>Did</u> the <u>phone</u> <u>ring</u>? (V S V)

◇ **PRACTICE 8, p. 111.**

1. The man opened the door <u>with</u> his <u>key</u>. (PREP — O of PREP)
2. The little girl put her shoes <u>on</u> the wrong <u>feet</u>. (PREP — O of PREP)
3. The student added and subtracted <u>with</u> a <u>calculator</u>. (PREP — O of PREP)
4. My father fixes breakfast <u>for</u> my <u>mother</u> every morning. (PREP — O of PREP)
5. Librarians work <u>in</u> <u>libraries</u>. (PREP — O of PREP)
6. The bird flew <u>into</u> the <u>window</u> <u>of</u> the <u>building</u>. (PREP — O of PREP — PREP — O of PREP)
7. I do all my homework <u>on</u> a <u>computer</u>. (PREP — O of PREP)
8. The artist drew scenes <u>of</u> the <u>beach</u> <u>in</u> his <u>notebook</u>. (PREP — O of PREP — PREP — O of PREP)
9. The children played <u>in</u> the <u>backyard</u> <u>until</u> <u>dinner</u>. (PREP — O of PREP — PREP — O of PREP)
10. It rained <u>for</u> two <u>weeks</u>. (PREP — O of PREP)
11. The painter splashed paint <u>on</u> the <u>floor</u> <u>of</u> his <u>studio</u>. (PREP — O of PREP — PREP — O of PREP)
12. A man <u>with</u> dark <u>glasses</u> stood <u>near</u> the <u>door</u>. (PREP — O of PREP — PREP — O of PREP)

◇ **PRACTICE 9, p. 112.**

        S   V   O
1. Bridges cross rivers.

              S   V   PP
2. A terrible earthquake occurred in Turkey.

       S   V   PP
3. Airplanes fly above the clouds.

      S   V   O
4. Trucks carry large loads.

      S   V   PP
5. Rivers flow toward the sea.

         S   V   O   PP
6. Salespeople treat customers with courtesy.

      S   V   O
7. Bacteria can cause diseases.

      S   V   PP
8. Clouds are floating across the sky.

       S   PP   V   O
9. The audience in the theater applauded the performers

         PP   PP
   at the end of the show.

       S   V   O   PP
10. Helmets protect bicyclists from serious injuries.

◇ **PRACTICE 10, p. 112.**

1. in	5. at	9. at	13. in
2. in	6. at	10. at	14. in
3. on	7. in	11. in	15. on
4. on	8. on	12. on	

◇ **PRACTICE 11, p. 113.**

1. 3	4. 2	7. 2
1	1	3
2	3	1
2. 1	5. 1	8. 3
2	3	1
3	2	2
3. 2	6. 3	9. 2
3	1	1
1	2	3

◇ **PRACTICE 12, p. 114.**

1. are	5. is	9. are
2. are	6. is	10. is
3. are	7. is	
4. is	8. is	

◇ **PRACTICE 13, p. 114.**

1. make	5. are	9. needs
2. need	6. comes	10. go
3. Do	7. is	11. work
4. are	8. are	12. are

◇ **PRACTICE 14, p. 114.**

1. old	9. hard	17. cheap/inexpensive
2. old	10. narrow	18. light
3. cold/cool	11. clean	19. light
4. slow	12. empty	20. public
5. happy	13. safe	21. right
6. bad	14. noisy	22. right
7. wet	15. deep	23. strong
8. easy	16. sour	24. long

◇ **PRACTICE 15, p. 115.**

adjective	→	*noun it describes*
1. loud	→	voice
2. sweet	→	Sugar
3. easy	→	test
4. free	→	Air
5. delicious	→	food
Mexican	→	restaurant
6. important	→	facts
wide	→	variety
7. sick	→	child
8. sick	→	child
warm	→	bed
hot	→	tea
9. camping	→	equipment
old, rusty	→	equipment
10. hungry	→	bear
garbage	→	cans
11. elderly	→	father
nursing	→	care
12. fresh	→	coffee
warm	→	cookies

◇ **PRACTICE 16, p. 116.**

1. newspaper articles	11. brick walls
2. page numbers	12. egg cartons
3. paper money	13. mountain views
4. apartment buildings	14. pocket knives
5. computer disks	15. traffic lights
6. birthday presents	16. picnic tables
7. rose gardens	17. apple pies
8. key chains	18. bicycle helmets
9. city governments	19. log cabins
10. duck ponds	20. steel bridges

◇ **PRACTICE 17, p. 117.**

1. mountains
2. Cats . . . **mice**
3. Mosquito**es**/Mosquito**s** . . . insects
4. eyelash**es**
5. Ge**es**e . . . ducks
6. programs
7. Forests . . . fires . . . fires . . . animals
8. kni**ves** . . . weapons
9. manners
10. tickets
11. li**ves** . . . ways . . . years . . . lamps . . . candles . . . houses . . . chickens . . . fires
12. kinds . . . flowers
13. reporters . . . jobs
14. universi**ties**
15. students
16. animals . . . horses . . . zebras [NOTE: *deer* is already plural]
17. students . . . experiments . . . class**es**
18. House**flies** . . . pests . . . germs
19. articles . . . experiences
20. devices . . . batte**ries** . . . flashlights . . . calculators . . . radios . . . recorders . . . kinds . . . toys . . . batte**ries**

◇ PRACTICE 18, p. 118

1. The teacher helped __me__ with the lesson.
   (O of V over "me")

2. I carry a dictionary with __me__ at all times.
   (S over "I"; O of PREP over "me")

3. Mr. Fong has a computer. __He__ uses __it__ for many things. __It__ helps __him__ in many ways.
   (S over "He"; O of V over "it"; S over "It"; O of V over "him")

4. Jessica went to Hawaii with Ann and __me__. __We__ like __her__, and __she__ likes __us__. __We__ had a good time with __her__.
   (O of PREP over "me"; S over "We"; O of V over "her"; S over "she"; O of V over "us"; S over "We"; O of PREP over "her")

5. Mike had dirty socks. __He__ washed __them__ in the kitchen sink and hung __them__ to dry in front of the window. __They__ dried quickly.
   (S over "He"; O of V over "them"; O of V over "them"; S over "They")

6. Joseph and __I__ are close friends. No bad feelings will ever come between __him__ and __me__. __He__ and __I__ share a strong bond of friendship.
   (O of PREP over "him"; O of PREP over "me"; S over "He"; S over "I")

◇ PRACTICE 19, p. 118.

pronoun	→	noun/noun phrase
1. She	→	Janet
it	→	a green apple
2. her	→	Betsy
3. They	→	Nick and Rob
4. They	→	phone messages
5. him	→	Louie
He	→	Louie
her	→	Alice
She	→	Alice
6. She	→	Jane
it	→	letter
them	→	Mr. and Mrs. Moore
They	→	Mr. and Mrs. Moore
her	→	Jane

◇ PRACTICE 20, p. 119.

1. me
2. He
3. him
4. he
5. her
6. She
7. me . . . He . . . us
8. her . . . They
9. I . . . They . . . us . . . it . . . We . . . them
10. them
11. me . . . him
12. she
13. I . . . him and me
14. them . . . They . . . her . . . it . . . She
15. me . . . him
16. me . . . him
17. me . . . he . . . him . . . us . . . We . . . We . . . him . . . he

◇ PRACTICE 21, p. 120.

1. friend's
2. friends'
3. son's
4. sons'
5. baby's
6. babies'
7. child's
8. children's
9. person's
10. people's
11. teacher's
12. teachers'
13. man's
14. men's
15. earth's

◇ PRACTICE 22, p. 120.

1. Dan's
2. (no change)
3. Jack's
4. (no change)
5. roommate's
6. roommates'
7. (no change)
8. Betty's . . . sister's
9. sisters'
10. woman's
11. women's . . . men's
12. Jupiter's surface
13. Mercury's atmosphere
14. Mars'/Mars's surface . . . Earth's surface
15. Earth's twin . . . Venus'/Venus's surface
16. planets' . . . Jupiter's son . . . Venus'/Venus's son

◇ PRACTICE 23, p. 122.

1. your . . . yours
2. her . . . hers
3. his . . . his
4. your . . . yours
5. their . . . our . . . theirs . . . ours

◇ PRACTICE 24, p. 122.

1. her
2. hers
3. Our
4. Ours
5. your
6. mine . . . my . . . yours
7. their . . . theirs
8. mine . . . yours
9. ours

◇ PRACTICE 25, p. 123.

1. myself
2. himself
3. ourselves
4. yourself
5. yourselves
6. herself
7. themselves
8. himself
9. herself
10. myself
11. ourselves
12. themselves
13. herself/himself
14. ourselves
15. themselves
16. herself
17. himself
18. themselves
19. yourself/yourselves

◇ PRACTICE 26, p. 124.

1. cut myself
2. be proud of yourself
3. talks to himself
4. taught myself
5. blamed herself
6. help yourselves
7. takes care of himself
8. enjoyed themselves
9. worked for himself
10. introduce themselves

◇ PRACTICE 27, p. 125.

1. me . . . him
2. yourselves
3. itself
4. its . . . its
5. hers
6. him
7. yourself . . . your
8. our . . . our
9. ours
10. themselves
11. itself
12. himself

◇ PRACTICE 28, p. 125.

1. his . . . He . . . himself . . . he . . . him
2. Her . . . She
3. Our . . . We
4. her
5. my . . . I
6. hers
7. mine

8. They . . . themselves . . . them . . . theirs . . . Their . . . their
9. hers . . . his
10. himself . . . him . . . he . . . his . . . He . . . him
11. her . . . she . . . herself (also possible: it) . . . she . . . her
12. your . . . ours

◇ PRACTICE 29, p. 126.
1. one . . . another . . . another . . . the other
2. one . . . another . . . the other
3. one . . . another . . . another . . . another . . . the other
4. one . . . the other
5. one . . . another . . . another . . . another . . . another . . . the other

◇ PRACTICE 30, p. 127.
1. another
2. The other
3. The other
4. Another
5. The other
6. a. Another
   b. the other
7. a. another
   b. another
c. another
d. another
e. another
8. another
9. The other
10. The other
11. another

◇ PRACTICE 31, p. 128.
1. The others
2. The others
3. Others
4. others
5. other
6. Others
7. Other
8. Others
9. Other
10. The others
11. The other
12. The other
13. Others . . . other
14. another . . . other
15. another . . . Other
16. The others
17. The other

◇ PRACTICE 32, p. 129.
1. A
2. C
3. D
4. B
5. B
6. A
7. D
8. B

◇ PRACTICE 33, p. 130.
1. are
2. potatoes
3. by myself
4. on . . . at
5. four-week
6. us
7. its
8. our . . . yours
9. himself
10. the others

◇ PRACTICE 34, p. 130.
1. Look at those **beautiful** mountains!
2. The children played **a game at the park** on Saturday afternoon.
3. There are two **horses,** several **sheep,** and a cow in the **farmer's** field.
4. The owner of the store is busy **at** the moment.
5. The teacher met **her** students at the park after school.
6. Everyone **wants** peace in the world.
7. I grew up in a **very large** city.
8. This apple tastes sour. Here's some more, so let's try **another** (OR **another one**).

9. Some **trees** lose their **leaves** in the winter.
10. I am going to wear my **brown** shirt ~~is~~ to the party.
11. I hurt **myself** at work last week.
12. Our neighbors invited my friend and **me** to visit **them.**
13. My **husband's** boss works for twelve **hours** every **day.**
14. The students couldn't find **their** books.
15. I always read **magazine** articles while I'm in the waiting room at my **dentist's** office.

Chapter 7: MODAL AUXILIARIES

◇ PRACTICE 1, p. 132.
(1) has to = *must*
(3) can't = *is not able to*
    may = *might*
(5) couldn't = *was not able to*
(7) got to = *must*
(10) have to = *must*
(12) 'd (had) better = *should*
(13) ought to = *should*
    has to = *must*
(17) might = *may*
(21) ought to = *should*

◇ PRACTICE 2, p. 133.
1. Ø
2. to
3. Ø
4. Ø
5. Ø
6. to
7. Ø
8. to
9. Ø
10. Ø . . . Ø
11. to . . . Ø
12. Ø
13. Ø

◇ PRACTICE 3, p. 134.
1. zebra
2. cat
3. Elephants
4. Monkeys
5. camels
6. cow
7. horse
8. donkey
9. squirrel
10. ants
11. baby
12. women

◇ PRACTICE 4, p. 134.
1. may/might . . . may not/might not
2. can't
3. can . . . may/might . . . may not/might not
4. may/might
5. can't
6. may/might . . . may/might
7. can't

◇ PRACTICE 5, p. 135.
1. I might take a nap.
2. Maybe she is sick.
3. Maybe there will be time later.
4. Our team may win.
5. You might be right.
6. We may hear soon.
7. It may rain.
8. It might snow.
9. Maybe she will come tomorrow.
10. Maybe she is at home right now.

◇ PRACTICE 6, p. 135.

1. possibility	6. permission
2. possibility	7. possibility
3. permission	8. permission
4. possibility	9. possibility
5. possibility	10. permission

◇ PRACTICE 7, p. 136.

1. b	4. a	7. b
2. b	5. b	8. a
3. a	6. a	

◇ PRACTICE 8, p. 137.

1. Can	6. A: Could
2. may	B: May
3. Would	7. A: Can
4. could	B: Will
5. Can	8. Could

◇ PRACTICE 9, p. 137.

1. Could/Can/Would
2. Could/May/Can
3. Would/Could/Will
4. Can/May/Could
5. Will/Can/Could

◇ PRACTICE 10, p. 138.

1. shouldn't drive a long distance
2. should quit
3. shouldn't exceed the speed limit
4. shouldn't give too much homework
5. shouldn't miss any classes
6. shouldn't be cruel to animals
7. should always be on time for an appointment
8. shouldn't throw trash out of your car window

◇ PRACTICE 11, p. 138.

1. soak it in cold water . . . wash it in hot water
2. take it back to the store . . . try to fix it herself
3. get a job
4. call the landlord and complain
5. find a new girlfriend
6. send it back to the kitchen . . . eat it

◇ PRACTICE 12, p. 139.

1. A	6. C
2. C	7. A
3. B	8. C
4. A	9. B
5. B	10. C

◇ PRACTICE 13, p. 140.

1. C	5. B
2. A	6. A
3. D	7. D
4. C	8. C

◇ PRACTICE 14, p. 140.

1. have to/must	5. has to
2. had to	6. had to
3. have to/must	7. have to/must
4. had to	8. had to

◇ PRACTICE 15, p. 141.

1. had to	4. had to
2. had to	5. have to
3. have to	6. had to

◇ PRACTICE 16, p. 141.

1. had to study	4. had to see
2. had to turn off	5. had to be
3. Did you have to work	6. had to close

◇ PRACTICE 17, p. 141.

1. must not	9. must not
2. don't have to	10. don't have to
3. don't have to	11. don't have to
4. don't have to	12. must not
5. must not	13. must not
6. don't have to	14. must not
7. must not	15. don't have to
8. must not	

◇ PRACTICE 18, p. 143.

1. must/have to	5. doesn't have to
2. doesn't have to	6. must/has to
3. don't have to	7. must not
4. must/has to	

◇ PRACTICE 19, p. 143.

People have to/must . . .
eat and drink in order to live
pay taxes
stop when they see a police car's lights behind them

People must not . . .
fall asleep while driving
drive without a license
take other people's belongings

People don't have to . . .
cook every meal themselves
say "sir" or "madam" to others
stay in their homes in the evening

◇ PRACTICE 20, p. 144.

1. 2	6. 2
2. 1	7. 2
3. 1	8. 2
4. 2	9. 1
5. 1	

◇ PRACTICE 21, p. 144.

1. Wait	6. Don't cross
2. Don't wait	7. Don't stand . . . Do
3. Read	8. Call
4. Don't put	9. Take . . . Go . . . Walk . . . give
5. Come . . . have	10. Capitalize . . . Put . . . use

◇ PRACTICE 22, p. 145.

1. 1	2. 2	3. 2	4. 4
4	1	1	2
3	4		1
2	3		3

◇ **PRACTICE 23, p. 145.**

1. A: go . . . fly
   B: see
2. A: get
   B: take/ask
3. A: go
   B: play
4. A: get/take
   B: take . . . save
5. A: stop . . . fill up
   B: get/pick up
6. go . . . call . . . ask/see

◇ **PRACTICE 24, p. 146.**

1. prefer
2. like
3. would rather
4. prefer
5. would rather
6. A: prefer
   B: likes . . . would rather
7. would rather
8. would rather
9. B: prefer
   A: like
10. prefer

◇ **PRACTICE 25, p. 147.**

1. Kim prefers salad to dessert.
2. In general, Nicole likes coffee better than tea.
3. Bill would rather teach history than work as a business executive.
4. When considering a pet, Sam likes dogs better than cats.
5. On a long trip, Susie prefers to drive than (to) ride in the back seat.
6. I would rather study in a noisy room than study in a completely quiet room.
7. Alex would rather play soccer than baseball.

◇ **PRACTICE 26, p. 148.**

1. C	6. C	11. B
2. A	7. B	12. B
3. C	8. C	13. A
4. A	9. B	14. C
5. B	10. C	15. A

◇ **PRACTICE 27, p. 149.**

1. Before I left on my trip last month, I **had to** get a passport.
2. Could you ~~to~~ bring us more coffee, please?
3. Ben can **drive**, but he prefers **to** take the bus.
4. My roommate **may be** at home this evening.
5. A few of our classmates can't ~~to~~ come to the school picnic.
6. **Could/Would/Will/Can** you take our picture, please?
7. Jane's eyes are red, and she is yawning. She must **be** sleepy.
8. Jim would rather **have** Fridays off in the summer than **have/take** a long vacation.
9. I must **read** several lengthy books for my literature class.
10. Take your warm clothes with you. It **may/might** snow. OR **Maybe it will** snow.
11. When the baby went to the doctor last week, she **had to have** several shots.
12. It's very cool in here. Please ~~you~~ turn up the heat. OR **Would/Could/Will/Can you** please turn up the heat?
13. You had better ~~to~~ call us before you come over. We're often away during the day.
14. The children would rather ~~to~~ see the circus than a baseball game.
15. It's such a gorgeous day. Why **don't we** go to a park or the beach?

◇ **PRACTICE 28, p. 150.**

(1) may . . . is . . . can . . . can
(2) should . . . can . . . should . . . should not . . . is . . . Will
(3) do not have to . . . do not have to . . . can
(4) have to . . . cannot . . . must . . . do . . . is . . . can . . . should
(5) ought to . . . prepare
(6) are . . . might . . . may . . . Maybe . . . could . . . is . . . are . . . should
(7) should . . . will . . . can change . . . should . . . should . . . should
(8) is . . . should

Chapter 8: CONNECTING IDEAS

◇ **PRACTICE 1, p. 152.**

1. The farmer has a <u>cow</u>, a <u>goat</u>, and a black <u>horse</u>.
       noun + noun + noun
2. Danny is a <u>bright</u> and <u>happy</u> child.
       adj. + adj.
3. I <u>picked</u> up the telephone and <u>dialed</u> Steve's number.
       verb + verb
4. The cook <u>washed</u> the vegetables and <u>put</u> them in boiling water.
       verb + verb
5. My feet were <u>cold</u> and <u>wet</u>.
       adj. + adj.
6. Anita is <u>responsible</u>, <u>considerate</u>, and <u>trustworthy</u>.
       adj. + adj. + adj.
7. The three largest land animals are the <u>elephant</u>, the <u>rhinoceros</u>, and the <u>hippopotamus</u>.
       noun + noun + noun
8. A hippopotamus <u>rests</u> in water during the day and <u>feeds</u> on land at night.
       verb + verb

◇ **PRACTICE 2, p. 153.**

1. *(no commas)*
2. I opened the door, walked into the room, and sat down at my desk.
3. *(no commas)*
4. Their flag is green, black, and yellow.
5. *(no commas)*
6. Tom made a sandwich, poured a glass of juice, and sat down to eat his lunch.
7. Ms. Parker is intelligent, friendly, and kind.
8. *(no commas)*
9. Did you bring copies of the annual report for Sue, Dan, Joe, and Mary?
10. *(no commas)*
11. Can you watch television, listen to the radio, and read the newspaper at the same time?
12. *(no commas)*
13. Doctors save lives, relieve suffering, and cure diseases.
14. The restaurant served a five-course dinner: soup, fish, entrée, salad, and dessert.
15. *(no commas)*
16. An invitation should include your name, address, the date, the time, the purpose of the party, and any special activities such as swimming or dancing.

◇ PRACTICE 3, p. 153.

S V S V
1. Birds fly, and fish swim.

S V S V
2. Birds fly. **F**~~f~~ish swim.

S V S V
3. Dogs bark. **L**~~l~~ions roar.

S V S V
4. Dogs bark, and lions roar.

S V S V
5. A week has seven days. **A**~~a~~ year has 365 days.

S V S V
6. A week has seven days, and a year has 365 days.

S V S V
7. Ahmed raised his hand, and the teacher pointed at him.

S V S V
8. Ahmed raised his hand. **T**~~t~~he teacher pointed at him.

◇ PRACTICE 4, p. 154.

1. I
2. C
3. C
4. I
5. I
6. C
7. C
8. C
9. I

◇ PRACTICE 5, p. 154.

1. I talked to Amy for a long time, but she didn't listen.
2. *(no change)*
3. *(no change)*
4. *(no change)*
5. Please call Jane, Ted, or Anna.
6. Please call Jane, Ted, and Anna.
7. I waved at my friend, but she didn't see me.
8. I waved at my friend, and she waved back.
9. *(no change)*
10. *(no change)*
11. My test was short and easy, but Ali's test was hard.

◇ PRACTICE 6, p. 155.

1. C
2. B
3. A
4. C
5. B
6. C
7. A
8. C

◇ PRACTICE 7, p. 155.

1. *(no change)*
2. I washed the dishes, and my son dried them.
3. I called their house, but no one answered the phone.
4. *(no change)*
5. I bought some apples, peaches, and bananas.
6. I was hungry, so I ate an apple.
7. *(no change)*
8. *(no change)*
9. My daughter is affectionate, shy, independent, and smart.
10. It started to rain, so we went inside and watched television.

◇ PRACTICE 8, p. 156.

1. . . . Every air traffic controller worldwide uses English, so it is important for Gina to become fluent in the language.
2. Gina has decided to take some intensive English courses at a private language institute, but she isn't sure which one to attend. There are many schools available, and they offer many different kinds of classes.
3. Gina has also heard of air traffic control schools that include English as part of their coursework, but she needs to have a fairly high level of English to attend.
4. Gina needs to decide soon, or the classes will be full . . . .

◇ PRACTICE 9, p. 156.

1. There are over 100,000 kinds of flies. **T**hey live throughout the world.
2. I like to get mail from my friends and family. **M**ail is important to me.
3. We are all connected by our humanity. **W**e need to help each other. **W**e can all live in peace.
4. There was a bad flood in Hong Kong. **T**he streets became raging streams. **L**uckily no one died in the flood.
5. People have used needles since prehistoric times. **T**he first buttons appeared almost two thousand years ago. **Z**ippers are a relatively recent invention. **T**he zipper was invented in 1890.

◇ PRACTICE 10, p. 157.

1. James has a cold. **H**e needs to rest and drink plenty of fluids, so he should go to bed and drink water, fruit juices, or soda pop. **H**e needs to sleep a lot, so he shouldn't drink fluids with caffeine, such as tea or coffee.
2. My friend and I were tired, so we went home early. **W**e wanted to stay until the end of the game, but it got too late for us. **B**oth of us had to get up early in the morning and go to our jobs.
3. The normal pulse for an adult is between 60 and 80 beats per minute, but exercise, nervousness, excitement, and a fever will all make a pulse beat faster. **T**he normal pulse for a child is around 80 to 90.
4. Many famous explorers throughout history set out on their hazardous journeys in search of gold, silver, jewels, or other treasures, but some explorers wanted only to discover information about their world.
5. Edward Fox was a park ranger for thirty-five years. **D**uring that time, he was hit by lightning eight times. **T**he lightning never killed him, but it severely burned his skin and damaged his hearing.
6. The Indian Ocean is bordered on four sides by the continents of Africa, Asia, Australia, and Antarctica. **S**ome of the important ports are Aden, Bombay, Calcutta, and Rangoon.
7. The Indian Ocean has many fish and shellfish, but it has less commercial fishing than the Atlantic or the Pacific. **T**he climate of the Indian Ocean is tropical, so fish spoil quickly out of the water. **I**t is difficult and expensive for commercial fishing boats to keep fish fresh.

◇ PRACTICE 11, p. 157.

1. did	10. are	19. does
2. does	11. will	20. don't
3. didn't	12. am	21. can't
4. do	13. won't	22. don't
5. does	14. will	23. is
6. doesn't	15. can	24. does
7. wasn't	16. has	25. did
8. is	17. did	26. is
9. isn't	18. would	27. isn't

◇ PRACTICE 12, p. 158.

1. does Tom . . . does too
2. does Brian . . . Brian doesn't
3. was I . . . I was
4. is Oregon . . . Oregon is
5. did Jean . . . Jean did
6. did Jason . . . Jason didn't
7. can Rick . . . Rick can't
8. does Laura . . . Laura does
9. does Alice . . . Alice doesn't
10. are porpoises . . . porpoises are
11. have I . . . I haven't
12. does my brother . . . my brother does
13. will Erin . . . Erin won't

◇ PRACTICE 13, p. 160.

PART I.

1. can't either	7. couldn't either
2. does too	8. did too
3. doesn't either	9. can't either
4. is too	10. does too
5. wasn't either	11. would too
6. didn't either	

PART II.

12. so is	18. neither is
13. neither do	19. so does
14. neither did	20. so is
15. so are	21. neither have
16. so do	22. so did
17. so is	23. neither did

◇ PRACTICE 14, p. 161.

1. Mr. Tanaka was late for work because [he] [missed] the bus. (s / v)

2. I closed the door because the [room] [was] cold. (s / v)

3. Because [I] [lost] my umbrella, I got wet on the way home. (s / v)

4. Joe didn't bring his book to class because [he] [couldn't find] it. (s / v)

5. The teacher couldn't hear the question because the [class] [was] so noisy. (s / v)

6. Because the [ice cream] [was beginning] to melt, I put it back in the freezer. (s / v)

◇ PRACTICE 15, p. 161.

1. I opened the window because the room was hot. **W**e felt more comfortable then.
2. Because his coffee was cold, Jack didn't finish it. **H**e left it on the table and walked away.
3. Because the weather was bad, we canceled our trip into the city. **W**e stayed home and watched TV.
4. Debbie is a cheerleader. **S**he woke up in the morning with a sore throat because she had cheered loudly at the basketball game.
5. Francisco is an intelligent and ambitious young man. **B**ecause he hopes to get a good job late in life, he is working hard to get a good education now.

◇ PRACTICE 16, p. 161.

1. *lose weight*—Eric went on a diet because he wanted to lose weight.
2. *didn't have money*—The family couldn't buy food because they didn't have money.
3. *have several children*—Our neighbors are very busy because they have several children.
4. *be tired*—Because I am tired, I am going to bed.
5. *exercise every day*—Because Susan exercises every day, she is in great shape.
6. *have a high fever*—Because Jennifer has a high fever, she is going to the doctor.

◇ PRACTICE 17, p. 162.

1. a. He was hungry, **so** he ate a sandwich.
   b. **Because** he was hungry, he ate a sandwich.
   c. He ate a sandwich **because** he was hungry.
2. a. **Because** my sister was tired, she went to bed.
   b. My sister went to bed **because** she was tired.
   c. My sister was tired, **so** she went to bed.
3. a. **Because** human beings have opposable thumbs, they can easily pick things up and hold them.
   b. Human beings have opposable thumbs, **so** they can easily pick things up and hold them.
   c. Human beings can easily pick things up and hold them **because** they have opposable thumbs.
4. a. Schoolchildren can usually identify Italy easily on a world map **because** it is shaped like a boot.
   b. **Because** Italy has the distinctive shape of a boot, schoolchildren can usually identify it easily.
   c. Italy has the distinctive shape of a boot, **so** schoolchildren can usually identify it easily on a map.

◇ PRACTICE 18, p. 163.

1. like	5. didn't change
2. don't like	6. didn't pass
3. is	7. ate
4. stayed	8. were

◇ PRACTICE 19, p. 164.

1. B	5. A	9. A
2. A	6. A	10. A
3. A	7. B	11. B
4. B	8. B	12. A

◇ PRACTICE 20, p. 165.

1. because
2. even though
3. even though
4. Even though
5. Because
6. Because
7. Even though
8. even though
9. because
10. even though
11. because . . . Even though . . . because

◇ PRACTICE 21, p. 166.

1. C
2. C
3. B
4. B
5. C
6. C
7. B
8. A
9. A
10. B
11. C
12. A
13. C

◇ PRACTICE 22, p. 168.

1. I don't drink coffee, and my roommate **doesn't** either.
2. The flight was overbooked, so I had to fly on another airline. OR The flight was overbooked. I had to fly on another airline.
3. Many people use computers for e-mail, the Internet, and word processing.
4. The room was stuffy and hot, but I didn't close the window.
5. The baby woke up crying **because** her diaper was wet.
6. Even **though** my father works two jobs, he always has time to play soccer or baseball on weekends with his family.
7. I saw a bad accident, and my sister **did** too.
8. Oscar always pays his bills on time, but his brother **doesn't**.
9. **Even though** my mother is afraid of heights, I took her up to the observation deck at the top of the building.
10. Janey doesn't like to get up early, and Joe **doesn't** either. OR Janey doesn't like to get up early, and **neither does** Joe.
11. Although it was raining quite hard, ~~but~~ we decided to go for a bike ride. OR ~~Although~~ It was raining quite hard, but we decided to go for a bike ride.
12. My mother and my father/ ~~They~~ immigrated to this country 30 years ago.
13. **Because** Maya is very intelligent, her parents want to put her in an advanced program at school.

Chapter 9: COMPARISONS

◇ PRACTICE 1, p. 169.

1. (just) as busy as Jason (is)
2. (nearly) as busy as Jason (is)
3. (nearly) as tired as Susan (was)
4. (nearly) as tired as Susan (was)
5. (just) as large as/as big as Po's (is)
6. (nearly) as big as Anna's (is)

◇ PRACTICE 2, p. 169.

1. aren't as noisy as
2. is as lazy as
3. aren't as strong as
4. is as tall as
5. isn't as comfortable as
6. isn't as big as
7. was as nervous as
8. isn't as fresh and clean as
9. am not as ambitious as
10. aren't as interesting as

◇ PRACTICE 3, p. 170.

PART I.
1. not nearly as
2. almost as / not quite as
3. not nearly as
4. just as

PART II.
5. just as
6. not nearly as
7. almost as / not quite as
8. not nearly as

PART III.
9. just as
10. not nearly as
11. almost as / not quite as

PART IV.
12. just as
13. almost as
14. just as
15. not nearly as
16. almost as / not quite as

◇ PRACTICE 4, p. 172.

1. E
2. C
3. D
4. G
5. B
6. H
7. F
8. A

◇ PRACTICE 5, p. 172.

PART I.
1. as snow
2. as ice
3. as a picture
4. as a bat
5. as a bone
6. as a pillow
7. as a wink
8. as a mouse
9. as a bird
10. as pie

PART II.
11. cold as ice
12. quick as a wink
13. blind as a bat
14. white as snow
15. quiet as a mouse
16. pretty as a picture
17. easy as pie
18. free as a bird
19. soft as a pillow
20. dry as a bone

◇ PRACTICE 6, p. 174.

1. stronger . . . the strongest
2. more important . . . the most important
3. softer . . . the softest
4. lazier . . . the laziest
5. more wonderful . . . the most wonderful
6. calmer . . . the calmest
7. tamer . . . the tamest
8. dimmer . . . the dimmest
9. more convenient . . . the most convenient
10. more clever/cleverer . . . the most clever/the cleverest
11. better . . . the best
12. worse . . . the worst
13. farther . . . the farthest
14. slower . . . the slowest
15. more slowly . . . the most slowly

◇ PRACTICE 7, p. 174.

1. colder than
2. older than
3. more expensive than
4. larger
5. hotter than
6. slower than
7. creamier than
8. worse than
9. faster than
10. more important
11. quicker than
12. heavier
13. safer than
14. more difficult than

◇ **PRACTICE 8, p. 175.**

1. colder
2. more generous
3. more slowly
4. more comfortable
5. friendlier/more friendly
6. more softly
7. softer
8. more careful
9. prettier
10. lazier

◇ **PRACTICE 9, p. 176.**

1. the worst
2. worse
3. the best
4. better
5. the worst
6. worse
7. the worst
8. better

◇ **PRACTICE 10, p. 176.**

1. A, B
2. B
3. A, B
4. B
5. B
6. B

◇ **PRACTICE 11, p. 177.**

1. more slowly (ADV)
2. slower (ADJ)
3. more serious (ADJ)
4. more seriously (ADV)
5. more politely (ADV)
6. more polite (ADJ)
7. more careful (ADJ)
8. more carefully (ADV)
9. more clearly (ADV)
10. clearer (ADJ)

◇ **PRACTICE 12, p. 177.**

1. I did
2. she is
3. I do
4. she did
5. I was
6. he will
7. he does
8. he has
9. she did
10. he can

◇ **PRACTICE 13, p. 178.**

	formal	*informal*
1.	I am	me
2.	he is	him
3.	I am	me
4.	she is	her
5.	I am	me
6.	I am	me

◇ **PRACTICE 14, p. 179.**

1. A
2. B, C, D
3. A
4. B, C, D
5. B, C, D
6. A
7. B, C, D
8. A
9. B, C, D

◇ **PRACTICE 15, p. 179.**

1. *(no change possible using **less**)*
2. I visit my brother less often than I visit my sister.
3. *(no change possible using **less**)*
4. Sam is less generous than his brother.
5. I'm less eager to go to the circus than the children are.
6. A notebook is less expensive than a textbook.
7. *(no change possible using **less**)*
8. Some people think that life in a city is less peaceful than life in a small town.
9. *(no change possible using **less**)*
10. I travel to Europe on business less frequently than I used to.

◇ **PRACTICE 16, p. 180.**

1. Sam enjoys football more than his best friend **does**.
2. OK
3. The coach helped Anna more than Nancy **did**. OR The coach helped Anna more than she/he **helped** Nancy.
5. Sara likes tennis more than her husband **does**.
5. OK
6. OK
7. Charles knows Judy better than Kevin **does**. OR Charles knows Judy better than he **knows** Kevin.

◇ **PRACTICE 17, p. 180.**

1. more newspapers (NOUN)
2. more homework (NOUN)
3. more snow (NOUN)
4. more friends (NOUN)
5. more pleasant/pleasanter (ADJ)
6. more easily (ADV)
7. more books (NOUN)
8. more carefully (ADV)
9. louder (ADJ)

◇ **PRACTICE 18, p. 181.**

1. better and better
2. bigger and bigger
3. colder and colder
4. louder and louder
5. angrier and angrier/more and more angry
6. longer and longer
7. more and more expensive
8. more and more tired
9. friendlier and friendlier/more and more friendly
10. faster and faster

◇ **PRACTICE 19, p. 181.**

1. The more . . . the stronger
2. The softer . . . the easier
3. the older . . . the wiser
4. The simpler . . . the more relaxed
5. The longer . . . the more tired
6. The harder . . . the more

◇ **PRACTICE 20, p. 182.**

1. more he talked, the more bored I became
2. older you are, the more you understand
3. more I thought about it, the more confused I became
4. more polluted the air, the greater the chances of developing respiratory diseases
5. faster he talked, the more confused I became
6. more the fans clapped and cheered, the more shots the basketball team made

◇ **PRACTICE 21, p. 183.**

1. the most familiar
2. the longest necks
3. the largest ears
4. the largest eyes
5. the most intelligent . . . the most intelligent

◇ PRACTICE 22, p. 183.

PART I.
1. the most difficult . . . ever
2. the friendliest . . . of
3. the most embarrassing . . . in
4. the wisest . . . ever
5. the best . . . in
6. the most artistic of
7. the hottest . . . in
8. the warmest . . . of
9. the brightest . . . ever
10. the highest . . . in
11. the most knowledgeable . . . of
12. the most important . . . in

PART II.
13. the least ambitious of
14. the least expensive . . . ever
15. the least populated . . . in
16. the least amount . . . ever

◇ PRACTICE 23, p. 184.

PART I.
1. A pencil . . . a telephone
2. A diamond ring . . . a paper clip
3. A cup of coffee . . . a can of coffee beans
4. Radios and CD players . . . big screen TVs
5. A compact car . . . a house
6. Footballs, soccer balls, and basketballs . . . ping-pong balls

PART II.
7. Angel Falls . . . than Niagara Falls
8. Giessbach Falls . . . as Cuquenán Falls
9. Angel Falls . . . of all
10. Niagara Falls . . . as Angel Falls
11. Giessbach Falls . . . as Cuquenán Falls

PART III.
12. Air . . . than iron
13. Iron . . . than wood
14. iron . . . of all
15. Air . . . as water
16. air . . . of all
17. Water . . . as air
18. Water and iron . . . than wood

◇ PRACTICE 24, p. 186.

1. a	4. a	7. a
2. b	5. a	8. b
3. b	6. b	

◇ PRACTICE 25, p. 186.

1. the funniest . . . funnier
2. sadder . . . the saddest
3. the best . . . better book
4. more exhausting . . . the most exhausting
5. happier . . . the happiest
6. more entertaining . . . the most entertaining
7. harder . . . the hardest
8. hotter . . . the hottest

◇ PRACTICE 26, p. 187.

1. more intelligent than . . . the smartest . . . in
2. the most popular . . . in
3. smaller than
4. More potatoes . . . than
5. the closest . . . faster than
6. the largest . . . in . . . the smallest . . . of
7. more important than . . . less important than
8. more information
9. kinder . . . more generous
10. more honest . . . than
11. the worst
12. the safest
13. faster . . . than
14. bigger than
15. more extensive . . . than

◇ PRACTICE 27, p. 188.

1. safer . . . than
2. the largest . . . in
3. more strength than
4. better
5. shortest
6. thinner . . . juicier
7. more comfortable . . . than
8. the most difficult of
9. the worst . . . in
10. harder than
11. lowest
12. the most complex . . . in
13. the funniest of
14. More people . . . than
15. less expensive . . . than

◇ PRACTICE 28, p. 189.

1. alike	5. like	9. like
2. like	6. like	10. alike
3. alike	7. alike	
4. alike	8. like	

◇ PRACTICE 29, p. 190.

1. from	7. to
2. to	8. as
3. as	9. to
4. from	10. from
5. as	11. as
6. to	12. from

◇ PRACTICE 30, p. 190.

PART I.
1. A is like D.
2. A and D are alike.
3. C is similar to A and D.
4. B is different from A, C, and D.

PART II.
5. similar to
6. the same as
7. different
8. the same as
9. different from

◇ PRACTICE 31, p. 191.

1. like
2. like
3. alike
4. A: alike
   B: alike/the same . . . the same . . . the same
5. like
6. A: like
   B: similar to
7. alike . . . alike . . . different
8. the same . . . the same . . . different

PRACTICE 32, p. 192.

1. My brother is older **than** me.
2. A sea is ~~more~~ deeper than a lake.
3. A donkey isn't as big **as** a horse.
4. Ellen is **the** happiest person I've ever met.
5. When I feel embarrassed, my face gets **redder** and **redder**.
6. One of **the** largest **animals** in the world is the hippopotamus.
7. The traffic on the highway is **worse** ~~from~~ than it was a few months ago.
8. Jack is the same **age as** Jerry.
9. Peas are similar **to** beans, but they have several differences.
10. Last winter was pretty mild. This winter is cold and rainy. It's much **rainier** than last winter.
11. Mrs. Peters, the substitute teacher, is **friendlier** than the regular instructor.
12. Although alligators and crocodiles are similar, alligators are **not as big as** crocodiles. OR alligators are **smaller** than crocodiles.
13. Mohammed and Tarek come from different countries, but they became friends easily because they speak **the** same language, Arabic.
14. Mothers of young children are **busier** than mothers of teenagers.
15. We'd like to go sailing, but the wind is not as strong today **as** it was yesterday.
16. We asked for a non-smoking room, but the air and furniture in our hotel room smelled **like** cigarette smoke.

Chapter 10: THE PASSIVE

◇ PRACTICE 1, p. 193.

	verb	active/passive
1.	grow	active
2.	is grown	passive
3.	wrote	active
4.	was written	passive
5.	explained	active
6.	was explained	passive
7.	are designed	passive
8.	design	active

◇ PRACTICE 2, p. 193.

1. <u>is</u> <u>delivered</u>
2. <u>has been</u> <u>eaten</u>
3. <u>was</u> <u>written</u>
4. <u>is going to be</u> <u>fixed</u>
5. <u>will be</u> <u>taught</u>
6. <u>is going to be</u> <u>brought</u>
7. <u>was</u> <u>won</u>
8. <u>will be</u> <u>treated</u>
9. <u>have been</u> <u>planted</u>
10. <u>are</u> <u>caught</u>

◇ PRACTICE 3, p. 194.

1.	brought	10.	left	19.	spent
2.	built	11.	lost	20.	taken
3.	bought	12.	made	21.	taught
4.	eaten	13.	found	22.	gone
5.	planned	14.	played	23.	visited
6.	given	15.	read	24.	worn
7.	grown	16.	saved	25.	written
8.	hit	17.	sent	26.	done
9.	hurt	18.	spoken		

◇ PRACTICE 4, p. 194.

1. was eaten
2. is spoken
3. are written
4. was hurt
5. is going to be visited
6. has been read
7. will be played
8. can be taught
9. are going to be taken
10. have been grown
11. is worn
12. will be built

◇ PRACTICE 5, p. 195.

1.	a	4.	b
2.	b	5.	b
3.	b	6.	a

◇ PRACTICE 6, p. 196.

PART I.
1. are collected
2. are written
3. is grown
4. are eaten
5. am paid
6. is understood

PART II.
7. were collected
8. was built
9. was written
10. were destroyed

PART III.
11. have been visited
12. has been spoken
13. have been read
14. has been worn

PART IV.
15. will be discovered
16. will be visited
17. will be saved

PART V
18. is going to be hurt
19. are going to be offered
20. is going to be elected

◇ PRACTICE 7, p. 197.

1. The government collects taxes.
2. Big fish eat small fish.
3. Everyone understands the meaning of a smile.
4. Leo Tolstoy wrote *War and Peace*.
5. The dog chased the cat.
6. XYZ Inc. is going to buy ABC Corporation.
7. Millions of tourists have visited the pyramids in Egypt.
8. Scientists in the twenty-first century will discover new information about the universe.

◇ PRACTICE 8, p. 197.

1. Mr. Rice signed the letter.
2. Did Mr. Foster sign the letter?
3. Ms. Owens sent the fax.
4. Did Mr. Chu send the other fax?
5. Will Mr. Berg meet Adam at the airport?
6. Has Mrs. Jordan invited you to the reception?
7. Mr. Lee has invited me to the reception.
8. Is the teacher going to collect the homework?

◇ PRACTICE 9, p. 198.

	verb	object
1.	TRANSITIVE	a letter
2.	INTRANSITIVE	(none)
3.	INTRANSITIVE	(none)
4.	INTRANSITIVE	(none)
5.	TRANSITIVE	the ball
6.	INTRANSITIVE	(none)
7.	INTRANSITIVE	(none)
8.	TRANSITIVE	my car
9.	TRANSITIVE	the book
10.	INTRANSITIVE	(none)

◇ PRACTICE 10, p. 198.

	object	passive sentence
1.	me	I was awakened by a noise.
2.	(no change)	
3.	the mistake	The mistake was discovered by Alice.
4.	(no change)	
5.	(no change)	
6.	the chair	The chair was fixed by Anita.
7.	(no change)	
8.	(no change)	
9.	(no change)	
10.	(no change)	
11.	a quiz	A quiz was announced by the teacher.
12.	(no change)	
13.	(no change)	
14.	(no change)	

◇ PRACTICE 11, p. 199.

Passive (checked) sentences: 2, 4, 6, 9

◇ PRACTICE 12, p. 199.

	passive verb	action performed by
1.	are used	unknown
2.	was opened	Shelley
3.	will be translated	unknown
4.	was stolen	unknown
5.	were taken	a professional photographer
6.	is going to be built	unknown
7.	has been rented	a young family
8.	has been rented	unknown

◇ PRACTICE 13, p. 200.

Unnecessary by-phrases: 1, 3, 6, 8

◇ PRACTICE 14, p. 200.

1. The soccer game has been canceled.
2. The meeting has been canceled by the president.
3. Beer and wine are served at that restaurant.
4. I was confused in class yesterday.
5. I was confused by the teacher's directions.
6. The dishes haven't been washed yet.
7. They should be washed soon.
8. Was this sweater washed in hot water?
9. Wool sweaters should not be washed in hot water.
10. I was invited to the party by Luis.
11. Have you been invited to the party?

◇ PRACTICE 15, p. 201.

1. Sometimes keys are hidden under cars.
2. Cats hide under cars.
3. Students are taught by teachers.
4. Students study a lot.
5. Cereal is often eaten at breakfast.
6. Cats eat cat food.
7. Mice are eaten by cats.
8. Songs are sung to children by their mothers.
9. Children sing songs in school.
10. Thai food is cooked in Thai restaurants.
11. Chefs cook in restaurants.

◇ PRACTICE 16, p. 201.

1. are considering . . . is being considered
2. are watching . . . are being watched
3. are painting . . . is being painted
4. is fixing . . . is being fixed
5. was fixing . . . was being fixed
6. are meeting . . . is being met
7. were moving . . . was being moved
8. were singing . . . was being sung
9. are discovering . . . are still being discovered

◇ PRACTICE 17, p. 202.

1. is being played
2. was being cleaned
3. is being built
4. is being read
5. were being watched
6. was being flown

◇ PRACTICE 18, p. 203.

1.	b	4.	a
2.	b	5.	b
3.	b		

◇ PRACTICE 19, p. 203.

	I/C	corrections
1.	I	It ~~was~~ happened many years ago.
2.	C	(none)
3.	I	I **went** to school yesterday.
4.	I	Two firefighters **were** injured while they were fighting the fire.
5.	I	Sara ~~was~~ accidentally **broke** the window.
6.	I	Kara **ate** a snack when she got home from school.
7.	C	(none)
8.	I	I ~~am~~ agree with you.
9.	I	The little boy **fell** down while he was running in the park.
10.	I	The swimmer ~~was~~ died from a shark attack.
11.	C	(none)
12.	I	I ~~was~~ slept for nine hours last night.

◇ PRACTICE 20, p. 204.

1. Class might be canceled.
2. Medicine can be prescribed by a doctor.
3. This report must be signed by Mr. Hook.
4. A new post office may be built on First Street.
5. Stamps have to be placed in the upper right-hand corner of an envelope.
6. That fence ought to be painted.
7. The assignment must be done by all of the students.

◇ PRACTICE 21, p. 204.

1. shouldn't be put off
2. must be written
3. can be taught
4. could be killed
5. ought to be divided
6. must be sold
7. will not be known
8. has to be torn down . . . can be built

◇ PRACTICE 22, p. 205.

1. has to be returned
2. should be returned
3. must be sent
4. could be sent
5. should be sent
6. can be put away
7. may be thrown away
8. might be picked up
9. will be cleaned up

◇ PRACTICE 23, p. 205.

	active/passive	verb
1.	ACTIVE	have used
2.	PASSIVE	have been used
3.	PASSIVE	are used
4.	ACTIVE	show
5.	PASSIVE	is shown
6.	PASSIVE	were made
7.	PASSIVE	were worn
8.	ACTIVE	became
9.	ACTIVE	wear
10.	PASSIVE	are sold
11.	PASSIVE	are made and sold
12.	PASSIVE	is being sold
13.	PASSIVE	can be bought
14.	ACTIVE	Do own
15.	PASSIVE	was made

◇ PRACTICE 24, p. 206.

1. is being repaired
2. was being repaired
3. repaired
4. is made
5. should not carry
6. ought to be kept
7. are sent
8. has already been hired
9. must be used . . . can produce
10. are manufactured
11. can be used . . . can be recycled . . . should not be thrown away
12. must be protected
13. can be found

◇ PRACTICE 25, p. 207.

1. are loved . . . brings . . . are often used . . . can be found
2. exist . . . are found . . . have
3. are carried . . . carries . . . were introduced
4. are appreciated . . . is made . . . is gathered . . . are eaten
5. are made . . . do not come . . . are made
6. may be planted . . . grown . . . survive

◇ PRACTICE 26, p. 207.

PART I.

1. to
2. about
3. from
4. of
5. with
6. of
7. with
8. in
9. about
10. with

PART II.

11. in
12. with
13. of
14. to
15. to
16. with
17. from

PART III.

18. of
19. in
20. with
21. for

◇ PRACTICE 27, p. 208.

1. The little girl is **excited about** her coming birthday party.
2. Mr. and Mrs. Rose **are devoted to** each other.
3. . . . I **am** lost.
4. The students are **bored with** their chemistry project.
5. . . . **are composed of** recycled products.
6. . . . He **is** hurt.
7. How well are you **prepared for** the driver's license test?
8. Mary has been **engaged to** Paul for five years.

◇ PRACTICE 28, p. 209.

1. interesting
2. interested
3. exciting
4. excited
5. fascinated
6. fascinating
7. bored . . . confused
8. boring . . . confusing
9. interesting
10. fascinating . . . surprising

◇ PRACTICE 29, p. 209.

1. boring
2. interested
3. confused
4. exciting
5. confused
6. interesting
7. surprising
8. bored
9. boring
10. fascinating
11. fascinated
12. fascinating
13. embarrassing
14. shocking . . . shocked
15. exciting . . . excited

◇ PRACTICE 30, p. 211.

1. confusing
2. frustrated
3. confusing
4. embarrassed
5. embarrassing
6. interested
7. interesting
8. exhausting . . . tired
9. frightening
10. frightened

◇ PRACTICE 31, p. 211.

Incorrect sentences:

1. c
2. a
3. b
4. a
5. c

◇ PRACTICE 32, p. 212.

1. sick
2. lost
3. dizzy
4. bored
5. hungry
6. late
7. rich
8. arrested
9. dressed
10. wet
11. invited
12. stolen

◇ **PRACTICE 33, p. 213.**

1. Get	10. got
2. got	11. 'm/am getting
3. am getting	12. got
4. to get	13. 's/is getting
5. got	14. get
6. getting . . . to get	15. 'm/am getting
7. 's/is getting	16. get
8. Get	17. 'm/am getting
9. got	18. getting

◇ **PRACTICE 34, p. 214.**

1. B, C	5. B, C
2. A	6. A
3. B, C	7. A
4. A	8. B, C

◇ **PRACTICE 35, p. 214.**

1. Ø	5. is
2. is	6. Ø
3. are . . . am	7. Ø
4. Ø	8. Ø

◇ **PRACTICE 36, p. 215.**

1. used to get	4. used to work
2. is used to working	5. is used to teaching
3. used to attend	6. am used to eating

◇ **PRACTICE 37, p. 215.**

1. I was supposed to return this book to the library.
2. We are supposed to read Chapter 9 before class tomorrow.
3. I was supposed to go to a party last night, but I stayed home.
4. We are supposed to do Exercise 10 for homework.
5. . . . is supposed to rain tomorrow.
6. . . . am supposed to take one pill every six hours.
7. I am supposed to dust the furniture and (to) vacuum the carpet.

◇ **PRACTICE 38, p. 216.**

1. are supposed to be
2. were supposed to sweep/clean
3. was supposed to send
4. are supposed to give
5. are supposed to clean
6. am . . . supposed to register
7. was supposed to cook
8. are supposed to take off

◇ **PRACTICE 39, p. 217.**

1. The moving boxes **were** packed by Pierre.
2. My uncle ~~was~~ died in the war.
3. Miami **is** located in Florida.
4. *(no change)*
5. Mr. Rivera **is** interested in finding a new career.
6. Did you tell everyone the **shocking** news?
7. After ten years, I **am** finally used to this wet and rainy climate.
8. The newspaper **is supposed** to come every morning before eight.

9. The Millers have been **married to** each other for 60 years.
10. I ~~am~~ **used** to drink coffee with cream, but now I drink it black.
11. What ~~was~~ **happened** at the party last night?
12. Several people almost **got killed** when the fireworks exploded over them.
13. A new parking garage **is** being **built** for our office.
14. I have been living in England for several years, so I **am accustomed to** driving on the left side of the road.

Chapter 11: COUNT/NONCOUNT NOUNS AND ARTICLES

◇ **PRACTICE 1, p. 218.**

1. **a** game	14. **an** hour
2. **an** office	15. **a** star
3. **a** car	16. **an** eye
4. **a** friend	17. **a** new car
5. **a** mountain	18. **an** old car
6. **a** rock	19. **a** used car
7. **an** army	20. **an** uncle
8. **an** egg	21. **a** house
9. **an** island	22. **an** honest mistake
10. **an** ocean	23. **a** hospital
11. **an** umbrella	24. **a** hand
12. **a** university	25. **an** ant
13. **a** horse	26. **a** neighbor

◇ **PRACTICE 2, p. 218.**

These do not complete the sentences:

1. b	3. c	5. a
d	e	c
e	4. d	f
h	f	h
2. c	g	6. d
f	h	g

◇ **PRACTICE 3, p. 219.**

	one	*some*
1.	words	words
2.	Ø	vocabulary
3.	Ø	slang
4.	Ø	homework
5.	assignment	assignments
6.	Ø	grammar
7.	dress	dresses
8.	Ø	clothes
9.	Ø	clothing
10.	parent	parents
11.	family	families
12.	Ø	knowledge
13.	Ø	information
14.	fact	facts
15.	Ø	luck
16.	Ø	garbage

◇ **PRACTICE 4, p. 220.**

1. bread, corn, peas, rice, sandwiches
2. apple trees, grass, lakes, mountains, plants, scenery
3. bracelets, jewels, jewelry, rings
4. equipment, hardware, machines, machinery, tools

◇ PRACTICE 5, p. 220.

1. **one** chair
2. **much** furniture
3. **many** vegetables
4. **much** clothing
5. **one** vegetable
6. **many** clothes
7. **much** fruit
8. **many** facts
9. **much** grammar
10. **one** word
11. **many** idioms
12. **much** vocabulary
13. **many** cars
14. **many** games
15. **much** water
16. **one** parent
17. **much** sand
18. **many** professors
19. **much** dust
20. **much** money
21. **much** stuff
22. **one** thing
23. **many** things
24. **much** English
25. **much** toast

◇ PRACTICE 6, p. 221.

1. is . . . snow
2. is . . . weather
3. Sunshine is
4. knowledge
5. fun
6. factories . . . pollution
7. pride . . . children
8. people . . . intelligence
9. peace
10. hospitality
11. beef . . . was
12. is . . . fog

◇ PRACTICE 7, p. 222.

1. many apples
2. much fruit
3. much mail
4. many letters
5. much English
6. much slang
7. many words are
8. much coffee
9. many sandwiches
10. much sugar
11. many courses
12. much homework
13. isn't much news
14. many articles are
15. much fun
16. many stars are
17. isn't much sunshine
18. Is . . . much pollution
19. much luck
20. are many kinds
21. is . . . much violence
22. much makeup
23. many cars
24. Is . . . much traffic

◇ PRACTICE 8, p. 223.

1. many letters are
2. much mail (/)
3. many **men** have
4. many famil**ies** are
5. many sentences are
6. much chalk (/) is
7. much English (/)
8. much . . . literature (/)
9. many . . . words
10. much gasoline (/)
    much petrol (/)
11. much homework (/)
12. many grandchild**ren**
13. many pag**es** are
14. many librar**ies** are
15. many glass**es**
16. much fun (/)
17. much education (/)
18. much soap (/)
19. many islands are
20. many people (/)
21. many zero**es**/zero**s** are

◇ PRACTICE 9, p. 224.

Circled words are in **boldface**:
1. **a** flower
2. **some/many** flowers
3. **a** coin
4. **some/much** money
5. **some/many** coins
6. **some/much** salt
7. **an** error
8. **a** mistake
9. **an** honest mistake
10. **some/many** mistakes
11. **a** dream
12. **an** interesting dream
13. **some/many** questions
14. **some/much** soap
15. **a** bar of soap
16. **some/much** beauty
17. **a** cup of tea
18. **an** unsafe place
19. **some/much** fruit
20. **some/many** pieces of fruit

◇ PRACTICE 10, p. 224.

1. a little music (/)
2. a few songs
3. a little help (/)
4. a little English (/)
5. a few . . . apples
6. a little honey (/)
7. a little advice (/)
8. a few suggestions
9. a few questions
10. a few people (/)
11. a few . . . minutes
12. a little light (/)
13. a little homework (/)
14. a little . . . grammar (/)
15. a few flowers
16. a little progress (/)

◇ PRACTICE 11, p. 225.

1. Kim has applied to **a** university in England.
2. . . . gave her **some** jewelry and a **poem** he **had written**.
3. The politician wanted specific **suggestions** for her speech on the economy.
4. Some of the **homework** for my English class was easy, but many of the **assignments** were unclear.
5. Diane has been to Rome several **times** recently. She always has **a** wonderful time.
6. Many parents need **advice** about raising children.
7. The boys played together in the **sand** and **dirt** for hours.
8. A person doesn't need **much** equipment to play baseball: just **a** ball and a bat.
9. **Much** happiness can come from enjoying the simple **things** in life.

◇ PRACTICE 12, p. 225.

1. Plants are the oldest living things on earth. (2)
2. Scientists divide living things into two groups: plants and animals. Generally speaking, plants stay in one place, but animals move around. (7)
3. Flowers, grass, and trees grow every place where people live. Plants also grow in deserts, in oceans, on mountaintops, and in polar regions. (7)
4. Plants are useful to people. We eat them. We use them for clothing. We build houses from them. Plants are also important to our health. We get many kinds of beneficial drugs from plants. In addition, plants provide beauty and enjoyment to all our lives. (7)
5. Crops are plants that people grow for food. Nature can ruin crops. Bad weather—such as too much rain or too little rain—can destroy fields of corn or wheat. Natural disasters such as floods and storms have caused farmers many problems since people first began to grow their own food. (9)
6. Food is a necessity for all living things. All animals and plants need to eat. Most plants take what they need through their roots and their leaves. The majority of insects live solely on plants. Many birds have a diet of worms and insects. Reptiles eat small animals, eggs, and insects. (15)

◇ PRACTICE 13, p. 226.

1. cup
2. pounds
3. bowl, cup
4. glass, bottle, quart
5. piece
6. gallons
7. bottle, gallon, quart
8. piece
9. bottle, glass
10. pieces
11. bowl, cup, piece, pound, kilo
12. sheets
13. loaf
14. spoonful
15. tube
16. bar, piece
17. piece
18. piece
19. pieces
20. pieces

◇ PRACTICE 14, p. 227.

1. jar
2. bottle, box
3. box, bottle
4. jar, bag, can/tin
5. can/tin
6. bag, box
7. jar
8. bottle
9. box, bag
10. can/tin

◇ PRACTICE 15, p. 227.

1. many suitcases
2. much suntan oil
3. many pairs of sandals
4. many tubes of toothpaste
5. many kilos of luggage
6. much money

◇ PRACTICE 16, p. 228.

1. **a** letter
2. **some** mail
3. **some** equipment
4. **a** tool
5. **some** food
6. **an** apple
7. **some** old clothing
8. **an** old shirt
9. **some** advice
10. **a** suggestion
11. **an** interesting story
12. **some** interesting news
13. **a** poem
14. **some** poetry
15. **a** song
16. **some** Indian music
17. **a** new word
18. **some** new slang

◇ PRACTICE 17, p. 228.

singular	*plural*
1. **a** bird	I saw some birds.
2. **some** corn	Ø *(none possible)*
3. **some** tea	Ø *(none possible)*
4. **a** flower	I picked some flowers.
5. **some** water	Ø *(none possible)*
6. **a** horse	I fed grass to some horses.
7. **some** jewelry	Ø *(none possible)*
8. **some** honey	Ø *(none possible)*
9. **a** new shirt	Tom bought some new shirts.
10. **some** soap	Ø *(none possible)*

◇ PRACTICE 18, p. 229.

1. **A** dog
2. **the** dog
3. **a** desk . . . **a** bed
   . . . **a** chest of drawers
4. **the** desk . . . **the** top
   drawer
5. **the** basement
6. **a** basement
7. **a** subject . . . **a** verb
8. **the** subject . . . **the** verb
9. **a** meeting
10. **the** meeting
11. **a** long distance . . .
    a telephone
12. **The** distance . . . **the** sun
    . . . **the** earth
13. **the** telephone
14. **the** cat
15. A: **a** cat
    B: **a** dog
16. **a** poem
17. A: **the** lecture
    B: **The** speaker . . .
    an interesting talk
18. A: **a** cup of coffee
    B: **the** cafe . . . **the**
    corner
19. **a** quiet street
20. A: **the** restaurant
    B: **the** street
21. A: **a** job
    B: **a** restaurant

◇ PRACTICE 19, p. 230.

1. Ø **D**ogs
2. **the** dogs
3. Ø **F**ruit
4. **The** fruit
5. **the** milk . . . **the**
   refrigerator . . . **the** table
6. Ø **M**ilk
7. Ø wine
8. **the** wine
9. Ø meat
10. **The** meat
11. **the** potatoes
12. Ø **P**otatoes . . .
    Ø vegetables
13. Ø **F**rogs . . . Ø small
    animals . . . Ø tails . . .
    Ø **T**urtles . . . Ø trails
    . . . Ø hard shells
14. **The** frogs . . . **The** turtles
15. **the** weather
16. Ø **C**opper
17. Ø candles . . . Ø light
    . . . Ø electricity
18. Ø books . . .
    Ø textbooks . . .
    Ø workbooks . . .
    Ø dictionaries . . .
    Ø encyclopedias . . .
    Ø entertainment . . .
    Ø novels . . . Ø poetry
19. **The** books

◇ PRACTICE 20, p. 231.

1. **some** coffee . . . **some** milk . . . **The** coffee . . .
   The milk
2. **some** soup . . . **a** sandwich . . . **The** soup . . .
   the sandwich
3. **some** clothes . . . **a** suit . . . **a** shirt . . . **a** tie . . .
   The suit . . . **The** shirt . . . **the** tie
4. A: **an** accident . . . **A** man . . . **a** Volkswagen . . . **a** bus
   B: **the** accident
   A: **The** man . . . **the** Volkswagen . . . **the** bus
5. **a** man . . . **a** woman . . . **an** argument . . . **The** man . . .
   the woman . . . **the** woman . . . **the** man . . .
   the argument
6. **some** birds . . . **a** tree . . . **a** cat . . . **the** tree . . .
   The birds . . . **the** cat . . . **the** cat . . . **the** birds

◇ PRACTICE 21, p. 233.

1. **a** man
2. **a** truck
3. **a** covered bridge
4. **The** bridge
5. **a** small river
6. **the** man
7. **the** man
8. **the** top
9. **the** bridge
10. **the** bridge
11. **a** solution
12. **the** solution
13. **the** truck
14. **the** bridge
15. **the** river
16. **a** great idea
17. **the** man
18. **the** tires
19. **the** river

◇ PRACTICE 22, p. 234.

1. B: **An** egg
   A: **the** egg
2. Ø **E**ggs
3. **a** scientific fact . . . Ø steam . . . Ø water
4. Ø **G**as
5. **The** gas
6. Ø **N**ewspapers . . . **an** important source . . .
   Ø information
7. **The** sun . . . **a** star . . . **the** sun . . . Ø heat . . . Ø light
   . . . Ø energy
8. Ø **D**ucks
9. Ø **P**izza . . . . Ø cheese . . . Ø tomatoes . . . Ø **P**izza
   . . . Ø Italian
10. A: **the** pizza
    B: **the** big piece . . . **the** small one
11. Ø **G**old . . . **an** excellent conductor . . . Ø electricity
    . . . **a** spaceship
12. **the** kitchen . . . **a** sandwich
13. A: **the** plumber . . . **The** sink
    B: **the** water supply . . . **the** house . . . **the** leak
14. **the** man . . . **the** president
15. **a** president

16. B: **a** blouse . . . Ø jewelry
    A: **the** blouse
17. **the** floor . . . **the** corner . . . **the** sofa
18. Ø furniture . . . **a** sofa . . . **an** easy chair
19. Ø F*f*urniture
20. **A** vegetarian . . . Ø meat
21. **the** continents . . . **the** world
22. **an** easy exam . . . **the** right answers . . . **the** questions
    . . . **the** exam
23. **a** job interview . . . Ø nice clothes
24. **a** mouse . . . Ø R*f*ats . . . Ø long, skinny tails
25. Ø wood . . . Ø coal . . . Ø heat . . . Ø gas . . . Ø oil . . .
    Ø electricity
26. **an** interesting experience . . . **A** man . . . **a** blue suit . . .
    a bouquet . . . Ø flowers . . . **the** man . . . **the** flowers
    . . . **the** door
27. Ø I*f*ce cream
28. Ø steamed rice . . . Ø fish . . . Ø vegetables . . . **The** rice
    . . . **The** fish . . . **The** vegetables
29. **an** exceptionally talented person
30. A: **the** letter
    B: **A** strong wind . . . **the** floor . . . **the** dog . . . **the**
    scraps . . . **the** wastebasket
31. A: **the** tape player
    B: **the** shelves
    A: **the** batteries
32. Ø C*f*halk . . . **a** necessity
33. **An** efficient transportation system . . . **an** essential part

◇ PRACTICE 23, p. 236.
1. Ø Paris
2. **The** Atlantic Ocean . . . **the** Pacific
3. Ø Dr. James
4. Ø Mt. Rainier . . . **the** Cascade Mountain Range
5. **The** Nile . . . Ø Africa
6. Ø Toronto . . . Ø Montreal
7. Ø Mt. Kilimanjaro . . . Ø Kenya
8. Ø New Zealand
9. **The** Himalayas . . . Ø Pakistan . . . Ø India . . . Ø Tibet
   . . . Ø Nepal
10. Ø President Davis
11. Ø Ho Chi Minh City . . . Ø Vietnam . . . Ø Saigon
12. **The** Andes Mountains

◇ PRACTICE 24, p. 237.
1. **the** Dead Sea
2. **the** Amazon River
3. Shanghai
4. **the** Sahara Desert
5. **the** Thames River
6. Europe
7. **the** Alps
8. Lake Tanganyika
9. North America
10. **the** Indian Ocean
11. **the** Netherlands
12. North America
13. Tibet
14. **The** Urals
15. Lagos
16. **the** United Arab Emirates

◇ PRACTICE 25, p. 238.
1. I'm taking **B**iology 101 this semester.
2. I'm taking history, biology, **E**nglish, and calculus this
   semester.
3. Some lab classes meet on **S**aturday.
4. Marta lives on a busy street. Marta lives at 2358 **O**live
   Street.
5. We went to **C**anada last summer. **W**e went to
   Montreal in **J**uly.

6. My roommate likes **V**ietnamese food, and **I** like **T**hai
   food.
7. The religion of **S**audi **A**rabia is **I**slam.
8. Shelia works for the **X**erox **C**orporation. **I**t is a very
   large corporation.
9. Pedro is from **L**atin **A**merica.
10. My uncle lives in **S**t. **L**ouis. I'm going to visit Uncle
    Bill next spring.
11. We went to a park. **W**e went to **W**aterfall **P**ark.
12. Are you going to the **U**niversity of **O**regon or **O**regon
    State **U**niversity?
13. Alice goes to a university in **O**regon.
14. The next assignment in literature class is to read *The
    Adventures of T*om *S*awyer*.
15. . . . In **F**rance, they call it "**B**astille **D**ay."

◇ PRACTICE 26, p. 238.
1. Do you know **R**obert **J**ones?
2. *(no change)*
3. I like **U**ncle **J**oe and **A**unt **S**ara.
4. *(no change)*
5. **S**usan **W**. **M**iller is a professor.
6. I am in **P**rof. **M**iller's class.
7. The weather is cold in **J**anuary.
8. *(no change)*
9. I have three classes on **M**onday.
10. I would like to visit **L**os **A**ngeles.
11. It's the largest city in **C**alifornia.
12. *(no change)*
13. There are fifty states in the **U**nited **S**tates of **A**merica.
14. *(no change)*
15. Today we can fly across the **A**tlantic **O**cean in hours.
16. *(no change)*
17. Mark lives on **M**arket **S**treet near **W**ashington **H**igh
    School.
18. *(no change)*
19. Our family stayed at the **H**ilton **H**otel in **B**angkok.
20. Yoko is **J**apanese, but she can also speak **G**erman.

◇ PRACTICE 28, p. 239.
1. The mail carrier brought only one **letter** today.
2. Mr. Dale gave his class **a** long history assignment for
   the weekend.
3. Tariq speaks several **languages**, including Arabic and
   Spanish.
4. Dr. **Kim** gives all her patients a toothbrush (OR
   toothbrushes) and toothpaste at their dental
   appointments.
5. I usually have **a** glass **of** water with my lunch.
6. A helpful policeman gave us ~~an~~ information about the
   city.
7. This cookie recipe calls for two **cups** of **nuts**.
8. **Many vegetables** are believed to have cancer-fighting
   ingredients.
9. Only applicants with the necessary experience*s* should
   apply for the computer position.
10. When Vicki likes a movie, she sees it several time**s**.
11. A popular children's story is *Snow White **and the** Seven
    Dwarfs*.
12. Is it possible to stop all violence*s* in the world?

Chapter 12: RELATIVE CLAUSES

◇ PRACTICE 1, p. 240.

1. who helped me move the refrigerator
   - *1:* I thanked
   - *2:* He helped
2. who was wearing a gray suit
   - *1:* A woman asked
   - *2:* She was wearing
3. who aided the rebels
   - *1:* The woman put
   - *2:* She aided
4. who was wearing a blue coat
   - *1:* I saw
   - *2:* He was wearing
5. who broke the vase
   - *1:* The girl apologized
   - *2:* She broke

◇ PRACTICE 2, p. 241.

1. The woman who answered the phone was polite.
2. The man who sang at the concert has a good voice.
3. We enjoyed the actors who played the leading roles.
4. The girl who fell down the stairs is hurt.
5. I read about the soccer player who was injured in the game yesterday.

◇ PRACTICE 3, p. 241.

1. The people who live next to me are nice.
   They live next to me.
2. The people whom Kate visited yesterday were French.
   Kate visited them yesterday.
3. The people whom I saw at the park were having a picnic.
   I saw them.
4. The students who go to this school are friendly.
   They go to this school.
5. The woman whom you met last week lives in Mexico.
   You met her last week.

◇ PRACTICE 4, p. 242.

1. The woman whom Jack met was polite.
2. I like the woman who manages my uncle's store.
3. The singer whom we heard at the concert was wonderful.
4. The people who came to dinner brought a small gift.
5. What is the name of the woman whom Tom invited to the dance?

◇ PRACTICE 5, p. 242.

1. who	6. who(m)	11. who(m)
2. who(m)	7. who	12. who(m)
3. who	8. who	13. who
4. who(m)	9. who	14. who(m)
5. who	10. who	15. who

◇ PRACTICE 6, p. 243.

1. O ~~that~~	6. S
2. S	7. S
3. S	8. O ~~that~~
4. O ~~who~~	9. S
5. S	10. O ~~that~~

◇ PRACTICE 7, p. 243.

1. That man ~~that~~ I saw was wearing a black hat.
2. *(no change)*
3. The fruit ~~that~~ I bought today . . . .
4. . . . a person ~~that~~ I will never forget.
5. *(no change)*
6. The girl that sits in front of Richard has long black hair ~~that~~ she wears . . . .
7. *(no change)*
8. *(no change)*

◇ PRACTICE 8, p. 244.

1. who/that	4. who/that
2. who(m)/that/Ø	5. who/that
3. who(m)/that/Ø	6. who(m)/that/Ø

◇ PRACTICE 9, p. 245.

1. C	5. B
2. A	6. A
3. C	7. C
4. C	8. C

◇ PRACTICE 10, p. 245.

1. who/that designs buildings.
2. who/that doesn't eat meat.
3. which/that forms when water boils.
4. which/that has a hard shell and can live in water or on land.
5. who/that leaves society and lives completely alone.
6. which/that grows in hot climates and produces large bunches of yellow fruit.
7. which/that can be shaped and hardened to form many useful things.
8. which/that cannot be understood or explained.

◇ PRACTICE 11, p. 246.

1. O ~~which~~	6. S
2. S	7. O ~~which~~
3. O ~~that~~	8. S
4. O ~~which~~	9. S
5. S	10. O ~~that~~

◇ PRACTICE 12, p. 246.

1. which/that/Ø	4. which/that
2. which/that	5. which/that/Ø
3. which/that/Ø	6. which/that

◇ PRACTICE 13, p. 247.

Incorrect (crossed out) pronouns:

1. them	4. him
2. it	5. her
3. them	6. him

◇ PRACTICE 14, p. 247.

1. A, C, D	8. C, D
2. A, D	9. A, C, D
3. C, D, E	10. C, D, E
4. A, C, D	11. A, C, D
5. A, D	12. A, C, D
6. C, D	13. C, D
7. C, D, E	

◇ PRACTICE 15, p. 248.

1. students . . . are	6. student . . . is
2. people . . . are	7. people . . . live
3. compound . . . consists	8. person . . . makes
4. students . . . speak	9. artists . . . make
5. people . . . know	

◇ PRACTICE 16, p. 249.

1. that . . . for	3. that . . . in
which . . . for	which . . . in
Ø . . . for	Ø . . . in
for which . . . Ø	in which . . . Ø
2. that . . . to	4. that . . . with
which . . . to	who(m) . . . with
Ø . . . to	Ø . . . with
to which . . . Ø	with whom . . . Ø

◇ PRACTICE 17, p. 250.

1. that . . . to	4. who(m) . . . for
who(m) . . . to	that . . . for
Ø . . . to	Ø . . . for
to whom . . . Ø	for whom . . . Ø
2. that . . . with	5. that . . . for
which . . . with	which . . . for
Ø . . . with	Ø . . . for
with which . . . Ø	for which . . . Ø
3. who(m) . . . about	6. that . . . in
that . . . about	which . . . in
Ø . . . about	Ø . . . in
about whom . . . Ø	in which . . . Ø

◇ PRACTICE 18, p. 250.

Adjective clauses:
1. we listened **to** at Sara's apartment
2. I accidentally broke Ø
3. we were waiting **for**
4. I always enjoy talking **to** about politics
5. I had just written Ø
6. I've been interested **in** for a long time
7. I talked **to** at the reception
8. I want to visit Ø next year
9. I was looking **at**
10. I wanted Ø
11. we were listening **to** at Jim's yesterday
12. I'm not familiar **with**
13. I was carrying Ø
14. I can always rely **on** for support and help
15. our fourteen-year-old is responsible **for**
16. I was reading Ø
17. I bought Ø
18. Ø which I enjoy studying the most
19. I waved **at**
20. **for** whom Alex was waiting

◇ PRACTICE 19, p. 251.

1. <u>whose daughter is a pilot</u>
   1: I know a man.
   2: His daughter is a pilot.
2. <u>whose husband is out of work</u>
   1: The woman found a job.
   2: Her husband is out of work.
3. <u>whose wallet I found</u>
   1: The man gave me a reward.
   2: I found his wallet.

◇ PRACTICE 20, p. 251.

1. The firefighters are very brave. <u>Their</u> department has won many awards.
   → The firefighters whose department has won many awards are very brave.
2. I talked to the boy. <u>His</u> kite was caught in a tree.
   → I talked to the boy whose kite was caught in a tree.
3. The family is staying in a motel. <u>Their</u> house burned down.
   → The family whose house burned down is staying in a motel.
4. I watched a little girl. <u>Her</u> dog was chasing a ball in the park.
   → I watched a little girl whose dog was chasing a ball in the park.
5. The reporter won an award. <u>Her</u> articles explained global warming.
   → The reporter whose articles explained global warming won an award.
6. I know a man. <u>His</u> daughter entered college at the age of fourteen.
   → I know a man whose daughter entered college at the age of fourteen.
7. We observed a language teacher. <u>Her</u> teaching methods included role-playing.
   → We observed a language teacher whose teaching methods included role-playing.
8. The teachers are very popular. <u>Their</u> methods include role-playing.
   → The teachers whose methods include role-playing are very popular.

◇ PRACTICE 21, p. 252.

True (checked) answers:

1. a, c	5. a
2. c	6. a, c
3. b, c	7. b
4. c	

◇ PRACTICE 22, p. 253.

1. which/that is used to carry boats with goods and/or passengers
2. whose children were doing poorly in her class
3. Ted bought for his wife on their anniversary
4. whose views I share
5. which/that had backbones
6. which/that disrupted the global climate and caused mass extinctions of animal life

◇ PRACTICE 23, p. 253.

1. who/that
2. who/that . . . whom
3. who/that . . . which/that . . . which/that
4. who/that
5. which/that/Ø
6. whose
7. which/that
8. who(m)/that/Ø
9. whose
10. which/that
11. who/that
12. who(m)/that/Ø

◇ PRACTICE 24, p. 254.

1. A movie that **looks** interesting opens tomorrow.
2. My family lived in a house which ~~it~~ was built in 1900.
3. The little boy **who** was lost asked for directions.
4. I don't know people **whose** ~~their~~ lives are carefree.
5. It is important to help people who **have** no money.
6. At the airport, I was waiting for friends **who(m)/that/Ø** I hadn't seen ~~them~~ for a long time.
7. The woman **who/that lives** next door likes to . . . .
8. My teacher has two cats **whose** ~~their~~ names are Ping and Pong.
9. A beautiful garden ~~that~~ separates my house from the street.
10. I asked the children who **were** sitting on the bench to help us.
11. The school that my children attend ~~it~~ is very good academically.
12. I enjoyed the songs which we sang ~~them~~.
13. One of the places that I like to visit **is** Central Park.
14. The movie we saw ~~it~~ last evening was very exciting.
15. I sent the parents **whose son** I hiked with a picture of us on Mt. Fuji.
16. Do you know the man who **works** in that office?
17. A mother **whose** daughter is in my class often brings cookies for the children.
18. The CD player **which/that/Ø** I bought can hold several CDs at once.
19. The bed which I sleep **in** is very comfortable. OR The bed **in** which I sleep is very comfortable.
20. . . . problems which I have had ~~them~~ since I came here.

Chapter 13: GERUNDS AND INFINITIVES

◇ PRACTICE 1, p. 256.

1. moving
2. living
3. taking
4. buying
5. giving
6. doing
7. reviewing
8. running
9. driving
10. retiring
11. getting married
12. working

◇ PRACTICE 2, p. 256.

1. went dancing
2. is going to go hiking
3. went shopping
4. go swimming
5. goes fishing
6. go sightseeing
7. go camping
8. go sailing
9. go skiing
10. went skydiving

◇ PRACTICE 3, p. 257.

1. INF   to wait
2. GER   walking
3. INF   to help
4. GER   writing
5. INF   to call
6. GER   quitting
7. INF   to work
8. INF   to grow

◇ PRACTICE 4, p. 258.

PART I.

1. to work
2. working
3. to work
4. working
5. to work
6. to work/working
7. to work
8. to work
9. working
10. to work
11. working
12. working

PART II.

13. to leave
14. to leave
15. leaving
16. leaving
17. leaving
18. leaving
19. to leave
20. to leave
21. leaving
22. to leave

PART III.

23. to know
24. to know
25. to know
26. knowing
27. to know
28. to know
29. to know/knowing
30. to know
31. to know
32. to know/knowing

◇ PRACTICE 5, p. 258.

1. B
2. A
3. B
4. B
5. A
6. B
7. B
8. B
9. A
10. A
11. A
12. B
13. B
14. B
15. A
16. B
17. B
18. B
19. A
20. B
21. B
22. B
23. B
24. A

◇ PRACTICE 6, p. 261.

1. B
2. A, B
3. A, B
4. B
5. A, B
6. A, B
7. A, B
8. B
9. A
10. A, B
11. A, B
12. A, B
13. B
14. A
15. B

◇ PRACTICE 7, p. 261.

1. to go
2. to buy
3. looking
4. to go shopping
5. passing
6. to go fishing
7. to cry/crying
8. to go/going
9. to go
10. to have
11. to meet
12. changing
13. camping
14. to arrive
15. writing
16. jogging
17. to call
18. to pass
19. hoping
20. to concentrate . . . to make
21. to go
22. to do/doing
23. to help
24. to learn
25. driving . . . to fly
26. to postpone
27. to be
28. teaching
29. to read/reading
30. to go dancing
31. building
32. to play/playing . . . to be . . . to be
33. to take

◇ PRACTICE 8, p. 262.

PART I.

1. of <u>flying</u>
2. for <u>hurting</u>
3. in <u>helping</u>
4. at <u>listening</u>
5. of <u>working</u>
6. about <u>walking</u>
7. of/about <u>owning</u>

PART II.

8. for <u>closing</u>
9. for <u>lending</u>
10. on <u>becoming</u>
11. for <u>taking</u>
12. on <u>eating</u>
13. to <u>finishing</u>
14. from <u>making</u>
15. about . . . <u>having</u>

◇ PRACTICE 9, p. 263.

1. for . . . for interrupting
2. in . . . in learning
3. for . . . for helping
4. on . . . on walking
5. for . . . for losing
6. like . . . like going
7. at . . . at drawing
8. in . . . in saving
9. about . . . about falling . . . making
10. about . . . about going
11. to . . . to going
12. of . . . of staying

◇ PRACTICE 10, p. 264.

PART I.

1. about asking
2. to ask
3. on asking
4. about asking
5. about asking
6. to ask
7. for asking
8. to ask
9. to ask/asking
10. to ask/asking

PART II.

11. to fix
12. to fix/fixing
13. to fix
14. to fix
15. to fix
16. about fixing
17. to fix/fixing
18. to fix
19. to fix
20. fixing

◇ PRACTICE 11, p. 265.

1. writing
2. to install
3. to cash
4. staying
5. to go
6. adopting
7. to take
8. in using
9. to be
10. to lower

◇ PRACTICE 12, p. 265.

1. going
2. of driving
3. to park/on parking
4. to watch/watching
5. to cook/cooking
6. baking
7. of going
8. of/about becoming
9. having
10. running
11. for watering
12. for speaking
13. on washing
14. from hitting
15. to be
16. repairing
17. to get
18. to have/on having
19. to taking
20. about seeing

◇ PRACTICE 13, p. 267.

1. by holding
2. by reading
3. by reading
4. by watching
5. by running
6. by treating

◇ PRACTICE 14, p. 268.

1. I arrived on time by taking a taxi instead of a bus.
2. I put out the fire by pouring water on it.
3. Giraffes can reach the leaves at the tops of trees by stretching their long necks.
4. I fixed the chair by tightening the loose screws.
5. Sylvia was able to buy an expensive stereo system by saving her money for two years.
6. A hippopotamus can cross a river by walking on the bottom of the riverbed.
7. I figured out how to cook the noodles by reading the directions on the package.
8. Pam finished her project on time by working all through the night.
9. You can figure out how old a tree is by counting its rings.

◇ PRACTICE 15, p. 268.

1. with
2. by
3. with
4. by
5. by
6. with
7. by
8. by
9. with
10. with
11. by
12. with
13. by
14. with
15. with
16. with

◇ PRACTICE 16, p. 269.

1. a. It is . . . to learn
   b. Learning . . . is
2. a. Eating . . . is
   b. It is . . . to eat
3. a. Driving . . . is
   b. It is . . . to drive
4. a. It is . . . to swim
   b. Swimming . . . is
5. a. Is it . . . to live
   b. Is living
6. a. Is it . . . to complete
   b. Is completing

◇ PRACTICE 17, p. 270.

1. It is difficult for shy people to meet
2. It is interesting for babies to look
3. it is customary for young children to sleep
4. It is necessary for airline pilots to have
5. It is hard for many teenagers to wake up
6. It is important for elderly people to keep
7. It is boring for people to listen
8. It is necessary for students to have
9. It is impossible for scientists to know
10. It is important for parents to teach
11. It is easy for people to be
12. It is dangerous for small children to cross

◇ PRACTICE 18, p. 271.

PART I.

1. for
2. to
3. to
4. for
5. to
6. to
7. for

PART II.

8. to
9. to
10. for
11. for
12. to
13. to
14. for
15. to

PRACTICE 19, p. 271.

1. to
2. for
3. for
4. to
5. for
6. to
7. to
8. for
9. to
10. for
11. for

PRACTICE 20, p. 271.

1. turned on the TV (in order) to watch the news.
2. goes to the laundromat (in order) to wash his clothes.
3. runs (in order) to get to class on time.
4. open the bedroom windows (in order) to let in some fresh air.
5. writes a letter to his parents (in order) to ask them for some money.
6. have the radio on (in order) to listen to a baseball game.
7. go to the library (in order) to study in peace and quiet.

PRACTICE 21, p. 272.

1. a. enough time to go
   b. too busy to go
2. a. tall enough
   b. too short
3. a. enough money
   b. too poor
4. a. too hot
   b. cool enough
5. a. too sick to eat anything
   b. well enough to eat anything
6. a. isn't old enough to stay home by herself
   b. too young to stay home by herself

PRACTICE 22, p. 273.

1. Ø . . . enough
2. too . . . Ø
3. enough . . . Ø
4. too . . . Ø
5. Ø . . . enough
6. Ø . . . enough
7. too . . . Ø
8. Ø . . . enough
9. enough . . . Ø
10. too . . . Ø
11. enough . . . Ø
12. Ø . . . enough

PRACTICE 23, p. 273.

1. being . . . to be
2. to stay
3. to help
4. to thank
5. going . . . to stay
6. to learn
7. to cause . . . to destroy
8. to recognize . . . to build . . . to knock
9. Predicting . . . to predict . . . reading . . . to act . . . running . . . counting . . . to be able to predict

PRACTICE 24, p. 274.

1. studying
2. jotting
3. to be
4. B: flying
   A: crashing
5. A: arguing . . . to disagree . . . be
   B: raising . . . to yell
   A: to get

6. A: to sneak . . . paying
   B: doing
   A: trying to sneak . . . to have . . . to like . . . liking . . . to do
7. to build
8. to do . . . to do . . . to do . . . to do
9. A: doing
   B: going shopping
   A: going . . . pretending to be . . . buying
   B: to do
   A: to get . . . to buy . . . to have
   B: Pretending to be . . . buying
10. B: putting . . . forgetting to send
    A: to get . . . not remembering
11. interrupting
12. to taste . . . to make

PRACTICE 25, p. 276.

1. I decided not **to buy** a new car.
2. The Johnsons are considering **selling** their antique store.
3. Sam finally finished **building** his vacation home in the mountains.
4. My wife and I go ~~to~~ dancing at the community center every Saturday night.
5. Suddenly, it began **to rain/raining** and the wind started to blow.
6. The baby is afraid **to be/of being** away from her mother for any length of time.
7. I am excited **about starting** college this September.
8. You can send your application **by** fax.
9. My country is **very** beautiful. OR My country is ~~too~~ beautiful.
10. **It is** exciting **to drive** a sports car.
11. My grandparents enjoy ~~to~~ traveling across the country in a motor home.
12. Elena made this sweater **by hand**.
13. Swimming ~~it~~ is one of the sports we can participate in at school.
14. That was very good, but I'm too full **to eat** any more.
15. My mother-in-law went to a tourist shop **to buy** a disposable camera.
16. Instead **of getting** her degree in four years, Michelle decided **to travel** abroad first.
17. **Swimming** with a group of people is more enjoyable than **swimming** alone.
18. **It is** interesting **to meet/meeting** new people.
19. **It is** hard **for** me to stay up past 9:00.
20. The professor thanked his students **for doing** well on the test.

Chapter 14: NOUN CLAUSES

PRACTICE 1, p. 278.

1. I don't know <u>where Jack bought his boots</u>. NOUN CLAUSE
2. Where did Jack buy his boots? QUESTION
3. I don't understand <u>why Ann left</u>. NOUN CLAUSE
4. Why did Ann leave? QUESTION
5. I don't know <u>where your book is</u>. NOUN CLAUSE
6. Where is your book? QUESTION
7. When did Bob come? QUESTION
8. I don't know <u>when Bob came</u>. NOUN CLAUSE

9. What does "calm" mean?   QUESTION
10. Tarik knows <u>what "calm" means</u>.   NOUN CLAUSE
11. I don't know <u>how long the earth</u> <u>has existed</u>.   NOUN CLAUSE
12. How long has the earth existed?   QUESTION

◇ PRACTICE 2, p. 278.

Noun clauses:

1. where [Patty] [went] last night
2. where [Joe's parents] [live]
3. where [Joe] [lives]
4. what time [the movie] [begins]
5. where [Brazil] [is]
6. what [Estefan] [said]
7. when [the packages] [will arrive]
8. how far [it] [is] to the post office
9. [who] [knocked] on the door
10. [what] [happened] at the party last night

◇ PRACTICE 3, p. 279.

question	*noun clause*
1. Why did Tim leave?	why Tim left
2. Where did he go?	where he went
3. Where does he live?	where he lives
4. Where is he now?	where he is now
5. What time will he return?	what time he will return
6. How far is it to his house?	how far it is to his house
7. Who lives next door to him?	who lives next door to him
8. What happened to him?	what happened to him

◇ PRACTICE 4, p. 279.

question	*noun clause*
1. did Marcos leave?	when Marcos left?
2. did he say?	what he said.
3. is the post office?	where the post office is?
4. is it?	what time it is?
5. did David arrive?	when David arrived.
6. is Anna from?	what country Anna is from.
7. was Kathy	why Kathy was
8. lives	who lives
9. did Eric invite	who(m) Eric invited
10. borrowed	who borrowed
11. are the restrooms located?	where the restrooms are located?

◇ PRACTICE 5, p. 281.

1. who(m) Helen talked to?
2. who lives in that apartment?
3. what he said.

4. what kind of car Pat has.
5. how old their children are.
6. why you said that.
7. where I can catch the bus?
8. who(m) Sara talked to.
9. how long Ted has been living here?
10. what this word means?

◇ PRACTICE 6, p. 281.

1.	A: were you	5.	A: Mr. Gow's office is ...
	A: you were		is Mr. Gow's office
2.	A: did Tom go	6.	A: did she come
	B: you said		B: she came
	A: Tom went		A: was she
3.	A: is a bumblebee ...		B: she was
	a bumblebee is		
4.	A: did Oscar borrow		
	B: Oscar borrowed		

◇ PRACTICE 7, p. 282.

Noun clauses:

1. who [that man] [is]
2. [who] [called]
3. who [those people] [are]
4. who [that person] [is]
5. [who] [lives] next door to me
6. who [my teacher] [will be] next semester
7. [who] [will teach] us next semester
8. what [a lizard] [is]
9. [what] [happened] in class yesterday
10. whose hat [this] [is]
11. [whose hat] [is] on the table

◇ PRACTICE 8, p. 282.

1. / ... is	6. / ... is
2. is ... /	7. is ... /
3. / ... is	8. / ... is
4. is ... /	9. / ... is
5. / ... is	10. is ... /

◇ PRACTICE 9, p. 283.

1. who she is.	7. what a clause is?
2. who they are.	8. what is in that drawer.
3. whose book that is.	9. who is in that room.
4. whose glasses those are?	10. what is on TV tonight.
5. what a wrench is?	11. what a carrot is?
6. who that woman is.	12. who I am.

◇ PRACTICE 10, p. 283.

1. whose car that is
2. whose car is in front of Sam's house
3. who the best students are
4. what time dinner is
5. who's next in line
6. whose purse this is
7. what the main ideas of the story are
8. whose shoes those are under the chair
9. what causes tornadoes

◇ PRACTICE 11, p. 284.

1. if (whether) Tom is coming
2. if (whether) Jin has finished medical school yet
3. if (whether) Daniel has any time off soon
4. if (whether) the flight is on time
5. if (whether) there is enough gas in the car
6. if (whether) Yuki is married
7. if (whether) the Petersons are going to move
8. if (whether) Khaled changed jobs

◇ PRACTICE 12, p. 285.

1. if I'm going to need
2. if chicken is
3. if the new teaching position includes
4. if there will be a movie
5. if Greg has to come
6. if penguins ever get
7. if you can drive
8. if Nasser has already left

◇ PRACTICE 13, p. 285.

1. if (whether) Karen is
2. where Karen went?
3. how Pat is feeling
4. if (whether) Pat is feeling
5. if (whether) the bus stops
6. where the bus stops.
7. why Elena is absent
8. if (whether) Elena is going to be absent
9. if (whether) I should buy
10. which book I should buy.
11. if (whether) we are going to have
12. if (whether) there is

◇ PRACTICE 14, p. 286.

1. rains
2. gets
3. like
4. runs
5. run
6. takes
7. enjoy
8. seems

◇ PRACTICE 15, p. 287.

1. I'm sorry that
2. I predict that
3. I'm surprised that
4. Are you certain that
5. Did you notice that
6. John is pleased that
7. Anna was convinced that
8. It's a fact that
9. A: Guido is delighted that
   B: I'm surprised that
10. A: How do you know that
    I'm still worried that

◇ PRACTICE 16, p. 288.

11. A: Mrs. Lane hopes that
    B: I don't think that
    A: I wish that
12. A: Do you think that
    B: Everyone knows that
    A: I'm not sure that that's true.

◇ PRACTICE 16, p. 288.

1. (that) I will have a peanut butter sandwich.
2. (that) I should study tonight
3. (that) flying in an airplane is safer than riding in a car.
4. (that) I'll get married someday.
5. (that) a huge monster was chasing me.
6. (that) John "Cat Man" Smith stole Mrs. Adams' jewelry.
7. (that) people are pretty much the same everywhere.
8. (that) high school students in the United States don't study as hard as the students in my country do.
9. (that) he always twirls his mustache when he's nervous?
10. (that) all people are equal.
11. (that) more than half of the people in the world go hungry every day?
12. (that) plastic trash kills thousands of marine animals every year?

◇ PRACTICE 17, p. 289.

1. I feel (don't feel) that smoking in public places should be prohibited.
2. I regret (don't regret) that I'm living in this country.
3. I would like to know (wouldn't like to know) when I will die.
4. I doubt (don't doubt) that there will be peace in the world soon.
5. I remember (can't remember) what I was like as a child.
6. I wonder (don't wonder) why the world exists.
7. I am afraid (am not afraid) that someone may make unwise decisions about my future.
8. I know (don't know) what I want to do with my life.

◇ PRACTICE 18, p. 290.

1. The Jensens are pleased that their granddaughter graduated from the university. They are pleased that she was offered a good job.
2. Po is lucky that the smoke alarm in his apartment rang. He is lucky that he woke up and discovered that his apartment building was on fire.
3. Ming Soo was surprised that she didn't fail the math exam. She was surprised that she got one of the highest grades in the class.
4. Karen is sorry that she lent her cousin Mark some money. She is sorry that she can't afford to buy her children new shoes.

◇ PRACTICE 19, p. 290.

1. that Alice has a car
2. that the library is open
3. that Ann speaks Spanish
4. that Alex passed his French course
5. that Mr. Kozari is going to be at the meeting
6. that the photos are ready to be picked up at the photo shop

◇ **PRACTICE 20, p. 291.**

1. Alex said, "**D**o you smell smoke?"
2. "Something is burning," he said.
3. He said, "**D**o you smell smoke? **S**omething is burning."
4. "**D**o you smell smoke?" he said. "**S**omething is burning."
5. Rachel said, "**T**he game starts at seven."
6. "The game starts at seven. **W**e should leave here at six," she said.
7. She said, "**T**he game starts at seven. **W**e should leave here at six. **C**an you be ready to leave then?"

◇ **PRACTICE 21, p. 291.**

1. Mrs. Hill said, "**M**y children used to take the bus to school."
2. She said, "**W**e moved closer to the school."
3. "Now my children can walk to school," Mrs. Hill said.
4. "Do you live near the school?" she asked.
5. "Yes, we live two blocks away," I replied.
6. "How long have you lived here?" Mrs. Hill wanted to know.
7. I said, "**W**e've lived here for five years. **H**ow long have you lived here?"
8. "We've lived here for two years," Mrs. Hill said. "How do you like living here?"
9. "It's a nice community," I said. "**I**t's a good place to raise children."

◇ **PRACTICE 22, p. 292.**

"Why weren't you in class yesterday?" Mr. Garcia asked me.
"I had to stay home and take care of my pet bird," I said. "He wasn't feeling well."
"What? Did you miss class because of your pet bird?" Mr. Garcia demanded to know.
I replied, "**Y**es, sir. That's correct. I couldn't leave him alone. He looked so miserable."
"Now I've heard every excuse in the world," Mr. Garcia said. Then he threw his arms in the air and walked away.

◇ **PRACTICE 23, p. 293.**

One day my friend Laura and I were sitting in her apartment. We were having a cup of tea together and talking about the terrible earthquake that had just occurred in Iran. Laura asked me, "Have you ever been in an earthquake?"
"Yes, I have," I replied.
"Was it a big earthquake?" she asked.
"I've been in several earthquakes, and they've all been small ones," I answered. "Have you ever been in an earthquake?"
"There was an earthquake in my village five years ago," Laura said. "I was in my house. Suddenly the ground started shaking. I grabbed my little brother and ran outside. Everything was moving. I was scared to death. And then suddenly it was over."
"I'm glad you and your brother weren't hurt," I said.
"Yes, we were very lucky. Has everyone in the world felt an earthquake sometime in their lives?" Laura wondered. "Do earthquakes occur everywhere on the earth?"
"Those are interesting questions," I said, "but I don't know the answers."

◇ **PRACTICE 24, p. 293.**

1. he . . . his
2. his . . . them
3. she . . . her
4. him . . . them
5. they . . . me . . . they
6. she . . . her
7. they . . . my
8. he . . . us . . . he . . . his

◇ **PRACTICE 25, p. 294.**

formal	*informal*
1. would meet	will meet
2. was going to be	is going to be
3. had	has
4. needed	needs
5. had flown	has flown
6. were planning	are planning
7. didn't want	doesn't want
8. could babysit	can babysit

◇ **PRACTICE 26, p. 295.**

1. (that) you didn't have
2. (that) you hadn't found
3. (that) the Smiths hadn't canceled
4. (that) it wouldn't rain
5. (that) the Whites hadn't gotten
6. (that) Mei didn't exercise
7. (that) your computer wasn't working
8. (that) Ali was coming

◇ **PRACTICE 27, p. 296.**

1. how old I was
2. if/whether he was going to be
3. if/whether she had
4. if/whether he had changed his
5. how long I had been
6. if/whether she could speak
7. if/whether he would be in his office
8. why she was laughing
9. if/whether I had ever considered

◇ **PRACTICE 28, p. 296.**

1. "Have you ever gone skydiving?"
2. "Will you be at the meeting?"
3. "Are you going to quit your job?"
4. "Where is your car?"
5. "What did you do after class yesterday?"
6. "Do you know Italian?"
7. "Can you guess what I have in my pocket?"
8. "Why aren't you working at your desk?"

◇ **PRACTICE 29, p. 297.**

1. where I was from.
2. how I liked it here.
3. how long I would stay.
4. why I had come here.
5. if/whether I had met many people.
6. what I was going to study.
7. if/whether the local people were friendly to me.
8. if/whether I liked the weather here.
9. how I had chosen this school.

◇ PRACTICE 30, p. 298.

1. he was going to call me
2. (that) he had to talk . . . her
3. (that) she could meet me
4. (that) she had written him
5. (that) I needed his
6. she would see him
7. (that) he was going to meet . . . me
8. what he was doing
9. (that) he was sure he had met me

◇ PRACTICE 31, p. 299.

1. told
2. said
3. asked
4. told
5. said
6. told . . . said
7. asked . . . asked . . . said
8. told . . . told
9. told
10. asked . . . said . . . asked . . . told

◇ PRACTICE 32, p. 299.

1. asked me where I lived.
2. asked me if/whether I lived
3. told him / replied / said that I had
4. told me / said that he was looking
5. told me / said that he didn't like living
6. asked him if / whether he wanted to move in with me.
7. asked me where my apartment was.
8. replied / told him / said that I lived
9. told me / said that he couldn't move
10. told me / said that he would cancel his
11. asked me if/whether that was okay.
12. told him / replied / said that I was looking forward to having him

◇ PRACTICE 33, p. 300.

Correct (checked) answers:
1. The teacher asked if I was finished.
   The teacher asked, "Are you finished?"
2. Aki said he was finished.
   Aki said that he was finished.
   Aki replied that he was finished.
   Aki answered that he was finished.
3. Ann told Tom she needed more time.
   Ann said she needed more time.
4. Donna answered that she was ready.
   Donna answered, "I am ready."
5. Mr. Wong wanted to know if Ted was coming.
   Mr. Wong wondered if Ted was coming.
   Mr. Wong wondered, "Is Ted coming?"

◇ PRACTICE 34, p. 300.

1. (that) he had forgotten
2. where his bicycle was . . . told me/said (that) he had sold
3. (that) we would miss
4. if/whether she could swim
5. if/whether she wanted . . . (that) she couldn't . . . had to study
6. (that) she had broken
7. was . . . (that) he wasn't . . . (that) he had gone
8. if/whether I would be . . . (that) I would be
9. if/whether he had . . . been . . . (that) he had been
10. where his cane was . . . (that) I didn't know . . . if/whether he needed . . . (that) he wanted to walk . . . (that) I would find it

◇ PRACTICE 35, p. 302.

The husband asked where the children were. His wife replied/said (that) they had already left for school.

The father said that they had forgotten to take their books with them. The mother wondered how they could be so irresponsible. She asked the father what they were going to do.

The father told her not to worry. He said (that) he would take the books with him and drop them off at the school on his way to work. The mother told him (that) that was okay and said goodbye. She told him to have a good day.

The children asked their mother where their schoolbooks were. They said (that) they had left them on the kitchen table. They said (that) they couldn't go to school without their books.

◇ PRACTICE 36, p. 303.

1. . . . May I ask ~~if~~ how old **you are**?
2. I wonder, **"Did** Rashed pick up something for dinner?"
3. I'm unsure what **Lawrence does** for a living.
4. Fernando said, **"The** best time for me to meet would be Thursday morning.**"**
5. Eriko **asked** me **if** I **was** coming to the graduation party. I **told** her that I wasn't.
   OR I said ~~her~~ I wasn't.
6. I hope ~~so~~ that I will do well on my final exams.
7. Antonio asked his mother what she **wanted** for her birthday**.**
8. I'm not sure if the price **includes** sales tax.
9. My mother **asked** me, "How many hours **did you spend** on your homework?"
10. Pedro asked **if/whether** that **was** okay.
    Pedro asked, **"Is** that okay?"
11. Mika told **me** she **was** going to stay home today.
12. I'd like to know how ~~do~~ you do that.
13. My parents knew what Sam and I **did**. OR . . . **know** what Sam and I do.
14. Beth said she had **been** working hard all week, but now **she** had some time off.
15. **It is** a fact that life always changes.

Appendix 1: PHRASAL VERBS

◇ PRACTICE 1, p. 305.

1. on
2. up
3. down . . . up
4. off
5. B: on
   A: off
6. away/out
7. A: down
   B: up
8. out . . . out
9. off . . . on
10. A: up
    B: off

◇ PRACTICE 2, p. 306.

Correct (circled) completions:
1. her socks
2. the TV, the stove
3. his new shoes
4. a story, a fairy tale, an excuse
5. some rotten food, an old shirt
6. a doctor's appointment, a meeting, a trip
7. a puzzle, a math problem, a riddle
8. a report, some late homework
9. a message, a phone number

10. a box, a sack of mail
11. my coat, my wedding ring
12. the light, the computer, the car engine

◇ PRACTICE 3, p. 307.
1. out of	4. over	7. from
2. on	5. into	8. in
3. off	6. into	9. on

◇ PRACTICE 4, p. 308.
1. B	5. F
2. C	6. D
3. A	7. E
4. G	

◇ PRACTICE 5, p. 308.
1. back
2. down/off
3. out
4. away
5. on
6. up . . . off
7. back
8. up
9. A: out
   B: up
   A: off
   B: back
10. back

◇ PRACTICE 6, p. 309.
1. out . . . out	7. down . . . X
2. on . . . X	8. X . . . up
3. into . . . X	9. away . . . X
4. into . . . X	10. up . . . up
5. up . . . up	11. off . . . X
6. away . . . away	12. from . . . X

◇ PRACTICE 7, p. 310.
1. over	6. down	11. out
2. out	7. around	12. up
3. in	8. out	13. over
4. out	9. up	
5. out	10. out	

◇ PRACTICE 8, p. 311.
1. a. off
   b. on
   c. down
   d. back
   e. out
   f. away
2. a. in
   b. out
3. a. over
   b. off
   c. on
   d. into
   e. out of
4. a. out
   b. up
   c. down
5. a. into
   b. up
   c. over
6. a. up
   b. off
   c. back
7. a. down
   b. back
   c. up
   d. over
8. a. in
   b. out
   c. up

◇ PRACTICE 9, p. 312.
1. on
2. up
3. out
4. out
5. out
6. A: out
   B: over
7. A: off
   B: over
8. back
9. up
10. on
11. A: up
    B: up

◇ PRACTICE 10, p. 313.
1. lay . . . off	6. cheer . . . up
2. take . . . back	7. clean . . . up
3. take . . . out	8. worked . . . out
4. blow . . . out	9. think . . . over
5. give . . . away	10. bring . . . up

◇ PRACTICE 11, p. 314.
1. off	8. out	15. out of
2. out	9. down	16. out
3. up	10. down	17. on
4. up	11. up	18. up
5. over	12. up	19. back
6. up	13. up	20. up
7. in . . . down	14. up	21. up

◇ PRACTICE 12, p. 316.
1. a. up
   b. up
   c. up
   d. out
   e. out
   f. out of
2. a. up
   b. up
   c. up
   d. up
   e. up
   f. up

◇ PRACTICE 13, p. 316.
1. out for	7. through with
2. in on	8. out for
3. up for	9. back from
4. along with	10. out of
5. around with	11. up in
6. out of	

◇ PRACTICE 14, p. 317.
1. gymnastics class	5. assignment
2. their neighbors	6. cord
3. paint	7. Hawaii
4. rocks	8. snakes

◇ PRACTICE 15, p. 317.
1. out . . . about
2. out for
3. back to
4. out with
5. away from
6. A: along with
   B: out of
7. over to
8. around with
9. over to
10. together with

◇ PRACTICE 16, p. 318.
1. out about	5. together with
2. out for	6. along with
3. back to	7. over to
4. around	8. out of

◇ PRACTICE 17, p. 319.
1. A	7. B	13. B	19. D
2. B	8. B	14. D	20. A
3. C	9. A	15. A	21. A
4. C	10. C	16. C	22. C
5. A	11. D	17. A	23. B
6. B	12. A	18. D	24. A

Appendix 2: PREPOSITION COMBINATIONS

◇ **PRACTICE 1, p. 321.**

1. of	6. to	11. with
2. to	7. about	12. for
3. to	8. of	13. for
4. with	9. from	
5. for	10. to	

◇ **PRACTICE 2, p. 322.**

1. B	5. C	9. D
2. F	6. I	10. G
3. J	7. A	
4. E	8. H	

◇ **PRACTICE 3, p. 322.**

1. at	6. for	11. with
2. at	7. for	12. to
3. in	8. from	13. with
4. with	9. about	
5. for	10. for	

◇ **PRACTICE 4, p. 323.**

1. A	5. B	9. A
2. C	6. A	10. A
3. B	7. C	
4. A	8. C	

◇ **PRACTICE 5, p. 323.**

1. A: with/to	6. to	13. about
B: about	7. for	14. with
2. for	8. of/about	15. about
3. to	9. for	
4. of	10. of	
5. A: in	11. for	
B: for	12. from	

◇ **PRACTICE 6, p. 324.**

1. a. of	2. a. about
b. for	b. about
c. of	c. of
d. with	d. of
e. with	e. of
f. of	f. about
g. in	g. for
h. to	h. for

◇ **PRACTICE 7, p. 325.**

1. for	6. in
2. A: to . . . about	7. of
B: at . . . for	8. with . . . about
3. to	9. to
4. from	10. to
5. A: on	11. with . . . about
B: about	

◇ **PRACTICE 8, p. 326.**

1. arrived at	6. talked about
2. wait on	7. is leaving for
3. invited . . . to	8. is . . . staring at
4. consists of	9. helped . . . with
5. waited for	10. borrowed . . . from

◇ **PRACTICE 9, p. 326.**

1. for	6. A: to	10. from
2. with	B: for	11. like
3. to	7. about/of	12. about
4. at	8. for	
5. to	9. about . . . about	

◇ **PRACTICE 10, p. 327.**

1. G	5. B	9. E
2. I	6. H	10. D
3. C	7. A	
4. J	8. F	

◇ **PRACTICE 11, p. 327.**

1. on	6. to . . . for . . .	10. for
2. from	for . . . on	11. from
3. of	7. for	12. from/of
4. on	8. to	13. of
5. to	9. of	

◇ **PRACTICE 12, p. 328.**

1. a. C	4. a. X	7. a. C
b. C	b. C	b. X
2. a. C	5. a. C	8. a. X
b. X	b. C	b. C
3. a. C	6. a. C	
b. C	b. C	

◇ **PRACTICE 13, p. 329.**

1. on	7. about . . . from
2. to . . . about	8. about
3. to . . . from . . . by . . . by	9. A: from
4. for	B: from
5. A: about	10. about
B: with	
6. A: from	
B: to	

◇ **PRACTICE 14, p. 330.**

1. hoped for	5. concentrates on
2. wonders about	6. escaped from
3. divided . . . into	7. am accustomed to
4. add . . . to	8. heard . . . about

◇ **PRACTICE 15, p. 331.**

Correct (circled) prepositions:

1. to	8. like	15. with
2. from/of	9. to	16. to/with
3. from	10. of	17. about
4. with/to	11. about . . . with	18. by
5. of/about	12. of/about	19. on
6. of/about	13. with	
7. for	14. at/with	

◇ **PRACTICE 16, p. 331.**

1. D	7. B	13. B	19. C
2. B	8. B	14. A	20. A
3. C	9. D	15. A	21. B
4. A	10. C	16. B	22. B
5. B	11. D	17. C	23. A
6. A	12. B	18. B	24. C

NOTES